SURVIVAL MODELS
AND THEIR ESTIMATION

(Second Edition)

Dick London, FSA

ACTEX Publications
Winsted and New Britain, Connecticut

To all my teachers,
but most of all DGG, B^2 and GC

Requests for permission should be addressed to
    ACTEX Publications
    P.O. Box 974
    Winsted, CT 06098

Manufactured in the United States of America

10 9 8 7 6 5 4 3 2

Cover design by MUF

Library of Congress Cataloging-in-Publication Data

London, Dick, 1943-
    Survival models and their estimation / Dick London, -- 2nd ed.
        p.   cm.
    Bibliography: p.
    Includes index.
    ISBN 0-936031-02-6 (pbk.) : $25.00
    1. Insurance--Statistical methods.   2. Mortality--Statistical
methods.   3. Population forecasting--Statistical methods.
I. Title
HG8782.L57 1988
304.6'4'015195--dc 19   88-22118
                                                               CIP

ISBN 0-936031-02-6

CONTENTS

PART II - ESTIMATION OF SURVIVAL MODELS FROM SAMPLE DATA

Chapter 6
TABULAR SURVIVAL MODELS
ESTIMATED FROM INCOMPLETE DATA SAMPLES
MOMENT PROCEDURES

Chapter 7
TABULAR SURVIVAL MODELS
ESTIMATED FROM INCOMPLETE DATA SAMPLES
MAXIMUM LIKELIHOOD PROCEDURES

Chapter 8
ESTIMATION OF PARAMETRIC SURVIVAL MODELS

PART III - PRACTICAL ASPECTS OF SURVIVAL MODEL ESTIMATION

Chapter 11

OTHER ISSUES REGARDING ACTUARIAL ESTIMATION

Appendix A

PROPERTIES OF ESTIMATORS

Appendix B

ASYMPTOTIC PROPERTIES OF
MAXIMUM LIKELIHOOD ESTIMATORS

Appendix C

DERIVATION OF FORMULA (8.49)   295

ANSWERS TO THE EXERCISES

Survival Models and Their Estimation is a general textbook describing the properties and characteristics of survival models, and statistical procedures for estimating such models from sample data. Although it is written primarily for actuaries, it is also intended to be of interest to a broader mathematical and statistical audience. Academically, the text is aimed at the fourth year undergraduate or the first year graduate level.

Actuaries and other applied mathematicians work with models which predict the survival pattern of humans or other entities (animate or inanimate), and frequently use these models as the basis for calculations of considerable financial importance. Specifically, actuaries use such models to calculate the financial values associated with individual life insurance policies, pension plans, and income loss coverages. Demographers and other social scientists use survival models for making predictive statements about the future make-up of a population to which the model is deemed to apply.

This text is not primarily concerned with the *uses* of survival models, but rather with the question of how such models are established. This exercise is sometimes referred to as survival model *development* or survival model *construction*; in this text, however, we prefer the more descriptive phrase survival model *estimation*.

It cannot be noted too strongly that the "real" survival distribution (or survival probabilities) which apply to a group of persons is unknown, and probably will forever be so. What we, therefore, attempt to do is *estimate* that distribution, based on the data of a sample and a chosen estimation procedure. It is vitally important that this be clearly understood. Since the name of the game is estimation, there are no "right" answers. There are only sound (or unsound) procedures.

Because the result of our exercise is an estimate of the theoretical, underlying, operative survival distribution, based on the particular experience of a sample, we recognize that the estimate is a realization of a *random variable*, called an *estimator*. In turn, this random variable has properties such as expected value and variance, and these properties tell us something about the quality of the estimator. Note that we do not judge the "accuracy" of the resulting estimate, but rather the quality (or validity) of the procedure which produced the estimate. Properties of estimator random variables are defined in Appendix A. Readers who are not entirely familiar with these properties may wish to review Appendix A before studying the specific estimators developed in the text.

Frequently the estimated survival model produced directly from a study is not entirely suitable for practical use, and is, therefore, systematically revised before such use. The process of revising the initial estimates into revised estimates is called *graduation*. This step in the development of a useable estimated survival model is the topic of a companion text to this one entitled *Graduation: The Revision of Estimates*.

Survival Models and Their Estimation is said to be a general text in that it treats survival model estimation from the viewpoint of several different practitioners, including the actuary, the demographer, and the biostatistician, without attempting to be an exhaustive treatment of any one of these traditions.

A more thorough treatment of the actuarial tradition, from a different perspective, can be found in texts by Gershenson [26], Benjamin and Pollard [9], and Batten [6]; demographic approaches are the main theme of the works by Keyfitz and Beekman [36], Spiegelman [58], Chiang [16], and Pollard et al. [50]; the medical, or biostatistical, tradition is more deeply pursued by Elandt-Johnson and Johnson [21]. Additional texts, which deal with the statistical analysis of survival data at the graduate level, include those by Lawless [39], Lee [40], Miller [45], and Kalbfleisch and Prentice [33].

How is an initial estimated survival model determined from sample data? There are many approaches to this. A survival model estimation problem will generally have three basic components: (1) the form and nature of the sample data (which might also be called the study design); (2) the chosen estimation procedure; and (3) any simplifying assumptions made along the way. All of these concepts will be further developed in this text. The traditional actuarial approach, for example, is characterized by a cross-sectional study design using the transactional data of an insurance company or pension fund operation, a method-of-moments estimation procedure, and the Balducci distribution assumption. In this text we will consider, as well, other study designs, primarily those encountered by the clinical statistician or the reliability engineer. In addition, we will consider other estimation procedures, especially the maximum likelihood and product limit methods. Finally, we will consider other simplifying assumptions, such as the uniform and exponential distributions.

The text presumes a basic familiarity with probability and statistics, including the topics of estimation and hypothesis testing. The application of these ideas specifically to the estimation of survival models is then developed throughout the text. An effort has been made to keep the mathematics and the pedagogy at a level which does not require a prior familiarity with the topic. Whenever a choice between mathematical rigor and pedagogic effectiveness appeared to be necessary, we opted for the latter. As a result, the level of mathematical rigor in the text may be somewhat less than that desired by the precise mathematician, but the increased clarity which results from sacrificing some rigor will hopefully be welcomed by the student reader.

The first edition of this text, published in 1986, included the subject matter contained in the first eight chapters of the new edition. Chapters 5 and 6 have been completely rewritten from the first edition, Chapter 7 has been substantially revised, and three entirely new chapters have been added. The first edition was adopted by the Society of Actuaries as a reference for its examination program in 1987, and many valuable suggestions for improvement were contributed by students and educators.

Drafts of the material in both editions of the text were submitted to a review team, whose many valuable comments are reflected in the final version. The indispensable assistance of this group is hereby gratefully acknowledged.

Warren R. Luckner, FSA, of the Society of Actuaries, coordinated the efforts of the review team and made many valuable comments himself.

Stuart A. Klugman, FSA, Ph.d., of the University of Iowa, was particularly adept at detecting mathematical errors in the drafts, and much of the precision that the text has attained is due to his careful efforts.

Stanley Slater, ASA, of Metropolitan Life Insurance Company, did a remarkable job of editing the drafts for improvements in writing style and clarity, especially for the benefit of the student reader.

Other members of the review team who made valuable contributions to the final text include Robert L. Brown, FSA, and Frank G. Reynolds, FSA, both of the University of Waterloo, Cecil J. Nesbitt, FSA, Ph.d., of the University of Michigan, Geoffrey Crofts, FSA, of the University of Hartford, and Robert Hupf, FSA, of United of Omaha Life Insurance Company.

Much of the research and writing time invested in this project was supported by a grant from the Actuarial Education and Research Fund. The author would like to express his appreciation to the directors of AERF for this support.

Special thanks and appreciation are expressed to Marilyn J. Baleshiski of ACTEX Publications who did the electronic typesetting for the entire text, through what must have appeared to be an endless series of revisions.

Despite the efforts of the review team and the author to attain pedagogic clarity and mathematical accuracy, errors and imperfections are undoubtedly still present in the text. For this the author and the publisher take full responsibility and sincerely apologize to the reader. We respectfully request that you report these errors to the author at ACTEX Publications, P.O. Box 974, Winsted, CT 06098.

Winsted, Connecticut　　　　　　　　　　　　　　　　Dick London, FSA
June, 1988

PART I

THE NATURE AND PROPERTIES OF SURVIVAL MODELS

The main topic of this text is the statistical estimation of survival models and the analysis of those estimated models.

Before we tackle the estimation idea, however, we must first develop a considerable familiarity with survival models themselves, and that is the purpose of the first three chapters of the text.

Chapter 1 introduces the general idea of survival models in a conceptual manner, and gives an overview of the entire text.

Chapter 2 presents a symbolic analysis of the survival model, and gives several examples of distributions that might be used as parametric survival models.

Chapter 3 describes the nature and properties of the traditional tabular survival model, the life table. A strong effort is made in this chapter to show that life tables, assisted by mortality distribution assumptions, have the same capabilities as the parametric models of Chapter 2.

CHAPTER 1

INTRODUCTION

1.1 *WHAT IS A SURVIVAL MODEL*

A *survival model* is a probability distribution for a special kind of random variable.

Suppose an air conditioning unit is being operated in a laboratory with the room temperature kept at a very high level. The unit begins to function at time $t=0$, and we are interested in the probability that the unit will still be functioning at any future time t in general. Symbolically we will denote this probability by $S(t)$.

The random variable we are considering here, called T, is defined to be the time of failure of the entity known to exist at time $t=0$, and is therefore frequently called the *failure time random variable*. Now if T is the time of failure, then the probability of still functioning at time t is the same as the probability that the failure time is later (mathematically greater) than the value of t. Formally,

$$S(t) = \Pr(T > t). \tag{1.1}$$

By the nature of T it is clear that $T \geq 0$, that $S(0) = 1$, and that $S(t)$ is a non-increasing function. We will assume $\lim_{t \to \infty} S(t) = 0$.

Now if T is the time of failure of an entity which exists at $t=0$, then T is also the future lifetime of this entity measured from $t=0$. Writers on this subject will somewhat freely interchange these equivalent definitions of T as "failure time" or "length of future lifetime." Although some consistency might be convenient, the reader should have no difficulty in dealing with these interchanges.

It is important to note in the above example that we are interested in the survival of the cooling unit as a function of time since an initial event, which occurred at time $t=0$. In this case, the initial event is the starting up of the unit under the test conditions. In particular, it is important to note that we are not concerned with the *age* of the unit at the time.

As a second example, consider a study of the survival of laboratory animals injected with a carcinogenic substance. The injection constitutes the initial event which defines time $t=0$. We are then interested in observing the survival pattern of these animals as a function of time since injection.

In each of the above two examples, the random variable of interest is T, the time to failure. The age of the study unit, animate or inanimate, at time t=0, and hence its attained age at time of failure, is not of interest to us, and might very well not even be known. The reason for this is that we believe the chance of failure to be a function of time under the study conditions, and not of the attained chronological age of the study unit. For this reason we use the notation S(t).

For the most part, cases where failure (or death) is reasonably viewed as a function of time since the initial event, and not of the chronological age of the study unit, will involve mechanical objects or laboratory animals, as in the above two examples. On the other hand, cases dealing with the survival patterns of humans, especially those of direct interest to actuaries, will normally recognize that chance of failure (death) is related to attained age. These cases where attained chronological age should be recognized are further explored in the next section.

We do recognize some situations, however, where the nature of the study group is such that attained chronological age is of minor importance, compared to that of time since the initial event. For example, consider a study of the survival of persons who have been diagnosed as having a certain disease, and who have begun treatment for such disease. If time t=0 is the date of diagnosis, we might again be interested in measuring the survival of such persons as a function of time since t=0 only, if we believe that the health condition (and the treatment program) would affect survival (or failure) to such a great extent that age is practically immaterial. In such a case we would again use S(t) for our survival function. Note that the various persons entering the study would be of many different chronological ages at t=0, the time of their respective initial events.

1.2 ACTUARIAL SURVIVAL MODELS

The three examples given in Section 1.1 illustrate cases which are of interest primarily to the reliability engineer, the clinical statistician, or the biostatistician. We stressed the idea that, in such cases, the actual chronological age of each individual under study is not of importance, and might very well not even be known.

In contrast, actuarial survival models, primarily for use in operating insurance or pension schemes, must recognize this chronological age, since we believe that survival is a function of age. Two versions of actuarial survival models will be explored.

1.2.1 *The Select Model*

Consider a survival model to be used for making insurance calculations with respect to persons selected for insurance coverage at age x (assumed to be an integer). We see that the issuance of insurance constitutes the initial event defining time $t=0$ as described in the prior section, and the model is to give probabilities of still being alive at time t in general. For example, if we are still thinking in terms of our S(t) function, then S(10) gives the probability of surviving to time $t=10$ (probably measured in years). But surely we would agree that S(10) should have a different value if $x=25$ when $t=0$ than if $x=55$ at that time. In other words, in such cases S(t) alone is insufficient for our needs. We need an S(t) which also depends, in one way or another, on the value of x when $t=0$. We will use the symbol S(t;x) in such cases.

In this context, the age at selection, x, is called a *concomitant variable*. We still view time since selection, t, as our primary variable of interest, but must reflect x, somehow, in our survival model S(t;x).

The standard actuarial approach is to simply have a *separate* S(t) for each value of x. Then the survival model for each selection age is viewed as a function of t only, but the appropriate model for use in any given case would depend on x.

Age at selection is not the only concomitant variable that is known to have an influence on survival. Another important one is sex, and this concomitant variable would probably also be reflected by having separate survival models for males and females. Still another example would be smokers vs. nonsmokers. If a survival model has been designed to reflect all three of these concomitant variables, as well as the primary variable of time since selection, then we might use the symbol S(t;x,m,s) to denote the model appropriate for use with male smokers who were age x at selection.

We will further discuss these survival models with concomitant variables later in the text. For now we are mainly concerned with introducing the idea that a factor other than time since the initial event can affect survival, and that age at the initial event (selection) is an obvious example of this.

1.2.2 *The Aggregate Model*

Next we consider the special case where the initial event defining time $t=0$ is the actual birth of the person whose survival probabilites are given by S(t). Then, using x for attained age in general, we see that $x=0$ when $t=0$, so attained age and elapsed time will run exactly together. In this case, one could use either x or t for the primary variable, with the usual convention being to use x. Thus the survival probabilities will be given by a function called S(x), $x \geq 0$, with $S(0) = 1$ and $S(x) \to 0$ as $x \to \infty$.

In this case, the random variable X is clearly the *age at death*, or the *future lifetime* random variable, just as T was the *time at death* (or *time at failure*), or the *future lifetime* random variable.

It should be clear that S(x) and S(t) are really identical functions (but different from S(t;x)). Thus as we explore the mathematical properties of either S(t) or S(x), we are really dealing with both of them at the same time. However, we prefer to use both symbols in this text, and to have a clear distinction between the use of x and the use of t.

To summarize, whenever the chronological age of the entities whose survival probablilities are being studied is not an important factor, so that survival is viewed only as a function of time since some initial event, we will use S(t). In the special case of the survival pattern of human beings from actual chronological birth, we will use S(x). Both S(t) and S(x) are functions of one variable. In the case of a study of the survival pattern of persons aged x at t=0, and where attained age *is* believed to affect survival, we will use S(t;x). This will be the least common of the three cases.

1.3 *FORMS OF THE SURVIVAL MODEL*

Thus far we have only referred to the function S(t) (or S(x)) conceptually, without being very specific about its form. Since we did refer to T as a univariate random variable, the reader might reasonably expect that we have specific distributions in mind, such as the exponential or the normal, and this is frequently the case. Whenever the survival probabilities, S(t), are given by a mathematical function of t, we say that S(t) is in *parametric* form. This name is chosen since values of S(t) will depend on one or more parameters, as well as on t. For example, if T is an exponentially distributed random variable, with $S(t) = e^{-\lambda t}$, then λ is a parameter in the survival model. Several specific parametric models are reviewed in the next chapter.

Traditionally, actuarial survival models have not been in parametric form. The shape of S(x), as suggested by empirical data, is too complex to be adequately represented by simple one-parameter distributions (such as the uniform or the exponential). Better representation is accomplished by the two-parameter Gompertz or Weibull distributions, and even better representation by the three-parameter Makeham distribution. (All five of these distributions are reviewed in Section 2.3.)

Although these distributions have had some use as parametric survival models, the actuarial profession has tended to favor *tabular* models over parametric ones. A tabular survival model is one in which numerical values of S(x) are presented for certian selected values of x, most commonly the integers. It is thus a *table of numbers*, from which it gets its name.

It has been argued that this table of numbers could still be said to represent a *parametric* survival model, wherein each and every one of the numbers is a parameter. There is some logic to this argument, but, as a matter of definition, we prefer to call such a model tabular, and reserve the term parametric for the situation defined above.

Now if a tabular model presents S(x) values only for x=0, 1, ⋯ , then the model lacks the ability to answer questions involving any fractional values of x. We might say that the survival model is not totally specified. To overcome this deficiency, it is customary to make an assumption about the form of S(x) *between adjacent integers*. When such assumption, called a mortality distribution assumption, is superimposed on the tabular model, then S(x) is defined for *all* x, x ≥ 0, and any calculation that could be made from a parametric model can now be made from the tabular-model-with-distribution-assumption combination.

The actuarial tabular survival model has been around for many years. It is alternatively referred to as a *life table*, or *mortality table*, depending, apparently, on whether one is an optimist or a pessimist. For the form of S(x) between adjacent integers, there are three common assumptions: linear (by far the most common), exponential, and hyperbolic.

Because the traditional tabular survival model is so important, we will describe it, along with the three common assumptions for S(x) between adjacent integers, at considerable length in Chapter 3.

In the special case of our select model S(t;x), actuarial uses of this model are nearly always in tabular form. Recently the development of parametric forms for S(t;x) in the actuarial context has been explored by Tenenbein and Vanderhoof [61]. Many others have explored this idea for S(t;x), as well as the more general S(t;z), where z is a vector of any number of concomitant variables, in the clinical setting. (See, for example, Chapter 13 of Elandt-Johnson and Johnson [21], where additional references are also given.) We briefly deal with this issue of parametric models with concomitant variables in Chapter 8.

1.4 *ESTIMATION*

Thus far we have defined the survival model as a function called S(t) (or S(x)) which gives probabilities of surviving to time t (or age x), either as a mathematical function of the variable, or as a table of numbers along with an assumption of form between adjacent integers. It is our intent to continue this exploration of the nature and properties of these two forms of the survival model in the next two chapters, so that a clear understanding of them can be established. We will then proceed to the main business of this text, which is to establish specific models for use. Because we take the point of view that there exists a conceptual, underlying, operative survival model, denoted by S(t) (or S(x)), then the specific model which we establish is an approximation to, or an *estimate* of, that "real," operative model. Thus we speak of estimating S(t), and will generally denote this estimate by Ŝ(t).

Various approaches to estimating $S(t)$ will be employed, depending on the nature of the sample data and the design of the study, and various distribution assumptions will be utilized as well.

It is important to note the meaning of "estimating" with respect to the two basic forms of the survival model. For the tabular model, we usually estimate the conditional probabilities of survival over short unit intervals (usually one-year periods), and produce our estimate of $S(t)$ from them. (The meaning of "conditional interval probabilities" will be clarified in the next two chapters.) Although there will be a few variations from this approach, it will be our most common route to $\hat{S}(t)$. Estimation of tabular models is pursued in Chapters 4 through 7.

By contrast, with respect to a parametric survival model, estimation of the unknown parameters of the assumed functional form of $S(t)$ produces the estimated $\hat{S}(t)$. Considerably fewer quantities are estimated here than in the tabular case if we estimate these parameters directly from the sample data. Frequently parametric survival model estimation is accomplished by first estimating the sequence of conditional interval probabilities, and then "fitting" them to the chosen parametric form. Both of these approaches, along with the topic of hypothesis testing of parametric models, are covered in Chapter 8.

1.5 *STUDY DESIGN*

In this text we will deal with approaches to survival model estimation that are followed by the clinical statistician, the actuary, and the demographer. In this section we give a brief description of the traditional design of the study with which each of these practitioners deals.

For the most part, it can be said that the actuary and the demographer deal with large sample studies, whereas most clinical studies are based on smaller samples. It is also generally true that actuarial and demographic studies have a cross-sectional design, whereas many clinical studies have a longitudinal design.

1.5.1 *Cross-sectional Studies*

In this study design, we begin by defining the *study group*, an identifiable group of persons whose survival pattern is to be studied (i.e., whose underlying, operative survival model is to be estimated). Examples of the study group would be the entire population of a city, state or nation (demographic), or the policyholders of a life insurance company or members of a pension plan (actuarial).

Next an *observation period* is chosen. At the beginning of this period there are many persons who are already members of the study group and they come under observation at that time. Others might join the study group during the observation period, and some could drop out of the study group without dying. This in-and-out movement during the study period is referred to as *migration*. By appropriately classifying and manipulating the data, especially the observed deaths, according to a chosen estimation procedure, age-specific death probabilities are estimated from the sample data. These probabilities constitute a tentative tabular survival model.

A major advantage of this study design is that the estimates can be based on the up-to-date experience of a group moving through time, where, in general, the time until failure is fairly lengthy.

1.5.2 *Longitudinal Studies*

In contrast to the large sample cross-sectional studies, clinical studies are frequently quite different in their design. Rather than selecting an interval of time, and observing failure data within that observation interval, these studies select a study group and follow the experience of that group *longitudinally* into the future. This study design is feasible when the time until failure is, in general, fairly short.

In many cases, clinical studies will have what we call a *cohort complete* design. In this study design, a cohort, or initial group, of study units are selected. These may be light bulbs, injected mice, or persons undergoing a certain medical treatment. In all cases, each study unit is selected at time $t=0$. Note that the respective $t=0$ times for each study unit could be the same date on the calendar (as would likely be true for the light bulb or injected mice studies), or could be different dates (as would likely be true for humans). Even in the latter case, however, the study would normally be conducted with respect to time since initial selection, regardless of the dates on which $t=0$ occurred. (This matter will be further clarified by example in Chapter 4.)

Once the initial group is selected, it is kept under observation until all have died (failed), and the time of each death is recorded. It is clear that in order to perform this type of study, the observer must have the ability to control the study group, in the sense that none of the study units may be allowed to "disappear" without dying (failing). For this reason, such studies are sometimes called *controlled-data* studies. By its nature, this study design is not feasible for large-sample studies of healthy lives; for such studies the cross-sectional design is used.

In some cases the cohort, longitudinal study may be terminated before all study units fail in order to avoid an unduly long study period. In such cases we have an *incomplete* data study, rather than a complete data

study. Two common approaches to terminating the study exist. If the study
is terminated at a fixed, pre-determined date, then we say the data have been
truncated. On the other hand, if a study is continued until a pre-determined
number of deaths has been observed, then we say the data have been
censored. The major reason for distinguishing between truncation and
censoring lies in the subsequent analysis of the estimation results.

1.6 *SUMMARY AND PREVIEW*

In this introductory chapter we have set the stage for a study of the nature
and properties of survival models and approaches to estimating these models,
which is the main topic of the text. The objectives of this chapter were to
define the concept of a survival model, to describe the two basic forms of
such a model, and to present a brief orientation to the idea of estimating the
model.

In Chapter 2 we will pursue the mathematical properties of the
conceptual survival model, and examine several specific parametric models.
In Chapter 3 we will explore the tabular survival model (the life table).

Chapters 4 through 9 comprise Part II of the text, and are concerned
with the theory of estimating survival models from sample data.

Chapter 4 addresses this issue in the convenient setting of complete
data samples, and the next five chapters all allow for incomplete data
samples.

Chapter 5 is devoted to an analysis of study design to discover the
types of estimation problems that we will encounter.

Chapter 6 describes moment estimation, including the traditional
actuarial approach.

Chapter 7 deals with maximum likelihood estimation, including the
product limit estimator.

Chapter 8 deals with the estimation of parametric survival models,
from both complete and incomplete data samples. It includes the topic of
hypothesis testing of such estimated models, and a brief discussion of
allowing for concomitant variables.

Chapter 9 is concerned with the special problem of estimating
tabular survival models from general population data, which is part of the
field of demography.

Chapters 10 and 11 comprise Part III of the text, and deal with the
practice, rather than the theory, of survival model estimation in an actuarial
setting.

Chapter 10 describes approaches to processing the data in large-
sample actuarial studies.

Chapter 11 includes some final, miscellaneous topics of a practical
nature.

CHAPTER 2

THE MATHEMATICS OF SURVIVAL MODELS

2.1 INTRODUCTION

Before we begin our exploration of the topic of estimating a survival model, we need to develop a complete understanding of the nature of survival models themselves.

Since a survival model is a special kind of probability distribution, most of the material in this chapter will be familiar to those with a good knowledge of probability. Furthermore, the survival model is discussed in many standard textbooks on actuarial mathematics. (See, for example, Bowers, et al. [10].)

2.2 THE DISTRIBUTION OF T

2.2.1 *The Survival Distribution Function*

In Chapter 1 we chose to define and describe a survival model in terms of the function $S(t)$, which represents $\Pr(T > t)$, where T is the *failure time* random variable. This function of the random variable T is called the Survival Distribution Function (SDF). We recall that it gives the probability that failure (death) will occur *after* time t, which is the same as the probability that the entity, known to exist at time $t=0$, will survive to *at least* time t. We also recall that $S(0) = 1$ and $S(\infty) = 0$.

2.2.2 *The Cumulative Distribution Function*

The Cumulative Distribution Function (CDF) of T is $F(t)$. The CDF gives the probability that the random variable will assume a value less than or equal to t. That is,

$$F(t) = \Pr(T \leq t). \tag{2.1}$$

In the special case of our failure time random variable, $F(t)$ gives the probability that failure (death) will occur *not later than* time t. It should be clear that

$$F(t) = 1 - S(t), \tag{2.2}$$

and that $F(0) = 0$ and $F(\infty) = 1$.

In most probability textbooks, the CDF, $F(t)$, is given greater emphasis than is the SDF, $S(t)$. But for our special kind of random variable, $S(t)$ will receive greater attention.

2.2.3 *The Probability Density Function*

For the special case of a continuous random variable, the Probability Density Function (PDF), $f(t)$, is defined as the derivative of $F(t)$. Thus

$$f(t) = \frac{d}{dt} F(t) = -\frac{d}{dt} S(t), \ \ t \geq 0. \tag{2.3}$$

Consequently, it is easy to see that

$$F(t) = \int_0^t f(y) \, dy, \tag{2.4}$$

and

$$S(t) = \int_t^\infty f(y) \, dy. \tag{2.5}$$

Of course it must be true that

$$\int_0^\infty f(y) \, dy = 1. \tag{2.6}$$

Although we have given mathematical definitions of $f(t)$, it will be useful to describe $f(t)$ more fully in the context of the failure time random variable. Whereas $F(t)$ and $S(t)$ are probabilities which relate to certain time *intervals*, $f(t)$ relates to a point of time, and is not a probability, *per se*. We prefer to refer to $f(t)$ by its conventional description as "probability density." It is the density of failure *at* time t, and is an *instantaneous* measure, as opposed to an interval measure.

It is important to recognize that $f(t)$ is the *unconditional* density of failure at time t. By this we mean that it is the density of failure at time t given *only* that the entity existed at $t = 0$. The significance of this point will become clearer in the next subsection.

2.2.4 *The Hazard Rate Function*

We have just established that the PDF of T, f(t), is the unconditional density of failure at time t. We now define a *conditional* density of failure at time t, such density to be conditional on survival to time t. This conditional instantaneous measure of failure at time t, given survival to time t, will be called the *hazard rate* at time t, or the Hazard Rate Function (HRF) when viewed as a function of t. It will be denoted by $\lambda(t)$.

In general, if a conditional measure is multiplied by the probability of obtaining the condition, then the corresponding unconditional measure will result. Specifically,

(Conditional density of failure at time t, given survival to time t)
X (Probability of survival to time t) =
(Unconditional density of failure at time t).

Symbolically this states that

$$\lambda(t) \cdot S(t) = f(t), \tag{2.7}$$

or

$$\lambda(t) = \frac{f(t)}{S(t)}. \tag{2.8}$$

Mathematically, formulas (2.8) and (2.3) define the HRF and the PDF of the failure time random variable, and these mathematical definitions are, of course, very important. However, it is equally important to have a clear understanding of the descriptive meanings of $\lambda(t)$ and f(t). They are both instantaneous measures of the density of failure at time t; they differ from each other in that $\lambda(t)$ is conditional on survival to time t, whereas f(t) is unconditional (i.e., given only existence at time $t=0$).

In the actuarial context of human survival models, failure means death, or mortality, and the hazard rate is normally called the *force of mortality*. We will discuss the actuarial context further in this chapter and in Chapter 3.

Some important mathematical consequences follow from formula (2.8). Since $f(t) = -\frac{d}{dt} S(t)$, it follows that

$$\lambda(t) = \frac{-\frac{d}{dt} S(t)}{S(t)} = -\frac{d}{dt} \ln S(t). \tag{2.9}$$

Integrating, we have

$$\int_0^t \lambda(y)\,dy = -\ln S(t), \tag{2.10}$$

or

$$S(t) = \exp\left[-\int_0^t \lambda(y)\,dy\right]. \tag{2.11}$$

The Cumulative Hazard Function (CHF) is defined to be

$$\Lambda(t) = \int_0^t \lambda(y)\,dy = -\ln S(t), \tag{2.12}$$

so that

$$S(t) = e^{-\Lambda(t)}. \tag{2.13}$$

2.2.5 *The Moments of the Random Variable T*

The first moment of a continuous random variable defined on $[0, \infty)$ is given by

$$E[T] = \int_0^\infty t \cdot f(t)\,dt, \tag{2.14}$$

if the integral exists, and otherwise the first moment is undefined. Integration by parts yields the alternative formula

$$E[T] = \int_0^\infty S(t)\,dt, \tag{2.15}$$

a form which is frequently used to find the first moment of a failure time random variable.

The second moment of T is given by

$$E[T^2] = \int_0^\infty t^2 \cdot f(t)\,dt, \tag{2.16}$$

if the integral exists, so the variance of T can be found from

$$\text{Var}(T) = E[T^2] - \{E[T]\}^2. \tag{2.17}$$

Specific expressions can be developed for the moments of T for specific forms of f(t). This will be pursued in the following section.

Another property of the future lifetime random variable that is of interest is its median value. We recall that the median of a random variable is the value for which there is a 50% chance that T will exceed (and thus also not exceed) that value. Mathematically, y is the median of T if

$$\Pr(T > y) = \Pr(T \le y) = \tfrac{1}{2}, \tag{2.18}$$

so that $S(y) = F(y) = \tfrac{1}{2}$.

2.2.6 *Actuarial Survival Models*

Thus far in this section we have considered only the random variable T, and have looked at various quantities related to that random variable and the interrelationships among those quantities. Exactly the same quantities and relationships exist for the actuarial survival model represented by the SDF $S(x)$, $x \ge 0$.

Special symbols are used in the actuarial context for some of the concepts defined in this section. The hazard rate, called the force of mortality, is denoted by μ_x, rather than $\lambda(x)$. Thus

$$\mu_x = \frac{-\frac{d}{dx} S(x)}{S(x)} = -\frac{d}{dx} \ln S(x). \tag{2.9a}$$

It is also customary to denote the first moment of X by $\overset{\circ}{e}_0$. Thus

$$\overset{\circ}{e}_0 = E[X] = \int_0^\infty x \cdot f(x)\, dx. \tag{2.19}$$

Since $\overset{\circ}{e}_0$ is the unconditional expected value of X, given only alive at $x=0$, it is called the *complete expectation of life at birth*.

For the select model $S(t;x)$, recall that t is a value of the random variable T, and x is the age at which the person to whom $S(t;x)$ refers was selected. The expected value of T, $E[T;x]$, gives the expected future lifetime (or expectation of life) for a person selected at age x, and is denoted by $\overset{o}{e}_{[x]}$. The HRF is denoted by $\mu_{[x]+t}$, and is given by

$$\mu_{[x]+t} \;=\; \frac{-\frac{d}{dt} S(t;x)}{S(t;x)} \;=\; -\frac{d}{dt} \ln S(t;x). \tag{2.9b}$$

We recognize that the moments of X or T given above are all unconditional. Conditional moments, and other conditional measures, are defined conceptually in Section 2.4, and the standard actuarial notation for them is reviewed in Chapter 3.

2.3 *EXAMPLES OF PARAMETRIC SURVIVAL MODELS*

In this section we explore several non-negative continuous probability distribuions which are candidates for serving as survival models. In practice, some distributions fit better than others to the *empirical* evidence of the shape of a failure time distribution, so we will comment on each distribution we present regarding its suitability as a survival model.

2.3.1 *The Uniform Distribution*

The uniform distribution is a simple two-parameter distribution, with a constant PDF. The parameters of the distribution are the limits of the interval on the real number axis over which it is defined, and its PDF is the reciprocal of that interval length. Thus if the random variable is defined over the interval [a, b], then $f(t) = \frac{1}{b-a}$ for $a \le t \le b$, and $f(t) = 0$ elsewhere.

For the special case of the future lifetime random variable, $a=0$. Therefore, b is the length of the interval, as well as the greatest value of t for which $f(t) > 0$. When the uniform distribution is used as a survival model, the Greek ω is frequently used for this parameter, so the distribution is defined by

$$f(t) \;=\; \frac{1}{\omega}, \;\; 0 \le t \le \omega. \tag{2.20}$$

The following properties of the uniform distribution easily follow, and should be verified by the reader:

$$F(t) \; = \; \int_0^t f(y) \, dy \; = \; \tfrac{t}{\omega} \tag{2.21}$$

$$S(t) \; = \; 1 - F(t) \; = \; \int_t^\omega f(y) \, dy \; = \; \tfrac{\omega - t}{\omega} \tag{2.22}$$

$$\lambda(t) \; = \; \frac{f(t)}{S(t)} \; = \; \tfrac{1}{\omega - t} \tag{2.23}$$

$$E[T] \; = \; \int_0^\omega t \cdot f(t) \, dt \; = \; \tfrac{\omega}{2} \tag{2.24}$$

$$\mathrm{Var}(T) \; = \; E[T^2] - \{E[T]\}^2 \; = \; \tfrac{\omega^2}{12} \tag{2.25}$$

The uniform distribution, as a survival model, is not appropriate over a broad range of time, at least as a model for *human* survival. It is of historical interest, however, to note that it was the first continuous probability distribution to be suggested for that purpose, in 1724, by Abraham de Moivre.

The major use of this distribution is over short ranges of time (or age). We will explore this use of the uniform distribution quite thoroughly in Section 3.5.1.

2.3.2 *The Exponential Distribution*

This very popular one-parameter distribution is defined by its SDF to be

$$S(t) \; = \; e^{-\lambda t}, \quad t \geq 0, \;\; \lambda \geq 0. \tag{2.26}$$

It then follows that the PDF is

$$f(t) \; = \; -\frac{d}{dt} S(t) \; = \; \lambda e^{-\lambda t}, \tag{2.27}$$

so that the HRF is

$$\lambda(t) \; = \; \frac{f(t)}{S(t)} \; = \; \lambda, \tag{2.28}$$

a constant. In the actuarial context, where the hazard rate is generally called the force of mortality, the exponential distribution is referred to as the "constant force" distribution.

EXAMPLE 2.1: Show that, for the exponential distribution,

$$E[T] = \frac{1}{\lambda} \tag{2.29}$$

and

$$Var(T) = \frac{1}{\lambda^2}. \tag{2.30}$$

SOLUTION: $E[T] = \int_0^\infty t \cdot f(t)\,dt = \int_0^\infty t\lambda e^{-\lambda t}\,dt.$ Integration by parts produces $\int_0^\infty e^{-\lambda t}\,dt$, whence $E[T] = -\frac{1}{\lambda}e^{-\lambda t}\Big|_0^\infty = \frac{1}{\lambda}.$ We also have $E[T^2] = \int_0^\infty t^2\lambda e^{-\lambda t}\,dt = 2\int_0^\infty t e^{-\lambda t}\,dt = \frac{2}{\lambda}\int_0^\infty e^{-\lambda t}\,dt = \frac{2}{\lambda^2}.$ Then $Var(T) = \frac{2}{\lambda^2} - \left\{\frac{1}{\lambda}\right\}^2 = \frac{1}{\lambda^2}.$

The exponential distribution, with its property of a constant hazard rate, is frequently used in reliability engineering as a survival model for inanimate objects such as machine parts. Like the uniform distribution, however, it is not appropriate as a model for human survival over a broad range, but is used extensively over short intervals, such as one year, due to its mathematical simplicity. This will be explored in Section 3.5.2.

Since we do not contemplate using the uniform or exponential as a model for human survival, we use T, rather than X for our failure time random variable. For the next three distributions, we use X to suggest that they are more useful as models of human survival.

2.3.3 *The Gompertz Distribution*

This distribution was suggested as a model for human survival by Gompertz [27] in 1825. The distribution is usually defined by its hazard rate as

$$\lambda(x) = Bc^x, \quad x \geq 0, \quad B > 0, \quad c > 1. \tag{2.31}$$

Then the SDF is given by

$$S(x) = \exp\left[-\int_0^x \lambda(y)\,dy\right] = \exp\left[\frac{B}{\ln c}\,(1-c^x)\right]. \tag{2.32}$$

The PDF is given by $\lambda(x) \cdot S(x)$, and is clearly not a very convenient mathematical form. In particular, the mean of the distribution, E[X], is not easily found.

2.3.4 *The Makeham Distribution*

In 1860 Makeham [42] modified the Gompertz distribution by taking the HRF to be

$$\lambda(x) \; = \; A + Bc^x, \;\; x \geq 0, \;\; B > 0, \;\; c > 1, \;\; A > -B. \tag{2.33}$$

Makeham was suggesting that part of the hazard at any age is independent of the age itself, so a constant was added to the Gompertz hazard rate.

The SDF for this distribution is given by

$$S(x) \; = \; \exp\left[-\int_0^x (A + Bc^y)\,dy\right] \; = \; \exp\left[\frac{B}{\ln c}\,(1 - c^x) - Ax\right]. \tag{2.34}$$

Again it is clear that the PDF for this distribution is not mathematically tractable, so the calculation of probabilities, moments, or other quantities is somewhat difficult.

2.3.5 *The Weibull Distribution*

This distribution is defined by

$$\lambda(x) \; = \; k \cdot x^n, \;\; x \geq 0, \;\; k > 0, \;\; n > 0. \tag{2.35}$$

Its SDF is given by

$$S(x) \; = \; \exp\left[-\int_0^x k \cdot y^n\,dy\right] \; = \; \exp\left[-\frac{k \cdot x^{n+1}}{n+1}\right]. \tag{2.36}$$

2.3.6 *Other Distributions*

Other probability distributions are very useful as models for other random variables, such as the *amount of claim* random variable in non-life insurance applications (see, for example, Hogg and Klugman [30]). These distributions, which include the Gamma, the Chi-square (a special case of the Gamma), the Normal, the Lognormal, the Pareto, and others, are not appropriate for the failure time random variable which we are considering in this text.

The Chi-square distribution, however, is useful in testing the fit of empirical data to a hypothesized parametric distribution (see Chapter 8).

2.3.7 *Summary of Parametric Models*

We have briefly explored five distributions here: two (uniform and exponential) which are mathematically simple, and three (Gompertz, Makeham
and Weibull) which are not.

For our actuarial survival model, denoted by S(x), the last three will
receive further consideration in Chapter 8. For many illustrations, where we
wish to avoid mathematical complexity, we will use the uniform or the
exponential for illustrative purposes only, not necessarily suggesting that they
are applicable in practice. The exponential has been assumed to be
applicable in many situations not involving healthy human lives, and has
been widely used in those situations.

2.4 *CONDITIONAL MEASURES AND TRUNCATED DISTRIBUTIONS*

Thus far we have only considered probabilities measured from age x=0,
denoting such probabilities by S(x) or F(x). Specifically, such probabilities
were unconditional, since we knew only that the person was alive at x=0.

Now we consider the case of a person known to be alive at age x>0,
and we seek probabilities (and densities) of survival (or failure) measured
from age x.

2.4.1. *Conditional Probabilities and Densities*

What is the probability that a person, known to be alive at age x, will still
be alive n years later (i.e., at age x+n)? We seek

$$\Pr(\text{survival to } x+n, \text{ given survival to } x).$$

If we multiply this conditional probability by the probability of obtaining the
condition, which is S(x), we obtain the unconditional probability of survival
to age x+n, which is S(x+n). Thus the desired probability, which we denote
by $_np_x$, is given by

$$_np_x = \frac{S(x+n)}{S(x)}. \tag{2.37}$$

The companion conditional probability for death prior to age x+n,
given alive at x, is given by

$$_nq_x = 1 - {_np_x} = \frac{S(x) - S(x+n)}{S(x)}. \tag{2.38}$$

It is important to distinguish $_np_x$, a conditional probability, from the unconditional probability represented by S(n;x). In each case we seek the probability that a person age x will survive to age x+n. When we determine this probability in accordance with the model S(x), it is conditional, it is denoted by $_np_x$, and it is given by $\dfrac{S(x+n)}{S(x)}$. If the desired probability is determined from S(t;x), then it is unconditional, it is given directly by S(n;x), and it is denoted by $_nP_{[x]}$, to distinguish it from $_np_x$.

Similar remarks hold for the companion probability of death prior to age x+n. If it is determined from S(x), then it is conditional (on survival to x), it is given by $\dfrac{S(x) - S(x+n)}{S(x)}$, and it is denoted by $_nq_x$. But if this probability is determined from S(t;x), then it is unconditional, it is given directly by F(n;x), and it is denoted by $_nq_{[x]}$.

This is not to suggest that we cannot have conditional probabilities in terms of S(t;x), as shown by the following example.

EXAMPLE 2.2: Find, in terms of S(t;x), the probability that a person selected at age x, but known to be alive at x+10, will die prior to age x+20.
SOLUTION: We seek the probability of death prior to age x+20, given alive at age x+10. We denote this probability by $_{10}q_{[x]+10}$. It is equal to $1 - \text{Pr}(\text{Survival to x+20, given survival to x+10}) = 1 - {}_{10}P_{[x]+10}$. Now if the conditional probability $_{10}P_{[x]+10}$ is multiplied by the probability of obtaining the condition, which is S(10;x), the result is the unconditional probability of survival to x+20, namely S(20;x). Thus

$$_{10}q_{[x]+10} = 1 - {}_{10}P_{[x]+10} = 1 - \frac{S(20;x)}{S(10;x)}.$$

Consider next the PDF for death at age y, given alive at age x (y>x). If this conditional density is multiplied by the probability of obtaining the condition, which is S(x), then the unconditional density, which is f(y), results. Thus the conditional density is

$$\frac{f(y)}{S(x)}. \tag{2.39}$$

We will derive this conditional density more formally in the next subsection.

Finally, consider the conditional HRF (or force of mortality) for death at age y, given alive at age x (y>x). Recall that the HRF is itself always conditional on survival to the age at which it applies. (There is no such thing as an unconditional HRF.) Thus, since y>x, and μ_y itself is conditional on survival to y, then the statement "given survival to x" is redundant. Therefore, this "conditonal" HRF to which we allude is clearly the same as μ_y itself. This intuitive result will be shown more formally in the following subsection.

2.4.2 *Lower Truncation of the Distribution of X*

When we speak of probabilities (or densities) conditional on survival to age x, we are dealing with the distribution of a subset of the sample space of the random variable X, namely those values of X which fall in excess of x. This distribution is called the distribution of X *truncated below* at x.

Our conditional survival probability $_np_x$ can now be stated formally as

$$_np_x \;=\; \Pr(X > x+n \,|\, X>x) \;=\; S(x+n \,|\, X>x). \tag{2.40}$$

In words, this asks for the probability that the age at death will exceed x+n, given that it does exceed x. It is easy to see that this is the same concept as "probability of survival to x+n, given survival to x." Thus, from formulas (2.37) and (2.40) we find that

$$S(x+n \,|\, X>x) \;=\; \frac{S(x+n)}{S(x)}. \tag{2.41}$$

Similarly,

$$\begin{aligned} _nq_x &= \Pr(X \leq x+n \,|\, X>x) \\ &= \Pr(x < X \leq x+n \,|\, X>x) \;=\; F(x+n \,|\, X>x). \end{aligned} \tag{2.42}$$

Comparison of formulas (2.38) and (2.42) shows that

$$F(x+n \,|\, X>x) \;=\; \frac{S(x) - S(x+n)}{S(x)} \;=\; \frac{F(x+n) - F(x)}{1 - F(x)}, \tag{2.43}$$

since $S(x) = 1 - F(x)$. Note that both (2.41) and (2.43) result from the general probability relationship $P(A\,|\,B) \cdot P(B) = P(A \cap B)$.

Next, the conditional density function for death at age y, given alive at age x (y>x), is denoted by $f(y\,|\,X>x)$. We have

$$f(y\,|\,X>x) \;=\; \frac{d}{dy}\, F(y\,|\,X>x) \;=\; \frac{d}{dy}\, \frac{F(y) - F(x)}{1 - F(x)} \;=\; \frac{f(y)}{1 - F(x)},$$

since $\frac{d}{dy}\, F(x) = 0$. Thus we have

$$f(y \,|\, X > x) = \frac{f(y)}{S(x)}, \qquad (2.39a)$$

as already established intuitively by (2.39).

Finally, the alleged "conditional HRF at y, given alive at x (y>x)", was shown intuitively to be the same as the basic μ_y (or $\lambda(y)$). This result can now be mathematically verified. Denoting this "conditional HRF" by $\lambda(y \,|\, X > x)$, we have

$$\lambda(y \,|\, X > x) = \frac{f(y \,|\, X > x)}{S(y \,|\, X > x)} = \frac{f(y)}{S(x)} \div \frac{S(y)}{S(x)} = \frac{f(y)}{S(y)} = \lambda(y). \qquad (2.44)$$

In summary, the functions $S(y \,|\, X > x)$, $F(y \,|\, X > x)$ and $f(y \,|\, X > x)$ are the functions for the truncated distribution of X, truncated below at x. The HRF for this truncated distribution, denoted by $\lambda(y \,|\, X > x)$, is identical to the untruncated $\lambda(y)$.

2.4.3 *Upper and Lower Truncation of the Distribution of X*

A more general view of truncated distributions is to consider the distribution of the subset of the sample space of X which falls between y and z. Still using X for the age at death random variable, the truncated SDF is given by

$$S(x \,|\, y < X \le z) = Pr(X > x \,|\, y < X \le z) = Pr(x < X \le z \,|\, y < X \le z), \qquad (2.45)$$

for $y < x \le z$. In words, we speak of the probability that death will occur after age x, given that it does occur between y and z. Since it must occur prior to z, then we are really talking about death between x and z. If this conditional probability is multiplied by the probability of obtaining the conditon, which is $S(y) - S(z)$, then the unconditional probability for death between x and z, which is $S(x) - S(z)$, results. Thus

$$S(x \,|\, y < X \le z) = \frac{S(x) - S(z)}{S(y) - S(z)}. \qquad (2.46)$$

The corresponding truncated CDF is given by

$$F(x \,|\, y < X \le z) = Pr(y < X \le x \,|\, y < X \le z) . \qquad (2.47)$$

Since $F(x \,|\, y < X \le z) = 1 - S(x \,|\, y < X \le z)$, we have

$$F(x \mid y < X \leq z) \;=\; \frac{S(y) - S(x)}{S(y) - S(z)} = \frac{F(x) - F(y)}{F(z) - F(y)}, \qquad (2.48)$$

directly from formula (2.46).

Next, the doubly-truncated PDF is given by

$$f(x \mid y < X \leq z) \;=\; -\frac{d}{dx}\, S(x \mid y < X \leq z) \;=\; -\frac{d}{dx}\, \frac{S(x) - S(z)}{S(y) - S(z)},$$

producing

$$f(x \mid y < X \leq z) \;=\; \frac{f(x)}{S(y) - S(z)}, \qquad (2.49)$$

since $-\dfrac{d}{dx} S(x) = f(x)$, and $-\dfrac{d}{dx} S(z) = 0$.

Finally, the doubly-truncated HRF is given by

$$\lambda(x \mid y < X \leq z) \;=\; \frac{f(x \mid y < X \leq z)}{S(x \mid y < X \leq z)},$$

producing

$$\lambda(x \mid y < X \leq z) \;=\; \frac{f(x)}{S(y) - S(z)} \div \frac{S(x) - S(z)}{S(y) - S(z)} \;=\; \frac{f(x)}{S(x) - S(z)}.$$

Since $f(x) = \lambda(x) \cdot S(x)$ in the untruncated distribution, then we have

$$\lambda(x \mid y < X \leq z) \;=\; \frac{\lambda(x) \cdot S(x)}{S(x) - S(z)}. \qquad (2.50)$$

Formula (2.50) shows that, whereas truncation only from below did not affect the HRF, truncation from above does (since the truncated HRF is a function of z). This result is intuitive. Since the HRF at x is conditional on survival to x, then truncation below x is immaterial. However, truncation above x has an effect on the HRF at x, since the time interval remaining for death is shortened. It should be clear that as $z \rightarrow x$ from above, $\lambda(x \mid y < X \leq z)$ becomes infinitely large, since the interval for death approaches zero. This result is clearly seen mathematically by taking the limit as $z \rightarrow x$ in formula (2.50).

2.4.4 *Moments of Truncated Distributions*

The first moment of the doubly-truncated distribution of X is given by

$$E[X \mid y < X \leq z] = \int_y^z x \cdot f(x \mid y < X \leq z) \, dx. \qquad (2.51)$$

Of special interest is the distribution of X truncated only below at y. Then

$$E[X \mid X > y] = \int_y^\infty x \cdot f(x \mid X > y) \, dx, \qquad (2.52)$$

if the expectation exists. Since X is the age at death of a person known to be alive at y, then formula (2.52) gives the expected age at death for such a person. If we subtract y from this expected age at death, we obtain the expected future lifetime of such a person. This expected future lifetime is denoted by $\overset{\circ}{e}_y$, and is called the "expectation of life at age y". Formally,

$$\overset{\circ}{e}_y = E[X \mid X > y] - y. \qquad (2.53)$$

Since $\int_y^\infty f(x \mid X > y) \, dx = 1$, we can write

$$\overset{\circ}{e}_y = \int_y^\infty (x - y) \cdot f(x \mid X > y) \, dx \qquad (2.54a)$$

$$= \int_0^\infty t \cdot f(t + y \mid X > y) \, dt, \qquad (2.54b)$$

and since $f(t+y \mid X > y)$ is the PDF of $(X - y \mid X > y)$, then "expected future lifetime" is a good name for $\overset{\circ}{e}_y$.

Furthermore, if it exists, then

$$E[X^2 \mid X > y] = \int_y^\infty x^2 \cdot f(x \mid X > y) \, dx. \qquad (2.55)$$

Then the variance of future lifetime is given by

$$Var(X - y \mid X > y) = Var(X \mid X > y) = E[X^2 \mid X > y] - \left\{ E[X \mid X > y] \right\}^2. \quad (2.56)$$

2.4.5 *The Central Rate*

Another type of conditional measure over the interval from age x to age x+1 is called the *central rate* of death, and is denoted by m_x. It is defined as the weighted average value of the HRF $\lambda(x)$ over the interval, using, as the weight for $\lambda(y)$, the probability of survival to age y. Formally,

$$m_x = \frac{\int_x^{x+1} S(y) \cdot \lambda(y)\,dy}{\int_x^{x+1} S(y)\,dy}, \tag{2.57}$$

where the denominator is the sum of the weights for a continuous case weighted average.

More generally, $_nm_x$ is the average hazard, or central rate of death, over the interval from x to x+n, and is given by

$$_nm_x = \frac{\int_x^{x+n} S(y) \cdot \lambda(y)\,dy}{\int_x^{x+n} S(y)\,dy} = \frac{\int_0^n S(x+s) \cdot \lambda(x+s)\,ds}{\int_0^n S(x+s)\,ds}, \tag{2.58}$$

the second expression resulting from the simple change of variable $y = x+s$. If we divide both numerator and denominator of (2.58) by $S(x)$, we obtain

$$_nm_x = \frac{\int_0^n \dfrac{S(x+s)}{S(x)} \cdot \lambda(x+s)\,ds}{\int_0^n \dfrac{S(x+s)}{S(x)}\,ds} = \frac{\int_0^n {}_sp_x\mu_{x+s}\,ds}{\int_0^n {}_sp_x\,ds}, \tag{2.59}$$

since $_sp_x$ is the conditional probability $\dfrac{S(x+s)}{S(x)}$, and μ_{x+s} is the standard actuarial symbol for $\lambda(x+s)$. The second expression in (2.59) is a common actuarial form for $_nm_x$. We will return to this function in the next chapter, and make some use of it in estimating the tabular survival model in Part II of the text.

EXAMPLE 2.3 : If X has an exponential distribution, show that this implies $m_x = -\ln p_x$.

SOLUTION : If X is exponential, the HRF is constant, with $\lambda(y) = \lambda$ for all y. Then, from formula (2.57), $m_x = \dfrac{\lambda \cdot \displaystyle\int_x^{x+1} S(y)\,dy}{\displaystyle\int_x^{x+1} S(y)\,dy} = \lambda.$

Furthermore, $p_x = \dfrac{S(x+1)}{S(x)} = \dfrac{e^{-\lambda(x+1)}}{e^{-\lambda(x)}} = e^{-\lambda}$. Thus $\lambda = -\ln p_x$, and since $m_x = \lambda$, then $m_x = -\ln p_x$.

2.4.6 *Use of Conditional Probabilities in Estimation*

We have noted that the main business of this text will be the estimation of an operative survival model, such estimation to be based on the data of a sample.

Suppose we wish to estimate, say, $S(10)$, the probability of survival from $t=0$ to $t=10$. In many cases the nature of the study (and the data) will suggest that we consider only the time interval from $t=i$ to $t=i+1$, and estimate the conditional probability of survival over that interval. That is, we will estimate $\dfrac{S(i+1)}{S(i)}$, the probability of survival to $i+1$, given alive at i. This conditional probability has been called p_i, so the *estimate* of it which we obtain will be called $\hat{p}_i$, for $i = 0,1,\cdots,9$. We will then obtain our estimate of $S(10)$ by multiplying these several $\hat{p}_i$. Thus we will obtain $\hat{S}(10) = \hat{p}_0 \cdot \hat{p}_1 \cdots \hat{p}_9$, or, in general

$$\hat{S}(t) \;=\; \hat{p}_0 \cdot \hat{p}_1 \cdots \hat{p}_{t-1}. \tag{2.60}$$

In many cases it will be natural to first estimate q_i, the conditional probability of failure (death) in $(i, i+1]$, given alive at i; then take $\hat{p}_i = 1-\hat{q}_i$, where $\hat{q}_i$ is the estimate of q_i; and finally obtain $\hat{S}(t)$ by multiplying these conditional $\hat{p}_i$ estimates. This approach to estimating the survival function will be utilized mainly in Chapters 6 and 7.

2.5 *TRANSFORMATION OF RANDOM VARIABLES*

Suppose we have a random variable X, with known probability distribution, and we consider a new random variable Y, which is some function of X. That is, let

$$y \;=\; g(x) \tag{2.61}$$

be a function of x such that the inverse function $x = g^{-1}(y) = h(y)$ exists. We seek the probability distribution of Y.

Let $y = g(x)$ be a strictly increasing function, as shown in Figure 2.1 on page 28. Since $g(x)$ is increasing, then if X is less than or equal to x, it follows that Y is less than or equal to the unique value of y which corresponds to the given value of x. Thus if $X \le x$, then $Y \le g(x)$. Conversely, if $Y \le y$, then $X \le h(y)$, and the probabilities of these events are equal. That is,

$$\Pr(Y \le y) \;=\; \Pr(X \le h(y)) , \tag{2.62}$$

or

$$F(y) = F[h(y)] . \tag{2.63}$$

Equation (2.63) can be confusing since the CDF's on opposite sides of the equation are not the same function. The one on the left is the CDF of the random variable Y, whereas the one on the right is for the random variable X. To clarify this we write

$$F_Y(y) = F_X[h(y)]. \tag{2.63a}$$

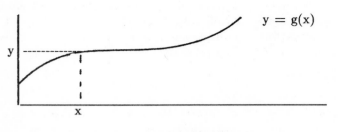

FIGURE 2.1

From (2.63a), which relates the CDF's of the random variables X and Y, we can derive relationships for the SDF's, PDF's and HRF's as well.

Since the SDF is the complement of the CDF, it follows from (2.63a) that $1 - S_Y(y) = 1 - S_X[h(y)]$, or that

$$S_Y(y) = S_X[h(y)]. \tag{2.64}$$

Next, the PDF is the derivative of the CDF, so we differentiate both sides of (2.63a) with respect to y, obtaining

$$f_Y(y) = \frac{d}{dy} F_Y(y) = \frac{d}{dy} F_X[h(y)] = f_X[h(y)] \cdot \frac{d}{dy} h(y),$$

using the chain rule to differentiate $F_X[h(y)]$. Since $h(y)$ is simply x, we can write

$$f_Y(y) = f_X[h(y)] \cdot \frac{dx}{dy} . \tag{2.65}$$

Finally, the HRF is the ratio of the PDF to the SDF. Thus

$$\lambda_Y(y) \;=\; \frac{f_Y(y)}{S_Y(y)} \;=\; \frac{f_X[h(y)] \cdot \frac{dx}{dy}}{S_X[h(y)]} \;=\; \lambda_X[h(y)] \cdot \frac{dx}{dy}. \qquad (2.66)$$

EXAMPLE 2.4: Suppose X has an exponential distribution with $\lambda = 1$. Let $y = g(x) = x^{1/2}$. Find the SDF, PDF and HRF of the transformed random variable Y.

SOLUTION: Note that $y = g(x)$ is strictly increasing, and that $x = h(y) = y^2$. Then $F_Y(y) = F_X(y^2)$. Since X is exponential, then $F_X(x) = 1 - e^{-x}$, so we have $F_Y(y) = 1 - e^{-y^2}$, and $S_Y(y) = e^{-y^2}$. Next,

$$f_Y(y) = \frac{d}{dy}F_Y(y) = 2y \cdot e^{-y^2}. \text{ Finally, } \lambda_Y(y) = \frac{f_Y(y)}{1 - F_Y(y)} = \frac{2y \cdot e^{-y^2}}{e^{-y^2}} = 2y.$$

Alternatively, since we have $\lambda_X(x) = \lambda_X[h(y)] = 1$, then, from (2.66), $\lambda_Y(y)$ is simply $\frac{dx}{dy} = 2y$. Note that Y has a Weibull distribution with $k = 2$ and $n = 1$.

If $y = g(x)$ is a strictly decreasing function, as shown in Figure 2.2, then our reasoning and our results change a bit.

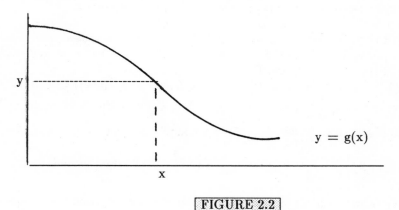

FIGURE 2.2

Here we can see that if X is less than x, then Y will be *greater* than the value of y which corresponds to the given value of x; or, conversely, if $Y > y$, then $X < h(y)$. In terms of probabilities, we have

$$\Pr(Y > y) \;=\; \Pr(X < h(y)) \;=\; \Pr(X \le h(y)) \qquad (2.67)$$

or

$$S_Y(y) = F_X[h(y)] = 1 - S_X[h(y)]. \qquad (2.68)$$

Then

$$F_Y(y) = 1 - S_Y(y) = 1 - F_X[h(y)] = S_X[h(y)], \qquad (2.69)$$

and

$$f_Y(y) = \frac{d}{dy} F_Y(y) = -\frac{d}{dy} F_X[h(y)] = -f_X[h(y)] \cdot \frac{dx}{dy}, \qquad (2.70)$$

by the chain rule. Since $x = h(y)$ is a decreasing function, then $\frac{dx}{dy}$ is negative and $f_Y(y)$ is positive, as required. Finally,

$$\lambda_Y(y) = \frac{f_Y(y)}{S_Y(y)} = \frac{-f_X[h(y)] \cdot \frac{dx}{dy}}{1 - S_X[h(y)]} = -\lambda_X[h(y)] \cdot \frac{S_X[h(y)]}{1 - S_X[h(y)]} \cdot \frac{dx}{dy}.$$

$$(2.71)$$

Note that the expression for $\lambda_Y(y)$ in terms of $\lambda_X(x)$ is not as convenient as it is for the case where $y = g(x)$ is a strictly increasing function.

EXAMPLE 2.5 : As in Example 2.4, let X have a standard exponential distribution, so that $F_X(x) = 1 - e^{-x}$, but this time let $y = g(x) = \frac{1}{x}$. Again find the SDF, PDF and HRF of Y.
SOLUTION : We have $x = h(y) = \frac{1}{y}$, so $S_Y(y) = F_X[h(y)] = 1 - e^{-(1/y)}$. Then, $f_Y(y) = -\frac{d}{dy} S_Y(y) = y^{-2} \cdot e^{-(1/y)}$. Finally, the HRF is given by

$$\lambda_Y(y) = \frac{f_Y(y)}{S_Y(y)} = y^{-2} \cdot \frac{e^{-(1/y)}}{1 - e^{-(1/y)}}. \qquad \text{Again note that with } \lambda_X(x) = 1$$

and $\frac{dx}{dy} = -y^{-2}$, the last expression of (2.71) can be used to find $\lambda_Y(y)$.

We now wish to explore two special cases of transformations of random variables.

2.5.1 *Linear Transformations*

If $y = g(x) = \frac{x - \alpha}{\beta}$, where α and β are constants, $\beta \neq 0$, then $x = h(y) = \alpha + \beta y$, and $\frac{dx}{dy} = \beta$. If the transformation is increasing ($\beta > 0$), then, from (2.66),

$$\lambda_Y(y) = \beta \cdot \lambda_X[\alpha + \beta y]. \tag{2.72}$$

This says that the hazard at a given value of the new variable is β times the hazard at the value of the original variable corresponding to the given value of the new variable.

For certain kinds of distributions, a linear transformation of that random variable produces a new random variable with the same kind of distribution as the original random variable.

EXAMPLE 2.6: Show that if X has a Gompertz distribution, then the transformed variable $Y = \dfrac{X - \alpha}{\beta}$ also has a Gompertz distribution when $\alpha = 0$.

SOLUTION: Since X is Gompertz, then $\lambda_X(x) = Bc^x$. From (2.72) we see that $\lambda_Y(y) = \beta \cdot Bc^{\alpha + \beta y} = \beta \cdot Bc^\alpha \cdot c^{\beta y} = B'c'^y$, where $c' = c^\beta$ and $B' = \beta \cdot Bc^\alpha$. This is not strictly a Gompertz distribution, since the domain of y is $[-\alpha/\beta, \infty)$, rather than $[0, \infty)$. When $\alpha = 0$, however, it is a Gompertz distribution.

2.5.2 *Probability Integral Transformations*

A special case of a transformation is one for which $y = g(x) = F_X(x)$, where $F_X(x)$ is a strictly increasing CDF of X. We note that $x = F_X^{-1}(y)$ is the inverse function $h(y)$. From (2.63a),

$$F_Y(y) = F_X[h(y)] = F_X\left[F_X^{-1}(y)\right] = y,$$

so, therefore, $f_Y(y) = \dfrac{d}{dy} F_Y(y) = 1$. This tells us that Y has a standard uniform distribution, with $f_Y(y) = 1$, for $0 \leq y \leq 1$.

If we let $y = g(x) = S_X(x)$, then we have a strictly decreasing function of x, but the result, namely that Y has a standard uniform distribution, will be the same. Note also that this result does not depend on the particluar probability distribution of X.

EXAMPLE 2.7: Let $y = g(x) = -\ln S_X(x)$. (Since $S_X(x)$ decreases from 1 to 0, then $\ln S_X(x)$ decreases from 0 to $-\infty$, and the transformed variable $y = g(x) = -\ln S_X(x)$ increases from 0 to ∞.) Find the distribution of Y.
SOLUTION: We have seen above that if $z = S_X(x)$, then Z has a standard uniform distribution. Thus we are considering $y = -\ln z$, with

inverse function $z = h(y) = e^{-y}$, so that $\frac{dz}{dy} = -e^{-y}$. Note that y is a decreasing function of z. From (2.70) we find $f_Y(y) = -f_Z[h(y)] \cdot \frac{dz}{dy}$. Now since Z is standard uniform, then $f_Z(z) = 1$ for all z, so (2.70) produces

$$f_Y(y) = -1 \cdot \frac{dz}{dy} = e^{-y}, \text{ for } y \geq 0.$$

Therefore, Y has a standard exponential distribution with $\lambda = 1$.

2.6   MEAN AND VARIANCE OF TRANSFORMED RANDOM VARIABLES

If $Y = g(x)$ is a random variable transformed from the random variable X, we may wish to find the expected value and variance of Y. Although $f_Y(y)$ is obtained in the transformation, it might turn out that the antiderivative of $y \cdot f(y)$ does not exist, so $E[Y]$ cannot be found in that manner. Note that this is the case in both Example 2.4 and Example 2.5, although $E[Y]$ in Example 2.4 can still be found, as we will see in the exercises.

Furthermore, the ability to find the mean of Y directly from the mean of X, and the variance of Y directly from the variance of X, is limited to linear transformations of X to Y. That is, if $Y = aX + b$, then we have $E[Y] = a \cdot E[X] + b$, and $Var(Y) = a^2 \cdot Var(X)$. But if $Y = X^{1/2}$ or $Y = X^{-1}$, as in our two examples, no such convenient result can be found.

For such cases we could use an approximate approach to finding $E[Y]$ and $Var(Y)$. One such approach would be the use of approximate integration to evaluate $\int_0^\infty y \cdot f(y) \, dy$ or $\int_0^\infty y^2 \cdot f(y) \, dy$. Another approach is the method of statistical differentials, which requires that $E[X]$ and $Var(X)$ be known, and that $y = g(x)$ be twice differentiable.

Let $E[X] = m$. We begin by expressing $g(X)$ in a Taylor series, expanded about $X = m$. Thus

$$g(X) = g(m) + (X-m) \cdot g'(m) + \tfrac{1}{2}(X-m)^2 \cdot g''(m) + \cdots, \quad (2.73)$$

where $g'(m)$ and $g''(m)$ are short-hand notation for $g'(x)|_{x=m}$ and for $g''(x)|_{x=m}$, respectively.

Next we take the expected value of both sides of (2.73), truncating the Taylor series after its third term, obtaining

$$E[Y] = E[g(X)] \approx g(m) + \tfrac{1}{2}g''(m) \cdot Var(X), \quad (2.74)$$

since $E[g(m)] = g(m)$, and $E[X-m] = 0$.

A rougher approximation is given by truncating the Taylor series after only two terms, obtaining

$$E[g(x)] \approx g(m). \qquad (2.75)$$

The variance of $g(X)$ is the expected value of $\{g(X) - E[g(X)]\}^2$. Using only the first two terms of (2.73) for $g(X)$, and using (2.75) for $E[g(X)]$, we have $g(X) - E[g(X)] \approx (X-m) \cdot g'(m)$. Then

$$\text{Var}\,[g(X)] = E\left[\left\{g(X) - E[g(X)]\right\}^2\right] \approx E\left[(X-m)^2[g'(m)]^2\right]$$

$$= [g'(m)]^2 \cdot \text{Var}(X). \qquad (2.76)$$

EXAMPLE 2.8 : Show that formulas (2.75) and (2.76) are exact for the linear transformation $Y = g(x) = aX + b$.
SOLUTION : We know that $E[Y] = a \cdot E[X] + b = am + b = g(m)$, so (2.75) is exact. Furthermore, $\text{Var}(Y) = a^2 \cdot \text{Var}(X)$. Since $g'(m) = a$, then $[g'(m)]^2 = a^2$, so (2.76) is exact. [Note: It is easy to see that the approximations will be exact for linear transformations, since $g''(x)$ and all higher order derivatives are zero.]

A major use of these results will arise in Part II of the text , where we wish to find the variance of an estimator. Frequently that estimator will be a complex function of another random variable, whose mean and variance are known (at least approximately), so the method of statistical differentials can be used.

In some cases, we may encounter a random variable which is a function of two (or more) other random variables, and we seek its mean and variance. For example, if $Y = g(X_1, X_2)$, and if $E[X_1] = m_1$, $E[X_2] = m_2$, $\text{Var}(X_1)$, $\text{Var}(X_2)$, and $\text{Cov}(X_1, X_2)$ are all known, then we can proceed similarly to the univariate case.

Expand $g(X_1, X_2)$ in a bivariate Taylor series as

$$g(X_1, X_2) = g(m_1, m_2) + (X_1 - m_1) \cdot g_1'(m_1, m_2) + (X_2 - m_2) \cdot g_2'(m_1, m_2)$$

$$+ \tfrac{1}{2}(X_1 - m_1)^2 \cdot g_1''(m_1, m_2) + \tfrac{1}{2}(X_2 - m_2)^2 \cdot g_2''(m_1, m_2)$$

$$+ (X_1 - m_1)(X_2 - m_2) \cdot g_{1,2}''(m_1, m_2) + \cdots , \qquad (2.77)$$

where $g_i'(m_1,m_2)$ represents $\left.\dfrac{\partial}{\partial x_i} g(x_1,x_2)\right|_{\substack{x_1=m_1 \\ x_2=m_2}}$, for $i=1,2$.   Similarly,

$g_i''(m_1,m_2)$ represents $\left.\dfrac{\partial^2}{\partial x_i^2} g(x_1,x_2)\right|_{\substack{x_1=m_1 \\ x_2=m_2}}$, $i=1,2$, and $g_{1,2}''(m_1,m_2)$ repre-

sents $\left.\dfrac{\partial^2}{\partial x_1 x_2} g(x_1,x_2)\right|_{\substack{x_1=m_1 \\ x_2=m_2}}$.   Taking the expected value of both sides of

(2.77), we obtain

$$E[g(X_1,X_2)] \approx g(m_1,m_2) + \tfrac{1}{2}g_1''(m_1,m_2) \cdot \mathrm{Var}(X_1) \tag{2.78}$$

$$+ \tfrac{1}{2}g_2''(m_1,m_2) \cdot \mathrm{Var}(X_2) + g_{1,2}''(m_1,m_2) \cdot \mathrm{Cov}(X_1,X_2).$$

Note that the expected value of each of the two first-order terms is zero.
    A rougher approximation is simply

$$E\big[g(X_1,X_2)\big] \approx g(m_1,m_2). \tag{2.79}$$

    For the variance of $g(X_1,X_2)$, we choose to retain only the first three terms of (2.77) for $g(X_1,X_2)$, and use (2.79) for $E[g(X_1,X_2)]$. Then

$$
\begin{aligned}
\mathrm{Var}[g(X_1,X_2)] &= E\left[\left\{g(X_1,X_2) - E[g(X_1,X_2)]\right\}^2\right] \\
&\approx E\left[\left\{(X_1-m_1)\cdot g_1'(m_1,m_2) + (X_2-m_2)\cdot g_2'(m_1,m_2)\right\}^2\right] \\
&= E\left[(X_1-m_1)^2[g_1'(m_1,m_2)]^2 + (X_2-m_2)^2[g_2'(m_1,m_2)]^2 \right. \\
&\qquad \left. + 2(X_1-m_1)(X_2-m_2)\cdot g_1'(m_1,m_2)\cdot g_2'(m_1,m_2)\right] \\
&= [g_1'(m_1,m_2)]^2 \cdot \mathrm{Var}(X_1) + [g_2'(m_1,m_2)]^2 \cdot \mathrm{Var}(X_2) \\
&\qquad + 2\cdot g_1'(m_1,m_2) \cdot g_2'(m_1,m_2) \cdot \mathrm{Cov}(X_1,X_2). \tag{2.80}
\end{aligned}
$$

If X_1 and X_2 are independent or uncorrelated, then the third term in (2.80) is zero. Extension to three or more random variables is analogous to the bivariate case.

2.7 *SUMMARY*

This chapter has attempted a thorough exploration of the theory and mathematics of survival models, using, for the most part, simply the concepts of the CDF, SDF, PDF, and HRF of a survival distribution. On occasion, some properties of the conceptual survival model were illustrated by using specific examples of continuous survival distributions, such as the exponential, Gompertz, and so on.

It is very important that the theoretical material of this chapter be thoroughly understood before dealing with the statistical estimation of survival models. In particular, the difference between conditional and unconditional distributions and mortality measures is very important, since conditional mortality probabilities are frequently used to develop the final, unconditional, survival distribution function.

EXERCISES

2.1 Introduction;   2.2 The Distribution of T

2-1. A survival distribution is defined by $S(t) = .1(100 - t)^{1/2}$, $0 \leq t \leq 100$. Find each of the following:
 (a) $f(36)$ (b) $\lambda(50)$ (c) $\Lambda(75)$ (d) $E[T]$ (e) $Var(T)$

2-2. Suppose the hazard rate of a survival distribution is a linear function, say, $\lambda(t) = a + bt$, where $a > 0$ and $b > 0$. Find each of the following:
 (a) $S(t)$ (b) $f(t)$ (c) The mode of the distribution

2-3. Suppose a survival distribution is defined by $S(x) = ax^2 + b$, for $0 \leq x \leq k$. If the expected value of X is 60, find the median of X.

2-4. Explain why the hazard rate $\lambda(t) = e^{-rt}$, $r > 0$, is not appropriate for a survival distribution.

2.3 Examples of Parametric Survival Models

2-5. If T is uniformly distributed over [1,3], find $Var(T)$.

2-6. Let X_1 and X_2 be independent random variables. Define the variables $Y = \min(X_1, X_2)$ and $Z = \max(X_1, X_2)$.
 (a) Show that the SDF of Y is the product of the SDF's of X_1 and X_2.

(b) Show that the CDF of Z is the product of the CDF's of X_1 and X_2.

(c) Show that if X_1 and X_2 both have exponential distributions, then Y has an exponential distribution, but Z does not.

2-7.   Suppose the independent random variables X_1 and X_2 both have exponential distributions, with parameters λ_1 and λ_2, repsectively, where $\lambda_1 > \lambda_2$. Let Y and Z be defined as in Exercise 2-6. If it is known that at time $t=2$, the SDF of Y has the value 0.24 and the SDF of Z has the value 0.86, then find the value of λ_1.

2-8. $_m|q_0 = S(m) - S(m+1)$ is the probability that an entity existing at time 0 will fail between $t=m$ and $t=m+1$. Determine whether $_m|q_0$ is an increasing, decreasing, or constant function of m for each of the following distributions:

(a) Uniform   (b) Exponential   (c) $f(t) = .00125t$, $0 \leq t \leq 40$.

2-9.   The distribution $f(x) = \dfrac{1}{2^{r/2}\Gamma(r/2)}\ x^{(r/2)-1}\ e^{-x/2}$, $x>0$, is the

Chi-square distribution with r degrees of freedom ($r>0$).

(a) Find each of the following for this distribution:

    (i) $E[X]$ (ii) $Var(X)$ (iii) $E[X^{-1}]$

(b) Find the hazard rate, $\lambda(x)$, for this distribution if $r=2$.

2.4   Conditional Measures and Truncated Distributions

2-10. Show that an exponential distribution truncated from below is still an exponential distribution.

2-11. Let $S(x) = ax+b$, $0 \leq x \leq k$. If it is known that $_2p_0 = .75$, find $_2m_3$.

2-12. The survival distribution for a certain laboratory unit known to exist at $t=5$ is given by an exponential distribution truncated above at $t=15$, with parameter $\lambda=.02$. Find the median future lifetime of this unit.

2-13. If $S(x) = 1-(.01x)^2$, $0 \leq x \leq 100$, find the expected future lifetime at the median age.

2-14   Find the hazard rate $\lambda(x \mid y \leq X \leq z)$ for a doubly-truncated exponential distribution. Why is the HRF not a constant?

2-15. The Type 1 Least Value distribution is defined by its SDF as

$$S(x) = \exp\left[\frac{-Bc^x}{\ln c}\right], \quad -\infty < x < \infty.$$

(a) Show that this distribution, when truncated below at $x=0$, becomes a Gompertz distribution.

(b) How does the HRF for the untruncated distribution compare with the HRF for the Gompertz distribution?

2.5 Transformations of Random Variables

2-16. Let X have a Weibull distribution, and let $Y = \ln X$. Find the SDF and HRF of Y. Can you give a name to this distribution?

2-17. Show that the transformation $y = S_X(x)$ leads to the same result as does $y = F_X(x)$, namely that $f_Y(y) = 1$ (i.e., that Y has a standard uniform distribution).

2-18. Let $y = -a\left[\ln F_X(x)\right]$, $a>0$. Find the distribution of Y.

2-19. If $f_X(x) = \dfrac{1}{\pi(1+x^2)}$, $-\infty < x < \infty$, find the distribution of $Y = X^2$.

2.6 Mean and Variance of Transformed Random Variables

2-20. Consider the transformed random variable Y defined in Example 2.4.
(a) Find E[Y] and Var(Y) directly from $f_Y(y)$. [*Hint: For E[Y], substitute $u=y^2$, and recognize that* $\int_0^\infty u^{1/2} \cdot e^{-u}\, du = \Gamma(1.5)$.]
(b) Approximate the mean and variance of Y by the method of statistical differentials; compare them with the exact values from part (a).

2-21. Approximate the mean and variance of the transformed random variable Y defined in Example 2.5.

2-22. Let X be normally distributed with mean μ and variance σ^2.
(a) Approximate the variance of $Y = e^X$.
(b) Since Y has a lognormal distribution, then $E[Y] = e^{\mu + \sigma^2/2}$ and $E[Y^2] = e^{2\mu + 2\sigma^2}$. If Var(Y) is expressed as a series in σ^2, and then truncated to agree with the approximate result in part (a), what is the first neglected term.

2-23. Two independent random variables X_1 and X_2 have PDF's given by $f_1(x_1) = 12x_1^2(1-x_1)$, $0 \le x_1 \le 1$, and $f_2(x_2) = 2x_2$, $0 \le x_2 \le 1$. Their product $Y = X_1 X_2$ has PDF $f_Y(y) = 12y(1-y)^2$, $0 \le y \le 1$. Calculate the exact mean and variance of Y, and compare them with the approximate values obtained by the method of statistical differentials.

CHAPTER 3

THE LIFE TABLE

3.1 *INTRODUCTION*

In this chapter we describe the nature of the traditional life table, showing that it can have all the properties of the survival models described in Chapter 2. Again we stress that a total understanding of the structure and properties of this model is essential for our main topic of model estimation.

When a survival model is presented in the life table format, it is customary to use notation and terminology which differ somewhat from that presented in Chapter 2. A major objective of this chapter will be to show clearly the correspondence between notation used in the conceptual model and that used in the specific life table model.

The reader should realize that life tables were developed by actuaries independently from (and a century earlier than) the development of the statistical theory of survival models as probability distributions, and the estimation thereof. For this reason, traditional life table notation and terminology will not tend to reveal the stochastic nature of the model as clearly as is done by the conceptual model in Chapter 2. By showing the correspondence of the life table symbols to those of the conceptual model, we intend to correct this.

The life table was defined in Section 1.3 as a table of numerical values of S(x) for certain values of x. Table 3.1 illustrates such a table.

TABLE 3.1

x	S(x)
0	1.00000
1	.97408
2	.97259
3	.97160
4	.97082
.	.
.	.
.	.
109	.00001
110	.00000

Typically a complete life table shows values of S(x) for all integral values of x, x=0,1,⋯. Since S(x) is represented by these values, it is clear that a practical upper limit on x must be adopted beyond which values of S(x) are taken to be zero. Traditionally we use ω for the smallest value of x for which S(x) = 0. That is, $S(\omega-1) > 0$, but $S(\omega) = 0$. In Table 3.1, $\omega = 110$.

From Table 3.1, one could calculate conditional probabilties represented by $_n p_x$ and $_n q_x$ for integral x and n. However, these are the only functions which can be determined from the tabular model. Functions such as f(x), $\lambda(x)$, m_x, and $\overset{\circ}{e}_x$ cannot be determined from the tabular model until one expands the model by adopting assumed values for S(x) between adjacent integers. We will pursue this in later sections of this chapter.

EXAMPLE 3.1 : From Table 3.1, calculate (a) the probability that a life age 0 will die before age 3; (b) the probability that a life age 1 will survive to age 4.

SOLUTION :   (a) This is given directly by F(3) = 1 − S(3) = .02840.

(b) This conditional probability is given by $_3 p_1 = \dfrac{S(4)}{S(1)} = .99665$.

3.2 *THE TRADITIONAL FORM OF THE LIFE TABLE*

The tabular survival model was developed by the early actuaries many years ago. The history of this model is reported throughout actuarial literature, and a brief summary of this history is presented by Dobson [19].

Traditionally, the tabular survival model differs from Table 3.1 in two respects. Rather than presenting decimal values of S(x), it is usual to multiply these values by, say, 100,000, and thereby present the S(x) values as integers. Secondly, since these integers are not probabilities (which S(x) values are), the column heading is changed from S(x) to ℓ_x, where ℓ stands for number *living*, or number of *lives*. Thus did the tabular survival model become known as the *life table*.

Since S(0) = 1, then clearly ℓ_0 is the same as the constant multiple which transforms all S(x) into ℓ_x. This constant is called the *radix* of the table. Formally,

$$\ell_x = \ell_0 \cdot S(x). \tag{3.1}$$

Using a radix of 100,000, we transform Table 3.1 into Table 3.1a.

TABLE 3.1a

x	ℓ_x
0	100,000
1	97,408
2	97,259
3	97,160
4	97,082
.	.
.	.
.	.
109	1
110	0

The basic advantage of the traditional form of the life table is its susceptibility to interpretation. If one views $\ell_0 = 100,000$ as a hypothetical cohort group of new-born lives, then each value of ℓ_x represents the survivors of that group to age x, according to the model. This is a convenient, deterministic, interpretation of the model. Of course, since $\ell_x = \ell_0 \cdot S(x)$, and $S(x)$ is a probability, then ℓ_x is the *expected* number of survivors to age x out of an original group of ℓ_0 new-borns. This connection between $S(x)$ and ℓ_x is also given in Chapter 1 of Jordan [32], and in Chapter 3 of Bowers, et al. [10].

The distinction between $S(x)$ and ℓ_x is sufficiently subtle to justify a second look at them. We first recognize that mathematically the two functions are identical. They embody the same information. The basic difference between them lies in their interpretation. $S(x)$ is a probability function, and therefore, has a probabilistic interpretation. ℓ_x is interpreted as a number of persons living at age x (out of an original cohort of ℓ_0), and thus has both a probabilistic and a deterministic interpretation.

Although the basic representation of the tabular survival model is in terms of the values of ℓ_x, it is customary for the table to also show the value of several other functions derived from ℓ_x. We define

$$d_x = \ell_x - \ell_{x+1}, \qquad (3.2)$$

or, more generally,

$$_n d_x = \ell_x - \ell_{x+n} . \qquad (3.3)$$

Since ℓ_x represents the size of the cohort at age x, and ℓ_{x+n} is the number of them still surviving at age x+n, then clearly $_n d_x$ gives the number who die between ages x and x+n. (This portrayal of number dying might be the

reason for the frequent reference to these models as *mortality* tables.)
Furthermore,

$$q_x = \frac{d_x}{\ell_x}, \tag{3.4}$$

or, more generally,

$$_nq_x = \frac{_nd_x}{\ell_x} \tag{3.5}$$

gives the conditional probability of death, given alive at age x. Finally, we
have

$$_np_x = 1 - {_nq_x} = \frac{\ell_x - {_nd_x}}{\ell_x} = \frac{\ell_{x+n}}{\ell_x} \tag{3.6}$$

as the conditional probability of surviving to age x+n, given alive at age x.
With n=1, we have the special case

$$p_x = \frac{\ell_{x+1}}{\ell_x}. \tag{3.7}$$

We recall that the conditional probabilities $_np_x$ and $_nq_x$ were first
defined in Section 2.4 in terms of S(x). The consistency of those definitions
with the ones presented in this section is easily seen since ℓ_x is simply
$\ell_0 \cdot S(x)$. We redefined $_np_x$ and $_nq_x$ in terms of ℓ_x here simply to complete
our description of the life table.

EXAMPLE 3.2 : From Table 3.1a, find (a) the number who die between
ages 2 and 4; (b) the probability that a life age 1 will survive to age 4.
SOLUTION : (a) This is given by $_2d_2 = \ell_2 - \ell_4 = 177$. (b) This is
given by $_3p_1 = \frac{\ell_4}{\ell_1} = .99665$. (Compare with part (b) of Example 3.1.)

3.3 *OTHER FUNCTIONS DERIVED FROM* ℓ_x

Although a life table only presents values of ℓ_x for certain (say, integral)
values of x, we wish to adopt the view that the ℓ_x function which produces
these values is a continuous and differentiable function. In other words, we
assume that a continuous and differentiable ℓ_x function *exists*, but only
certain values of it are presented in the survival model. The reason we make
this assumption is that there are several other mortality functions which can
be derived from ℓ_x if ℓ_x is continuous and differentiable.

If values of ℓ_x are known only at integral x, the question of how to *evaluate* these additional functions then arises, and the usual way to accomplish this evaluation is to make an assumption about the form of ℓ_x between adjacent integral values of x. (Recall that we earlier referred to the assumptions of a form for S(x) as mortality distribution assumptions.)

In this section we will derive these several new functions from ℓ_x symbolically, assuming ℓ_x to be continuous and differentiable. In Section 3.5 we will discuss the common mortality distribution assumptions, and show how they allow us to evaluate the functions of this section from a table of ℓ_x values at integral x only. We will also interpret these mortality distribution assumptions in terms of both ℓ_x and S(x).

3.3.1 *The Force of Mortality*

The derivative of ℓ_x can be interpreted as the absolute instantaneous annual rate of change of ℓ_x. Since ℓ_x represents the number of persons alive at age x, then the derivative, which is the annual rate at which ℓ_x is changing, gives the annual rate at which people are dying at age x. This derivative is negative since ℓ_x is a decreasing function. To obtain the absolute magnitude of this instantaneous rate of death, we will use the negative of the derivative. Finally, since the magnitude of the derivative depends on the size of ℓ_x itself, we obtain the *relative* instantaneous rate of death by dividing the negative derivative of ℓ_x by ℓ_x itself. Thus we have

$$\mu_x = \frac{-\frac{d}{dx}\ell_x}{\ell_x}, \qquad (3.8)$$

which we call the *force of mortality* at age x. Now since $\ell_x = \ell_0 \cdot S(x)$, then we see that (3.8) is the same as

$$\lambda(x) = \frac{-\frac{d}{dx}S(x)}{S(x)} = \frac{f(x)}{S(x)}. \qquad (3.9)$$

Thus the hazard rate and the force of mortality are identical.

If we multiply both sides of equation (2.11) by ℓ_0, replace t with x, and substitute μ_y for $\lambda(y)$, we obtain

$$\ell_x = \ell_0 \cdot S(x) = \ell_0 \cdot \exp\left[-\int_0^x \mu_y \, dy\right]. \qquad (3.10)$$

In the life table context, $S(x) = {}_xp_0 = \exp\left[-\int_0^x \mu_y\,dy\right]$ can be interpreted as a decremental factor which reduces the initial cohort of size ℓ_0 to size ℓ_x at age x.

By a simple variable change we can write (3.8) as

$$\mu_{x+s} = \frac{-\dfrac{d}{ds}\,\ell_{x+s}}{\ell_{x+s}}, \tag{3.8a}$$

a form in which the force of mortality will frequently be expressed.

EXAMPLE 3.3 : Show that the force of mortality, μ_x, is the limiting value of the probability of death over an interval divided by the interval length (in years), as the interval length approaches zero.

SOLUTION : Consider first a one-year interval, with $q_x = \dfrac{d_x}{\ell_x}$. Then consider a half-year interval with $\dfrac{{}_{1/2}q_x}{1/2} = \dfrac{\ell_x - \ell_{x+1/2}}{1/2\cdot\ell_x}$. Now, in general, consider $\dfrac{{}_{\Delta x}q_x}{\Delta x} = \dfrac{\ell_x - \ell_{x+\Delta x}}{\Delta x \cdot \ell_x}$, and show that $\lim\limits_{\Delta x \to 0} \dfrac{{}_{\Delta x}q_x}{\Delta x} = \mu_x$. This is

$$\lim_{\Delta x \to 0}\left[\frac{\ell_x - \ell_{x+\Delta x}}{\Delta x \cdot \ell_x}\right] = \frac{1}{\ell_x}\cdot\lim_{\Delta x \to 0}\left[\frac{\ell_x - \ell_{x+\Delta x}}{\Delta x}\right] = \frac{1}{\ell_x}\left[-\frac{d}{dx}\,\ell_x\right] = \mu_x,$$

by (3.8).

3.3.2 *The Probability Density Function of X*

With the force of mortality, which is the same as the hazard rate, now defined, the next function to develop from ℓ_x is the PDF of the age-at-death random variable X. (Remember that we wish to show that the life table is a representation of the distribution of this random variable.)

From formula (2.7) we have $f(x) = \lambda(x)\cdot S(x)$. In the life table context, we have $\lambda(x) = \mu_x$ and $S(x) = \ell_x/\ell_0$. Thus we have

$$f(x) = \mu_x(\ell_x/\ell_0) = {}_xp_0\mu_x, \quad x \geq 0. \tag{3.11}$$

Since, from (3.8), $\dfrac{d}{dx}\,\ell_x = -\ell_x\mu_x$, then dividing both sides by ℓ_0 gives

$$\frac{d}{dx}\,{}_xp_0 = -{}_xp_0\mu_x. \tag{3.12}$$

[**EXAMPLE 3.4**]: Show that $\int_0^\infty f(x)\,dx = 1$.

[**SOLUTION**]: Since $f(x) = {}_xp_0\mu_x$, we have $\int_0^\infty {}_xp_0\mu_x\,dx = - \left. {}_xp_0 \right|_0^\infty$,

from (3.12). Thus we have ${}_0p_0 - {}_\infty p_0 = 1$, since ${}_0p_0 = 1$ and ${}_\infty p_0 = 0$.

With the PDF in hand, we can now find E[X], which we recall is denoted by $\overset{\circ}{e}_0$. (Throughout this and the following section, all expectations are assumed to exist.) We have

$$\overset{\circ}{e}_0 = E[X] = \int_0^\infty x \cdot f(x)\,dx = \int_0^\infty x \cdot {}_xp_0\mu_x\,dx. \tag{3.13}$$

Integration by parts produces the alternative formula

$$\overset{\circ}{e}_0 = E[X] = \int_0^\infty {}_xp_0\,dx = \frac{1}{\ell_0} \cdot \int_0^\infty \ell_x\,dx. \tag{3.14}$$

If we define

$$T_0 = \int_0^\infty \ell_x\,dx, \tag{3.15}$$

then we have

$$\overset{\circ}{e}_0 = E[X] = \frac{T_0}{\ell_0}. \tag{3.16}$$

The function T_0 is a special case of T_x, defined by

$$T_x = \int_x^\infty \ell_y\,dy. \tag{3.17}$$

This function T_x is very important. We will encounter it again, and in Section 3.3.5 we will give an interpretation of it.

The second moment of X is found from

$$E[X^2] = \int_0^\infty x^2 \cdot {}_xp_0\mu_x\,dx. \tag{3.18}$$

Integration by parts produces $2 \cdot \int_0^\infty x \cdot {}_xp_0\,dx = \frac{2}{\ell_0} \cdot \int_0^\infty x \cdot \ell_x\,dx$. From formula (3.17),

$$\frac{d}{dx} T_x = -\ell_x, \tag{3.19}$$

by the fundamental theorem of calculus, so $\int \ell_x \, dx = -T_x$. Then integrating by parts $\frac{2}{\ell_0} \cdot \int_0^\infty x \cdot \ell_x \, dx$, we obtain $\frac{2}{\ell_0} \cdot \int_0^\infty T_x \, dx$ (since the term $-\frac{2x}{\ell_0} \cdot T_x$ evaluates to zero at both limits). We define

$$Y_0 = \int_0^\infty T_x \, dx, \tag{3.20}$$

obtaining

$$E[X^2] = \frac{2 \cdot Y_0}{\ell_0}. \tag{3.21}$$

Finally, from (3.21) and (3.16), we have

$$Var(X) = E[X^2] - \left\{ E[X] \right\}^2 = \frac{2 \cdot Y_0}{\ell_0} - \left(\frac{T_0}{\ell_0} \right)^2. \tag{3.22}$$

3.3.3 *Conditional Probabilities and Densities*

We have already discussed the conditional probabilities $_np_x$ and $_nq_x$ in terms of both $S(x)$ and ℓ_x.

Another conditional probability of some interest is denoted by $_{n|m}q_x$. It represents the probability that a person known to be alive at age x will die between ages x+n and x+n+m. In terms of the formal probability notation of Chapter 2, $_{n|m}q_x = \Pr[(x+n) < X \leq (x+n+m) \,|\, X > x]$. This can also be expressed as the probability that a person age x will survive n years, but then die within the next m years. This way of stating the probability suggests that we can write

$$_{n|m}q_x = {}_np_x \cdot {}_mq_{x+n}. \tag{3.23}$$

Here $_mq_{x+n}$ is the conditional probability of dying between x+n and x+n+m, given alive at age x+n. In turn, $_np_x$ is the conditional probability of surviving to age x+n, given alive at age x. Their product gives the probability of dying between ages x+n and x+n+m, given alive at age x. In terms of ℓ_x, we have, from (3.6) and (3.5),

$$_{n|m}q_x = \frac{\ell_{x+n}}{\ell_x} \cdot \frac{_md_{x+n}}{\ell_{x+n}} = \frac{_md_{x+n}}{\ell_x}. \tag{3.24}$$

EXAMPLE 3.5: Show that $_{n|m}q_x = {_n}p_x - {_{n+m}}p_x$, and give an interpretation of this result.

SOLUTION: Since, from (3.3), $_m d_{x+n} = \ell_{x+n} - \ell_{x+n+m}$, then (3.24) becomes $_{n|m}q_x = \dfrac{\ell_{x+n} - \ell_{x+n+m}}{\ell_x} = {_n}p_x - {_{n+m}}p_x$. Since $_n p_x$ is the probability of surviving to age x+n, we can think of it as containing the probability of surviving to any age beyond x+n. If we remove from $_n p_x$ the probability of surviving to x+n+m, which is $_{n+m}p_x$, we have the probability of surviving to x+n, but not to x+n+m, which is $_{n|m}q_x$.

Next we wish to explore the conditional PDF for death at age y, given alive at age x (y>x). From (2.39), we know this conditional PDF is $f(y\,|\,X>x) = \dfrac{f(y)}{S(x)}$. Now from (3.11) we have $f(y) = \dfrac{1}{\ell_0} \cdot \ell_y \mu_y$, and from (3.1) we have $S(x) = \ell_x/\ell_0$. Thus

$$f(y\,|\,X>x) = \frac{\ell_y \mu_y}{\ell_x} = {_{y-x}}p_x \mu_y. \qquad (3.25)$$

Letting $s = y - x$, so $y = x+s$, we have

$$f(s\,|\,X>x) = {_s}p_x \mu_{x+s}, \qquad (3.26)$$

where the random variable S denotes the length of future lifetime of a person alive at age x. The conditional PDF given by (3.26) is a very useful function for developing other results.

If both numerator and denominator of (3.8a) are divided by ℓ_x, we obtain

$$\mu_{x+s} = \frac{-\dfrac{d}{ds}\, {_s}p_x}{{_s}p_x}, \qquad (3.27)$$

which shows that

$$\frac{d}{ds}\, {_s}p_x = -\,{_s}p_x \mu_{x+s}. \qquad (3.28)$$

The expected future lifetime of a person alive at age x is given by

$$\overset{\circ}{e}_x = E[S] = \int_0^\infty s \cdot {_s}p_x \mu_{x+s}\, ds = \int_0^\infty {_s}p_x\, ds, \qquad (3.29)$$

since, in the integration by parts, $\int {}_sP_x\mu_{x+s}\,ds = -{}_sP_x$ (from (3.28)), and $-s\cdot{}_sP_x$ evaluates to zero at both limits. Furthermore, ${}_sP_x = \frac{\ell_{x+s}}{\ell_x}$, so (3.29) becomes

$$\overset{\circ}{e}_x = \frac{1}{\ell_x}\cdot\int_0^\infty \ell_{x+s}\,ds = \frac{1}{\ell_x}\cdot\int_x^\infty \ell_y\,dy = \frac{T_x}{\ell_x}, \tag{3.30}$$

from (3.17).

By steps parallel to those leading from (3.18) to (3.21), we find

$$E[S^2] = \frac{2\cdot Y_x}{\ell_x}, \tag{3.31}$$

where

$$Y_x = \int_x^\infty T_y\,dy. \tag{3.32}$$

Finally, from (3.31) and (3.30), we have

$$\text{Var}(S) = E[S^2] - \{E[S]\}^2 = \frac{2\cdot Y_x}{\ell_x} - \left(\frac{T_x}{\ell_x}\right)^2. \tag{3.33}$$

EXAMPLE 3.6 : A survival model is defined by $\ell_x = \dfrac{10{,}000}{(x+1)^3}$, $x\geq 0$. Determine $\text{Var}(X\,|\,X>x)$, where X is the age-at-death random variable.

SOLUTION : We recognize that the age-at-death random variable X and the future-lifetime random variable S are related by $X = x+S$, where x is a constant. Thus, $\text{Var}(X\,|\,X>x) = \text{Var}(S\,|\,X>x)$. From (3.33) this variance is given by $\dfrac{2\cdot Y_x}{\ell_x} - \left(\dfrac{T_x}{\ell_x}\right)^2$. Thus we first find

$$T_x = \int_x^\infty \ell_y\,dy = 10{,}000\int_x^\infty (y+1)^{-3}\,dy = 5000(x+1)^{-2}$$

and

$$Y_x = \int_x^\infty T_y\,dy = 5000\int_x^\infty (y+1)^{-2}\,dy = 5000(x+1)^{-1}.$$

Then $\text{Var}(X\,|\,X>x) = \dfrac{(x+1)^{-1}}{(x+1)^{-3}} - \left(\dfrac{(x+1)^{-2}}{2(x+1)^{-3}}\right)^2 = \dfrac{3(x+1)^2}{4}.$

3.3.4 *The Central Rate*

In Section 2.4.5, the central rate of death was defined by formula (2.59) as

$$_n\text{m}_x \;=\; \frac{\displaystyle\int_0^n {}_s\text{P}_x\mu_{x+s}\,\text{ds}}{\displaystyle\int_0^n {}_s\text{P}_x\,\text{ds}}. \tag{2.59}$$

Since $_s\text{P}_x = \dfrac{\ell_{x+s}}{\ell_x}$, multiplication of both numerator and denominator of (2.59) by ℓ_x produces

$$_n\text{m}_x \;=\; \frac{\displaystyle\int_0^n \ell_{x+s}\mu_{x+s}\,\text{ds}}{\displaystyle\int_0^n \ell_{x+s}\,\text{ds}}. \tag{3.34}$$

Now $\displaystyle\int_0^n \ell_{x+s}\mu_{x+s}\,\text{ds} = -\ell_{x+s}\Big|_0^n = \ell_x - \ell_{x+n} = {}_n\text{d}_x$, so (3.34) becomes

$$_n\text{m}_x \;=\; \frac{_n\text{d}_x}{\displaystyle\int_0^n \ell_{x+s}\,\text{ds}} \;=\; \frac{_n\text{d}_x}{_n\text{L}_x}, \tag{3.35}$$

where

$$_n\text{L}_x \;=\; \int_0^n \ell_{x+s}\,\text{ds}. \tag{3.36}$$

If n=1, we have the one-year interval function

$$\text{L}_x \;=\; \int_0^1 \ell_{x+s}\,\text{ds}, \tag{3.37}$$

and the central rate over the interval (x, x+1] is given by

$$\text{m}_x \;=\; \frac{\text{d}_x}{\text{L}_x}. \tag{3.38}$$

Note that there is a simple relationship between L_x and T_x, as defined by (3.17). There we saw that

$$\text{T}_x \;=\; \int_x^\infty \ell_y\,\text{dy} \;=\; \int_x^{x+1} \ell_y\,\text{dy} + \int_{x+1}^{x+2} \ell_y\,\text{dy} + \cdots \;=\; \text{L}_x + \text{L}_{x+1} + \cdots,$$

Thus

$$T_x = \sum_{y=x}^{\infty} L_y . \qquad (3.39)$$

We have developed L_x and T_x simply as mathematical concepts. It is now necessary to give descriptive meanings to them, since these interpretations will be helpful in understanding the use of m_x, T_x and L_x in the estimation of survival models from general population data.

3.3.5 *The Concept of Exposure*

A survival model, expressed by the SDF S(x), is a probability distribution with all the properties that such distributions possess. The simple transformation of $\ell_x = \ell_0 \cdot S(x)$, where ℓ_0 is a constant, expresses the same probability distribution. The function ℓ_x is the same function as is S(x), except for the trivial difference that whereas $1 \geq S(x) \geq 0$, we now have $\ell_0 \geq \ell_x \geq 0$. Any function or result that can be derived from S(x) can also be derived from ℓ_x.

However, an advantage in using ℓ_x, instead of S(x), is the ability to interpret the values of ℓ_x as the survivors of an initial, closed, cohort of newborn lives of size of ℓ_0. Successive values of S(x) are probabilities, which are somewhat abstract, especially to non-mathematicians. But values of ℓ_x have a "real world" meaning, notwithstanding the fact that we are dealing with hypothetical situations.

In turn, the interpretive nature of ℓ_x allows for concrete (albeit hypothetical) interpretations of several functions derived from ℓ_x. Of particular usefulness is the function L_x, defined by (3.37).

Recall, from (3.26), that ${}_sp_x\mu_{x+s}$ is the PDF for death at age x+s, given alive at age x. If we multiply this PDF by ℓ_x, which we interpret as the number of persons alive in a group at age x, we obtain $\ell_{x+s}\mu_{x+s}$, which is the *rate* of deaths occurring in the group at exact age x+s. In turn, $\ell_{x+s}\mu_{x+s}$ ds is the differential *number* of deaths occurring at exact age x+s. Then $s \cdot \ell_{x+s}\mu_{x+s}$ ds is the total number of years lived by those deaths after attaining age x. Finally, $\int_0^1 s \cdot \ell_{x+s}\mu_{x+s}$ ds gives the aggregate number of years lived, after age x, by all those who die between age x and age x+1.

Most of the ℓ_x group, of course, survive to age x+1, ℓ_{x+1} being the number who do so. Each of these persons live one year from age x to age x+1, so ℓ_{x+1} also represents the aggregate number of years lived, between ages x and x+1, by those who survive to age x+1. Together,

$$\ell_{x+1} + \int_0^1 s \cdot \ell_{x+s}\mu_{x+s}\, ds \qquad (3.40)$$

gives the aggregate number of years lived between ages x and x+1 by the ℓ_x persons who comprised the group at age x.

This quantity is measured in units of *life-years*, and is called *exposure*, since it is a measure of the extent to which the group is *exposed to* the risk of dying. Note that persons who do die contribute to our exposure aggregation only up to the time of death. This is an important point, since in Chapter 6 we will encounter two different meanings of the exposure concept, where this rule will not hold.

We can simplify (3.40) by performing integration by parts, to obtain

$$\ell_{x+1} - s \cdot \ell_{x+s}\Big|_0^1 + \int_0^1 \ell_{x+s}\, ds = \int_0^1 \ell_{x+s}\, ds,$$

which has already been defined in (3.37) to be L_x.

This result suggests the possibility of directly interpreting L_x, as defined by (3.37), as the exposure concept. The definite integral in (3.37) is, by definition, the limit of the Riemann sum

$$R = \sum_{i=1}^n \ell_{x+s_i^*} \cdot \Delta s_i, \tag{3.41}$$

where $\ell_{x+s_i^*}$ represents the number of persons alive at some point in the ith sub-interval of (x, x+1]. Multiplying by Δs_i, the width of that subinterval, gives the number of life-years lived in the subinterval. Since ℓ_{x+s} is constantly changing, R is only an approximation to the precise number of life-years lived in (x, x+1]. But

$$L_x = \int_0^1 \ell_{x+s}\, ds = \lim_{||\Delta|| \to 0} R$$

gives the exact value of the exposure concept, where $||\Delta||$ is the largest Δs_i.

By extension,

$$_nL_x = \int_0^n \ell_{x+s}\, ds \tag{3.36}$$

gives the exact exposure in the interval (x, x+n]. Further,

$$T_x = \sum_{y=x}^{\infty} L_y \tag{3.39}$$

clearly gives the exact exposure over the interval (x, ∞), which can be viewed as the total aggregate number of life-years lived in the future by the ℓ_x group. Then $\dfrac{T_x}{\ell_x}$ gives the *average* future lifetime per person in the ℓ_x group.   We have already seen, from (3.30), that $\dfrac{T_x}{\ell_x}$ is $\overset{\circ}{e}_x$, the *expected* future lifetime for a person age x (i.e., in the ℓ_x group).   The correspondence of these two concepts, average and expected, is a very familiar one.

In turn,

$$Y_x = \int_x^\infty T_y \, dy \qquad (3.32)$$

also has an exposure interpretation.   However, this first requires an understanding of the concept and properties of the stationary population, which we do not wish to presume.

Now that we have the exposure interpretation of L_x, we can give further meaning to m_x, defined by (3.38) as

$$m_x = \frac{d_x}{L_x}. \qquad (3.38)$$

Recall that in Chapter 2 we defined m_x as a continuously weighted average of the hazard function $\lambda(y)$, over the interval (x, x+1]. Formula (3.38) shows us that, in the life table model, d_x persons died in (x, x+1], and the associated quantity of exposure to the risk of dying for the group was L_x. The ratio, m_x, is thus the (annual) rate of death (rate of mortality) in this one-year age interval.   Note how this rate differs from the probability q_x, given by (3.4); in particular, it is possible for m_x to exceed one, whereas q_x cannot.

For the interval (x, x+n], we have

$$_n m_x = \frac{_n d_x}{_n L_x}. \qquad (3.35)$$

Note that, although $_n m_x$ relates to an n-year age interval, it is an average *annual* rate, rather than a rate for an n-year period. This can easily be seen by comparing (3.35) and (3.38). In (3.38), we have a "years's worth" of deaths in the numerator, and a "year's worth" of exposure in the denominator. In (3.35), we have "n years' worth" in both the numerator and denominator, so the relative magnitude of the ratio is still annual.

A modification of this concept of exposure would be to count only the exposure in (x, x+1] contributed by the *survivors* of that interval. Since there are ℓ_{x+1} survivors, and each contributes exactly one year, then ℓ_{x+1} is also the exposure. In similar manner, ℓ_{x+2} is the exposure in (x+1, x+2], and so on. Summing over all years from age x to infinity, we have

$$T_x^* = \sum_{y=x+1}^{\infty} \ell_y .$$ (3.42)

We can describe T_x^* as the total future lifetime of the ℓ_x group, in which only whole years of future lifetime are counted. Then

$$e_x = \frac{T_x^*}{\ell_x}$$ (3.43)

is the average (or expected) number of whole years of future lifetime per person in the ℓ_x group. It is called the *curtate* expectation of life at age x, as distinguished from the *complete* expectation denoted by $\overset{o}{e}_x$.

We can derive an alternate formula for e_x as

$$e_x = \frac{1}{\ell_x} \cdot \sum_{y=x+1}^{\infty} \ell_y = \frac{1}{\ell_x} \cdot \sum_{k=1}^{\infty} \ell_{x+k} = \sum_{k=1}^{\infty} {}_kP_x .$$ (3.44)

Finally, if we make the assumption that a person lives approximately one-half year in the year of death, then we see that $\overset{o}{e}_x$ exceeds e_x by that half-year. Thus

$$\overset{o}{e}_x \approx e_x + \tfrac{1}{2}.$$ (3.45)

Later in this chapter we will formalize this approximate, intuitive result.

3.3.6 *Relationship Between ${}_nq_x$ and ${}_nm_x$*

Familiarity with the concept of exposure allows us to develop a very useful formula which relates the functions ${}_nq_x$ and ${}_nm_x$. Let us first explore this relationship with n=1. Since $q_x = \frac{d_x}{\ell_x}$, and $m_x = \frac{d_x}{L_x}$, then we are, in effect, exploring the relationship between ℓ_x and L_x. To do this, we first need to define a new function.

From (3.40), we recall that

$$\int_0^1 s \cdot \ell_{x+s} \mu_{x+s} \, ds = \int_0^1 \ell_{x+s} \, ds - \ell_{x+1} = L_x - \ell_{x+1}$$ (3.46)

gives the aggregate number of life-years lived in (x, x+1] by those who die in that age interval, namely d_x. Then if (3.46) is divided by d_x, we obtain the *average* number of years lived in (x, x+1] by those who die in that interval.

It is clear that this average number is necessarily less than one, and could also be called the average *fraction* of (x, x+1] lived through by those who die in that interval. We define this average fraction to be f_x, so that

$$f_x = \frac{L_x - \ell_{x+1}}{d_x}. \tag{3.47}$$

Further, since $d_x = \ell_x - \ell_{x+1}$, then $\ell_{x+1} = \ell_x - d_x$, so we have

$$f_x \cdot d_x = L_x - \ell_x + d_x,$$

or

$$L_x = \ell_x - (1-f_x)d_x. \tag{3.48}$$

Then

$$m_x = \frac{d_x}{L_x} = \frac{d_x}{\ell_x - (1-f_x)d_x} = \frac{q_x}{1 - (1-f_x)q_x}. \tag{3.49}$$

Alternatively,

$$\ell_x = L_x + (1-f_x)d_x, \tag{3.50}$$

so

$$q_x = \frac{d_x}{\ell_x} = \frac{d_x}{L_x + (1-f_x)d_x} = \frac{m_x}{1 + (1-f_x)m_x}. \tag{3.51}$$

Note that, since ℓ_x is non-increasing on (x, x+1], then $L_x \leq \ell_x$, so $m_x \geq q_x$.

More generally, if we consider the n-year age interval (x, x+n], then

$$\int_0^n s \cdot \ell_{x+s}\mu_{x+s}\, ds = \int_0^n \ell_{x+s}\, ds - n \cdot \ell_{x+n} = {}_nL_x - n \cdot \ell_{x+n} \tag{3.46a}$$

gives the aggregate number of life-years lived in (x, x+n] by those who die in that interval, and there were ${}_nd_x$ such deaths. Division of (3.46a) by ${}_nd_x$ gives the *average number* of years lived in (x, x+n] by those who die in that interval, and further division by n, the interval length, gives the average *fraction* of the interval lived through by those who die in it. We define this average fraction to be ${}_nf_x$, obtaining

$$_nf_x = \frac{{}_nL_x - n \cdot \ell_{x+n}}{n \cdot {}_nd_x}. \tag{3.47a}$$

Further, $\ell_{x+n} = \ell_x - {}_nd_x$, so we have

$$n \cdot {}_nf_x \cdot {}_nd_x = {}_nL_x - n \cdot \ell_x + n \cdot {}_nd_x,$$

or

$$_nL_x = n \cdot \ell_x - n(1 - _nf_x)_nd_x \, . \tag{3.48a}$$

Then

$$_nm_x = \frac{_nd_x}{_nL_x} = \frac{_nd_x}{n \cdot \ell_x - n(1 - _nf_x)_nd_x} = \frac{_nq_x}{n[1 - (1 - _nf_x)_nq_x]}. \tag{3.49a}$$

Alternatively,

$$n \cdot \ell_x = _nL_x + n(1 - _nf_x)_nd_x,$$

or

$$\ell_x = \frac{1}{n}\Big[\,_nL_x + n(1 - _nf_x)_nd_x\Big], \tag{3.50a}$$

so

$$_nq_x = \frac{_nd_x}{\ell_x} = \frac{_nd_x}{\frac{1}{n}[_nL_x + n(1 - _nf_x)_nd_x]} = \frac{_nm_x}{\frac{1}{n}[1 + n(1 - _nf_x)_nm_x]}. \tag{3.51a}$$

Formula (3.51a) gives the general relationship for deriving $_nq_x$ from $_nm_x$. This formula is important in the estimation of a life table from population data. The concept of exposure is also extensively used in that exercise.

EXAMPLE 3.7: The following values are taken from a certain life table:
$\ell_0 = 100{,}000 \quad \ell_1 = 97{,}408 \quad \ell_5 = 97{,}015 \quad L_0 = 97{,}764 \quad _4L_1 = 388{,}713.$
What are the values of f_0 and $_4f_1$?
SOLUTION: $d_0 = \ell_0 - \ell_1 = 2592$. From (3.47), $f_0 = \dfrac{L_0 - \ell_1}{d_0} = .13734.$

Similarly, $_4d_1 = \ell_1 - \ell_5 = 393$. From (3.47a), $_4f_1 = \dfrac{_4L_1 - 4 \cdot \ell_5}{4 \cdot {_4d_1}} = .41539.$

EXAMPLE 3.8: If $_5q_{80} = .400$, and $_5m_{80} = .102$, find $_5f_{80}$.
SOLUTION: (3.49a) leads to $n \cdot {_nm_x} - n \cdot {_nm_x} \cdot {_nq_x}(1 - _nf_x) = {_nq_x}$, so
$(1 - _nf_x) = \dfrac{n \cdot {_nm_x} - _nq_x}{n \cdot {_nm_x} \cdot {_nq_x}}$. Substituting the given values, along with n=5, we obtain $(1 - _5f_{80}) = .53921$, whence $_5f_{80} = .46079$.

3.4 SUMMARY OF CONCEPTS AND NOTATION

Thus far we have been striving for an understanding of the nature and properties of survival models, both in the notation of the stochastic model of Chapter 2 and the life table model of Chapter 3. It might be useful at this point to summarize the concepts developed thus far, and give the standard formulas or symbols for them in the notation of both chapters.

TABLE 3.2

Concept	Chapter 2 Formulas	Chapter 3 Formulas
1. (Unconditional) probability of survival from age 0 to age x	$S(x)$	$_xp_0 = \dfrac{\ell_x}{\ell_0}$
2. (Unconditional) probability of death not later than age x	$F(x)$	$_xq_0 = \dfrac{\ell_0 - \ell_x}{\ell_0}$
3. (Conditional) probability of survival from age x to age x+n	$\dfrac{S(x+n)}{S(x)}$	$_np_x = \dfrac{\ell_{x+n}}{\ell_x}$
4. (Conditional) probability of death before age x+n, given alive at age x	$\dfrac{S(x) - S(x+n)}{S(x)}$	$_nq_x = \dfrac{\ell_x - \ell_{x+n}}{\ell_x} = \dfrac{_nd_x}{\ell_x}$
5. Hazard rate (force of mortality) at exact age x	$\lambda(x) = \dfrac{-\frac{d}{dx} S(x)}{S(x)}$ $= -\dfrac{d}{dx} \ln S(x)$	$\mu_x = \dfrac{-\frac{d}{dx} \ell_x}{\ell_x}$ $= -\dfrac{d}{dx} \ln \ell_x$
6. (Unconditional) density function for death at exact age x	$f(x) = \dfrac{d}{dx} F(x)$ $= -\dfrac{d}{dx} S(x)$	$_xp_0\mu_x = -\dfrac{d}{dx} \,_xp_0$
7. (Unconditional) expectation of future lifetime at birth	$E[X] = \displaystyle\int_0^\infty x \cdot f(x)\, dx$ $= \displaystyle\int_0^\infty S(x)\, dx$	$\overset{\circ}{e}_0 = \displaystyle\int_0^\infty x \cdot {}_xp_0\mu_x\, dx$ $= \displaystyle\int_0^\infty {}_xp_0\, dx = \dfrac{T_0}{\ell_0}$
8. (Unconditional) variance of future lifetime at birth	$\mathrm{Var}(X) = \displaystyle\int_0^\infty x^2 \cdot f(x)\, dx$ $- \{E[X]\}^2$	$= \displaystyle\int_0^\infty x^2 \cdot {}_xp_0\mu_x\, dx - \overset{\circ}{e}_0{}^2$ $= 2 \cdot Y_0/\ell_0 - (T_0/\ell_0)^2$ (no specific symbol)

$$\boxed{\text{TABLE 3.2 (Cont.)}}$$

Concept	Chapter 2 Formula	Chapter 3 Formulas
9. (Conditional) density function for death at age y, given alive at age x(y>x)	$f(y \mid X>x) = \dfrac{f(y)}{S(x)}$	$= {}_{y-x}p_x \mu_y$ $= {}_{s}p_x \mu_{x+s}$, where s=y−x
10. (Conditional) expectation of future lifetime at age x	$E[X{-}x \mid X>x] = E[S \mid X>x]$ $= \displaystyle\int_0^\infty s \cdot f(x+s \mid X>x)\,ds$ $= \displaystyle\int_0^\infty \dfrac{S(x+s)}{S(x)}\,ds$	$\overset{\circ}{e}_x = \displaystyle\int_0^\infty s \cdot {}_s p_x \mu_{x+s}\,ds$ $= \displaystyle\int_0^\infty {}_s p_x\,ds = T_x/\ell_x$
11. (Conditional) variance of future lifetime at age x	$\mathrm{Var}(S \mid X>x)$ $= \mathrm{Var}(X \mid X>x)^*$ $= \displaystyle\int_0^\infty s^2 \cdot f(x+s|X>x)\,ds$ $\qquad - \{E[S \mid X>x]\}^2$	$= \displaystyle\int_0^\infty s^2 \cdot {}_s p_x \mu_{x+s}\,ds - \overset{\circ}{e}_x{}^2$ $= 2 \cdot Y_x/\ell_x - (T_x/\ell_x)^2$ (no specific symbol)
12. Central rate of death over (x, x+n]	${}_n m_x =$ $\dfrac{\displaystyle\int_0^n S(x+s) \cdot \lambda(x+s)\,ds}{\displaystyle\int_0^n S(x+s)\,ds}$	$= \dfrac{\displaystyle\int_0^n \ell_{x+s}\mu_{x+s}\,ds}{\displaystyle\int_0^n \ell_{x+s}\,ds} = \dfrac{{}_n d_x}{{}_n L_x}$
13. Exposure Concepts	Do not exist in the Chapter 2 model	${}_n L_x = \displaystyle\int_0^n \ell_{x+s}\,ds$ $T_x = \displaystyle\int_x^\infty \ell_y\,dy = \sum_{y=x}^\infty L_y$

*Variance of future lifetime and variance of age at death are equal, since S=X−x, and x is a constant.

$$T_x^* = \sum_{y=x+1}^\infty \ell_y$$

$$Y_x = \int_x^\infty T_y\,dy$$

3.5 *METHODS FOR NON-INTEGRAL AGES*

A review of the functions that we have developed, and summarized in Table 3.2, shows that not many of them can be numerically determined from a life table that gives values of ℓ_x only for integral x. Actually, only the probability function $_np_x$ (and its complement $_nq_x$) for *integral* x and n can be so determined. (Note that $_xp_0$ and $_xq_0$, for integral x, are special cases of $_np_x$ and $_nq_x$.)

The determination of all other functions requires that values of ℓ_{x+s} be available for all s, $0\leq s\leq1$. This is obtained in the life table model by assuming that ℓ_{x+s} has a certain mathematical form between x and x+1. This assumed form for ℓ_{x+s} will be differentiable on the open interval $0<s<1$, but not at s=0 or s=1.

The ability to determine ℓ_{x+s} numerically for any s, $0\leq s\leq1$, will allow us to calculate probabilities of the form $_sp_x$ and $_{1-s}p_{x+s}$, and their complements $_sq_x$ and $_{1-s}q_{x+s}$. The differentiability of ℓ_{x+s} will allow us to evaluate μ_{x+s}, and hence the conditional density function $f(s\,|\,X>x) = \,_sp_x\,\mu_{x+s}$, for all s on the open interval, $0<s<1$. The integrability of ℓ_{x+s} will allow us to calculate L_x, T_x and Y_x, and hence m_x, $\overset{\circ}{e}_x$ and the conditional variance of future lifetime (or age at death), $Var(X\,|\,X>x)$.

These between-the-integral-ages assumptions are extremely important and useful, so we want to acquire a complete familiarity with them. We will later see that they are essential elements in the estimation of the model, as well as being useful for making calculations from the life table model.

We should not lose sight of the fact that we assume a mathematical form for ℓ_{x+s} *only* between x and x+1, *not* for the entire domain of x; the latter case would return us to the continuous parametric models described in Chapter 2. We will also see that each particular mathematical form that we assume for ℓ_{x+s} will correspond to a certain interpolation method.

To recapitulate, we assume that we have a life table with numerical values of ℓ_x given for all integral x. We then assume a mathematical form for ℓ_{x+s}, $0\leq s\leq1$, and show how to calculate, from the given life table, values of $_sp_x$, $_{1-s}p_{x+s}$, L_x, T_x, m_x and $\overset{\circ}{e}_x$. (The functions Y_x and $Var(X\,|\,X>x)$ can also be evaluted, but with greater difficulty. Since we will not need them for our estimation work, we will not develop them in this text.) We will now pursue each of the following three assumptions of a mathematical form for ℓ_{x+s}: linear, exponential, and hyperbolic.

3.5.1 *Linear Form for* ℓ_{x+s}

If ℓ_{x+s} is a linear function between x and x+1, then it is of the form $a+bs$. To provide continuity for ℓ_{x+s}, we require that, at s=0, we have $\ell_x = a$, and at s=1, we have $\ell_{x+1} = a+b$, so that $b = \ell_{x+1} - a$, or $b = \ell_{x+1} - \ell_x = -d_x$. Thus we have

$$\ell_{x+s} = \ell_x - s \cdot d_x. \tag{3.52}$$

An alternate form is to use $\ell_x - \ell_{x+1}$ in place of d_x, obtaining

$$\ell_{x+s} = \ell_x - s(\ell_x - \ell_{x+1}) = s \cdot \ell_{x+1} + (1-s) \cdot \ell_x. \tag{3.52a}$$

Both (3.52) and (3.52a) reveal that the linear assumption for ℓ_{x+s} allows us to determine values of ℓ_{x+s} from ℓ_x and ℓ_{x+1} by linear interpolation.

The determination of other functions follows easily from (3.52). Thus

$$_s p_x = \frac{\ell_{x+s}}{\ell_x} = 1 - s \cdot \frac{d_x}{\ell_x} = 1 - s \cdot q_x, \tag{3.53}$$

and

$$_s q_x = 1 - {}_s p_x = s \cdot q_x. \tag{3.54}$$

We also have

$$_{1-s}P_{x+s} = \frac{\ell_{x+1}}{\ell_{x+s}} = \frac{\ell_{x+1}}{\ell_x - s \cdot d_x} = \frac{p_x}{1 - s \cdot q_x}, \tag{3.55}$$

and

$$_{1-s}q_{x+s} = 1 - {}_{1-s}P_{x+s} = \frac{1 - s \cdot q_x - p_x}{1 - s \cdot q_x} = \frac{(1-s) \cdot q_x}{1 - s \cdot q_x}. \tag{3.56}$$

Next,

$$\mu_{x+s} = \frac{-\dfrac{d}{ds} \ell_{x+s}}{\ell_{x+s}} = \frac{d_x}{\ell_x - s \cdot d_x} = \frac{q_x}{1 - s \cdot q_x}, \tag{3.57}$$

which, when multiplied by (3.53), leads to the very convenient result

$$f(s \mid X > x) = {}_s p_x \mu_{x+s} = q_x. \tag{3.58}$$

Note that μ_{x+s}, and hence $f(s \mid X > x)$, are not defined at s=0 and s=1, since ℓ_{x+s} is not differentiable there.

Finally we have

$$L_x = \int_0^1 \ell_{x+s}\, ds = \int_0^1 (\ell_x - s \cdot d_x)\, ds = \ell_x - \tfrac{1}{2}d_x = \ell_{x+1} + \tfrac{1}{2}d_x, \tag{3.59}$$

so

$$T_x = \sum_{y=x}^{\infty} L_y = \sum_{y=x}^{\infty} (\ell_{y+1} + \tfrac{1}{2} d_y) = T_x^* + \tfrac{1}{2}\ell_x. \tag{3.60}$$

Then

$$m_x = \frac{d_x}{L_x} = \frac{d_x}{\ell_x - \tfrac{1}{2} d_x} = \frac{q_x}{1 - \tfrac{1}{2} \cdot q_x}, \tag{3.61}$$

and

$$\overset{\circ}{e}_x = \frac{T_x}{\ell_x} = \frac{T_x^* + \tfrac{1}{2}\ell_x}{\ell_x} = e_x + \tfrac{1}{2}, \tag{3.62}$$

which we developed intuitively in (3.45).

Turning to the question of the associated probability distribution over the interval (x, x+1], we note that the PDF for time at death within the interval is a constant, and the CDF, which is $_s q_x$, is a linear function. This shows that the random variable S has a uniform distribution over (x, x+1]. Furthermore, the linear nature of (3.52) shows that ℓ_{x+s} decreases uniformly (i.e., persons are dying uniformly) over the interval. For these reasons, this linear assumption for ℓ_{x+s} has traditionally been called the *uniform distribution of deaths* assumption, which we will refer to as UDD.

Without question the UDD assumption is extremely useful, both for the purpose of making calculations from the life table, and for the purpose of estimating the life table in the first place. No doubt the ability to analyze the assumption in terms of the uniform (or even) distribution pattern of the occurring deaths, along with the mathematical simplicity afforded by the constant PDF, are the major reasons for this assumption's popularity.

EXAMPLE 3.9: Evaluate f_x, defined in Section 3.3.6, under the UDD assumption.

SOLUTION: From (3.47), $f_x = \dfrac{L_x - \ell_{x+1}}{d_x} = \dfrac{\ell_{x+1} + \tfrac{1}{2} d_x - \ell_{x+1}}{d_x} = \tfrac{1}{2}$,

using (3.59) for L_x. The uniform nature of the time-of-death distribution makes this result intuitively obvious.

3.5.2 *Exponential Form for* ℓ_{x+s}

If ℓ_{x+s} is an exponential function between x and x+1, then it is of the form $\ell_{x+s} = a \cdot b^s$. To assure continuity, at s=0, we have $\ell_x = a$, and at s=1, we have $\ell_{x+1} = ab$, so that $b = \frac{\ell_{x+1}}{a} = \frac{\ell_{x+1}}{\ell_x}$. Thus we have

$$\ell_{x+s} = \ell_x \left(\frac{\ell_{x+1}}{\ell_x} \right)^s = (\ell_{x+1})^s \cdot (\ell_x)^{1-s}, \qquad (3.63)$$

which shows that the exponential assumption for ℓ_{x+s} allows us to determine values of ℓ_{x+s} from values of ℓ_x and ℓ_{x+1} by exponential interpolation. (Note the similarity of (3.63) and (3.52a).) An alternative form of (3.63), which results from substituting $\ell_{x+1} = \ell_x \cdot p_x$, is

$$\ell_{x+s} = \ell_x (p_x)^s. \qquad (3.63a)$$

The determination of other functions follows from (3.63) or (3.63a). Thus

$$_s p_x = \frac{\ell_{x+s}}{\ell_x} = (p_x)^s, \qquad (3.64)$$

and

$$_s q_x = 1 - _s p_x = 1 - (p_x)^s = 1 - (1-q_x)^s. \qquad (3.65)$$

We also have

$$_{1-s} p_{x+s} = \frac{\ell_{x+1}}{\ell_{x+s}} = \frac{\ell_{x+1}}{\ell_x (p_x)^s} = \frac{p_x}{(p_x)^s} = (p_x)^{1-s}, \qquad (3.66)$$

and

$$_{1-s} q_{x+s} = 1 - _{1-s} p_{x+s} = 1 - (p_x)^{1-s} = 1 - (1-q_x)^{1-s}. \qquad (3.67)$$

Next,

$$\mu_{x+s} = \frac{-\frac{d}{ds} \ell_{x+s}}{\ell_{x+s}} = \frac{-\ell_x (p_x)^s \cdot \ln p_x}{\ell_x (p_x)^s} = -\ln p_x, \qquad (3.68)$$

a constant, for $0 < s < 1$. Thus we have the useful result that, if ℓ_{x+s} is exponential, then the force of mortality, μ_{x+s}, is constant over $(x, x+1)$. We will call this constant force simply μ. Then (3.68), which says $\mu = -\ln p_x$, can be rearranged to read

$$p_x = e^{-\mu}, \qquad (3.68a)$$

from which (3.64) becomes

$$_sP_x \;=\; e^{-\mu s},\tag{3.64a}$$

and (3.66) becomes

$$_{1-s}P_{x+s} \;=\; e^{-\mu(1-s)}.\tag{3.66a}$$

The conditional PDF is then found by multiplying (3.64a) and (3.68), obtaining

$$f(s \,|\, X > x) \;=\; {}_sP_x\,\mu_{x+s} \;=\; \mu \cdot e^{-\mu s}.\tag{3.69}$$

The PDF of S, given by (3.69), and its SDF, given by (3.64a), clearly show us that S has an exponential distribution over (x, x+1]. (Recall from Section 2.3.2 that this distribution has a constant hazard rate, which is the same as the force of mortality.) This constant force of mortality has led to this assumption being traditionally called the *constant force* assumption.

We will find that the exponential assumption is not as convenient as the linear assumption for making calculations from the life table, but, on the other hand, it is sometimes more convenient than the linear for the purpose of model estimation. We will make frequent use of both assumptions in Part II of this text.

With respect to the exposure functions L_x and T_x, we find

$$L_x \;=\; \int_0^1 \ell_{x+s}\,ds \;=\; \int_0^1 \ell_x (p_x)^s\,ds \;=\; \frac{-\ell_x \cdot q_x}{\ln p_x} \;=\; \frac{-d_x}{-\mu} \;=\; \frac{d_x}{\mu}.\tag{3.70}$$

Then the central rate is found to be

$$m_x \;=\; \frac{d_x}{L_x} \;=\; \frac{d_x}{d_x/\mu} \;=\; \mu.\tag{3.71}$$

This result comes as no surprise, since, from (2.59), m_x is the weighted average value of μ_{x+s}. If μ_{x+s} is constant, then clearly its weighted average is the same as that constant, which is μ.

Of course this μ is the constant value of μ_{x+s}, $0 < s < 1$. For clarity let us call it μ_x. For the interval (x+1, x+2) we have a different constant force, namley $\mu_{x+1} = -\ln p_{x+1}$, so $L_{x+1} = d_{x+1}/\mu_{x+1}$. Then we have

$$T_x \;=\; \sum_{y=x}^{\infty} L_y \;=\; \sum_{y=x}^{\infty} \frac{d_y}{\mu_y}.\tag{3.72}$$

There is no convenient way to further simplify (3.72), but it does show that T_x can be precisely calculated from a life table under the exponential assumption.

Finally, $\overset{\circ}{e}_x$ can be obtained as T_x/ℓ_x. Again there is no convenient, simple formula for $\overset{\circ}{e}_x$.

EXAMPLE 3.10 : Evaluate f_x, as defined in Section 3.3.6, in terms of p_x under the constant force assumption.

SOLUTION : We know that $L_x = \dfrac{d_x}{\mu} = \dfrac{d_x}{-\ln p_x}$. Then from (3.47) we have

$$f_x = \frac{(d_x/-\ln p_x) - \ell_{x+1}}{d_x} = \frac{1}{-\ln p_x} - \frac{\ell_{x+1}}{d_x}$$

$$= \frac{1}{-\ln p_x} - \frac{p_x}{q_x} = \frac{1}{-\ln p_x} - \frac{p_x}{1 - p_x}.$$

3.5.3 *Hyperbolic Form for ℓ_{x+s}*

If ℓ_{x+s} is a hyperbolic function between x and x+1, then it is of the form $\ell_{x+s} = (a + bs)^{-1}$. To assure continuity, at s=0, we have $\ell_x = \frac{1}{a}$, or $a = \frac{1}{\ell_x}$, and at s=1, we have $\ell_{x+1} = \frac{1}{a+b}$, so that $b = \frac{1}{\ell_{x+1}} - a = \frac{1}{\ell_{x+1}} - \frac{1}{\ell_x}$.

Thus

$$\ell_{x+s} = \left(\frac{1}{\ell_x} + s\left\{ \frac{1}{\ell_{x+1}} - \frac{1}{\ell_x} \right\} \right)^{-1}, \tag{3.73}$$

or

$$\frac{1}{\ell_{x+s}} = \frac{1}{\ell_x} + s\left(\frac{1}{\ell_{x+1}} - \frac{1}{\ell_x} \right) = s \cdot \frac{1}{\ell_{x+1}} + (1-s) \cdot \frac{1}{\ell_x}, \tag{3.73a}$$

which shows that values of $\dfrac{1}{\ell_{x+s}}$ can be determined by linear interpolation between the reciprocals of ℓ_x and ℓ_{x+1}. Linear interpolation on the reciprocal of a function is called harmonic interpolation on the function itself.

From (3.73) we can determine expressions for other functions. To obtain $_sp_x$, we consider first

$$(_sp_x)^{-1} = \frac{\ell_x}{\ell_{x+s}} = \ell_x\left(\frac{1}{\ell_x} + s\left\{ \frac{1}{\ell_{x+1}} - \frac{1}{\ell_x} \right\} \right)$$

$$= 1 + s\left(\frac{1}{p_x} - 1 \right) = \frac{p_x + s(1 - p_x)}{p_x},$$

so that

$$_sP_x \;=\; \frac{P_x}{P_x + s(1-P_x)} \;=\; \frac{1 - q_x}{1 - (1-s)q_x}. \tag{3.74}$$

Then

$$_sq_x \;=\; 1 - {_sP_x} \;=\; \frac{s \cdot q_x}{1 - (1-s)q_x}. \tag{3.75}$$

We also have

$$_{1-s}P_{x+s} \;=\; \frac{\ell_{x+1}}{\ell_{x+s}} \;=\; \ell_{x+1}\left(\frac{1}{\ell_x} + s\left\{ \frac{1}{\ell_{x+1}} - \frac{1}{\ell_x} \right\} \right)$$

$$\;=\; P_x + s(1-P_x) \;=\; 1 - (1-s)q_x, \tag{3.76}$$

from which we find the very convenient result

$$_{1-s}q_{x+s} \;=\; 1 - {_{1-s}P_{x+s}} \;=\; (1-s)q_x. \tag{3.77}$$

Next, using $_sP_x = \dfrac{P_x}{P_x + s \cdot q_x}$, we find

$$\mu_{x+s} \;=\; \frac{-\dfrac{d}{ds}{_sP_x}}{_sP_x} \;=\; \frac{P_x \cdot q_x}{(P_x + s \cdot q_x)^2} \div \frac{P_x}{P_x + s \cdot q_x}$$

$$\;=\; \frac{q_x}{P_x + s \cdot q_x} \;=\; \frac{q_x}{1 - (1-s)q_x}, \tag{3.78}$$

and so

$$f(s \,|\, X > x) \;=\; {_sP_x}\mu_{x+s} \;=\; \frac{q_x \cdot (1 - q_x)}{[1 - (1-s)q_x]^2}. \tag{3.79}$$

Again we note that μ_{x+s} and $f(s \,|\, X > x)$ are not defined at $s=0$ and $s=1$.

The hyperbolic assumption is somewhat illogical, in that it implies a decreasing μ_{x+s} over $(x,\, x+1)$, whereas the linear assumption implies an increasing μ_{x+s}, and the exponential assumption implies a constant μ_{x+s}, as we have seen. It is not often used for making calculations from the life table model, and is not widely used in estimation work outside of actuarial science. For these reasons it might be thought that this assumption need not be considered any further. However, the convenient relationship

$$_{1-s}q_{x+s} \;=\; (1-s)q_x \tag{3.77}$$

is used in what has been the traditional actuarial approach to survival model estimation for over a century. This approach is not without merit, and will no doubt continue to be used in actuarial circles, so the hyperbolic assumption will continue to receive some attention.

The Italian actuary Gaetano Balducci made major use of the hyperbolic distribution in several of his writings, such as [4] and [5]. Although he did not originate the use of this assumption, it has come to be called the Balducci assumption, or Balducci distribution.

With respect to the exposure functions L_x and T_x, we note first that, from (3.73), $\ell_{x+s} = \frac{1}{a+bs}$, where $a = \frac{1}{\ell_x}$ and $b = \frac{1}{\ell_{x+1}} - \frac{1}{\ell_x}$. Then

$$L_x = \int_0^1 \ell_{x+s} \, ds = \int_0^1 \frac{ds}{a+bs} = \frac{1}{b} \cdot \ln\left(\frac{a+b}{a}\right).$$

Substituting for a and b, we find $\frac{a+b}{a} = \frac{1}{p_x}$ and $\frac{1}{b} = \frac{\ell_{x+1}}{q_x}$. Thus we have

$$L_x = \frac{\ell_{x+1}}{q_x} \cdot \ln\frac{1}{p_x} = -\ell_{x+1}\left(\frac{\ln p_x}{q_x}\right). \tag{3.80}$$

From L_x we can find T_x, m_x and $\overset{\circ}{e}_x$ from the usual formulas.

EXAMPLE 3.11 : In a certain life table, $\ell_x = 1000$ and $\ell_{x+1} = 900$. Evaluate m_x under each of the UDD, constant force, and Balducci assumptions.

SOLUTION : From the given values we find $d_x = 100$, $\ln p_x = -.10536$, and $\mu = -\ln p_x = .10536$. Under UDD, $L_x = \ell_x - \frac{1}{2}d_x = 950$, so $m_x = \frac{d_x}{L_x} = .10526$; under constant force, we directly have $m_x = \mu = .10536$; under Balducci, we have $L_x = \frac{-\ell_{x+1} \cdot \ln p_x}{q_x} = 948.24$, so $m_x = \frac{100}{948.24} = .10545$.

3.5.4 *Summary*

Table 3.3 summarizes most of the results developed in this section. Our purpose is to establish a sufficient familiarity with the three common assumptions to allow an understanding of their use in survival model estimation. A deeper analysis of these assumptions is given by Batten [6], and Mereu [44] gives a presentation of the use of these assumptions in actuarial calculations.

TABLE 3.3

Function	Linear (UDD)	Exponential (Constant Force)	Hyperbolic (Balducci)
ℓ_{x+s}	$\ell_x - s \cdot d_x$ $= s \cdot \ell_{x+1}$ $+ (1-s) \cdot \ell_x$	$\ell_x(p_x)^s$ $= (\ell_{x+1})^s \cdot (\ell_x)^{1-s}$	$\left(s \cdot \dfrac{1}{\ell_{x+1}} + (1-s) \cdot \dfrac{1}{\ell_x} \right)^{-1}$
$_sp_x$	$1 - s \cdot q_x$	$(p_x)^s = e^{-\mu s}$	$\dfrac{p_x}{p_x + s(1-p_x)}$ $= \dfrac{1 - q_x}{1 - (1-s)q_x}$
$_sq_x$	$s \cdot q_x$	$1 - (1-q_x)^s$	$\dfrac{s \cdot q_x}{1 - (1-s)q_x}$
$_{1-s}p_{x+s}$	$\dfrac{p_x}{1 - s \cdot q_x}$	$(p_x)^{1-s} = e^{-\mu(1-s)}$	$p_x + s(1-p_x)$ $= 1 - (1-s)q_x$
$_{1-s}q_{x+s}$	$\dfrac{(1-s)q_x}{1 - s \cdot q_x}$	$1 - (1-q_x)^{1-s}$	$(1-s)q_x$
μ_{x+s}	$\dfrac{q_x}{1 - s \cdot q_x}$	$\mu = -\ln p_x$	$\dfrac{q_x}{1 - (1-s)q_x}$
$_sp_x\mu_{x+s}$	q_x	$\mu \cdot e^{-\mu s}$	$\dfrac{q_x(1-q_x)}{[1 - (1-s)q_x]^2}$
L_x	$\ell_x - \frac{1}{2}d_x$ $= \ell_{x+1} + \frac{1}{2}d_x$	$\dfrac{d_x}{\mu}$	$-\ell_{x+1}\left(\dfrac{\ln p_x}{q_x} \right)$
m_x	$\dfrac{q_x}{1 - \frac{1}{2} \cdot q_x}$	μ	$\dfrac{(q_x)^2}{-p_x \cdot \ln p_x}$

3.6 *SELECT LIFE TABLES*

In this section we consider life tables developed from the select survival distribution defined in Section 1.2 as $S(t;x)$, $t \geq 0$.

It is easy to see that a life table based on this SDF is completely parallel to one based on $S(x)$. Thus we begin with a radix which represents a hypothetical cohort of lives selected at age x, which we call $\ell_{[x]}$. Then subsequent values are developed from

$$\ell_{[x]+t} = \ell_{[x]} \cdot S(t;x). \tag{3.81}$$

If values of $\ell_{[x]+t}$ are specified for all integral t, the resulting select life table (for age at selection x) can then be used to obtain other values, just as we did for the aggregate life table earlier in this chapter. It is important to specify the age at selection in the symbols for the functions derived from a select table. For example, if selection is at age x, the conditional probability of death between ages x+7 and x+10, for a person known to be alive at age x+5, is given by

$$_{2|3}q_{[x]+5} = \frac{\ell_{[x]+7} - \ell_{[x]+10}}{\ell_{[x]+5}}. \tag{3.82}$$

Select life tables do not normally extend to all values of t in a manner that is unique to the selection age. For example, consider two persons, one selected at age 20 and now age 30 (t=10), and the other selected at age 21 and now age 30 (t=9). Their respective conditional probabilities of survival for another n years are $_nP_{[20]+10} = \frac{\ell_{[20]+10+n}}{\ell_{[20]+10}}$ and $_nP_{[21]+9} = \frac{\ell_{[21]+9+n}}{\ell_{[21]+9}}$. If it is felt that selection no longer has an effect on mortality at these durations, then the two probabilities should have the same value, denoted by $\frac{\ell_{30+n}}{\ell_{30}}$. A life table with this characteristic is called a *select and ultimate* table.

The first step in developing a select and ultimate table is to determine the length of the *select period*, the time over which selection is assumed to have an effect on mortality. Although there is evidence that effects of selection can persist for many years, published tables will seldom show a select period greater than 15 years. For illustration in this text, however, we will assume only a four-year select period. This means that for persons four and more years beyond selection, mortality is a function of attained age only.

Suppose [x] is the youngest age at selection in the table which we wish to construct. Then we select a radix, $\ell_{[x]}$, and generate

$$\ell_{[x]+t} = \ell_{[x]} \cdot S(t;x) \quad \text{for } t=1,2,3$$

$$\ell_{x+t} = \ell_{[x]} \cdot S(t;x) \quad \text{for } t \geq 4 \tag{3.83}$$

Instead of arranging these values of $\ell_{[x]+t}$ and ℓ_{x+t} in a column, as in our earlier Table 3.1a, we arrange them in the row-and-column format shown in Table 3.4.

TABLE 3.4

$\ell_{[x]}$	$\ell_{[x]+1}$	$\ell_{[x]+2}$	$\ell_{[x]+3}$	ℓ_{x+4}
				ℓ_{x+5}
				ℓ_{x+6}
				.
				.
				.

Next, consider age at selection [x+1]. If a radix, $\ell_{[x+1]}$, were arbitrarily chosen, then we would generate

$$\ell_{[x+1]+t} = \ell_{[x+1]} \cdot S(t;x+1) \quad \text{for } t=1,2,3$$

$$\ell_{x+1+t} = \ell_{[x+1]} \cdot S(t;x+1) \quad \text{for } t \geq 4 \tag{3.84}$$

But the basic idea of the select and ultimate table is that the same values of ℓ_{x+t}, $t \geq 5$, should be common to the cohorts $\ell_{[x]}$ and $\ell_{[x+1]}$. Thus $\ell_{[x+1]}$ must be chosen so that $\ell_{[x+1]} \cdot S(4;x+1)$ produces the same ℓ_{x+5} as was produced by $\ell_{[x]} \cdot S(5;x)$. This is easily accomplished by taking

$$\ell_{[x+1]} = \frac{\ell_{x+5}}{S(4;x+1)}. \tag{3.85}$$

Then $\ell_{[x+1]+1}$, $\ell_{[x+1]+2}$, and $\ell_{[x+1]+3}$ can be found from this $\ell_{[x+1]}$ using the first line of (3.84). Note that values of $S(t;x+1)$ for $t>4$ are not utilized once it has been decided to use a four-year select period.

Similarly, $\ell_{[x+2]}$ would be found from the already established value of ℓ_{x+6} by

$$\ell_{[x+2]} = \frac{\ell_{x+6}}{S(4;x+2)}, \tag{3.86}$$

and then values of $\ell_{[x+2]+t}$, $t=1,2,3$, are found from

$$\ell_{[x+2]+t} = \ell_{[x+2]} \cdot S(t;x+2). \tag{3.87}$$

The complete select and ultimate table is in the format of Table 3.5, where we assume age 20 is the youngest age at selection.

TABLE 3.5

[x]	$\ell_{[x]}$	$\ell_{[x]+1}$	$\ell_{[x]+2}$	$\ell_{[x]+3}$	ℓ_{x+4}	x+4
[20]	$\ell_{[20]}$	$\ell_{[20]+1}$	$\ell_{[20]+2}$	$\ell_{[20]+3}$	ℓ_{24}	24
[21]	$\ell_{[21]}$	$\ell_{[21]+1}$	$\ell_{[21]+2}$	$\ell_{[21]+3}$	ℓ_{25}	25
[22]	$\ell_{[22]}$	$\ell_{[22]+1}$	$\ell_{[22]+2}$	$\ell_{[22]+3}$	ℓ_{26}	25
.	.	.	.	.	.	.
.	.	.	.	.	.	.
.	.	.	.	.	.	.

From this table, conditional probabilities can be calculated for integral ages and durations. Other calculations can be made by assuming one of the mortality distribution assumptions, as described in Section 3.5, between pairs of adjacent integers.

EXAMPLE 3.12: Express the conditional probabilities (a) $_{2|4}q_{[20]+1}$ and (b) $_{2|4}q_{[22]+3}$ in terms of ℓ's, assuming a 4-year select period.

SOLUTION: (a) This is the probability of death between ages 23 and 27 for a person age 21, selected at age 20. The number of such deaths, from Table 3.5, is $\ell_{[20]+3} - \ell_{27}$, so the desired probability is $\dfrac{\ell_{[20]+3} - \ell_{27}}{\ell_{[20]+1}}$.

(b) Here we seek the probability of death between ages 27 and 31 for a person age 25, selected at age 22. For this person, age 27 is already beyond the select period, so the probability is $\dfrac{\ell_{27} - \ell_{31}}{\ell_{[22]+3}}$.

In this section we have developed the select and ultimate life table from values of S(t;x). Alternatively, a set of $q_{[x]+t}$, t=0,1,2,3, for all ages at selection, and q_{x+t}, t≥4, might be available. Since $p_{[x]+t} = 1 - q_{[x]+t}$ and $p_{x+t} = 1 - q_{x+t}$, then values of S(t;x) can easily be found. Thus the development of a select life table from a set of q's is totally parallel to its development from S(t;x). For a description of this select table development from q's, specifically oriented to the idea of selection for issuance of insurance, see Section 1.8 of Jordan [32].

3.7 *SUMMARY*

The life table is a very common form in which survival models are expressed, expecially in actuarial and demographic work. In this chapter we have tried to provide a very thorough description of this model, including an understanding of the correspondence between the life table and the conceptual survival distribution expressed by S(x) and its related functions.

Detailed *uses* of the life table is not the subject of this text. We have described tabular models in this chapter as background for the material on estimating such models, which comprises Part II of the text. In particular, the material in Section 3.5 on mortality distribution assumptions will be useful in the estimation of models.

Some explanation would be useful at this point concerning our notation (x, x+1] for the interval from x to x+1. We take the view that we are addressing the question of death (or survival) over this interval, *given alive at x*. If the given condition is *alive at x*, then it follows that death *at* x is not possible for this interval. Death *at* x+1 is possible for this interval, however. In other words, death at an integral age, which is an interval boundary, is defined to "belong" to the interval *closing* at that boundary, not the one *opening* there.

It must be understood that this choice was somewhat arbitrary, and other texts might choose the opposite, thereby using [x, x+1). Our choice is based on a literal interpretation of the condition *alive at x*, as well as a desire to be consistent with the unconditional probability F(x) = Pr(X≤x).

The reader should also be aware that when one calculates the conditional probability $q_x = \frac{d_x}{\ell_x}$, the issue of whether this is the probability of death *prior to* x+1, or *not later than* x+1 is not numerically crucial, since we may take Pr(X = x+1 | X>x) to be zero. But for the estimation work in Part II of the text, if a death is observed *at* age x, then, as a practical matter, one *must* decide whether to consider it as being "between x−1 and x" or "between x and x+1". We will choose the former, and this is indicated by the notation $(x-1, x]$ and $(x, x+1]$.

EXERCISES

3.1 Introduction;   3.2 The Traditional Form of the Life Table

3-1.   A tabular survival model is defined by the following values of p_x:

x	p_x
0	.9
1	.8
2	.6
3	.3
4	0

(a)   What are the corresponding values of $S(x)$, for x=0,1,2,3,4,5?
(b)   Using a radix of 10,000, derive a life table showing the values of ℓ_x and d_x.
(c)   What is the value of ω in this table?
(d)   Verify that $\sum_{x=0}^{\omega-1} d_x = \ell_0$.

3-2.   From the life table developed in Exercise 3-1, calculate each of the following:
(a) $_3d_0$ (b) $_2q_1$ (c) $_3p_1$ (d) $_3q_2$

3-3.   The unconditional probability of death between ages x and x+1 is given by $_x|q_0$.
(a)   Define $_x|q_0$ in terms of $S(x)$ and in terms of ℓ_x.

(b)   Show that $\sum_{x=0}^{\omega-1} {_x|q_0} = 1$.

3-4.   A survival distribution function is defined by $S(x) = \frac{c-x}{c+x}$, $0 \le x \le c$. A life table is developed from this SDF using $\ell_0 = 100,000$. In the resulting life table, $\ell_{35} = 44,000$.
(a)   Find the value of ω in the table.
(b)   Find the probability of surviving from birth to age 60.
(c)   Find the probability that a life age 10 will die between age 30 and age 45.

3.3   Other Functions Derived from ℓ_x;
3.4   Summary of Concepts and Notation

3-5.   If $\mu_x = \frac{2}{x+1} + \frac{2}{100-x}$, $0 \leq x < 100$, find the number of deaths which occur between ages 1 and 4 in a life table with a radix of 10,000.

3-6.   Find each of the following derivatives: (a) $\frac{\partial}{\partial s} {}_sP_x$ (b) $\frac{\partial}{\partial x} {}_sP_x$

3-7.   A simple approximation to $\frac{d}{dx} \ell_x$ is $\frac{\ell_{x+1} - \ell_{x-1}}{2}$.   Use this approximation to determine a value for μ_2 from the life table shown in Table 3.1a.

3-8.   If $\ell_x = 2500(64 - .8x)^{1/3}$, $0 \leq x \leq 80$, find each of the following:
(a) f(x)   (b) E[X]   (c) Var(X)

3-9.   Find each of the following derivatives: (a) $\frac{d}{dx} \left[\frac{T_x}{\ell_x} \right]$ (b) $\frac{d}{dx} (\ln T_x)$

3-10.   For the ℓ_x function given in Exercise 3-8, find $\overset{\circ}{e}_{70}$ and the variance of future lifetime for a person age 70.

3-11.   Show that $L_{x+1} = L_x \cdot \exp\left[-\int_x^{x+1} m_y \, dy \right]$.   (c.f., Equation 3.10)

3-12.   Evaluate ${}_{10}m_{70}$ from the ℓ_x function given in Exercise 3-8.

3-13.   Find each of the following derivatives: (a) $\frac{\partial}{\partial_x} {}_nL_x$ (b) $\frac{\partial}{\partial_n} {}_nL_x$

3-14.   Consider the ℓ_x value in a life table to represent a hypothetical group of persons all age x. Give symbolic answers to each of the following:
(a)   What is the aggregate number of life-years that this group will live in the future (their total future lifetime)?
(b)   How many life-years will they live prior to reaching age x+n?
(c)   What is the average (or expected) lifetime for a person in this group prior to age x+n (denoted by $\overset{\circ}{e}_{x:\overline{n}|}$)?
(d)   How many in this group survive to age x+n?
(e)   How many life-years did the survivors in (d) live from age x to age x+n?
(f)   Then how many years were lived between the ages of x and x+n by the persons who died in that age interval?
(g)   How many persons died between ages x and x+n?
(h)   What was the average number of life-years lived between ages x and x+n, by those who died in that age interval?

3-15. Show that $e_x = p_x(1 + e_{x+1})$.

3-16. Let e_x be the curtate expectation of life at age x according to a certain life table, and let e'_x be the same concept according to a second life table. For all x it is known that $\frac{1+e_x}{1+e'_x} = 1+k$, where k is a constant. Show that $q'_x = q_x + \frac{k}{1+e_{x+1}}$.

3-17. Let μ_x^I denote the force of mortality in Life Table I, and μ_x^{II} denote the force of mortality in Life Table II. If $\mu_x^{II} = \mu_x^I + \frac{1}{\overset{\circ}{e}_x^I}$, show that $\overset{\circ}{e}_x^{II} = \frac{1}{2} \cdot \overset{\circ}{e}_x^I$.

3-18. Consider the function f_x defined by (3.47). Which of the following correctly define f_x?

(a) $\displaystyle\int_0^1 s \cdot {}_sp_x\mu_{x+s}\,ds$

(b) $E[X-x\,|\,x \le X \le x+1]$

(c) $\dfrac{\displaystyle\int_x^{x+1}(y-x) \cdot S(y) \cdot \lambda(y)\,dy}{S(x) - S(x+1)}$

3-19. Determine ${}_5f_{70}$ from the following data:

x	ℓ_x	T_x
70	54,900	573,800
75	40,900	332,800
80	26,100	165,800
85	13,700	67,600

3-20. Let ${}_na_x$ be the average *number* of years lived beyond age x by persons who die between ages x and x+n. Given that $\ell_{35} = 1060$, $\ell_{40} = 960$, ${}_5m_{35} = .020$, and ${}_5m_{40} = .018$, find ${}_5a_{35}$.

3.5 Methods for Non-integral Ages

3-21. Show that linear interpolation on the log of a function is the same as exponential interpolation on the function itself.

3-22. If $\ell_x = 1000\sqrt{100-x}$, $0 \le x \le 100$, calculate the exact value of $\mu_{36+1/4}$, and compare it with the value obtained from each of the linear, exponential and hyperbolic assumptions. (Round the value of ℓ_{37} to the nearest integer.)

3-23. If $\ell_x = 15,120$ and $q_x = \frac{1}{3}$, find $\ell_{x+1/4}$ under the hyperbolic assumption.

3-24. The following values are given by a certain life table:

$\ell_x = 10,000$ $L_{x+1} = 8,000$ $q_{x+1} = .2500$

$\ell_{x+1} = 8,100$ $L_{x+2} = 6,000$ $m_{x+2} = .3645$

Using exponential interpolation, find $_2q_{x+1/2}$.

3-25. Let μ_{x+k} denote the constant force of mortality for the age interval $(x+k, x+k+1)$. Determine $\overset{\circ}{e}_{x:\overline{3}|}$, the expected number of years to be lived over the next three years by a life age x, given the following data:

k	$\exp(-\mu_{x+k})$	$\dfrac{1 - \exp(-\mu_{x+k})}{\mu_{x+k}}$
0	.9512	.9754
1	.9493	.9744
2	.9465	.9730

3-26. If $_{.1}q^H_{x+1/2} = {_zq^L_{x+1/2}} = k$, find z in terms of k. (H and L refer to the hyperbolic and linear assumptions for ℓ_{x+s}, respectively.)

3-27. Which of the following relationships are correct under the linear assumption for ℓ_{x+s}, $0<s<1$?
(a) $_{1/2}q_x < {_{1/2}q_{x+1/2}}$ (b) $_sq_x = {_{1-s}p_x} \cdot {_sq_{x+1-s}}$ (c) $\mu_{x+s} > {_sq_x}$

3-28. Show that $Y_x = \sum\limits_{k=0}^{\infty} (k+1) \cdot \ell_{x+k+1} + \frac{1}{6} \cdot \ell_x$, under the uniform assumption.

3-29. Given the following excerpt from a life table, find the median of future lifetime for a person age 50, assuming (a) uniform, and (b) constant force.

$\ell_{50} = 80,000$ $\ell_{74} = 42,693$ $\ell_{75} = 40,280$ $\ell_{76} = 37,480$

3.6 Select Life Tables

3-30. For a select and ultimate table with a four-year select period, show that $\overset{\circ}{e}_{[20]} = \overset{\circ}{e}_{[20]:\overline{4}|} + {_4p_{[20]}} \cdot \overset{\circ}{e}_{24}$.

3-31. A select and ultimate table with a three-year select period begins at selection age 0. Given the following, find the radix $\ell_{[0]}$.

$\ell_6 = 90,000$ $q_{[0]} = \frac{1}{6}$ $_5p_{[1]} = \frac{4}{5}$

$d_x = 5,000$ for $x \ge 3$ $_3p_{[0]+1} = \frac{9}{10} \cdot {_3p_{[1]}}$

PART II

ESTIMATION OF SURVIVAL MODELS FROM SAMPLE DATA

This part of the text deals with the mathematics of various approaches to estimating a survival model from sample data.

Once a sample is selected, a basic distinction is made between the case where the sample is kept under observation until all have died (complete data sample), versus the case where units in the sample may terminate observation while still alive (incomplete data sample). Estimation from complete data samples is considerably more straightforward than estimation from incomplete data samples. The former case is considered in Chapter 4, and the latter in Chapters 5 through 9.

Chapter 5 is devoted to an analysis of study design to discover the types of estimation problems that we will encounter.

Chapter 6 describes moment estimation procedures, including the traditional actuarial approach.

Chapter 7 deals with maximum likelihood estimation, including the product limit estimator.

Chapter 8 deals with the estimation of parametric survival models, from both complete and incomplete data samples. It includes the topic of hypothesis testing of such estimated models, and a brief discussion of allowing for concomitant variables as well.

Chapter 9 deals with the special problem of estimating survival models from general population data, illustrated by the development of the most recent United States and Canadian National Life Tables.

In all cases, an attempt is made to analyze the nature and quality of the resulting estimates.

CHAPTER 4

TABULAR SURVIVAL MODELS ESTIMATED
FROM COMPLETE DATA SAMPLES

4.1 INTRODUCTION

We begin our study of the estimation of survival models with a very simple study design. This design is found in clinical studies where the observer can keep each study unit under observation for the fairly short time until it fails, and no units are permitted to withdraw from the study without failing (dying). This situation is referred to as *complete data*. In those situations where study units can withdraw, or are otherwise lost from observation before death, some information regarding the survival pattern of the entities under study is lost, and we say that the data are incomplete.

To say that the presence of withdrawals complicates the estimation problem is a huge understatement. We will see that survival model estimation from complete data and the analysis of such estimates are considerably more straightforward than will be the case with incomplete data.

Because complete data situations are generally found only in clinical studies, we use S(t), rather than S(x), for the operative survival function which we wish to estimate. The variable of interest is, therefore, time of survival (hence failure) since some initial event. Our estimate of S(t) will be denoted by Ŝ(t) in most cases.

4.2 STUDY DESIGN

In this chapter we are dealing with the longitudinal study design defined in Section 1.5. All study units come under observation at a well-defined time t=0, and are observed over time until all have died; the exact time of each death is recorded. The initial group of study units forms a *cohort* group. By this we mean a closed group which allows no entrants after time t=0.

The cohort could be gathered in either of two ways. Suppose, for example, that 100 laboratory mice are injected with a dose of nicotine on a certain day. Then time t=0 is obtained on the same day for all study units, and, furthermore, a death observed at duration t would occur on the tth day of the study. In this case it is easy to see the idea of survival viewed as time since the initial event.

Contrast this with a second example. Suppose a study is made of the survival pattern of persons diagnosed as having a certain terminal disease. The study includes all persons so diagnosed during calendar years 1980 and 1981, and each person has his own date on which t=0. Together the dates of diagnosis and of death give the observed value of t at death, and this is the variable of interest for our study. Note that the chronological ages of the persons are not of concern to us.

EXAMPLE 4.1 :   Person A was diagnosed on March 1, 1980 and died on March 11, 1981. Person B was diagnosed on July 1, 1981 and died on August 1, 1981. What are their observed times of death, measured in days.
SOLUTION :   Person A died at t=375 and Person B died at t=31. It is a simple matter, but a very important one, to distinguish between calendar time (or chronological time), and time under observation (frequently called *follow-up* time). A time diagram of the contributions of Persons A and B to our study, in terms of calendar time, is shown in Figure 4.1a.

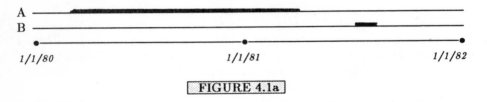

FIGURE 4.1a

In terms of follow-up time, the contributions of Persons A and B are shown in Figure 4.1b.

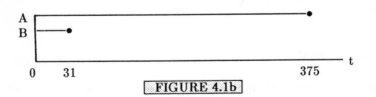

FIGURE 4.1b

The idea that we wish to reinforce is that all persons come under observation at t=0, even though these generally occur at different dates for different persons. It should also be understood that our procedures for estimating the survival model will not depend on whether each t=0 occurs on different days or on the same day.

4.3 *EXACT TIME OF DEATH*

Suppose a cohort of 5 study units is observed, with deaths occurring at ordered times t_1, t_2, t_3, t_4, and t_5. Based on this sample data we wish to estimate the survival distribution applicable to these entities.

4.3.1 *The Empirical Survival Distribution*

A very natural approach would be to estimate the operative $S(t)$ by the observed proportion of the sample surviving to each time point t. A graph of the observed (or empirical) survival distribution would be helpful, and is shown in Figure 4.2 . We will use $S^o(t)$ to denote this distribution.

Values of $S^o(t)$, which estimate $S(t)$, are easy to read from the graph. For all $t < t_1$, the proportion surviving to that t is 1.00, and we take this as our estimate of $S(t)$. We are not saying that death prior to time t_1 is *impossible*, but rather that $S^o(t) = 1.00$ is the estimate of $S(t)$ which results from this data and this estimation procedure.

Similarly, we take our estimate of $S(t_1)$, which we call $S^o(t_1)$, to be .80, since this is the proportion which we observe surviving to time t_1. Actually, we take $S^o(t) = .80$ for *all* t such that $t_1 \leq t < t_2$, since .80 is the surviving proportion at all such t. In like manner we take $S^o(t) = .60$ for all t such that $t_2 \leq t < t_3$.

What should be our estimate of $S(t)$ for all $t \geq t_5$? Since our estimation procedure has been defined to be simply the observed proportion surviving, it follows that we take $S^o(t) = 0$ for all such t. Here we are not saying that survival beyond t_5 is *impossible*, but rather that $S^o(t) = 0$ is the estimate of $S(t)$ from *this* data, according to *this* procedure.

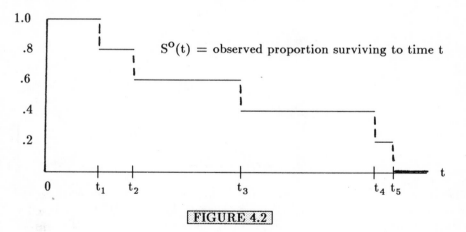

FIGURE 4.2

To summarize, for an initial cohort of size n, this simple estimation approach produces the estimate

$$S^o(t) = \begin{cases} 1.0 & \text{for } t < t_1 \\ \frac{n-i}{n} & \text{for } t_i \leq t < t_{i+1}, \quad i = 1, 2, \cdots, n-1 \\ 0 & \text{for } t \geq t_n. \end{cases} \qquad (4.1)$$

To some extent the constancy of $S^o(t)$ for all t between t_i and t_{i+1} is not intuitively appealing. We would expect S(t) to be a strictly decreasing function of t, and thus our estimate $S^o(t)$ should show this property as well. We recognize that the "step-down" nature of $S^o(t)$ results from the finite sample size from which it was produced. Suppose that, for the entities under study here, very few ever survive beyond time t=10. Suppose also that we have a cohort of n=50 study units, rather than only 5. Then the empirical proportion surviving graph would step down .02 each death, and would pack 50 such steps between t=0 and t=10. The graph would look something like Figure 4.3.

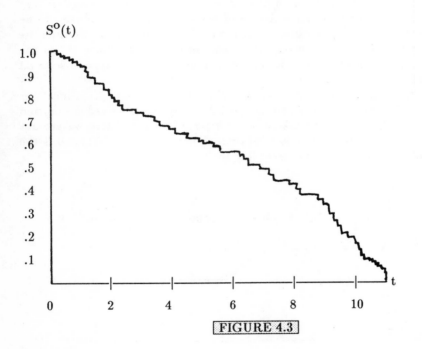

FIGURE 4.3

The greater number of steps, resulting from the greater sample size, packed into a maximum practical range (here taken to be 10), results in estimated values of S(t) that are "smoother" than those produced from the smaller sample. If we wish, we could revise the $S^o(t)$ shown in Figure 4.3 by superimposing a smooth curve which closely fits the observed step pattern. This revision is called *graduation*, and would be done as part of the process of producing an estimate of S(t) for practical use. In this text we are concerned only with procedures which produce the initial estimate of S(t), and will not pursue the issue of graduation. (For a thorough treatment of graduation, see London [41].)

Note that in the estimation procedure described here we assume that time of death is recorded with sufficient accuracy such that there is no more than one death at each time point. If the recording unit (i.e., week, day, etc.) is not sufficiently fine, or if the sample is sufficiently large, or both, then *multiple deaths* will occur at one time point. When this occurs, our step graph of $S^o(t)$ will merely step down $\frac{2}{n}$ if there are two deaths at that point, or, in general, $\frac{r}{n}$ for r deaths at the same time point. This is illustrated in Example 4.2 and Figure 4.4.

EXAMPLE 4.2 : A cohort of eight individuals is observed from time t=0 until all have failed. Only the day of failure is recorded. (By assuming that the initial event defining t=0 occurs in the middle of the day, and failure also occurs in the middle of the day, then all durations at failure are integral.) The observed durations at failure were 3, 4, 5, 5, 7, 10, 10, 12. The observed proportion of the sample surviving, $S^o(t)$, is used to estimate the operative (but unknown) S(t). (a) What are our estimates of S(2), S(5), S(12)? (b) Graph $S^o(t)$.

SOLUTION : (a) $S^o(2) = 1.00$, the proportion still surviving. Since we have defined $S^o(t)$ to be right continuous, by (4.1), the observed proportion surviving at t=5 is $S^o(5) = .50$. Similarly, since $t_8 = 12$ is the time of the last death, then $S^o(12) = 0$.

(b)

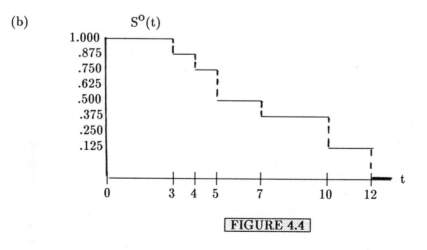

FIGURE 4.4

In general, we might use the procedure of this section for cohorts small enough to avoid a prohibitive amount of computation. For larger samples, we can use the approach described in Section 4.4.

4.3.2 *Analysis of the Empirical Survival Distribution*

We note that $S^o(t)$ is an estimate of $S(t)$, such estimate depending on the *random* occurrence of deaths prior to (and hence following) time t. For any fixed value of t, we define $S^o(t)$ as

$$S^o(t) = \frac{\text{number of survivors at time t}}{n} = \frac{N_t}{n}, \qquad (4.2)$$

where N_t denotes the (random) number of survivors at time t. (It will be our convention to use capital letters for random variables.) Equation (4.2) is the estimator for $S(t)$. Recall that $S(t)$ represents the "real," or operative, probability of survival to time t for an entity in our study. Then N_t is a binomial random variable with parameters n (sample size) and $S(t)$, if the standard characteristics of a binomial model are assumed to hold. We recall that

$$E[N_t] = n \cdot S(t) \qquad (4.3a)$$

and

$$\text{Var}(N_t) = n \cdot S(t) \cdot F(t), \qquad (4.3b)$$

since $F(t) = 1 - S(t)$.

Since N_t is a binomial random variable, then $S^o(t) = \frac{N_t}{n}$ is a binomial proportion random variable, with

$$E[S^o(t)] = \frac{1}{n} \cdot E[N_t] = S(t) \qquad (4.4a)$$

and

$$\text{Var}[S^o(t)] = \frac{1}{n^2} \cdot \text{Var}(N_t) = \frac{S(t) \cdot F(t)}{n}. \qquad (4.4b)$$

Equation (4.4a) shows that $S^o(t)$ is an unbiased estimator of $S(t)$.

Of course $S(t)$ is not known, so if we seek numerical values of $\text{Var}[S^o(t)]$ the best we can obtain are approximate, or estimated, values by using $S^o(t)$ in place of $S(t)$. Thus we have

$$\text{est. Var}[S^o(t)] = \frac{S^o(t) \cdot F^o(t)}{n}, \qquad (4.5)$$

where $F^o(t) = 1 - S^o(t)$.

EXAMPLE 4.3 : Suppose it is known that the survival distribution to which our sample in Example 4.2 is actually subject is uniform on (0,15]. (a) What is the variance of the random variable $S^o(6)$? (b) If the uniform distribution assumption is not made, how would we estimate $\text{Var}[S^o(6)]$?

SOLUTION : (a) If T is uniform on (0,15], then $S(6) = .6$, so that $\text{Var}[S^O(6)] = \dfrac{(.6)(.4)}{8} = .03$. (b) Note that $S^O(6) = .5$, so (4.5) gives

est. $\text{Var}[S^O(6)] = \dfrac{(.5)(.5)}{8} = .03125$. [Note: The data of this sample could

be used to test the hypothesis that the applicable distribution is uniform on (0,15]. We will do this in Chapter 8.]

4.4 GROUPED TIMES OF DEATH

If the cohort group under observation is large, so that the procedure of the preceding section is not practical, we might use a grouped deaths approach. We begin by dividing the time continuum into an indefinite number of fixed intervals of equal length. This time line is shown in Figure 4.5.

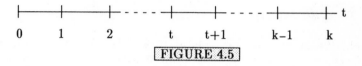

FIGURE 4.5

Although intervals of equal length are not required for this procedure, it is convenient to assume them. The notation and formulas for the estimators are simplified by the use of equal length intervals.

4.4.1 *Notation*

As before, let n be the initial size of the cohort under study. Since we are dealing with complete data, all n study units are observed to die, and each of the n deaths falls into one of k intervals, where k is set large enough so that survival to time k is impossible.

Let D_t be the random variable for the number of deaths which occur in the $(t+1)^{st}$ interval (i.e., between t and t+1), $0 \le t \le k-1$, and let d_t represent the realized value of D_t in an actual study. We note that

$$n = \sum_{t=0}^{k-1} d_t. \qquad (4.6)$$

Let N_t be the random variable for the number of survivors at time t, and let n_t represent the realized value of N_t in an actual study. Note that, necessarily, $N_0 = n$, and $N_k = 0$, so N_0 and N_k are degenerate random variables. We note the relationship

$$N_{t+1} = N_t - D_t, \quad \text{for } t = 0, 1, \cdots, k-1. \tag{4.7}$$

Let q_t represent the conditional probability of death between t and $t+1$, given alive at t, and let $p_t = 1 - q_t$ be the complementary survival probability.

Since $S(t)$ is already understood to be the unconditional probability of survival to time t (from time 0), then $S(t) \cdot q_t$ is the unconditional probability of death between t and $t+1$. In standard actuarial notation we would use $_t|q_0$ for $S(t) \cdot q_t$.

In an actual study using a cohort, complete data, grouped deaths design, our objective will be to estimate the operative $S(t)$, along with some other functions of the survival model, and to analyze the estimates we obtain. To do this it will be important to have a clear understanding of the basic random variables in our study, since our estimators will depend on those random variables.

4.4.2 The Distributions of N_t and D_t

Each N_t, the number of survivors at time t, is a binomial random variable with parameters n and $S(t)$. The mean and variance of each N_t are given by (4.3a) and (4.3b), respectively.

Together the set of random variables $D_0, D_1, \cdots, D_{k-1}$ has a joint multinomial distribution. The multinomial probability for D_t is $S(t) \cdot q_t = {_t|q_0}$. We recall the following properties of the multinomial distribution:

$$P_n(d_0, d_1, \cdots, d_{k-1}) = \frac{n!}{d_0! \, d_1! \cdots d_{k-1}!} \prod_{t=0}^{k-1} ({_t|q_0})^{d_t} \tag{4.8}$$

$$E[D_t] = n \cdot {_t|q_0} \tag{4.9}$$

$$\text{Var}(D_t) = n({_t|q_0})(1 - {_t|q_0}) \tag{4.10}$$

$$\text{Cov}(D_r, D_t) = - n({_r|q_0})({_t|q_0}). \tag{4.11}$$

Note that for this distribution, the mean, variance and covariance are all unconditional, i.e., given only n study units existing at time $t=0$.

Conditional on $N_t = n_t$ survivors at time t, D_t is a binomial random variable, with mean $n_t \cdot q_t$ and variance $n_t \cdot q_t \cdot p_t$.

4.4.3 *Estimation of S(t) and* $_t|q_0$

It should be clear that $S(t)$ can be estimated by using the observed proportion surviving to t. Thus

$$\hat{S}(t) = \frac{N_t}{n} \tag{4.12}$$

is a binomial proportion random variable, with mean and variance given by (4.4a) and (4.4b), respectively, with $S^o(t)$ replaced by $\hat{S}(t)$.

Similarly, $_t|q_0$ is naturally estimated by using the observed relative frequency of deaths between t and t+1. Thus

$$_t|\hat{q}_0 = \frac{D_t}{n}, \quad t = 0, 1, \cdots, k-1 \tag{4.13}$$

is a multinomial proportion, with mean and variance given by

$$E\left[_t|\hat{q}_0\right] = \frac{1}{n} \cdot E[D_t] = {}_t|q_0 \tag{4.14}$$

and

$$\text{Var}(_t|\hat{q}_0) = \frac{1}{n^2} \cdot \text{Var}(D_t) = \frac{_t|q_0 \cdot (1 - {}_t|q_0)}{n}. \tag{4.15}$$

We observe from (4.14) that the multinomial proportion estimator $_t|\hat{q}_0 = \frac{D_t}{n}$ is unbiased, as defined in Appendix A.

4.4.4 *Estimation of* q_t *and* p_t

Recall that q_t is the conditional probability of death not later than time t+1, given alive at time t. It is natural to estimate this probability by

$$\hat{q}_t = \frac{D_t}{n_t} . \tag{4.16}$$

Here we recognize that, conditional on there being n_t survivors at time t, D_t is binomial, so $\hat{q}_t = \frac{D_t}{n_t}$ is binomial proportion, with conditional mean and variance given by

$$E\left[\hat{q}_t|n_t\right] = \frac{1}{n_t} \cdot E[D_t] = q_t \tag{4.17}$$

and

$$\text{Var}(\hat{q}_t|n_t) = \frac{1}{n_t^2} \cdot \text{Var}(D_t) = \frac{q_t(1-q_t)}{n_t}. \qquad (4.18)$$

Furthermore,

$$\hat{p}_t = 1 - \hat{q}_t = \frac{n_t - D_t}{n_t} = \frac{N_{t+1}}{n_t} \qquad (4.19)$$

is also a binomial proportion, so

$$E[\hat{p}_t|n_t] = p_t \qquad (4.20)$$

and

$$\text{Var}(\hat{p}_t|n_t) = \frac{p_t(1-p_t)}{n_t}. \qquad (4.21)$$

Since $q_t = 1-p_t$, then, clearly, (4.18) and (4.21) are the same.

$\boxed{\text{EXAMPLE 4.4}}$: Consider a sample of 20 individuals existing at t=0. All fail within 5 weeks, and only the week of failure is recorded. The observed outcome of this sample is that two individuals failed in the first week, three in the second, eight in the third, six in the fourth, and one in the fifth. Using the data of this sample, estimate (a) $_2|q_0$;   (b) S(3);   (c) q_3.
$\boxed{\text{SOLUTION}}$: Figure 4.6 is a diagram of this study:

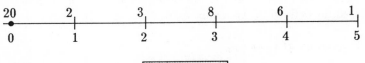

$\boxed{\text{FIGURE 4.6}}$

(a) $_2|q_0$ is estimated by the multinomial proportion of deaths in the third interval, so $_2|\hat{q}_0 = \frac{d_2}{n} = \frac{8}{20} = .40$.   (b) S(3) is estimated by the proportion surviving to t=3, so $S^o(3) = \frac{7}{20} = .35$.   (c) q_3, a conditional probability, is estimated by the binomial proportion of deaths in the fourth interval, out of those alive at the beginning of that interval, so $\hat{q}_3 = \frac{d_3}{n_3} = \frac{6}{7}$.

EXAMPLE 4.5 : Suppose our sample in Example 4.4 is known to be subject to a survival distribution that is uniform on $(0,5]$. (a) Calculate the variance of $_2|\hat{q}_0$ and the conditional variance of $\hat{p}_3$. (b) Estimate these variances if no distribution is assumed.

SOLUTION : (a) $_2|q_0 = F(3) - F(2) = .2$, under the uniform distribution. Then, by (4.15), $Var(_2|\hat{q}_0) = \frac{(.2)(.8)}{20} = .008$. $p_3 = \frac{S(4)}{S(3)} = .5$, and $n_3 = 7$, so, from (4.21), $Var(\hat{p}_3|n_3) = .03571$. (b) In this case we use $_2|\hat{q}_0$ in place of $_2|q_0$, and $\hat{p}_3$ in place of p_3, obtaining est. $Var(_2|\hat{q}_0) = .012$, and est. $Var(\hat{p}_3|n_3) = .01749$.

4.4.5 *Estimation of S(t) from* $\{\hat{p}_i\}$

We recall that $S(t)$ is the unconditional probability of surviving from time 0 to time t, and the direct approach to estimating $S(t)$ given by (4.12) is an unconditional approach.

As an alternative to estimating $S(t)$ by (4.12), we could use the approach introduced in Section 2.4.6, producing

$$\hat{S}(t) = \hat{p}_0 \cdot \hat{p}_1 \cdot \cdots \cdot \hat{p}_{t-1}. \qquad (4.22)$$

This estimation approach follows logically from the conceptual relationship

$$S(t) = p_0 \cdot p_1 \cdot \cdots \cdot p_{t-1}. \qquad (4.23)$$

It is easy to see by general reasoning that, although each p_i in (4.23) is a conditional probability, the product of them, which is $S(t)$, is unconditional. Thus $S(t)$ is the same unconditional probability concept, whether estimated by the direct (unconditional) approach of (4.12) or the indirect (conditional) approach of (4.22). Furthermore, for a given sample outcome in the cohort, complete data study design of this chapter, it is easy to see that the same numerical value of $\hat{S}(t)$ will result from both (4.12) and (4.22), provided each $\hat{p}_i$ in (4.22) is determined by (4.19). The demonstration of this is left as an exercise.

In studies which are not restricted to an initial cohort, or which allow for withdrawals or termination of observation before all have died, the (4.12) approach to $\hat{S}(t)$ will not be possible. In these studies, described in Chapters 5-7, the (4.22) approach to $\hat{S}(t)$ will be taken.

4.4.6 *Estimation of Other Functions*

For our cohort, complete, grouped deaths situation, we have estimated each conditional p_t and the survival distribution function $S(t)$. In this section we will consider the estimation of the HRF and the PDF of T. The approach in each case will be to express the new function in terms of a function whose estimation has already been discussed, and then to substitute the estimator of that function.

Let $t^* = t + \frac{1}{2}$ represent the midpoint of the interval $(t, t+1]$. (Recall that the HRF and the PDF relate to a point of time, not an interval.) To express the hazard rate $\lambda(t^*)$ in terms of p_t (or q_t), we need to make a distribution assumption, such as one of those described in Section 3.5 in the context of the life table.

For example, assuming that T is exponentially distributed over $(t, t+1]$, so that $\lambda(t)$ is a constant, we recall from (3.67) that

$$\lambda(t^*) \ = \ - \ln p_t, \qquad (4.24)$$

so $\lambda(t^*)$ is estimated by

$$\hat{\lambda}(t^*) \ = \ - \ln \hat{p}_t. \qquad (4.25)$$

Recall that p_t is estimated by the binomial proportion estimator $\frac{N_{t+1}}{n_t}$, conditional on the value of n_t being given. (Note that N_{t+1} is the random variable here.) Thus the estimator for $\lambda(t^*)$ can be written as

$$\hat{\lambda}(t^*) \ = \ - \ln \frac{N_{t+1}}{n_t}, \qquad (4.26)$$

which is a biased estimator. The random variable $\hat{\lambda}(t^*)$ is a natural log function of the binomial random variable N_{t+1}, so the variance of $\hat{\lambda}(t^*)$, conditional on n_t, can be approximated by the method of statistical differentials using formula (2.76). This results in

$$\text{Var}\Big[\hat{\lambda}(t^*) \mid n_t\Big] \ \approx \ \frac{q_t}{p_t \, n_t} \, . \qquad (4.27)$$

To approximate the PDF at the interval midpoint, $f(t^*)$, we first express it in terms of the SDF, using a standard approximation. Let

$$f(t^*) \ = \ -\frac{d}{dt} S(t)\Big|_{t=t^*} \ \approx \ S(t) - S(t+1) \ = \ S(t) \cdot q_t \ = \ {}_t|q_0, \qquad (4.28)$$

so that $f(t^*)$ is estimated by

$$\hat{f}(t^*) \ = \ {}_t|\hat{q}_0. \qquad (4.29)$$

Recall from (4.13) that $_t|\hat{q}_0 = \frac{D_t}{n}$, a multinomial proportion. Thus the estimator for $f(t^*)$ can be written as

$$\hat{f}(t^*) = \frac{D_t}{n}. \tag{4.30}$$

This time we see that the random variable $\hat{f}(t^*)$ is a simple linear function of the multinomial random variable D_t, so the variance of $\hat{f}(t^*)$ can be found without approximation (beyond that already involved in the derivative) as

$$\mathrm{Var}\left[\hat{f}(t^*)\right] = \frac{\mathrm{Var}(D_t)}{n^2} = \frac{_t|q_0 \cdot (1 - _t|q_0)}{n}. \tag{4.31}$$

EXAMPLE 4.6: Again using the sample data given in Example 4.4, estimate $\lambda(3\frac{1}{2})$ and $f(3\frac{1}{2})$. Also estimate the variance of $\hat{\lambda}(3\frac{1}{2})$ and the variance of $\hat{f}(3\frac{1}{2})$, using the sample outcomes.

SOLUTION: We will need the sample results $\hat{p}_3 = \frac{1}{7}$, $\hat{q}_3 = \frac{6}{7}$, $n_3 = 7$, and $_3|\hat{q}_0 = \frac{6}{20}$. From (4.25), $\hat{\lambda}(3\frac{1}{2}) = -\ln\hat{p}_3 = 1.94591$, and from (4.27), evaluated by sample results, we calculate the estimated variance as est. $\mathrm{Var}\left[\hat{\lambda}(3\frac{1}{2})\,|\,n_3\right] = \frac{6/7}{(1/7)(7)} = .85714$. From (4.29), we then find $\hat{f}(3\frac{1}{2}) = _3|\hat{q}_0 = .3$, and from (4.31), evaluated by sample results, we find est. $\mathrm{Var}\left[\hat{f}(3\frac{1}{2})\right] = \frac{(.3)\,(.7)}{20} = .0105$.

4.5 *SUMMARY*

In this chapter we have introduced the topic of estimating a tabular survival distribution from sample data. The estimation exercise was fairly straightforward here due to the convenient properties of complete data samples. With the general idea of survival model estimation now familiar to us, we can deal with the complications created by incomplete data, which we will do in the remaining chapters.

But first we need to make some final observations on the material of this chapter.

The observed survival distribution defined and analyzed in Section 4.3 is somewhat special. We can describe it as an exact and complete representation, or description, of the survival pattern *actually experienced* by the sample. It can be used as an estimate of the operative (but unknown) $S(t)$ to which this sample was subject. We must become totally comfortable with the idea that a sample is subject to a survival distribution, which we call S(t), which is likely to be different from the $S^o(t)$ that the sample actually experiences. We never know how different S(t) and $S^o(t)$ are, since S(t) is forever unknown. Thus, to summarize, $S^o(t)$ is the precise survival pattern of *this* sample, and it plays the role of an estimate of S(t).

In later cases, we will again derive an estimate of S(t), to be called $\hat{S}(t)$, from sample date, but it will not be correct to call such $\hat{S}(t)$ the *exact* survival pattern of the sample. That property belongs exclusively to the cohort, complete data, exact time of death situation. It is because of this property that we use the special symbol $S^o(t)$ in this case; in other cases the general $\hat{S}(t)$ is used.

Finally, it should also be noted that $S^o(t)$, defined by (4.1), does provide an estimate of S(t) for *all t*. In light of this, this $S^o(t)$ is in the nature of a parametric, rather than a tabular, survival model. We introduced it in this chapter, rather than in Chapter 8, because its simplicity makes it an excellent first lesson in survival model estimation.

The grouped deaths study design of Section 4.4 is associated directly with the estimation of a tabular model, that is, one which gives values of S(t) only for certain, evenly spaced, values of t.

Some observations should be made with regard to the properties of the estimators developed in Section 4.4.

It should be clear that those estimators which are binomial or multinomial proportions, which include $_t|\hat{q}_0$, $\hat{q}_t$, $\hat{p}_t$, and the unconditional (4.12) approach to $\hat{S}(t)$, are also maximum likelihood estimators (MLE), with the optimality properties of unbiasedness, consistency, and efficiency, as described in Appendix A.

The conditional (4.22) approach to $\hat{S}(t)$ is through the product of the MLE's $\hat{p}_0$ through $\hat{p}_{t-1}$. $\hat{S}(t)$ is also an MLE, and is unbiased.

The estimator $\hat{\lambda}(t^*)$, defined by (4.25), is derived from the MLE $\hat{p}_t$ under the exponential assumption. *Under this assumption*, $\hat{\lambda}(t^*)$ is also a MLE, but it is biased.

The unconditional $\hat{f}(t^*)$ is a linear function of an unbiased MLE, so it is also an unbiased MLE, *within the approximation* used to develop (4.28). Since the approximation is present, the estimator is not truly unbiased.

As a final observation on the results derived in this chapter, we note that to estimate $\lambda(t^*)$ we made the exponential distribution assumption. This was our first use of a distribution assumption for the purpose of aiding our estimation work. In the following chapters frequent use of this and other assumptions will be made.

The results of Section 4.4, and some properties of those results, are summarized in Table 4.1.

TABLE 4.1

Function to be Estimated	Estimator	Unconditional or Conditional	Biasedness	Variance	
$_t|q_0$	$\dfrac{D_t}{n}$	Unconditional	Unbiased	$\dfrac{_t|q_0(1-_t|q_0)}{n}$	(Exact)
$S(t)$	$\dfrac{N_t}{n}$	Unconditional	Unbiased	$\dfrac{S(t)\cdot F(t)}{n}$	(Exact)
p_t	$\dfrac{N_{t+1}}{n_t}$	Conditional on n_t	Unbiased	$\dfrac{p_t q_t}{n_t}$	(Exact)
q_t	$\dfrac{D_t}{n_t}$	Conditional on n_t	Unbiased	$\dfrac{p_t q_t}{n_t}$	(Exact)
$\lambda(t^*)$	$-\ln\dfrac{N_{t+1}}{n_t}$	Conditional on n_t	Biased	$\dfrac{q_t}{p_t n_t}$	(Approximate)
$f(t^*)$	$_t|\hat{q}_0 = \dfrac{D_t}{n}$	Unconditional	Unbiased (within the derivative approximation)	$\dfrac{_t|q_0(1-_t|q_0)}{n}$	(Exact within derivative approximation)

EXERCISES

4.1 Introduction; 4.2 Study Design; 4.3 Exact Time of Death

4-1. Let $\hat{e}_0$ represent the observed average lifetime of a cohort whose times at death are exactly recorded. Find $\hat{e}_0$ for the sample described in Example 4.2.

4-2. Let $\hat{e}_t$ be the observed average remaining lifetime for those in the cohort who survive to time t. Find $\hat{e}_6$ for the sample of Example 4.2.

4-3. Suppose the cohort of Example 4.2 is actually subject to a uniform survival distribution on $(0,15]$. Compare the observed average lifetimes $\hat{e}_0$ and $\hat{e}_6$ to the expected, according to the assumed distribution.

4-4.   We recognize that $\hat{e}_0$ is a random variable, since it depends on the random lifetimes of the n units in the cohort. Find expressions for the expected value and variance of $\hat{e}_0$, assuming that the lifetimes of different units in the cohort are independently and identically distributed.

4-5.   The following values are taken from a standard life table: $\ell_{70} = 80{,}000$, $\ell_{83} = 42{,}000$ and $\ell_{84} = 37{,}000$. Four individuals, each exact age 70, are observed until death. The deaths of these individuals occur at the following exact ages: 83.30, 83.34, 83.36, 83.47. Assuming that the operative survival model for these individuals is given by the standard table, determine the probability that the number of individuals whose lifetimes exceed their expected median future lifetimes is greater than the number actually observed.

4.4 Grouped Times of Death

4-6.   Find $\text{Cov}(_t|\hat{q}_0, {}_r|\hat{q}_0)$.

4-7.   Find $\text{Cov}[\hat{S}(t),\hat{S}(r)]$, where $t<r$. Hint: consider the trinomial distribution of the random variables (1) deaths before t, (2) deaths between t and r, and (3) deaths beyond r (i.e., survivors at r).

4-8.   A cohort of n persons is observed until all die, with deaths grouped in fixed intervals. If $\text{Var}[\hat{S}(t)] = .0009$, $\text{Var}[\hat{S}(r)] = .0016$, and their covariance is $\text{Cov}[\hat{S}(t),\ \hat{S}(r)] = .0008$, find $E[\hat{S}(t)]$.

4-9.   Let $n=500$ and let $t<r$. If $\text{Var}[\hat{S}(t)] = .000420$, $\text{Var}[\hat{S}(r)] = .000255$, and if $S(t) > 2 \cdot S(r)$, then find $\text{Cov}[\hat{S}(t),\hat{S}(r)]$.

4-10.   Demonstrate that, if each value of $\hat{p}_i$ is determined by (4.19), then the estimated value $\hat{S}(t)$ will be the same whether obtained by the approach of (4.12) or by the approach of (4.22).

4-11.   A complete mortality study is made on a sample of 7 lives. The cohort is believed to be subject to the survival pattern given by the following life table.

t	ℓ_t
0	100
1	?
2	10
3	0

The value of ℓ_1 in the table is not given, but it is known that the unconditional variance of D_1, the random variable for the number of deaths in $(1, 2]$ for this sample is 1.68. It is also known that, in the life table, $d_0 > d_1$. Find the probability that the outcome for this sample will be one death in $(0, 1]$, one death in $(1, 2]$, and five deaths in $(2, 3]$.

4-12. A complete mortality study was made of $n = 1000$ persons all exact age 100. The following is a partially completed record of results, by duration since age 100.

Duration (t)	Observed Deaths (d_t)	Observed Survivors (n_t)	Observed Conditional Probability $(\hat{q}_t)$	Estimate of Survival Function $[\hat{S}(t)]$
0		1000	.200	1.000
1	150			
2				
3			.100	
4	50			
5			.250	
6	100			
7		200		
8		100		
Total	1000			

Complete the missing entries in the table.

4-13. Derive formula (4.27).

4-14. Assume that T is uniformly distributed over $(t, t+1]$.

(a) Express $\lambda(t^*)$ in terms of p_t.

(b) Express the estimator $\hat{\lambda}(t^*)$ in terms of the binomial random variable N_{t+1}. (Note that this is conditional on n_t being given.)

(c) Find the approximate variance of $\hat{\lambda}(t^*)$

(d) Is $\hat{\lambda}(t^*)$ biased or unbiased?

4-15. Show that the expression for $Var[\hat{\lambda}(t^*)]$ derived in Exercise 4-14(c) can also be written as

$$\frac{[\lambda(t^*)]^2}{n_t \, q_t} \cdot \left\{ 1 - \tfrac{1}{4}\big[\lambda(t^*)\big]^2 \right\}.$$

4-16. Of 100 persons surviving to time t, four die before time t+1. Use this data to estimate the central rate m_t, under both the exponential and uniform distribution assumptions. Also estimate the variances of these estimators for m_t.

4-17. Out of a cohort of laboratory mice all born on January 1, the following table gives the number still alive at selected durations.

Duration	Alive
10 weeks	270
15 weeks	252
20 weeks	198
25 weeks	162

The unconditional probability density function at time 12.5 weeks is approximately .05. Estimate the unconditional variance for the number of deaths from the end of week 20 to the end of week 25.

4.5 Summary

4-18. Show that $\hat{f}(t^*)$, defined by (4.30), is an unbiased estimator of $f(t^*)$, within the derivative approximation.

4-19. Show that $_t|\hat{q}_0$ is a maximum likelihood estimator.

4-20. Find a general expression for est. $\text{Var}[\hat{S}(t)]$, when the sample estimate is used to estimate $S(t)$.

CHAPTER 5

TABULAR SURVIVAL MODELS ESTIMATED
FROM INCOMPLETE DATA SAMPLES

STUDY DESIGN

5.1 *INTRODUCTION*

The situation described in Chapter 4, in which values of the survival function at various times were estimated by the proportion of the study sample still surviving, was a special situation usually found only in laboratory or other closely controlled environments. We recall that the properties of that situation were that all members of the sample came under observation at time t=0, none left the sample other than by death, and observation was continued until all had died. In such a situation we say that the data are complete.

Many estimation situations encountered in practice, including those encountered by the actuary in a life insurance or pension setting, do not exhibit the properties of complete data. Rather it will be common to find persons coming under observation at times (or ages) greater than zero, and not all persons will remain under observation until death. This termination of observation (other than by death) can occur in the one of two ways described in the next two paragraphs.

In some situations there will be one or more *random* events (in addition to death) to which members of the sample are susceptible, the occurrence of which eliminates the member from the sample. For example, in a pension plan, active members might be eliminated from the study sample through disability, retirement or voluntary termination. In a sample of life insurance policyholders, members might lapse their policies. In general, we will collectively refer to all random decrements (other than death) as *withdrawals* from the study. It is important to note that withdrawal is a random event in the same sense that death is a random event.

The longitudinal study design of Chapter 4 is feasible only when the sample consists of relatively few members with a relatively short lifetime, such as mechanical devices, laboratory animals, or unhealthy humans. Most studies conducted by actuaries deal with large samples of healthy humans; to keep a longitudinal study open until all persons have died is simply not feasible. Instead a *cross-sectional* study design is used, in which period of observation is chosen, and sample members are observed only during that period. When the observation period closes, most members are still alive and in the sample, and observation terminates for them at that time. These members are called *enders*, since their observation terminates as a result of the ending of the observation period.

It is important to note that whereas withdrawals are random events, enders are not. By setting a date at which the observation period will end, the maximum age at which a particular sample member will cease observation is thereby established. Thus we say that each sample member has a *scheduled* ending age. If the member remains in the group to that age, the event of "ending" is then certain to occur. An example will make this clear.

EXAMPLE 5.1 :   The period of observation for a sample of pension plan participants is January 1, 1985 to December 31, 1988. Participant A, who joined the plan in 1980, was born on April 1, 1950. At what age does Participant A come under observation, and at what age is Participant A *scheduled* to cease observation?

SOLUTION :   Since Participant A is already in the plan on January 1, 1985, then observation begins on that date. This person will be age 35 on April 1, 1985, so he comes under observation at age 34.75 on January 1, 1985. If neither death nor withdrawal intervenes, Participant A will be age 38.75 on December 31, 1988, so this is his scheduled ending age.

Example 5.1 illustrates the basic information that will be required on each sample member for the estimation approaches that will be presented in the next several chapters. This information consists of

(1) dates of the observation period;
(2) date of joining the group under observation;
(3) date of birth;
(4) date of death or withdrawal, where applicable.

From items (1), (2) and (3), each sample member's age at the start of observation and scheduled age at the close of observation can be established. For the ith sample member, we will refer to these two ages as y_i and z_i, respectively. Note that, necessarily, $y_i < z_i$. Thus the scheduled age span of observation is represented by the ordered pair (y_i, z_i) for the ith member. If death or withdrawal occurs while under observation (i.e., before age z_i), then observation will actually end prior to the scheduled ending age. In no case can observation continue beyond the scheduled ending age.

EXAMPLE 5.2 :   The members of a fraternal organization form a study sample with observation period of July 1, 1980 to June 30, 1986. Member B was born on June 30, 1933 and joined the organization on January 1, 1982. What is the ordered pair (y_i, z_i) for Member B?

[SOLUTION]: Since Member B joined the organization during the observation period, her observation began at that time, rather than at the start of the period. On January 1, 1982, Member B was $y_i = 48.5$. Her scheduled ending age on June 30, 1986 is $z_i = 53$. Thus her ordered pair is (48.5, 53).

A practical question arises as to the computation of fractional ages whenever the dates have not been so conveniently chosen. Since all large studies of the type contemplated here will be totally computerized, it will be an easy matter to count ages in days, and then convert them to fractions of a year. This is illustrated in the final example of this section.

[EXAMPLE 5.3]: An alumni association membership forms a study sample. The observation period begins for each member on the member's birthday in 1984 and ends on December 31, 1988. Member C is born on July 12, 1958, joins the alumni association in 1981, and dies on March 20, 1988. What is Member C's ordered pair (y_i, z_i)? At what age does observation actually cease for Member C?

[SOLUTION]: Observation begins on Member C's birthday in 1984, which is exactly age $y_i = 26$. Observation is scheduled to end December 31, 1988. Member C will be age 30 on July 12, 1988. Counting days from there to December 31 produces $19 + 31 + 30 + 31 + 30 + 31 = 172$ days, so the scheduled ending age is $z_i = 30\frac{172}{365} = 30.47$. However, death intervenes on March 20, 1988, on which date Member C has attained age 29 years plus $19 + 31 + 30 + 31 + 30 + 31 + 31 + 29 + 20 = 252$ days, or 29.69 years. This is the age at which observation actually ceases.

5.2 *INTERVAL ESTIMATES*

The overall approach to estimating S(x), or, equivalently, ℓ_x, which we will use in the presence of incomplete data will be to first estimate p_x, the conditional probability of survival to age x+1, given alive at age x. Then, since $S(x) = p_0 \cdot p_1 \cdot \cdots \cdot p_{x-1}$, it follows that a natural estimator of S(x) is

$$\hat{S}(x) = \hat{p}_0 \cdot \hat{p}_1 \cdot \cdots \cdot \hat{p}_{x-1}. \tag{5.1}$$

In turn, we will frequently find it convenient to estimate q_x, rather than p_x, from the sample data, and then to obtain an estimate of p_x as

$$\hat{p}_x = 1 - \hat{q}_x. \tag{5.2}$$

The generalized estimation interval (x, x+1] is illustrated in Figure 5.1.

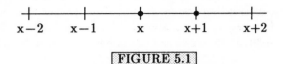

x−2   x−1   x   x+1   x+2

FIGURE 5.1

The notation (x, x+1] is used to indicate that deaths *at* age x+1 are assigned
to this interval, whereas deaths *at* age x belong to the previous interval
(x−1, x]. This assignment is somewhat arbitrary, and indeed the alternative
[x, x+1) has been used by some writers. We prefer (x, x+1], since existence
at age x is assumed in the concept of q_x as "the probability of death within a
year for a person *known to be alive* at age x." Thus death *at* age x is not
possible in this interval.

In order to estimate q_x, we need to know what contribution, if any,
each member of the sample makes within the interval (x, x+1]. In other
words, we need to know the *survival experience* of each member between ages
x and x+1. To obtain this, we need to see how the ordered pair (y_i, z_i) for
person i relates to the interval (x, x+1].

First we note that if $z_i \leq x$, then person i makes no contribution to
(x, x+1], since he left the study without moving into that estimation
interval. Similarly, if $y_i \geq x+1$, then person i again makes no contribution to
(x, x+1], this time as a result of coming under observation after age x+1.
These cases are illustrated in Figure 5.2.

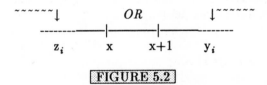

z_i x   x+1 y_i

FIGURE 5.2

If $y_i \leq x$ *and* $z_i \geq x+1$, as shown in Figure 5.3, then person i is
scheduled to be under observation for the entire interval (x, x+1].

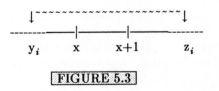

y_i x   x+1 z_i

FIGURE 5.3

Finally, it is possible that $x < y_i < x+1$ *or* $x < z_i < x+1$, *or both*, as shown in Figure 5.4.

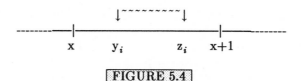

$$\text{x} \qquad \text{y}_i \qquad \text{z}_i \qquad \text{x+1}$$

FIGURE 5.4

Disregarding the cases where $z_i \leq x$ or $y_i \geq x+1$, so that person i does not contribute to $(x, x+1]$ at all, we can say that person i enters $(x, x+1]$ at age $x+r_i$ and is *scheduled* to exit $(x, x+1]$ at age $x+s_i$. If $y_i \leq x$, as in Figure 5.3, then person i enters $(x, x+1]$ at exact age x, so that $r_i = 0$. If $x < y_i < x+1$, as in Figure 5.4, then entry into $(x, x+1]$ is at age $x+r_i$ with $0 < r_i < 1$. If $z_i \geq x+1$, as in Figure 5.3, then person i is scheduled to exit $(x, x+1]$ at exact age $x+1$, so that $s_i = 1$. If $x < z_i < x+1$, as in Figure 5.4, then scheduled exit from $(x, x+1]$ is at age $x+s_i$ with $0 < s_i < 1$. Note, overall, that $0 \leq r_i < 1$ and $0 < s_i \leq 1$. That is, r_i can be 0 but not 1, whereas s_i can be 1 but not 0.

This correspondence between the entry and scheduled exit ages *for the study*, represented by (y_i, z_i), and the entry and scheduled exit ages *for the estimation interval* $(x, x+1]$, represented by $(x+r_i, x+s_i)$, is very important. The basic data for the study implies the pair (y_i, z_i), as illustrated in Examples 5.1, 5.2 and 5.3. But in order to estimate q_x for the interval $(x, x+1]$, the necessary information is given by $(x+r_i, x+s_i)$, or, more simply, by (r_i, s_i), with x being understood. Practice with the conversion from (y_i, z_i) to (r_i, s_i), for a given $(x, x+1]$, is provided in Examples 5.4 and 5.5, and in the exercises.

It should also be noted that person i might not contribute to $(x, x+1]$ even if $z_i > x$. Recall that z_i is the age at which observation is *scheduled* to end due to the closing of the observation period. If person i actually dies or withdraws at an age less than x, then no contribution is made to $(x, x+1]$ even though such a contribution had been scheduled. For this person, r_i and s_i are not defined for the interval $(x, x+1]$.

EXAMPLE 5.4 : For Participant A in Example 5.1, what is the ordered pair (r_i, s_i) for the estimation interval $(38, 39]$?
SOLUTION : Since $y_i = 34.75 < 38$, then $r_i = 0$. Since $z_i = 38.75$, then $s_i = .75$.

EXAMPLE 5.5 : For Member C in Example 5.3, what is the ordered pair (r_i, s_i) for the estimation interval $(30, 31]$?

[SOLUTION]:   Here $y_i = 26$, implying $r_i = 0$, and $z_i = 30.47$, implying $s_i = .47$.   However, death occurred at age 29.69, so Member C does not contribute to (30, 31] at all.   Thus (r_i, s_i) is simply not defined for the interval (30, 31].

The approaches to estimating q_x which are described in Chapters 6 and 7 are designed to accept ordered pairs (r_i, s_i) for the estimation interval (x, x+1] satisfying the general conditions $0 \leq r_i < 1$ and $0 < s_i \leq 1$.   There are several special cases, however, under which the estimation mathematics is simplified.

If, for a certain (x, x+1], $r_i = 0$ *and* $s_i = 1$ for all i, so that all persons enter the estimation interval at its beginning and are scheduled to remain under observation to age x+1, the estimation of q_x is considerably simplified. We call this convenient situation Special Case A.

If, for a certain (x, x+1], $s_i = 1$ for all i but the general $0 \leq r_i < 1$ exists, then persons can enter (x, x+1] at any age but all are scheduled to exit the interval at age x+1. This is referred to as Special Case B.

If, for a certain (x, x+1], $r_i = 0$ for all i but the general $0 < s_i \leq 1$ holds, then all persons enter (x, x+1] at age x but have scheduled exit ages scattered throughout the interval. This is called Special Case C.

The significance of these special cases, in terms of the simplification that they introduce to the process of estimating q_x, will be illustrated in Chapters 6 and 7.   In particular, the simplification provided under Special Case A is so delightful that one is motivated to design studies in a manner so as to produce this case. This issue is explored in Part III of the text.

How are Special Cases A, B and C obtained?   One way is by grouping, or averaging, values of y_i and z_i.   For example, for all y_i such that $x - \frac{1}{2} < y_i < x + \frac{1}{2}$, one could substitute x for the actual value of each y_i.   Then all persons would be entering observation at an estimation interval boundary, so r_i would be zero for all i.   Similarly, all z_i such that $x - \frac{1}{2} < z_i < x + \frac{1}{2}$, could be replaced by x.   Then all scheduled exits would be at interval boundaries, and we would have $s_i = 1$ for all i.   This grouping approach to estimation simplification will be pursued in Chapters 10 and 11.

Even without grouping, the various special cases can be obtained as a result of the definition of the observation period.   In Example 5.3 we saw that having an observation period begin on a member's birthday necessarily resulted in an integral value for y_i.   Then if x is also an integer, it follows that all y_i occur at estimation interval boundaries, so that $r_i = 0$ for all i. Similarly, $s_i = 1$ for all i if the observation period ends on the member's birthday.   If the observation period opens on a fixed date for all members, then $r_i > 0$ for some i; if it closes on a fixed date for all members, then $s_i < 1$ for some i.

EXAMPLE 5.6: An observation period opens on January 1, 1985 and closes, for a given member, on that member's birthday in 1986. Three members, all in the study group as of January 1, 1985, have the following dates of birth:

Member	Date of Birth
1	April 1, 1964
2	July 1, 1964
3	Oct. 1, 1965

Which special cases are created for estimation intervals (20, 21] and (21, 22]?

SOLUTION: The ordered pairs (y_i, z_i) are $(y_1, z_1) = (20.75, 22)$, $(y_2, z_2) = (20.50, 22)$, and $(y_3, z_3) = (19.25, 21)$. For estimation interval (20, 21], the values of (r_i, s_i) are (.75, 1), (.50, 1) and (0, 1), for $i = 1,2,3$, respectively, which is Special Case B since $s_i = 1$ for all i but $r_i > 0$ for some i. For estimation interval (21, 22], Member 3 is not involved, and we have $(r_1, s_1) = (0,1)$ and $(r_2, s_2) = (0, 1)$. Since all $r_i = 0$ and all $s_i = 1$, we have Special Case A for this interval. The data of this example are shown in Figure 5.5.

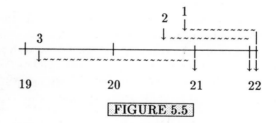

FIGURE 5.5

5.3 SINGLE- AND DOUBLE-DECREMENT ENVIRONMENTS

We have established that the ith person in a study sample enters the estimation interval (x, x+1] at age $x+r_i$, $0 \leq r_i < 1$, and is scheduled to exit the interval at age $x+s_i$, $0 < s_i \leq 1$, as shown in Figure 5.6.

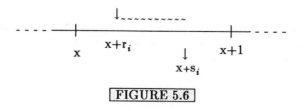

FIGURE 5.6

Suppressing the subscript i for convenience, we note that the probability of survival to age x+s for this person is $_{s-r}p_{x+r}$, and the probability of death while under observation in this interval is

$$_{s-r}q_{x+r} \; = \; 1 - {_{s-r}p_{x+r}} \cdot \tag{5.3}$$

Note that these probabilities are conditional on being alive at age x+r. The density function for death at age x+t, given alive at age x+r, is given by

$$_{t-r}p_{x+r}\mu_{x+t} \cdot \tag{5.4}$$

This notation is adequate, however, only if the study is being conducted in an environment in which death is the only random event to which sample members are subject, i.e., if we are working in a single-decrement environment. If both death and withdrawal are random events, so that we are in a double-decrement environment, the estimation mathematics is more complex. In this section we will review basic double-decrement theory to the extent needed for our estimation work. (For a more thorough review of this theory, the reader is referred to Chapter 14 of Jordan [32] or Chapter 9 of Bowers, et al. [10].)

We begin with the basic function $_{t}p_x$, which has been understood to represent the probability of *not dying* before age x+t, given alive at age x, in a single-decrement environment. When a life age x is in a double-decrement environment, however, it is necessary to specify the random event for which $_{t}p_x$ represents the probability on nonoccurrence before age x+t. We do this by using $_{t}p_x'^{(d)}$ for the probability that *death* will not occur prior to age x+t, and by using $_{t}p_x'^{(w)}$ for the probability that *withdrawal* will not occur prior to age x+t, where each probability has its meaning in its own single-decrement environment.

Note that we use $_{t}p_x'^{(d)}$ to represent *exactly* the same concept as represented earlier by the unadorned $_{t}p_x$. We have simply added the extra notation to identify the idea of "survival against death." Similarly, we will now use $q_x'^{(d)}$ to mean the probability of death in (x, x+1], and note that $q_x'^{(d)}$ represents exactly the same concept as represented by the simpler q_x used heretofore in the text.

Associated with $_{t}p_x'^{(d)}$ and $q_x'^{(d)}$ is the force of mortality $\mu_{x+t}^{(d)}$ (previously denoted as μ_{x+t} when it was clear that it represented the force of *mortality*). The reader should recall the relationships

$$_{t}p_x'^{(d)} \; = \; \exp\left[- \int_0^t \mu_{x+u}^{(d)}\, du \right] \tag{5.5}$$

and

$$q'^{(d)}_x = 1 - \exp\left[-\int_0^1 \mu^{(d)}_{x+u}\,du\right]. \tag{5.6}$$

Now that withdrawal is also viewed as a random event, there exists a force of withdrawal, $\mu^{(w)}_{x+t}$, at age x+t, and the relationships

$$_tp'^{(w)}_x = \exp\left[-\int_0^t \mu^{(w)}_{x+u}\,du\right] \tag{5.7}$$

and

$$q'^{(w)}_x = 1 - \exp\left[-\int_0^1 \mu^{(w)}_{x+u}\,du\right]. \tag{5.8}$$

If the random events death and withdrawal are independent, then

$$_tP^{(\tau)}_x = {}_tP'^{(d)}_x \cdot {}_tP'^{(w)}_x \tag{5.9}$$

is the probability of neither dying nor withdrawing prior to age x+t, given alive and not withdrawn at age x. In this text we will assume the independence of these events. The reader should be aware that this independence is not always assumed in basic multiple-decrement theory (see, for example, Benjamin and Pollard [9], or Bowers, et al. [10]).

The density functions for death and withdrawal, respectively, at age x+t, given alive at age x, are

$$_tP^{(\tau)}_x \mu^{(d)}_{x+t} \tag{5.10}$$

and

$$_tP^{(\tau)}_x \mu^{(w)}_{x+t}. \tag{5.11}$$

The more general relationships

$$_{s-r}q'^{(d)}_{x+r} = 1 - {}_{s-r}p'^{(d)}_{x+r} = 1 - \exp\left[-\int_r^s \mu^{(d)}_{x+u}\,du\right] \tag{5.12}$$

and

$$_{s-r}q'^{(w)}_{x+r} = 1 - {}_{s-r}p'^{(w)}_{x+r} = 1 - \exp\left[-\int_r^s \mu^{(w)}_{x+u}\,du\right] \tag{5.13}$$

will arise in our estimation work, as will the relationship

$$_{t-r}\mathrm{p}^{(T)}_{x+r} \;=\; _{t-r}\mathrm{p}'^{(d)}_{x+r} \cdot \; _{t-r}\mathrm{p}'^{(w)}_{x+r} \tag{5.14}$$

and the density functions

$$_{t-r}\mathrm{p}^{(T)}_{x+r}\mu^{(d)}_{x+t} \tag{5.15}$$

for death and

$$_{t-r}\mathrm{p}^{(T)}_{x+r}\,\mu^{(w)}_{x+t} \tag{5.16}$$

for withdrawal.

Finally, we let $\mathrm{q}^{(d)}_x$ and $\mathrm{q}^{(w)}_x$ represent the probabilities of death and withdrawal, respectively, prior to age x+1 for a life age x, in the presence of the other decrement (i.e., in the double-decrement environment). Note how these two probabilities differ in concept from $\mathrm{q}'^{(d)}_x$ and $\mathrm{q}'^{(w)}_x$. Mathematically,

$$\mathrm{q}^{(d)}_x = \int_0^1 {}_u\mathrm{p}^{(T)}_x \mu'^{(d)}_{x+u}\,du = \int_0^1 \left[1 - {}_u\mathrm{q}'^{(d)}_x\right]\left[1 - {}_u\mathrm{q}'^{(w)}_x\right]\mu'^{(d)}_{x+u}\,du \tag{5.17}$$

and

$$\mathrm{q}^{(w)}_x = \int_0^1 {}_u\mathrm{p}^{(T)}_x \mu'^{(w)}_{x+u}\,du = \int_0^1 \left[1 - {}_u\mathrm{q}'^{(d)}_x\right]\left[1 - {}_u\mathrm{q}'^{(w)}_x\right]\mu'^{(w)}_{x+u}\,du. \tag{5.18}$$

The probability of surviving from age x to age x+1 is

$$\mathrm{p}^{(T)}_x \;=\; 1 - \mathrm{q}^{(T)}_x \;=\; 1 - \mathrm{q}^{(d)}_x - \mathrm{q}^{(w)}_x. \tag{5.19}$$

More generally, $_{s-r}\mathrm{q}^{(d)}_{x+r}$ and $_{s-r}\mathrm{q}^{(w)}_{x+r}$ represent the probabilities of death and withdrawal, respectively, prior to age x+s for a life age x+r, in the presence of the other decrement. Corresponding to (5.17), (5.18), and (5.19) we have

$$_{s-r}\mathrm{q}^{(d)}_{x+r} \;=\; \int_r^s {}_{u-r}\mathrm{p}^{(T)}_{x+r}\mu^{(d)}_{x+u}\,du$$

$$=\; \int_r^s \left[1 - {}_{u-r}\mathrm{q}'^{(d)}_{x+r}\right]\left[1 - {}_{u-r}\mathrm{q}'^{(w)}_{x+r}\right]\mu^{(d)}_{x+u}\,du, \tag{5.20}$$

$$_{s-r}q_{x+r}^{(w)} = \int_r^s {}_{u-r}p_{x+r}^{(\tau)}\mu_{x+u}^{(w)}\,du$$

$$= \int_r^s \left[1 - {}_{u-r}q_{x+r}'^{(d)}\right]\left[1 - {}_{u-r}q_{x+r}'^{(w)}\right]\mu_{x+u}^{(w)}\,du, \qquad (5.21)$$

and

$$_{s-r}p_{x+r}^{(\tau)} = 1 - {}_{s-r}q_{x+r}^{(\tau)} = 1 - {}_{s-r}q_{x+r}^{(d)} - {}_{s-r}q_{x+r}^{(w)}. \qquad (5.22)$$

5.4 *SUMMARY*

The purpose of this chapter is to provide an orientation to the problem of estimating q_x over the interval $(x, x+1]$, given alive at age x, from which an estimate of $S(x)$ can then be produced.

Our approach to the estimation of q_x is to first process the basic information on the ith life in the sample to obtain the ordered pair (y_i, z_i), the entry age and scheduled exit age for person i for the study as a whole. (It is important that the concept of *scheduled* exit age be clearly understood.)

The pair (y_i, z_i) then implies the pair $(x+r_i, x+s_i)$, the entry age and scheduled exit age for person i with respect to the estimation interval $(x, x+1]$. The importance of the distinction between entry and scheduled exit ages *for the study*, and those *for a particular estimation interval*, cannot be overemphasized.

We saw how certain definitions of the observation period led to convenient values of r_i and s_i, which, in turn, led to simplified estimation situations. We also saw, briefly, how this simplification could be achieved by grouping, or averaging, neighboring values of y_i and z_i. This practical approach to large-sample studies will be explored further in Part III of the text.

Finally, we reviewed basic double-decrement theory for the purpose of becoming familiar with the necessary relationships and notation before we encounter estimation in a double-decrement environment in later chapters. We will then be able to concentrate on the estimation theory without being diverted by the development of the basic mathematics.

5.1 Introduction

5-1.   The members of a pension plan form a study sample over the observation period January 1, 1982 to December 31, 1987. Member D was born April 1, 1956. What other information is needed in order to obtain the ordered pair (y_i, z_i) for Member D?

5-2.   Find the value of y_i for Member D of Exercise 5-1, if he joined the pension plan on (a) April 1, 1981; (b) April 1, 1984; (c) April 1, 1988.

5-3.   Find the value of z_i for Member D of Exercise 5-1 if he joined the pension plan on April 1, 1981, and if he (a) is still alive and in the plan on December 31, 1987; (b) dies on September 23, 1987.

5.2 Interval Estimates

5-4.   Under what condition on y_i is it true that $y_i = x + r_i$?

5-5.   Under what condition on z_i is it true that $z_i = x + s_i$?

5-6.   Assume that Member D of Exercise 5-1 joins the pension plan on April 1, 1981, and dies on September 23, 1987. Find the ordered pair (r_i, s_i) for
   (a)   estimation interval (25, 26] ;
   (b)   estimation interval (28, 29] ;
   (c)   estimation interval (31, 32] .

5-7.   Which of the special cases defined in the text is represented by each of Exercise 5-6 (a), (b), (c)?

5.3 Single- and Double-Decrement Environments

5-8.   If $q_x'^{(d)} = .1$ and $q_x'^{(w)} = .2$, find $q_x^{(T)}$.

5-9.   If the force of mortality is given by $\mu_x^{(d)} = \dfrac{2}{3(100-x)}$, and the force of withdrawal is given by $\mu_x^{(w)} = \dfrac{4}{3(100-x)}$, find the conditional density function for death at age $80+t$, given alive at age 80.

5-10. If both $\mu_{60+t}^{(d)}$ and $\mu_{60+t}^{(w)}$ are constant over $0 < t < 1$, and if $q_{60}'^{(d)} = q_{60}'^{(w)} = .2$, find $q_{60}^{(d)}$.

CHAPTER 6

TABULAR SURVIVAL MODELS ESTIMATED
FROM INCOMPLETE DATA SAMPLES

MOMENT PROCEDURES

6.1 INTRODUCTION

The foundation which underlies estimation by a moment procedure is the statistical principle that the expected number of deaths to be observed in $(x, x+1]$ from a certain sample should be equated to the number actually observed. Assuming that the number of actual deaths in the age interval, to be denoted by d_x, is readily available, then the estimation problem consists of two steps:

(1) Finding an expression for the expected number of deaths in $(x, x+1]$;

(2) Solving the moment equation for the desired estimate.

Generally a simplifying assumption will be required to solve the moment equation.

6.2 MOMENT ESTIMATION IN A SINGLE-DECREMENT ENVIRONMENT

Assume that the basic data regarding an observation period, dates of birth and membership into the group under observation, and dates of death have been analyzed to produce the orderd pair $(x+r_i, x+s_i)$ for person i's scheduled contribution to $(x, x+1]$, as illustrated in Figure 5.6. Recall that $s_i = 1$ is possible but $s_i = 0$ is not, whereas, $r_i = 0$ is possible but $r_i = 1$ is not.

For person i, the probability of death while under observation in the single-decrement environment is the conditional probability of death before age $x+s_i$, given alive at age $x+r_i$, which is $_{s_i-r_i}q_{x+r_i}$, and this is also the expected number of deaths from this sample of size one. This is easily seen, since the number of deaths will be one (with probability $_{s_i-r_i}q_{x+r_i}$), or zero (with probability $_{s_i-r_i}p_{x+r_i}$). Thus the expected

107

number is

$$1 \cdot {}_{s_i - r_i}q_{x+r_i} + 0 \cdot {}_{s_i - r_i}p_{x+r_i} = {}_{s_i - r_i}q_{x+r_i} \cdot \qquad (6.1)$$

6.2.1 *The Basic Moment Relationship*

If n_x is the total number of persons who contribute to $(x, x+1]$, then the total number of expected deaths is $\sum\limits_{i=1}^{n_x} {}_{s_i - r_i}q_{x+r_i}$. (For convenience we will use n for n_x in our summations.) When equated to the actual number of observed deaths, we obtain the moment equation

$$E[D_x] = \sum_{i=1}^{n} {}_{s_i - r_i}q_{x+r_i} = d_x , \qquad (6.2)$$

where D_x is the random variable for deaths in $(x, x+1]$, and d_x is the observed number.

To solve (6.2) for our estimate of q_x, we will use the approximation

$${}_{s_i - r_i}q_{x+r_i} \approx (s_i - r_i) \cdot q_x. \qquad (6.3)$$

Then (6.2) becomes

$$E[D_x] = q_x \cdot \sum_{i=1}^{n} (s_i - r_i) = d_x, \qquad (6.4)$$

from which we easily obtain

$$\hat{q}_x = \frac{d_x}{\sum\limits_{i=1}^{n} (s_i - r_i)} , \qquad (6.5)$$

the general form of the moment estimator in a single-decrement environment.

6.2.2 *Special Cases*

If $r_i = 0$ and $s_i = 1$ for all n_x persons who contribute to $(x, x+1]$, then we have ${}_{s_i - r_i}q_{x+r_i} = q_x$, and (6.2) becomes

$$E[D_x] = n_x \cdot q_x = d_x , \qquad (6.6)$$

so that (6.5) becomes

$$\hat{q}_x = \frac{d_x}{n_x} . \qquad (6.7)$$

Recall that this is Special Case A, as defined in Section 5.2.

We recognize (6.7) as the binomial proportion estimator already encountered in Chapter 4. We also recognize it as the maximum likelihood estimator of the conditional mortality probability q_x, where the model for the likelihood is a simple binomial model. Thus the number of persons in the sample, n_x, can be thought of as a number of binomial trials. The standard characteristics of a binomial model are assumed to apply. Thus each trial is considered to be independent, and the probability of death on a single trial (q_x) is assumed constant for all trials. In such a situation, the sample proportion of deaths, which is given by (6.7), is a natural estimator for this parameter q_x.

If $s_i=1$ for all, but $r_i>0$ for some of the n_x persons who contribute to the (x, x+1], then we have $_{s_i-r_i}q_{x+r_i} = {}_{1-r_i}q_{x+r_i}$, and (6.2) becomes

$$E[D_x] = \sum_{i=1}^{n} {}_{1-r_i}q_{x+r_i} = d_x . \qquad (6.8)$$

The general approximation given by (6.3) then becomes

$$_{1-r_i}q_{x+r_i} \approx (1-r_i) \cdot q_x, \qquad (6.9)$$

which is the same as (3.77). Substituting (6.9) into (6.8), we obtain the result

$$\hat{q}_x = \frac{d_x}{\sum_{i=1}^{n}(1-r_i)} , \qquad (6.10)$$

the moment estimator for Special Case B.

If $r_i=0$ for all, but $s_i<1$ for some of the n_x persons who contribute to the interval (x, x+1], then we have $_{s_i-r_i}q_{x+r_i} = {}_{s_i}q_x$, and (6.2) becomes

$$E[D_x] = \sum_{i=1}^{n} {}_{s_i}q_x = d_x . \qquad (6.11)$$

The general approximation given by (6.3) then becomes

$$_{s_i}q_x = s_i \cdot q_x , \qquad (6.12)$$

which is the same as (3.54). When (6.12) is substituted into (6.11) we obtain the result

$$\hat{q}_x = \frac{d_x}{\sum_{i=1}^{n} s_i} , \qquad (6.13)$$

the moment estimator for Special Case C.

EXAMPLE 6.1 : From the sample of five persons whose basic data is given below, estimate q_{30}, using an observation period of calendar year 1987.

Person	Date of Birth	Date of Death
1	July 1, 1957	---
2	Apr. 1, 1957	---
3	Jan. 1, 1957	Oct. 1, 1987
4	July 1, 1956	---
5	Apr. 1, 1956	Apr. 22, 1987

SOLUTION : The data are shown in Figure 6.1:

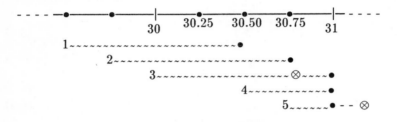

FIGURE 6.1

The ordered pairs (r_i, s_i) are $(0, .50)$, $(0, .75)$, $(0, 1)$, $(.50, 1)$, and $(.75, 1)$, for $i = 1,2,3,4,5$, respectively. Thus the denominator of estimator (6.5) is $.50 + .75 + 1.00 + .50 + .25 = 3.00$. The numerator of (6.5) is $d_x = 1$, because person 5 died *after* reaching age 31. Thus $\hat{q}_{30} = \frac{1}{3}$.

6.2.3 *Exposure*

The concept of exposure was defined in Section 3.3.5 in the context of a life table model. At this time, and at several other places throughout the text, we will make use of this concept in the context of a study sample.

The ordered pair (r_i, s_i) for person i represents the interval of age, within $(x, x+1]$, over which person i is potentially under observation. We say that person i is *exposed to* the risk of death from age $x+r_i$ to age $x+s_i$. Numerically, $s_i - r_i$ is the length of time (in years) that person i is exposed, so it also represents the amount of exposure, measured in units of life-years, contributed by that person. The total exposure contributed by the sample is $\sum_{i=1}^{n} (s_i - r_i)$, the denominator of estimator (6.5).

The exposure interpretation of the denominators of estimators (6.7), (6.10), and (6.13) is the same as that for estimator (6.5).

It is important to recognize that the denominator of the moment estimator represents the *scheduled* exposure of the sample. When a sample member dies while under observation, not all of the scheduled exposure is realized. Henceforth in this text we will refer to the realized exposure as *exact* exposure, to distinguish it from scheduled exposure. Note that exact exposure cannot exceed scheduled exposure.

EXAMPLE 6.2 : Calculate the exact exposure, for the interval (30,31], of the sample described in Example 6.1.
SOLUTION : Only person 3 has exact exposure less than scheduled exposure, and it is less by .25 years. Thus the total exact exposure of the sample is 2.75.

Exact exposure plays an extremely important role in estimation, as we shall see in Chapter 7. Intuitively, the observed deaths divided by exact exposure provides an estimate of the central death rate, m_x, for the interval (x, x+1]. From the derived value of $\hat{m}_x$, one could then estimate q_x by

$$\hat{q}_x = \frac{\hat{m}_x}{1 + \frac{1}{2} \cdot \hat{m}_x}, \tag{6.14}$$

which uses the linear distribution assumption for ℓ_{x+s}. Alternatively, if we assume an exponential ℓ_{x+s} (the constant force of mortality assumption), then this constant force, μ, is the same as m_x, so that $\hat{\mu} = \hat{m}_x$, and thus

$$\hat{q}_x = 1 - e^{-\hat{\mu}} = 1 - e^{-\hat{m}_x}. \tag{6.15}$$

In the next chapter we will see that this $\hat{\mu}$ (and thus $\hat{q}_x$) are maximum likelihood estimators.

To summarize, scheduled exposure is divided into observed deaths to estimate q_x in a single-decrement environment by the moment estimation approach, coupled with the approximation $_{s-r}q_{x+r} \approx (s-r) \cdot q_x$. Exact exposure is divided into observed deaths to estimate m_x, or to estimate a constant force of mortality over (x, x+1]. This latter case will arise regularly in Chapter 7.

6.2.4 *Grouping*

Consider Special Case B in which the n_x persons who contribute to (x, x+1] enter this interval at various ages, but all are scheduled to exit the interval at age x+1. That is, all are scheduled to survive (x, x+1]; none are scheduled to be study enders at an age z_i such that $x < z_i < x+1$. It may reasonably be assumed that many of these n_x persons enter the interval at exact age x (i.e., have $r_i = 0$); let us say that b_x is the subset of n_x which has

$r_i = 0$. (b_x is chosen to stand for "beginner," since these persons are exposed from the beginning of $(x, x+1]$.)

The remainder of the sample, say $k_x = n_x - b_x$, all have r_i such that $0 < r_i < 1$. Let us assume that the *average* value of these r_i's is r, $0 < r < 1$. (Alternatively, it might be possible that the study was designed such that k_x persons all had $r_i = r$, and no averaging is needed.) This situation is illustrated in Figure 6.2.

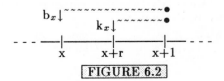

$$\boxed{\text{FIGURE 6.2}}$$

As a result of this grouping, the expected number of deaths in $(x, x+1]$ is $b_x \cdot q_x + k_x \cdot {}_{1-r}q_{x+r}$, so that the moment equation becomes

$$E[D_x] = b_x \cdot q_x + k_x \cdot {}_{1-r}q_{x+r} = d_x . \tag{6.16}$$

Under the hyperbolic assumption, ${}_{1-r}q_{x+r} = (1-r) \cdot q_x$, so (6.16) is easily solved for the estimator

$$\hat{q}_x = \frac{d_x}{b_x + (1-r) \cdot k_x}. \tag{6.17}$$

The exposure interpretation of the denominator of (6.17) is readily apparent.

Next we consider Special Case C, in which all n_x persons are exposed from age x (i.e., have $r_i = 0$), but are scheduled to exit $(x, x+1]$ at various ages z_i such that $x < z_i \leq x+1$. Let c_x represent the subset of n_x scheduled to exit at $z_i < x+1$ (i.e., $s_i < 1$); the remainder, $n_x - c_x$, are scheduled to remain under observation to age $x+1$.

Let us assume that the *average* value of the s_i's for the c_x subset is s, $0 < s < 1$. This situation is illustrated in Figure 6.3.

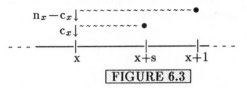

$$\boxed{\text{FIGURE 6.3}}$$

The expected number of deaths in $(x, x+1]$ is now $(n_x - c_x) \cdot q_x + c_x \cdot {}_s q_x$, so that the moment equation becomes

$$E[D_x] = (n_x - c_x) \cdot q_x + c_x \cdot {}_s q_x = d_x. \tag{6.18}$$

Under the linear assumption, $_sq_x = s \cdot q_x$, (6.18) is easily solved for the estimator

$$\hat{q}_x = \frac{d_x}{n_x - (1-s) \cdot c_x}. \qquad (6.19)$$

Again the exposure interpretation of the denominator is apparent.

Our Special Case C is one that frequently arises in clinical studies. As seen in Chapter 4, these studies often are designed so that all members of the study sample come under observation at time t=0. It follows that all members who reach the estimation interval (t, t+1] must enter it at exact time t, so that $r_i = 0$ for all i. But if the study is terminated before all have died, then there will be enders at various times, so that $s_i < 1$ for some i. Because of the frequent occurrence of Special Case C in practice, we will refer to it several more times as we develop the theory of estimation in this text.

6.2.5 *Properties of Moment Estimators*

In this section we will explore the bias and the variance of the moment estimators derived thus far in the chapter. It is assumed that the reader is familiar with these two properties of estimators. Formal definitions of them are given in Appendix A.

A characteristic of the moment estimators for q_x which we will derive is that they are always unbiased under the assumption, or other approximation, used to derive them. We will demonstrate this for the general form of the moment estimator given by (6.5).

To investigate bias, we need to compare the expected value of the estimator with the true value of the parameter, q_x, which it seeks to estimate. We are using $\hat{q}_x$ to represent the realized value of the estimator random variable when the random variable for number of deaths, D_x, has realized value d_x. Thus we use $\hat{Q}_x$ for the estimator random variable, so that

$$\hat{Q}_x = \frac{D_x}{\sum\limits_{i=1}^{n} (s_i - r_i)} \qquad (6.5a)$$

is the relationship between the random variables $\hat{Q}_x$ and D_x for the general single-decrement moment estimator. Then the expected value of $\hat{Q}_x$ is

$$E[\hat{Q}_x] = \frac{E[D_x]}{\sum\limits_{i=1}^{n} (s_i - r_i)}, \text{ where } E[D_x] = \sum_{i=1}^{n} {}_{s_i - r_i}q_{x+r_i}. \text{ When } {}_{s_i - r_i}q_{x+r_i} \text{ is}$$

approximated by (6.3), we obtain

$$E[\hat{Q}_x] = \frac{\sum_{i=1}^{n} {}_{s_i-r_i}q_{x+r_i}}{\sum_{i=1}^{n} (s_i-r_i)} = \frac{q_x \cdot \sum_{i=1}^{n} (s_i-r_i)}{\sum_{i=1}^{n} (s_i-r_i)} = q_x. \qquad (6.20)$$

This shows that estimator (6.5) is unbiased under the approximation used to derive it. It is biased to the extent that (6.3) deviates from the mortality distribution to which the sample is actually subject. This last point is illustrated in the following example.

EXAMPLE 6.3 : Analyze the degree of bias contained in estimator (6.10) for Special Case B.

SOLUTION : For Special Case B, we have $E[D_x] = \sum_{i=1}^{n} {}_{1-r_i}q_{x+r_i}$ and the

estimator $\hat{Q}_x = \dfrac{D_x}{\sum_{i=1}^{n} (1-r_i)}$. Then $E[\hat{Q}_x] = \dfrac{E[D_x]}{\sum_{i=1}^{n} (1-r_i)} = \dfrac{\sum_{i=1}^{n} {}_{1-r_i}q_{x+r_i}}{\sum_{i=1}^{n} (1-r_i)}$.

If we assume that ${}_{1-r_i}q_{x+r_i} = (1-r_i) \cdot q_x$, then $E[\hat{Q}_x] = q_x$, so estimator (6.10) is unbiased under this assumption. However, as shown in Chapter 3, this assumption implies that the force of mortality decreases over $(x, x+1)$. Thus if the force is constant or increasing, as is true over most ages other than juvenile ages, then ${}_{1-r_i}q_{x+r_i} > (1-r_i) \cdot q_x$. In this case we find that

$E[D_x] > \sum_{i=1}^{n} (1-r_i) \cdot q_x$, and thus $E[\hat{Q}_x] > \dfrac{\sum_{i=1}^{n} (1-r_i) \cdot q_x}{\sum_{i=1}^{n} (1-r_i)} = q_x$, which shows

that, for most ages, estimator (6.10) is positively biased.

To determine the variance of the general moment estimator (6.5), note first that the random variable for number of deaths in $(x, x+1]$, D_x, can be written as

$$D_x = \sum_{i=1}^{n} D_i, \qquad (6.21)$$

where D_i is the random variable (either 0 or 1) for number of deaths from person i. We hypothesize that all D_i, for $i = 1, 2, \cdots, n$, are mutually independent. Since D_i is binomially distributed, with sample size 1 and probability of occurrence ${}_{s_i-r_i}q_{x+r_i}$, we have

$$\text{Var}(D_x) = \sum_{i=1}^{n} \text{Var}(D_i) = \sum_{i=1}^{n} {}_{s_i-r_i}q_{x+r_i}(1 - {}_{s_i-r_i}q_{x+r_i}), \qquad (6.22)$$

so that

$$\text{Var}(\hat{Q}_x | n_x, \{r_i, s_i\}) = \frac{\sum\limits_{i=1}^{n} {}_{s_i - r_i} q_{x + r_i} (1 - {}_{s_i - r_i} q_{x + r_i})}{\left[\sum\limits_{i=1}^{n} (s_i - r_i) \right]^2}. \tag{6.23}$$

The notation $\text{Var}(\hat{Q}_x | n_x, \{r_i, s_i\})$ is used to remind us that the variance is conditional on the size of the sample, n_x, and the set of times at which persons enter and are scheduled to exit $(x, x+1]$. Expression (6.23) could then be simplified by using approximation (6.3).

Alternatively, the variance of (6.5) can be approximated by noting that $\hat{Q}_x$ is approximately a binomial proportion with sample size $\sum\limits_{i=1}^{n} (s_i - r_i)$. Thus the approximate variance is

$$\text{Var}(\hat{Q}_x | n_x, \{r_i, s_i\}) \approx \frac{p_x q_x}{\sum\limits_{i=1}^{n} (s_i - r_i)}. \tag{6.24}$$

Expressions for the variance of estimators (6.7), (6.10) and (6.13), for Special Cases A, B, and C, respectively, are analogous to expressions (6.23) and (6.24), and their derivations are pursued in the exercises.

EXAMPLE 6.4 : Find an exact expression for the variance of the Special Case C estimator (6.19).

SOLUTION : Let D'_x be the random variable for deaths out of the c_x group, and D''_x be the random variable for deaths out of the $(n_x - c_x)$ group. Note that $D_x = D'_x + D''_x$, that D'_x and D''_x are both binomial random variables, and that they are independent. From these properties we find that $\text{Var}(D_x) = \text{Var}(D'_x) + \text{Var}(D''_x) = c_x \cdot {}_s q_x (1 - {}_s q_x) + (n_x - c_x) \cdot q_x (1 - q_x)$, so that $\text{Var}(\hat{Q}_x | n_x, c_x) = \dfrac{c_x \cdot {}_s q_x (1 - {}_s q_x) + (n_x - c_x) \cdot q_x (1 - q_x)}{\left[n_x - (1 - s) \cdot c_x \right]^2}$.

6.2.6 *A Different Moment Approach for Special Case C*

We saw in Section 6.2.4 that the expected deaths out of the c_x, all scheduled to exit at age $x+s$, was given by $c_x \cdot {}_s q_x$. The fractional-interval probability required an assumption (such as the uniform) in order to solve the resulting moment equation. As an alternative to making such a distribution assumption, we now consider a different approach.

Assume that the c_x scheduled enders are subject to the same probability of death in $(x, x+1]$ as are the remaining $n_x - c_x$, namely q_x. Now consider *all* of the deaths out of c_x in $(x, x+1]$; let us call this d^c_x. Some of these deaths occur before exit from the study, and are thus observed, whereas others occur after exit, and are not observed. Let d'_x denote the number of observed deaths out of c_x, and let α represent the *proportion* of d^c_x that are observed. Thus $d'_x = \alpha \cdot d^c_x$.

Note well that d^c_x is not known, so α is not calculated. Rather, α is an input parameter, presumably derived from other data, or merely assumed. The assumption of α takes the place of a distribution assumption.

Of the c_x group, $c_x \cdot q_x$ are expected to die in (x, x+1], and $\alpha \cdot c_x \cdot q_x$ is the expected number of observable deaths. $(n_x - c_x) \cdot q_x$ is the expected observable deaths out of $n_x - c_x$, so total expected observable deaths, equated to the actual observed deaths, gives the moment equation

$$(n_x - c_x) \cdot q_x + \alpha \cdot c_x \cdot q_x \;=\; n_x \cdot q_x - (1-\alpha) \cdot c_x \cdot q_x \;=\; d_x. \qquad (6.25)$$

A person scheduled to exit observation at age x+s as a study ender, and who survives to that age, is then observed to be an actual ender. Let e_x denote the number of actual enders in the sample. Now let us consider the expected number of observable enders in the sample. We have $c_x(1-q_x)$ not expected to die in (x, x+1] at all, and $(1-\alpha) \cdot c_x \cdot q_x$ expected to die, but *after* departure so that they are observed enders. Then total expected observable enders, equated to actually observed enders, gives the moment equation

$$c_x \cdot (1-q_x) + (1-\alpha) \cdot c_x \cdot q_x \;=\; c_x - \alpha \cdot c_x \cdot q_x \;=\; e_x. \qquad (6.26)$$

Note that there can be no observed enders in (x, x+1] from the $n_x - c_x$ group.

The estimator of q_x is derived by eliminating c_x from equations (6.25) and (6.26). From equation (6.26), we have $c_x = \dfrac{e_x}{1 - \alpha \cdot q_x}$; substituting this into (6.25) gives us

$$n_x \cdot q_x - \frac{(1-\alpha) \cdot e_x \cdot q_x}{1 - \alpha \cdot q_x} \;=\; d_x,$$

which leads to the quadratic equation

$$\alpha \cdot n_x \cdot q_x{}^2 - \Big[n_x - (1-\alpha) \cdot e_x + \alpha \cdot d_x\Big] q_x + d_x \;=\; 0, \qquad (6.27)$$

the solution of which is

$$\hat{q}_x \;=\; \frac{b - \sqrt{b^2 - 4\alpha \cdot n_x \cdot d_x}}{2\alpha \cdot n_x}, \qquad (6.28)$$

where $b = n_x - (1-\alpha) \cdot e_x + \alpha \cdot d_x$. The negative radical is used in (6.28) because the positive radical would result in $\hat{q}_x > 1$.

It turns out that estimator (6.28) is also a maximum likelihood estimator, which we will show in Chapter 7 (see Exercise 7-9). We also defer to Chapter 7 the derivation of the variance of this estimator (see Exercise 7-24).

One advantage of estimator (6.28) over estimator (6.19) is that (6.28) does not require knowing the value of c_x, but rather depends on the number of actually observed enders, e_x. Also, it has some of the desirable properties of an MLE. Although it does not require a distribution assumption, as does (6.19), it does require an assumed value for α.

This estimator was derived by Schwartz and Lazar [54].

EXAMPLE 6.5 : In a Special Case C study, $n_x = 1000$, $c_x = 100$ (all scheduled to be enders at age $x+\frac{1}{4}$), and $d_x = 20$, of which $d'_x = 2$. What value of α will produce the same estimate of q_x by estimator (6.28) as that produced by estimator (6.19)?

SOLUTION : Estimator (6.19) gives $q_x = \dfrac{20}{1000 - (.75)(100)} = \dfrac{4}{185}$. Since $e_x = c_x - d'_x = 98$, then $b = 1000 - 98 + 98\alpha + 20\alpha = 902 + 118\alpha$. It is easier to solve for α from (6.27) than from (6.28). Substituting, we have $(1000\alpha)(\frac{4}{185})^2 - (902 + 118\alpha)(\frac{4}{185}) + 20 = 0$, which produces $\alpha = .23864$. Since α is the proportion of deaths out of c_x which occur in the first quarter of $(x, x+1]$, this result, which is close to .25, is very reasonable.

6.3 MOMENT ESTIMATION IN A DOUBLE-DECREMENT ENVIRONMENT

As in the case of estimation in a single-decrement environment, we assume that the sample data have been analyzed to produce the ordered pair $(x+r_i, x+s_i)$ for person i's scheduled contribution to $(x, x+1]$, as illustrated in Figure 5.6.

The probability of death for person i while under observation in the double-decrement environment is ${}_{s_i - r_i}q^{(d)}_{x+r_i}$, and this is also the expected number of deaths from this sample of size one, as demonstrated by (6.1) for the single-decrement case.

6.3.1 The Basic Moment Relationships

As explained in Section 5.3, we now consider both death and withdrawal to be random events. Thus, analogous to the moment Equation (6.2) in the single-decrements case, we now write the *pair* of moment equations

$$E[D_x] = \sum_{i=1}^{n} {}_{s_i - r_i}q^{(d)}_{x+r_i} = d_x \qquad (6.29a)$$

and

$$E[W_x] = \sum_{i=1}^{n} {}_{s_i-r_i}q_{x+r_i}^{(w)} = w_x \qquad (6.29b)$$

where W_x is the random variable for withdrawals in $(x, x+1]$, and w_x denotes the observed number of withdrawals in the sample.

A simple way to solve (6.29a) and (6.29b) for estimates of the double-decrement probabilities $q_x^{(d)}$ and $q_x^{(w)}$ would be to use approximations analogous to (6.3), namely

$$ {}_{s_i-r_i}q_{x+r_i}^{(d)} \approx (s_i-r_i) \cdot q_x^{(d)} \qquad (6.30a)$$

and

$$ {}_{s_i-r_i}q_{x+r_i}^{(w)} \approx (s_i-r_i) \cdot q_x^{(w)}, \qquad (6.30b)$$

producing

$$\hat{q}_x^{(d)} = \frac{d_x}{\sum\limits_{i=1}^{n} (s_i-r_i)} \qquad (6.31a)$$

and

$$\hat{q}_x^{(w)} = \frac{w_x}{\sum\limits_{i=1}^{n} (s_i-r_i)}. \qquad (6.31b)$$

However, our objective is usually to estimate the *single-decrement* probabilities $q'^{(d)}_x$ and $q'^{(w)}_x$, in this case from data that have been collected in a double-decrement environment. To accomplish this, we could calculate estimates of $q'^{(d)}_x$ and $q'^{(w)}_x$ from the estimates $\hat{q}_x^{(d)}$ and $\hat{q}_x^{(w)}$, produced by (6.31a) and (6.31b), using one of the approximate relationships between single-decrement and double-decrement probabilities presented in Chapter 14 of Jordan [32] or Chapter 9 of Bowers, et al. [10].

Alternatively, we could calculate estimates of $q'^{(d)}_x$ and $q'^{(w)}_x$ directly from our sample data by expressing ${}_{s_i-r_i}q_{x+r_i}^{(d)}$ and ${}_{s_i-r_i}q_{x+r_i}^{(w)}$ directly in terms of $q'^{(d)}_x$ and $q'^{(w)}_x$, under a chosen assumption, without using the preliminary approximations (6.30a) and (6.30b). This approach normally results in equations which must be solved numerically for $\hat{q}'^{(d)}_x$ and $\hat{q}'^{(w)}_x$.

6.3.2 *Uniform Distribution Assumptions*

If the random events, death and withdrawal, are each assumed to have uniform distributions over $(x, x+1)$ in the single-decrement context, we know from Section 3.5 that $_{u-r}q'^{(d)}_{x+r} = \dfrac{(u-r)\cdot q'^{(d)}_x}{1 - r\cdot q'^{(d)}_x}$, $0 \le r < u \le 1$, and also that

$\mu^{(d)}_{x+u} = \dfrac{q'^{(d)}_x}{1 - u\cdot q'^{(d)}_x}$, so that $(1 - {_{u-r}q'^{(d)}_{x+r}})\mu^{(d)}_{x+u} = \dfrac{q'^{(d)}_x}{1 - r\cdot q'^{(d)}_x}$. Then

equation (5.20) becomes

$$_{s-r}q^{(d)}_{x+r} = \int_r^s \left[1 - {_{u-r}q'^{(w)}_{x+r}}\right]\left[1 - {_{u-r}q'^{(d)}_{x+r}}\right]\mu^{(d)}_{x+u}\,du$$

$$= \int_r^s \frac{q'^{(d)}_x}{1 - r\cdot q'^{(d)}_x} \cdot \frac{1 - u\cdot q'^{(w)}_x}{1 - r\cdot q'^{(w)}_x}\,du$$

$$= \frac{q'^{(d)}_x}{\left[1 - r\cdot q'^{(d)}_x\right]\left[1 - r\cdot q'^{(w)}_x\right]} \int_r^s \left[1 - u\cdot q'^{(w)}_x\right]du$$

$$= \frac{q'^{(d)}_x\left[(s-r) - \tfrac{1}{2}(s^2 - r^2)\cdot q'^{(w)}_x\right]}{\left[1 - r\cdot q'^{(d)}_x\right]\left[1 - r\cdot q'^{(w)}_x\right]}. \tag{6.32a}$$

Similarly, equation (5.21) would lead to

$$_{s-r}q^{(w)}_{x+r} = \frac{q'^{(w)}_x\left[(s-r) - \tfrac{1}{2}(s^2 - r^2)\cdot q'^{(d)}_x\right]}{\left[1 - r\cdot q'^{(d)}_x\right]\left[1 - r\cdot q'^{(w)}_x\right]}. \tag{6.32b}$$

Substitution of (6.32a) and (6.32b) into the basic moment equations (6.29a) and (6.29b), respectively, results in

$$E[D_x] = \sum_{i=1}^n \frac{q'^{(d)}_x\left[(s_i - r_i) - \tfrac{1}{2}(s_i^2 - r_i^2)\cdot q'^{(w)}_x\right]}{\left[1 - r_i\cdot q'^{(d)}_x\right]\left[1 - r_i\cdot q'^{(w)}_x\right]} = d_x \tag{6.33a}$$

and

$$E[W_x] = \sum_{i=1}^{n} \frac{q_x'^{(w)} \left[(s_i - r_i) - \frac{1}{2}(s_i^2 - r_i^2) \cdot q_x'^{(d)} \right]}{\left[1 - r_i \cdot q_x'^{(d)} \right] \left[1 - r_i \cdot q_x'^{(w)} \right]} = w_x. \tag{6.33b}$$

The complexity of equations (6.33a) and (6.33b), necessitating a numerical solution, is obvious.

If Special Case A, in which $r_i = 0$ and $s_i = 1$ for all i prevails, then equations (6.33a) and (6.33b) are considerable simplified. With $r_i = 0$, both denominators are 1; with $s_i = 1$ and $r_i = 0$, $(s_i - r_i) = (s_i^2 - r_i^2) = 1$. Thus we have

$$E[D_x] = \sum_{i=1}^{n} q_x'^{(d)} \left[1 - \frac{1}{2} \cdot q_x'^{(w)} \right] = d_x \tag{6.34a}$$

and

$$E[W_x] = \sum_{i=1}^{n} q_x'^{(w)} \left[1 - \frac{1}{2} \cdot q_x'^{(d)} \right] = w_x . \tag{6.34b}$$

To simplify notation, let $q_x'^{(d)} = \theta$ and $q_x'^{(w)} = \phi$. Then we have

$$n_x \cdot \theta(1 - \tfrac{1}{2}\phi) = d_x \tag{6.35a}$$

and

$$n_x \cdot \phi(1 - \tfrac{1}{2}\theta) = w_x. \tag{6.35b}$$

To solve for $\hat{\theta} = \hat{q}_x'^{(d)}$, we determine $\phi = \dfrac{w_x}{n_x(1 - \tfrac{1}{2}\theta)}$ from (6.35b), and substitute into (6.35a), producing

$$n_x \cdot \theta \left[1 - \frac{\tfrac{1}{2}w_x}{n_x(1 - \tfrac{1}{2}\theta)} \right] = d_x. \tag{6.36}$$

This leads to the quadratic equation

$$\tfrac{1}{2}n_x \cdot \theta^2 - \theta(n_x - \tfrac{1}{2}w_x + \tfrac{1}{2}d_x) + d_x = 0, \tag{6.37}$$

which leads to the result

$$\hat{\theta} = \hat{q}_x'^{(d)} = \frac{b - \sqrt{b^2 - 2n_x d_x}}{n_x} , \tag{6.38}$$

where $b = n_x - \frac{1}{2}w_x + \frac{1}{2}d_x$. Again the positive radical is not taken since it would produce $\hat{q}_x'^{(d)} > 1$. In Chapter 7 we will see that estimator (6.38) is a maximum likelihood estimator.

EXAMPLE 6.6 : 100 persons enter the estimation interval $(20,21]$ at exact age 20. None are scheduled to exit before exact age 21, but one death and two random withdrawals are observed before age 21. Assuming a uniform distribution of both random events, estimate $q_{20}'^{(d)}$.

SOLUTION : Using equation (6.38), $b = 100 - \frac{1}{2}(2) + \frac{1}{2}(1) = 99.5$, so that $\hat{q}_{20}'^{(d)} = \dfrac{99.5 - \sqrt{(99.5)^2 - 200}}{100} = .0101015.$

The solution of (6.34a) and (6.34b) for $\hat{q}_x'^{(w)}$ is analogous to the solution for $\hat{q}_x'^{(d)}$, and is left to the exercises. The simplification of (6.33a) and (6.33b), and the resulting solution of them for $\hat{q}_x'^{(d)}$ and $\hat{q}_x'^{(w)}$, under Special Cases B and C, are also left to the exercises.

6.3.3 *Exponential Distribution Assumptions*

If both death and withdrawal are assumed to have exponential distributions (constant forces) over $(x, x+1)$, then, from Section 3.5, $\mu_{x+u}^{(d)} = \mu^{(d)}$, $1 - {}_{u-r}q_{x+r}'^{(d)} = e^{-(u-r)\mu^{(d)}}$, and $1 - {}_{u-r}q_{x+r}'^{(w)} = e^{-(u-r)\mu^{(w)}}$. Then equation (5.20) becomes

$$
\begin{aligned}
{}_{s-r}q_{x+r}^{(d)} &= \int_r^s \left[1 - {}_{u-r}q_{x+r}'^{(w)}\right]\left[1 - {}_{u-r}q_{x+r}'^{(d)}\right]\mu_{x+u}^{(d)}\,du \\
&= \mu^{(d)} \int_r^s e^{-(u-r)(\mu^{(d)} + \mu^{(w)})}\,du \\
&= \frac{\mu^{(d)}}{\mu^{(d)} + \mu^{(w)}}\left[1 - e^{-(s-r)(\mu^{(d)} + \mu^{(w)})}\right].
\end{aligned} \tag{6.39a}
$$

Similarly, equation (5.21) becomes

$$
{}_{s-r}q_{x+r}^{(w)} = \frac{\mu^{(w)}}{\mu^{(d)} + \mu^{(w)}}\left[1 - e^{-(s-r)(\mu^{(d)} + \mu^{(w)})}\right]. \tag{6.39b}
$$

Substitution of (6.39a) and (6.39b) into the basic moment equations (6.29a) and (6.29b), respectively, results in

$$E[D_x] = \sum_{i=1}^{n} \frac{\mu^{(d)}}{\mu^{(d)} + \mu^{(w)}} \left[1 - e^{-(s_i - r_i)(\mu^{(d)} + \mu^{(w)})} \right] = d_x \qquad (6.40a)$$

and

$$E[W_x] = \sum_{i=1}^{n} \frac{\mu^{(w)}}{\mu^{(d)} + \mu^{(w)}} \left[1 - e^{-(s_i - r_i)(\mu^{(d)} + \mu^{(w)})} \right] = w_x. \qquad (6.40b)$$

Again, the necessity of a numerical solution of these equations for $\hat{\mu}^{(d)}$ and $\hat{\mu}^{(w)}$ is obvious.

If Special Case A prevails, with $r_i = 0$ and $s_i = 1$ for all i, then (6.40a) and (6.40b) are simplified to

$$E[D_x] = \sum_{i=1}^{n} \frac{\mu^{(d)}}{\mu^{(d)} + \mu^{(w)}} \left[1 - e^{-(\mu^{(d)} + \mu^{(w)})} \right] = d_x \qquad (6.41a)$$

and

$$E[W_x] = \sum_{i=1}^{n} \frac{\mu^{(w)}}{\mu^{(d)} + \mu^{(w)}} \left[1 - e^{-(\mu^{(d)} + \mu^{(w)})} \right] = w_x, \qquad (6.41b)$$

respectively.

To simplify notation, let $\mu^{(d)} = \alpha$ and $\mu^{(w)} = \beta$. Then we have

$$\frac{\alpha \cdot n_x}{\alpha + \beta} \left[1 - e^{-(\alpha + \beta)} \right] = d_x \qquad (6.42a)$$

and

$$\frac{\beta \cdot n_x}{\alpha + \beta} \left[1 - e^{-(\alpha + \beta)} \right] = w_x . \qquad (6.42b)$$

To solve for $\hat{\alpha} = \hat{\mu}^{(d)}$, we see from (6.42a) that $\dfrac{n_x \left[1 - e^{-(\alpha + \beta)} \right]}{\alpha + \beta} = \dfrac{d_x}{\alpha}$.

Substituting this into (6.42b) we obtain $\beta \cdot \dfrac{d_x}{\alpha} = w_x$, or

$$\beta = \frac{w_x}{d_x} \cdot \alpha . \qquad (6.43)$$

This implies that

$$\alpha + \beta = \alpha + \frac{w_x}{d_x} \cdot \alpha = \alpha\left(\frac{d_x + w_x}{d_x}\right), \tag{6.44}$$

so that (6.42a) becomes

$$\frac{n_x \cdot d_x}{d_x + w_x}\left\{1 - \exp\left[-\alpha\left(\frac{d_x + w_x}{d_x}\right)\right]\right\} = d_x,$$

or

$$\exp\left[-\alpha\left(\frac{d_x + w_x}{d_x}\right)\right] = \frac{n_x - d_x - w_x}{n_x},$$

which solves for

$$\hat{\alpha} = \hat{\mu}^{(d)} = -\ln\left[\frac{n_x - d_x - w_x}{n_x}\right]^{d_x/(d_x + w_x)}. \tag{6.45}$$

Finally,

$$\hat{q}_x'^{(d)} = 1 - e^{-\hat{\alpha}} = 1 - \left[\frac{n_x - d_x - w_x}{n_x}\right]^{d_x/(d_x + w_x)}. \tag{6.46}$$

In Chapter 7 we will see that estimator (6.46) is a maximum likelihood estimator.

EXAMPLE 6.7 : Use the data of Example 6.6 to estimate $q_{20}'^{(d)}$, assuming an exponential distribution for both death and withdrawal.

SOLUTION : Using Equation (6.46), we have $\frac{n_x - d_x - w_x}{n_x} = .97$ and $\frac{d_x}{d_x + w_x} = \frac{1}{3}$. Thus $\hat{q}_{20}'^{(d)} = 1 - (.97)^{1/3} = .0101017$.

The solution of equations (6.41a) and (6.41b) for $\hat{q}_x'^{(w)}$ is analogous to the solution for $\hat{q}_x'^{(d)}$, and is left to the exercises. The simplification of (6.40a) and (6.40b), and the resulting solution of them for $\hat{q}_x'^{(d)}$ and $\hat{q}_x'^{(w)}$, under Special Cases B and C, are also left to the exercises.

6.3.4 Hoem's Approach to Moment Estimation in a Double-Decrement Environment

The mathematical difficulty inherent in the solution of (6.29a) and (6.29b) for $\hat{q}_x'^{(d)}$ and $\hat{q}_x'^{(w)}$, under either the uniform or exponential distribution, motivates us to find a different, simpler, approach to moment estimation in the double-decrement environment. One such approach is the actuarial approach, to be described in Section 6.4; another is Hoem's approach (see Hoem [29]), which we present at this time.

For person i, who enters $(x, x+1]$ at age $x+r_i$, Hoem contemplates a theoretical age scheduled for *withdrawal*, say $x+t_i$, in the same manner that there is an age scheduled for exit due to the ending of the observation period, which we have called $x+s_i$. The difference is that $x+s_i$ is known when person i enters $(x, x+1]$, whereas $x+t_i$ is not known (except, according to Hoem, to a Laplacian demon). For those persons with $t_i < s_i$, the values of t_i become known, *a posteriori*, as the sample experience unfolds and the withdrawals are observed.

Using the exposure interpretation of the moment estimator developed in Section 6.2.3, we find exposure of $(s_i - r_i)$ if person i survives to the scheduled ending age, and exposure of $(t_i - r_i)$ if person i withdraws at $x+t_i < x+s_i$ (i.e., survives to the "scheduled" withdrawal age). But what is the exposure for those who die in $(x, x+1]$?

In Section 6.2.3 it was stressed that the appropriate exposure for a death was the *scheduled* exposure $(s_i - r_i)$, within a single-decrement environment. Now in our double-decrement environment, we will still use the scheduled exposure for a death, but the scheduled exposure is now $(s_i - r_i)$ or $(t_i - r_i)$, *whichever is less*. In other words, if a person had an unknown scheduled withdrawal time of $t_i < s_i$, and died before time t_i, this scheduled withdrawal time would never become known. This person *should* contribute $(t_i - r_i)$, but we can never know what t_i is (or would have been).

Hoem deals with this dilemma by simply assuming that no one who died in $(x, x+1]$ had a t_i value that was less than s_i. In other words, *all* deaths contribute $(s_i - r_i)$ to the exposure. Then the estimate of $q_x'^{(d)}$ is produced as the ratio of number of deaths to the exposure.

An example will make this procedure clear. The important point is that all persons have a known value of s_i *at entry* into $(x, x+1]$, regardless of the outcome for person i (survival, death or withdrawal). Each person's value of t_i becomes known *only if* that person actually withdraws. Since t_i can never become known for a person who dies, s_i values are used for all deaths.

EXAMPLE 6.8 : The basic data on a sample of four persons has been analyzed to produce the following ordered pairs (r_i, s_i) with respect to the estimation interval $(x, x+1]$. In addition, it is known that one person died and one person withdrew while under observation, at the times shown. Estimate $q_x'^{(d)}$.

Person	(r_i, s_i)	Time of Death	Time of Withdrawal
1	(0, .4)	--	--
2	(0, 1)	.7	--
3	(.3 1)	--	--
4	(.5, .8)	--	.75

SOLUTION : Persons 1 and 3 contribute exposure of .4 and .7, respectively. Person 4 contributes .25, the theory being that he was scheduled to withdraw at age x+.75, since, in fact, he did! Person 2 contributes 1, under the assumption that she was *not* scheduled to withdraw before age x+1. The total exposure is $.4 + .7 + .25 + 1 = 2.35$, so we obtain

$$\hat{q}'^{(d)}_x = \frac{1}{2.35} = .42553.$$

6.4 THE ACTUARIAL APPROACH TO MOMENT ESTIMATION

Of the various approaches to the estimation of q_x over the interval (x, x+1] described in this text, the actuarial approach was the first to be developed, dating from the middle of the nineteenth century. There are two significant implications of this early origin:

(1) The method predates the formal, scientific development of statistical estimation theory.
(2) The method predates any kind of mechanical or electronic calculating equipment.

It will be easy to see the reflection of these two observations in the features of the actuarial method. The method was developed primarily in an intuitive manner, in the absence of a guiding statistical theory, and a key theoretical concession was made in the interest of simpler record-keeping and calculation.

We will present the actuarial method assuming a double-decrement environment. The simplification that results if the environment is single-decrement will be easily seen.

6.4.1 The Concept of Actuarial Exposure

The key difference between the traditional actuarial approach to estimation and the moment approaches presented thus far in this chapter is that the actuarial approach does not make major use of the concept of scheduled exposure, as defined in Section 6.2.3. Rather it makes use of a type of observed exposure, which we will call *actuarial* exposure, to distinguish it from the two other types of exposure (scheduled and exact) described earlier.

Recall that person i is scheduled to be an ender to the study at age z_i, and this is known at entry to the study. Recall also that if $x < z_i < x+1$, then we say that person i is scheduled to exit $(x, x+1]$ at age $z_i = x+s_i$, where $0 < s_i < 1$. On the other hand, if $z_i \geq x+1$, we say that person i is scheduled to survive $(x, x+1]$, which is the same as to say scheduled to exit at $x+s_i$, where $s_i = 1$.

Suppose person i enters $(x, x+1]$ at age $x+r_i$, $0 \leq r_i < 1$. Under the actuarial method, if person i is an *observed ender* at $x+s_i$, he contributes exposure of $(s_i - r_i)$. If he is an *observed withdrawal* at $x+t_i$, where, necessarily, $t_i \leq s_i$, he contributes exposure of $(t_i - r_i)$. But what if person i is an *observed death* in $(x, x+1]$? We have seen that a proper moment estimation procedure would have person i contribute exposure to age $x+s_i$, the scheduled exit age, and early in the development of the actuarial method this was intuitively recognized. However, the identification of scheduled exit age, for a person who died before reaching it, required more extensive data analysis than the early manual procedures allowed. To resolve the problem of an unknown $x+s_i$ for an observed death, it was simply assumed that $s_i = 1$ for all deaths.

The important point here is that the traditional actuarial approach to handling the data, as thoroughly described by Batten [6] and Gershenson [26], simply does not identify $x+s_i$ *a priori*. Rather $x+s_i$ becomes known *a posteriori* only if person i is, in fact, an ender, just as Hoem's "scheduled" withdrawal age $x+t_i$ becomes known, *a posteriori*, only if person i is an observed withdrawal. Thus, in the actuarial approach, $x+s_i$ does not become known for a death, so it is assumed to be $x+1$, just as, in Hoem's approach, a death that might otherwise have been a withdrawal has an unknown $x+t_i$, and is therefore assumed to be $x+s_i$.

Note that if, in fact, $s_i = 1$, then the actuarial method of giving exposure to age $x+1$ is correct; it is only if a death has $s_i < 1$ that the method "over-credits" exposure to age $x+1$ rather than only to age $x+s_i$.

EXAMPLE 6.9 : Three persons in a study sample all have the ordered pair $(r_i, s_i) = (0, .75)$. Person 1 remains in the sample to age $x+.75$, Person 2 withdraws at age $x+.5$, and Person 3 dies at age $x+.5$. How much exposure does each person contribute (a) under the actuarial approach; (b) under Hoem's moment approach?

SOLUTION : (a) Person 1 contributes .75, from age x to age $x+.75$; Person 2 contributes .50, from age x to age $x+.50$, where exposure ceases due to withdrawal; Person 3 contributes 1.00, from age x to age $x+1$. (b) Person 1 and Person 2 again contribute .75 and .50, respectively; Person 3 contributes only to scheduled exit age, which is .75, under the moment approach.

It cannot be overemphasized that the historical reason for crediting Person 3 in Example 6.9(a) with exposure to age x+1, rather than only to age x+.75, was that the scheduled exit age was not conveniently available information in the actuarial approach to processing the sample data. *Assuming* such scheduled exit age to be x+1 was simply a practical expedient.

Since age $z_i = x+s_i$ is person i's age when the observation period closes, then it follows that crediting exposure to age x+1, whenever $s_i < 1$, means that person i is viewed as contributing exposure after the observation period has closed. Ackland [1] refers to this as an "odd procedure" which is "in strictness" incorrect, but nevertheless acceptable for reasons of expediency. Seal [55], [56] and [57] has repeatedly criticized this facet of actuarial moment estimation, particularly later attempts to justify it by a statistical principle. It would appear that today, with large-scale studies totally computerized, the argument for this archaic practice loses any merit that it once had.

In a single-decrement environment the possibility of withdrawals does not exist. Then observed enders contribute exposure to their observed ending ages, and observed deaths contribute exposure to age x+1, regardless of a possibly earlier scheduled ending age.

6.4.2 *Statistical Justification*

Attempts to statistically justify the nineteenth century actuarial approach to the calculation of exposure appear to have originated with Cantelli [15] in 1914, and Balducci [4] a few years later. We will illustrate their argument first in a single-decrement environment.

Suppose n_x persons come under observation at age x+r, $0 \leq r < 1$, e_x persons, a subset of n_x, leave observation at age x+s as a result of the end of the observation period, d_x persons die in (x, x+1], and the remaining $n_x - e_x - d_x$ stay under observation to age x+1, as illustrated in Figure 6.4.

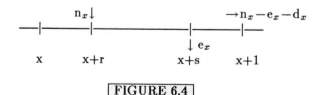

FIGURE 6.4

Cantelli's statistical principle for the estimation of q_x is that the expected number of deaths to be observed in (x, x+1] should be equated to the number actually observed, which is the moment approach we have already defined. However, Cantelli defined expected observable deaths to be

$n_x \cdot {}_{1-r}q_{x+r} - e_x \cdot {}_{1-s}q_{x+s}$, which can be read as "*all* deaths expected to occur before age x+1 out of a sample of n_x persons, less those *unobservable* deaths expected to occur before age x+1 out of the subsample of e_x persons who leave observation at age x+s." The resulting moment equation is then

$$E[D_x] = n_x \cdot {}_{1-r}q_{x+r} - e_x \cdot {}_{1-s}q_{x+s} = d_x. \qquad (6.47)$$

Note that Cantelli's equation uses the actual number of enders, whereas equation (6.2) makes use of scheduled ending ages. We have already noted that scheduled ending ages were not readily available information to Cantelli, but the observed number of enders was.

If there were no *scheduled* ending ages x+s_i with $s_i < 1$, then there could be no *observed* enders prior to age x+1, and Special Case B prevails. Then Cantelli's expression for expected deaths has no subtractive term, and the actuarial approach is easily seen to be identical to the moment approach defined by equation (6.8). This is also true for Special Case A defined by equation (6.6).

In a double-decrement environment, Cantelli's approach treats observed withdrawals the same as observed enders. If there are w_x observed withdrawals at age x+t, then we have

$$E[D_x] = n_x \cdot {}_{1-r}q_{x+r} - e_x \cdot {}_{1-s}q_{x+s} - w_x \cdot {}_{1-t}q_{x+t} = d_x, \qquad (6.48)$$

where ${}_{1-r}q_{x+r}$ is being used for the more notationally proper ${}_{1-r}q'^{(d)}_{x+r}$. If the ith person in the n_x group had entry age x+r_i, the jth person in e_x had observed ending age x+s_j, and the kth person in w_x had observed withdrawal age x+t_k, then the general form of the actuarial estimation equation is

$$\sum_{i=1}^{n} {}_{1-r_i}q_{x+r_i} - \sum_{j=1}^{e} {}_{1-s_j}q_{x+s_j} - \sum_{k=1}^{w} {}_{1-t_k}q_{x+t_k} = d_x. \qquad (6.49)$$

Since all probability symbols in these equations are of the form ${}_{1-u}q_{x+u}$, Cantelli and Balducci naturally chose the hyperbolic distribution to allow the substitution $(1-u) \cdot q_x$. (Recall that this distribution is known in the actuarial literature as the Balducci hypothesis.) Then equation (6.48) leads to the actuarial estimator

$$\hat{q}_x = \frac{d_x}{(1-r) \cdot n_x - (1-s) \cdot e_x - (1-t) \cdot w_x}, \qquad (6.50)$$

where the denominator represents the actuarial exposure. Note that there are deductions from the maximum exposure $(1-r) \cdot n_x$ for exposure "cancelled" by the observed enders and the observed withdrawals, but no deduction for exposure "cancelled" by the deaths. This implies that the deaths contribute exposure to age x+1, as already stated in Section 6.4.1.

6.4.3 *Critique of the Statistical Justification*

Cantelli's argument appears to have been widely accepted, at least in North America. Subsequent papers by Wolfenden [62], Beers [7] and Marshall [43], and textbooks by Gershenson [26] and Batten [6], in effect repeated his demonstration. But the preponderance of modern statistical thought would indicate that Cantelli's expression for expected deaths, although correct for Special Cases A and B, is seriously flawed in the cases involving enders within the estimation interval. (See, for example, Hoem [29] and Seal [56].)

Referring to equation (6.47), we note that each person in e_x is *necessarily* also in n_x. Now the expected value $n_x \cdot {}_{1-r}q_{x+r}$ is conditional on being alive at age x+r, and the expected value $e_x \cdot {}_{1-s}q_{x+s}$ is conditional on being alive at age x+s, where x+s > x+r, so there is a questionable "mixed conditionality" in the expected value expression. Saying it another way, $n_x \cdot {}_{1-r}q_{x+r}$ assumes that a person in our sample is alive at x+r, and $e_x \cdot {}_{1-s}q_{x+s}$ assumes the *same* person is alive at x+s, without first specifying the survival of this person from x+r to x+s.

Another way to view the questionable aspect of Cantelli's moment expression is to note that all e_x observed enders at age x+s were scheduled to do so when they were age x+r. Actually there were c_x such scheduled enders, as defined in Section 6.2.4, and e_x is the subset of c_x that survived to the scheduled ending age. Thus e_x is the sample realization of E_x, the binomial random variable for number of survivors to x+s out of the sample c_x, so Cantelli's expression for $E[D_x]$, by depending on the outcome of the random variable E_x, is itself a random variable, and is therefore not a correct expectation.

6.4.4 *Properties of the Actuarial Estimator*

In the single-decrement environment, the actuarial estimators for Special Cases A and B are the same as the moment estimators, so the discussion in Section 6.2.5 regarding bias and variance is applicable to the actuarial estimators as well.

In situations involving enders within (x, x+1], that is, enders at $x+s_i$ where $s_i < 1$, various investigations have shown under simulation, or otherwise, that the actuarial estimator is negatively biased. It has also been shown to be inconsistent. (See, for example, Breslow and Crowley [11], and Broffitt [12].) In large-scale actuarial studies of insurance data, there will always be a considerable number of enders for the observation period, and it follows that there could therefore be a significant number in any estimation interval (unless the study design places them at the interval boundary). The moment estimator will always produce a larger estimate $\hat{q}_x$ than will the actuarial estimator, so a natural way to counteract the negative bias in the latter is thereby suggested.

Finally it should be repeated that all estimators of the form $\dfrac{\text{Deaths}}{\text{Exposure}}$, which includes most of the ones in this chapter, are approximately binomial proportions, so all are approximately unbiased with variance given by $\dfrac{p_x q_x}{\text{Exposure}}$. This fact plays a crucial role in the next section.

6.5 *ESTIMATION OF S(x)*

Thus far in this chapter we have concentrated on obtaining estimates of q_x or p_x over the estimation interval (x, x+1]. To estimate S(x) we will use the approach introduced in Section 2.4.6, whereby

$$\hat{S}(x) = \hat{p}_0 \cdot \hat{p}_1 \cdot \cdots \cdot \hat{p}_{x-1}. \qquad (6.51)$$

To find the expected value and variance of $\hat{S}(x)$, we make two important assumptions:

(1) We assume that each $\hat{p}_i$, $i = 0,1,\cdots,x-1$, is approximately an unbiased binomial proportion, with mean p_i and variance $\dfrac{p_i q_i}{n'_i}$, where n'_i is the exposure used to calculate $\hat{q}_i$ (and hence $\hat{p}_i$). Note that this exposure is being interpreted as an approximate binomial sample.

(2) We assume that, conditional on the set $\{n'_i\}$, the $\hat{p}_i$'s are mutually independent. (In Chapter 10 we will explore a study design in which the $\hat{p}_i$'s are unconditionally independent.)

The important consequence of the first assumption is that, being unbiased, $E[\hat{p}_i \,|\, n'_i] = p_i$. The importance of the second assumption is that the expected value of a product of independent random variables is the product of their expected values.

6.5.1 *Expected Value of $\hat{S}(x)$*

It is important to note that this expected value is conditional on the set of exposures (approximate binomial samples) underlying the estimates of $\hat{q}_i$, for $i = 0,1,\cdots,x-1$. We will reflect this by using the notation $E[\hat{S}(x) \,|\, \{n'_i\}]$.

With $\hat{S}(x)$ given by (6.51), we have

$$E[\hat{S}(x) \,|\, \{n_i'\}] \;=\; E[\hat{p}_0 \cdot \hat{p}_1 \cdot \cdots \cdot \hat{p}_{x-1} \,|\, \{n_i'\}] \;=\; \prod_{i=0}^{x-1} E[\hat{p}_i \,|\, \{n_i'\}], \qquad (6.52)$$

as a consequence of the independence assumption. Then from the assumption of unbiasedness, we have

$$E[\hat{S}(x) \,|\, \{n'\}] \;=\; p_0 \cdot p_1 \cdot \cdots \cdot p_{x-1} \;=\; S(x). \qquad (6.53)$$

Thus we see that $\hat{S}(x)$ is unbiased under our pair of assumptions.

6.5.2 *Variance of $\hat{S}(x)$*

Again we note that this variance is conditional on the set of exposures, and we reflect this in the notation $\mathrm{Var}[\hat{S}(x) \,|\, \{n_i'\}]$.

Proceeding from first principles,

$$\mathrm{Var}\Big[\hat{S}(x)\,|\,\{n_i'\}\Big] \;=\; E\Big[\hat{S}(x)^2\,|\,\{n_i'\}\Big] - \left(E\Big[\hat{S}(x)\,|\,\{n_i'\}\Big]\right)^2 \qquad (6.54)$$

$$= \; E\Big[\hat{p}_0^2 \cdot \hat{p}_1^2 \cdot \cdots \cdot \hat{p}_{x-1}^2 \,|\, \{n_i'\}\Big] - \left(E\Big[\hat{p}_0 \cdot \hat{p}_1 \cdot \cdots \cdot \hat{p}_{x-1}\,|\,\{n_i'\}\Big]\right)^2$$

by the definition of $\hat{S}(x)$ given by (6.51). The independence assumption then allows us to write (6.54) as

$$\mathrm{Var}\Big[\hat{S}(x)\,|\,\{n_i'\}\Big] = \prod_{i=0}^{x-1} E\Big[\hat{p}_i^2\,|\,\{n_i'\}\Big] - \left[\prod_{i=0}^{x-1} E\Big[\hat{p}_i\,|\,\{n_i'\}\Big]\right]^2. \qquad (6.55)$$

Now for each $\hat{p}_i$, $\mathrm{Var}(\hat{p}_i\,|\,\{n_i'\}) = E[\hat{p}_i^2\,|\,\{n_i\}] - (E[\hat{p}_i\,|\,\{n_i'\}])^2$, so that $E[\hat{p}_i^2\,|\,\{n_i'\}] = \mathrm{Var}(\hat{p}_i\,|\,\{n_i'\}) + (E[\hat{p}_i\,|\,\{n_i'\}])^2$. But since $\hat{p}_i$ is taken to be an unbiased binomial proportion, the first moment is

$$E\Big[\hat{p}_i\,|\,\{n_i'\}\Big] \;=\; p_i, \qquad (6.56)$$

and the second moment is

$$E\Big[\hat{p}_i^2\,|\,\{n_i'\}\Big] \;=\; \frac{p_i q_i}{n_i'} + p_i^2 \;=\; (p_i)^2 \cdot \left(\frac{q_i}{p_i n_i'} + 1\right). \qquad (6.57)$$

Substituting (6.56) and (6.57) into (6.55), we have

$$\text{Var}\left[\hat{S}(x) \,|\, \{n_i'\}\right] = \prod_{i=0}^{x-1} (p_i)^2 \cdot \left(\frac{q_i}{p_i n_i'}+1\right) - \left[\prod_{i=0}^{x-1} p_i\right]^2$$

$$= \left[\prod_{i=0}^{x-1} p_i\right]^2 \cdot \prod_{i=0}^{x-1} \left(\frac{q_i}{p_i n_i'}+1\right) - \left[\prod_{i=0}^{x-1} p_i\right]^2$$

$$= \left[S(x)\right]^2 \cdot \left[\prod_{i=0}^{x-1} \left(\frac{q_i}{p_i n_i'}+1\right) - 1\right], \qquad (6.58)$$

since $S(x) = p_0 \cdot p_1 \cdots p_{x-1} = \prod_{i=0}^{x-1} p_i$.

The exact expression for the conditional variance of $\hat{S}(x)$, given by (6.58), is sometimes approximated in the following manner. Expanding the product of the binomial terms, we obtain

$$\prod_{i=0}^{x-1} \left(\frac{q_i}{p_i n_i'}+1\right) = \left(1+\frac{q_0}{p_0 n_0'}\right)\left(1+\frac{q_1}{p_1 n_1'}\right)\cdots\left(1+\frac{q_{x-1}}{p_{x-1} n_{x-1}'}\right)$$

$$= 1 + \frac{q_0}{p_0 n_0'} + \frac{q_1}{p_1 n_1'} + \cdots + \frac{q_{x-1}}{p_{x-1} n_{x-1}'} + \text{(higher order terms)}.$$

Since these second and higher order terms are quite small, we ignore them, and approximate $\prod_{i=0}^{x-1}\left(\frac{q_i}{p_i n_i'}+1\right)$ by $1+\sum_{i=0}^{x-1}\frac{q_i}{p_i n_i'}$. Thus (6.58) is approximated by

$$\text{Var}\left[\hat{S}(x) \,|\, \{n_i'\}\right] \approx \left[S(x)\right]^2 \cdot \sum_{i=0}^{x-1} \frac{q_i}{p_i n_i'}. \qquad (6.59)$$

This formula for the conditional variance of $\hat{S}(x)$ is known as Greenwood's formula (see Greenwood [28]). Since the terms which we ignored were all positive, Greenwood's approximation understates the true value of this variance.

Greenwood's approximation to the variance can also be derived by the method of statistical differentials, described in Section 2.6. We note that $\hat{S}(x)$ is a function of the x random variables $\hat{p}_0, \cdots, \hat{p}_{x-1}$, specifically, the product of them. Thus formula (2.80), extended from two to x random variables, can be used to approximate the variance of $\hat{S}(x)$. Because the $\hat{p}_i$'s are conditionally independent, then all covariance terms in (2.80) are zero.

The general term in (2.80) is the derivative of $\hat{S}(x)$ with respect to $\hat{p}_i$, evaluated at $\hat{p}_j = p_j$ (i.e., the mean of $\hat{p}_j$), for $j = 0,1,\cdots,x-1$, squared, times $Var(\hat{p}_i)$. Thus

$$Var\left[\hat{S}(x) \mid \{n'_i\}\right] = \sum_{i=0}^{x-1}\left(\frac{\partial}{\partial \hat{p}_i}\hat{S}(x)\Big|_{\hat{p}_j=p_j}\right)^2 \cdot Var(\hat{p}_i) . \qquad (6.60)$$

The simplification of (6.60) into (6.59) is left as an exercise.

EXAMPLE 6.10 : In a study using a moment estimation approach, we observe the following numbers of deaths in estimation interval (x, x+1], based on the given exposure amounts.

Interval	Deaths	Exposure
(0,1]	10	1040
(1,2]	8	1120
(2,3]	7	1191
(3,4]	7	1307
(4,5]	8	1612

Estimate S(5) and $Var[\hat{S}(5) \mid \{n'_i\}]$ from this sample data.

SOLUTION : From the sample data we obtain the following:

i	n'_i	$\hat{q}_i$	$\hat{p}_i$	$\hat{p}_i n'_i$	$\hat{q}_i / \hat{p}_i n'_i$
0	1040	10/1040	1030/1040	1030	9.335×10^{-6}
1	1120	8/1120	1112/1120	1112	6.423×10^{-6}
2	1191	7/1191	1184/1191	1184	4.964×10^{-6}
3	1307	7/1307	1300/1307	1300	4.120×10^{-6}
4	1612	8/1612	1604/1612	1604	3.094×10^{-6}

Then $\hat{S}(5) = \hat{p}_0 \cdot \hat{p}_1 \cdot \hat{p}_2 \cdot \hat{p}_3 \cdot \hat{p}_4 = .96747$. The variance is estimated as $(.96747)^2$ $[(1.000009335)(1.000006423)(1.000004964)(1.000004120)(1.000003094) - 1]$, which is $(.96747)^2 \cdot (27.93631 \times 10^{-6}) = .000026148336$. If the Greenwood approximation to (6.58) is used, the approximate estimated variance is $(.96747)^2 \cdot [(9.335 + 6.423 + 4.964 + 4.120 + 3.094) \times 10^{-6}]$, which is $(.96747)^2 \cdot (27.936 \times 10^{-6}) = .000026148046$. This gives us a good picture of the small understatement inherent in the Greenwood approximation.

6.6 *SUMMARY*

Most of the estimators for q_x (or for $q'^{(d)}_x$ in double-decrement notation) derived in this chapter are in the form of a ratio of observed deaths over a measure of exposure from which those deaths arose. In addition we noted that an estimator for m_x (or $m_x^{\prime(d)}$ in double-decrement notation) is also in that ratio form, and this quantity is an estimator for μ, the constant force over $(x, x+1)$ as well. Therefore, much of this chapter is summarized according to the methods by which exposure may be calculated.

Recall that the ith life in the sample begins contributing exposure to the estimation interval $(x, x+1]$ at age $x+r_i$, $0 \le r_i < 1$, and is scheduled to cease contributing exposure to that interval at age $x+s_i$, $0 < s_i \le 1$, either by reaching the end of the interval, in which case $s_i = 1$, or by the intervention of the end of the observation period, in which case $s_i < 1$. It is possible that the ith life dies at age $x+t_i$, where, neccesarily, $t_i \le s_i$, or that it withdraws at age $x+t_i$, $t_i \le s_i$. If neither random event occurs, then person i is called an observed ender at $x+s_i$, if $s_i < 1$, or an interval survivor at $x+1$, if $s_i = 1$.

For each of the estimators of the general form $\dfrac{\text{Deaths}}{\text{Exposure}}$, Table 6.1 summarizes the determination of exposure.

TABLE 6.1

Estimator	Type of Exposure	Calculation of Exposure
$\hat{m}_x$, or (constant) $\hat{\mu}$	Exact	$s_i - r_i$ for observed enders and survivors $t_i - r_i$ for observed deaths and withdrawals
$\hat{q}_x$, by Hoem's moment approach	Scheduled	$s_i - r_i$ for observed enders and survivors $t_i - r_i$ for observed withdrawals $s_i - r_i$ for observed deaths
$\hat{q}_x$, by the actuarial approach	Actuarial	$s_i - r_i$ for observed enders and survivors $t_i - r_i$ for observed withdrawals $1 - r_i$ for observed deaths

In the single decrement case, the moment estimator is derived using the general approximation $_{b-a}q_{x+a} \approx (b-a) \cdot q_x$. Under Special Case B this approximation is the same as the hyperbolic assumption, and under Special Case C it is the same as the linear assumption.

The actuarial estimator is derived from a type of moment equation which naturally involves the function $_{1-u}q_{x+u}$. Thus it is natural to use the hyperbolic assumption indentity $_{1-u}q_{x+u} = (1-u) \cdot q_x$, commonly called the Balducci hypothesis in the actuarial literature.

Some investigation of the bias and the variance of moment and actuarial estimators was presented.

A different moment approach in the double-decrement environment that is more complex than either the actuarial or the Hoem approach is given by Equations (6.33a) and (6.33b) under uniform distributions, and by Equations (6.40a) and (6.40b) under exponential distributions. If a computer routine to solve these equations is readily available, they are an excellent approach to the estimation of $q'^{(d)}_x$ and $q'^{(w)}_x$. In particular, if Special Case A prevails, convenient solutions for $\hat{q}'^{(d)}_x$ and $\hat{q}'^{(w)}_x$ are available.

A different moment approach for Special Case C in the single-decrement environment was presented in Section 6.2.6. This approach, called the Schwartz-Lazar estimator, is used in clinical studies where the single-decrement Special Case C frequently arises.

Finally, as an overall observation on moment procedures, there seems to be no totally satisfactory way to deal with the presence of withdrawals in the estimation of $q'^{(d)}_x$. The actuarial approach makes use of a questionable moment relationship and the illogical hyperbolic assumption with its decreasing force of mortality over $(x, x+1)$. Hoem's approach requires the assumption of a mystical "scheduled withdrawal age," and the convenient assumption that no deaths would otherwise have been withdrawals. The more analytical moment approach requires a numerical solution of the pair of moment equations.

In light of these difficulties, and since random withdrawals occur frequently in actuarial and other mortality estimation problems, moment approaches are not generally recommended. We will see in the next chapter that maximum likelihood procedures, although still requiring simplifying assumptions at times, are generally superior to moment approaches.

EXERCISES

6.1 Introduction;
6.2 Moment Estimation in a Single-Decrement Environment

6-1. Find an expression for $_{s-r}q_{x+r}$, in terms of q_x, under the linear assumption for ℓ_{x+s}.

6-2. Find an expression for $_{s-r}q_{x+r}$, in terms of q_x, under the hyperbolic assumption for ℓ_{x+s}.

6-3. Consider the approximation $_{s-r}q_{x+r} \approx (s-r) \cdot q_x$.
(a) Show that this implies a linear ℓ_{x+s} if $r = 0$.
(b) Show that this implies a hyperbolic ℓ_{x+s} if $s = 1$.

(c) Show that there exists no decreasing ℓ_{x+s} function for which $_{s-r}q_{x+r} = (s-r)\cdot q_x$ for all r and s. (For this reason, this relationship does not represent a mortality distribution assumption in the same sense as is true for the linear, exponential, and hyperbolic assumptions.)

6-4. Show that the expression for $_{s-r}q_{x+r}$ in terms of q_x, under each of the linear, exponential and hyperbolic assumptions for ℓ_{x+s}, reduces to $(s-r)\cdot q_x$ if quadratic and higher powers of q_x are ignored.

6-5. Suppose, of the n_x persons who contribute to $(x, x+1]$, k_x of them have $r_i = r$, a constant, and the remaining $(n_x - k_x)$ have $r_i = 0$. Suppose all n_x have $s_i = 1$. Derive the moment estimator of q_x.

6-6. Over the estimation interval $(x, x+1]$, the central rate of mortality is estimated as $\hat{m}_x = .015$. There were two observed deaths in the interval, one at age $x+\frac{1}{2}$ and one at age $x+\frac{1}{3}$, and both deaths had $s_i = 1$. Find the moment estimate of q_x.

6-7. Show that estimator (6.7) for Special Case A is unbiased.

6-8. (a) Show that estimator (6.13) for Special Case C is unbiased under the linear assumption for ℓ_{x+s}.
      (b) If the force of mortality were actually constant over $(x, x+1)$, what is the bias in estimator (6.13)?

6-9. Find exact expressions for the variances of each of the following estimators:
      (a) Estimator (6.7)
      (b) Estimator (6.10)
      (c) Estimator (6.13)

Exercises 6-10 through 6-12 relate to the Schwartz-Lazar moment estimator described in Section 6.2.6.

6-10. Suppose all c_x persons have a common scheduled ending age of $x+s$. Find an expression for α under each of the following assumptions for ℓ_{x+s}:
       (a) Uniform   (b) Exponential   (c) Hyperbolic

6-11. Now suppose the c_x scheduled enders have scheduled ending ages that are distributed over (x, x+1] with PDF g(u) and CDF G(u).

(a) Show that, in general, $\alpha = \dfrac{\displaystyle\int_0^1 {}_tP_x\mu_{x+t}\,[1-G(t)]\,dt}{\displaystyle\int_0^1 {}_tP_x\mu_{x+t}\,dt}$.

(b) Find the expression for α if g(u) = 1 (i.e., if U has a uniform distribution over (x, x+1)), and if the mortality assumption is a linear ℓ_{x+s}.

(c) Repeat part (b) assuming that U has a uniform distribution, but the mortality assumption is an exponential ℓ_{x+s}.

6-12. Find an estimator of q_x by eliminating α from equations (6.25) and (6.26). (This is the reduced sample estimator proposed by Drolette [20].)

6.3 Moment Estimation in a Double-Decrement Environment

6-13. A traditional formula to approximate $q_x'^{(d)}$ from $q_x^{(d)}$ and $q_x^{(w)}$ is

$q_x'^{(d)} \approx \dfrac{q_x^{(d)}}{1 - \frac{1}{2} \cdot q_x^{(w)}}$. Use this relationship, along with (6.31a) and

(6.31b) to estimate $q_x'^{(d)}$.

6-14. Solve equations (6.34a) and (6.34b) for $\hat{q}_x'^{(w)}$.

6-15. Assuming grouped Special Case B prevails, with $r_i = r$ for all i, solve equations (6.33a) and (6.33b) for (a) $\hat{q}_x'^{(d)}$, and (b) $\hat{q}_x'^{(w)}$.

6-16. Assuming grouped Special Case C prevails, with $s_i = s$ for all i, solve equations (6.33a) and (6.33b) for (a) $\hat{q}_x'^{(d)}$, and (b) $\hat{q}_x'^{(w)}$.

6-17. Solve equations (6.41a) and (6.41b) for $\hat{q}_x'^{(w)}$.

6-18. Assuming grouped Special Case B prevails, with $r_i = r$ for all i, solve equations (6.40a) and (6.40b) for (a) $\hat{q}_x'^{(d)}$, and (b) $\hat{q}_x'^{(w)}$.

6-19. Assuming grouped Special Case C prevails, with $s_i = s$ for all i, solve equations (6.40a) and (6.40b) for (a) $\hat{q}_x'^{(d)}$, and (b) $\hat{q}_x'^{(w)}$.

6-20. Suppose 100 persons come under observation at age x, and an additional 30 persons come under observation at age $x+\frac{1}{2}$. There are 2 deaths in $(x, x+1]$. Solve equation (6.16) for $\hat{q}_x$, under each of the hyperbolic, linear, and exponential assumptions.

6-21. A study sample has 10,000 persons at age x. There are 1000, 100, and 10 intermediate entrants at ages $x+\frac{1}{4}$, $x+\frac{1}{2}$, and $x+\frac{3}{4}$, respectively, and 3730 deaths in $(x, x+1]$. If μ_{x+t} is constant for $0 < t < 1$, find the moment estimator of q_x.

6.4 The Actuarial Approach to Moment Estimation

6-22. A group of 100 insureds are observed for a period of one year. During the year there are two deaths and six withdrawals. Deaths and withdrawals occur centrally in the year. Estimate the annual central rate of withdrawal, m^w, and the annual probability of withdrawal, q^w, by the actuarial approach.

6-23. A study over the period January 1, 1980 to December 31, 1981 yields the following information:

Individual	Date of Entry	Date of Death	Date of Withdrawal
V	Jan. 1, 1980		September 30, 1981
W	Jan. 1, 1981	June 30, 1981	
X	Jan. 1, 1980		March 31, 1980
Y	July 1, 1980		
Z	??		December 31, 1980

The estimation interval is one year. The central rate m_0 is estimated by $\hat{m}_0 = .3\dot{3}$. Using the traditional actuarial estimator, estimate q_0.

6-24. Ten individuals were observed for all or part of the two-year period following attainment of age 100. Five persons survived to age 102. One person withdrew at .75 of the two-year period. Four persons died, at durations .20, .55, .70 and .80 of the two-year period. Estimate $_2m_{100}$.

6-25. Suppose n lives come under observation at age x+a, and will leave observation at age x+b, $0 \le a < b \le 1$, unless death intervenes. Let d be the number of deaths that do intervene.
    (a) Verify the moment equation $n \cdot {}_{b-a}q_{x+a} = d$.

(b) Show that $_{b-a}q_{x+a} = {_{1-a}q_{x+a}} - {_{b-a}p_{x+a}} \cdot {_{1-b}q_{x+b}}$.

(c) Substitute (b) into (a), make the hyperbolic assumption substitution for $_{1-a}q_{x+a}$ and $_{1-b}q_{x+b}$, and reach the moment equation $n(1-a) \cdot q_x - n \cdot {_{b-a}p_{x+a}} \cdot (1-b) \cdot q_x = d$.

(d) Note that $n \cdot {_{b-a}p_{x+a}}$ is the *expected* number of survivors at age x+b. Substitute for it (n−d), the *actual* number of survivors in the sample, and solve the resulting equation for the traditional actuarial estimator. (This derivation of the actuarial estimator is given by Broffitt and Klugman [13].)

6-26. In a Special Case C study, there are c_x scheduled enders at age x+s out of n_x alive at age x, of which e_x survive to age x+s and are thus observed enders.

(a) What is the expected number of deaths to occur in (x, x+1] out of the n_x beginners?

(b) What is the expected number of deaths to occur in (x+s, x+1] to persons who have left the sample
  (i) conditional on being alive at age x?
  (ii) conditional on the number actually leaving the sample at age x+s?

(c) Equate (a) − (b) to the number of observed deaths. Solve the equation using the linear assumption under (b), (i) for the moment estimator, and using the hyperbolic assumption under (b), (ii) for the actuarial estimator.

(d) Compare our alternatives (b), (i) and (b), (ii) with the derivation in Exercise 6-25.

6-27. Consider the Special Case C study of Exercise 6-26. Let D_n be the random variable for *all* deaths in (x, x+1] out of the n_x beginners, and let D_c be the random variable for the (unobservable) deaths in (x+s, x+1] of those who terminate observation at age x+s. Then $D_x = D_n - D_c$, and in Exercise 6-26 we found

$$E[D_x] = n_x \cdot q_x - c_x \cdot {_sp_x} \cdot {_{1-s}q_{x+s}} = n_x \cdot q_x - c_x(q_x - {_sq_x}),$$

which led to estimator (6.19).

(a) Is it true that $\text{Var}(D_x) = \text{Var}(D_n) + \text{Var}(D_c)$? Why?

(b) If X_1 and X_2 are nonindependent binomial random variables with parameters (n, p_1) and (c, p_2), respectively, with $c \leq n$, and where x_2 cannot exceed the smaller of c and x_1, then it can be shown that $\text{Cov}(X_1, X_2) = c \cdot p_2(1-p_1)$. Use this fact to derive $\text{Var}(D_x)$.

6-28. Show that, in a Special Case C study, $\hat{q}_x$ by the traditional actuarial approach cannot exceed unity, whereas $\hat{q}_x$ by the moment approach can.

6.5   Estimation of S(x)

6-29. Evaluate expression (6.60) to reach Greenwood's formula (6.59).

6-30. Explain by general reasoning why formula (2.80) produces the same approximation to $\text{Var}\left[\hat{S}(x)\,|\,\{n_i'\}\right]$ as does Greenwood's approximation.

CHAPTER 7

TABULAR SURVIVAL MODELS ESTIMATED
FROM INCOMPLETE DATA SAMPLES

MAXIMUM LIKELIHOOD PROCEDURES

7.1 INTRODUCTION

In this chapter we consider maximum likelihood estimation (MLE) as an alternative to the actuarial and other moment estimators developed in Chapter 6. It is assumed that the reader has a basic familiarity with MLE from a study of statistical estimation in general. Here we will be applying MLE theory specifically to estimate q_x over the basic interval (x, x+1], considering both single-decrement and double-decrement environments. As in Chapter 6, we will see that the single decrement environment is the more convenient one within which to estimate q_x.

In our moment approaches of Chapter 6 we were equating the expected number of deaths in (x, x+1] to the number actually observed. This meant that we needed only the observed *number* of deaths in (x, x+1], which we called d_x, and not the *age location* of those deaths within (x, x+1], Recall that we did make use of the specific ages at which a person began observation and was scheduled to end observation, or was observed to withdraw, but we never used the precise ages at death of the d_x group to estimate q_x.

In MLE, the precise age at death is information that can be incorporated into the estimation procedure if it is available. Thus we distinguish two important subdivisions of MLE: the situation in which precise age at death is used will be referred to as a *full data* situation; that in which only the number of deaths in the interval (x, x+1] is used will be referred to as a *partial data* situation. Note that the very nature of moment estimation calls for partial data only on the deaths, whereas maximum likelihood estimation can be based on either partial data or full data.

Thus we will find that an MLE problem will begin with a recognition of the available data, including the question of whether we have full data or partial data on the deaths. This information will lead us to the likelihood function. We will then need to make certain simplifying assumptions, such as mortality distribution assumptions, in order to solve the likelihood equation for $\hat{q}_x$.

The concept of scheduled exit age, $x+s_i$, for person i with respect to the estimation interval (x, x+1] will not play a major role in this chapter.

Maximum likelihood estimation of interval mortality probabilities is discussed in many other texts on survival analysis and survival model estimation. The work of Broffitt [12] is a particularly good one, and parts of this chapter are based on that work.

7.2 SINGLE-DECREMENT ENVIRONMENT, SPECIAL CASE A

We wish to start with this case as a way of obtaining familiarity with the maximum likelihood approach in the simplest possible situation. We can then deal with more complex situations knowing that the basic theory is comfortably understood.

7.2.1 *Partial Data*

As defined in Section 6.2.2, this situation simply states that, of n_x lives exactly age x, d_x of them die in (x, x+1], and $n_x - d_x$ survive to age x+1. We recognize this as a binomial model, so the likelihood is simply the binomial probability of obtaining the sample result actually obtained. That is,

$$L(q_x | n_x, d_x) \; = \; \frac{n_x!}{d_x!(n_x - d_x)!} \, (q_x)^{d_x} \, (1 - q_x)^{n_x - d_x}. \tag{7.1}$$

One of the basic properties of MLE is that any multiplicative constants can be ignored, and the same estimate of q_x will still result. When this is done, the likelihood is no longer the probability of the sample *per se*, but is proportional to it. Thus many writers prefer to write

$$L(q_x | n_x, d_x) \; \propto \; (q_x)^{d_x} \cdot (1 - q_x)^{n_x - d_x} , \tag{7.2}$$

where $\propto$ is read "is proportional to." We wish to take the point of view that it is just as reasonable to call the right side of (7.2) the likelihood itself, as to call it something to which the likelihood is proportional. Thus we would write simply

$$L(q_x | n_x, d_x) \; = \; (q_x)^{d_x} \cdot (1 - q_x)^{n_x - d_x}. \tag{7.3}$$

The notation $L(q_x | n_x, d_x)$ reminds us that the likelihood is a function of the unknown q_x, and that n_x and d_x are given values, namely those observed in the sample upon which our estimate of q_x is to be based. When there is no doubt as to the unknown and the given values, we will simply use L instead of $L(q_x | n_x, d_x)$. Finally, for convenience we will frequently suppress the subscript x. Thus we will write the likelihood for the Special Case A partial data situation as

$$L = q^d \cdot (1-q)^{n-d}. \tag{7.4}$$

The idea now is to find the value of q, called $\hat{q}$, which maximizes (7.4). Formally, if $\hat{q}$ exists, such that $L(\hat{q}) \geq L(q)$ for all other q, then $\hat{q}$ is the maximum likelihood estimator (MLE) of q.

To find $\hat{q}$ by the calculus technique of setting $\frac{dL}{dq} = 0$ would require an application of the product rule for differentiating (7.4). Although this is not difficult in this case, we will see that likelihood functions can become much more complex, and several applications of the product rule might be required. To avoid this, we take the natural log of L before differentiating. That is, we solve the equation $\frac{d}{dq} \ln L = 0$ for $\hat{q}$. The same value of $\hat{q}$ will result from solving this equation as from solving $\frac{dL}{dq} = 0$, since the natural log is a one-to-one monotonic transformation.

Thus we define the *log-likelihood*, ℓ, to be ln L, obtaining, in this case

$$\ell = \ln L = d \cdot \ln q + (n-d) \cdot \ln(1-q). \tag{7.5}$$

Then

$$\frac{d\ell}{dq} = \frac{d}{q} - \frac{n-d}{1-q} = 0 \tag{7.6}$$

is the likelihood equation which easily produces

$$\hat{q}_x = \frac{d_x}{n_x}, \tag{7.7}$$

which is the same as (6.7), already noted in Section 6.2.2 to be an MLE.

EXAMPLE 7.1 : Show that the same $\hat{q}_x$ will result for Special Case A partial data even if the log transformation is not used.
SOLUTION : We differentiate (7.4) to obtain

$$\frac{dL}{dq} = q^d[-(n-d)(1-q)^{n-d-1}] + (1-q)^{n-d}[dq^{d-1}] = 0,$$

so $d \cdot q^{d-1}(1-q)^{n-d} = (n-d)q^d(1-q)^{n-d-1}$, or $d(1-q) = (n-d)q$, which is the same as (7.6).

EXAMPLE 7.2 : Show that $\hat{q}_x$ defined by (7.7) maximizes, rather than minimizes, (7.5).

SOLUTION : Since $\dfrac{d\ell}{dq} = \dfrac{d}{q} - \dfrac{n-d}{1-q}$, then $\dfrac{d^2\ell}{dq^2} = -\dfrac{d}{q^2} - \dfrac{n-d}{(1-q)^2}$. Since d, $(n-d)$, q^2 and $(1-q)^2$ are all positive, then the second derivative is negative, so $\hat{q}_x$ maximizes ln L.

7.2.2 *Full Data*

Now we assume that we have the precise age at death for each of the d_x deaths in the interval. Since this age is different for each death, we consider them individually, and take the product of each death's contribution to the likelihood function.

The likelihood for the ith death is given by the probability density function for death at that particular age, given alive at age x. That is, for death at age x_i,

$$L_i = f(x_i | X > x) = \frac{f(x_i)}{S(x)} = \frac{S(x_i) \cdot \lambda(x_i)}{S(x)} \qquad (7.8)$$

is the contribution to L of the ith death. If we let $s_i = x_i - x$ be the time of the ith death within $(x, x+1]$, where $0 < s_i \le 1$, then we have

$$L_i = \frac{S(x+s_i) \cdot \lambda(x+s_i)}{S(x)} = {}_{s_i}p_x \mu_{x+s_i}, \qquad (7.9)$$

in standard actuarial notation. The contribution to L for all deaths combined is

$$\prod_{i=1}^{d} {}_{s_i}p_x \mu_{x+s_i}, \qquad (7.10)$$

which is commonly written as $\prod_{\mathfrak{D}} {}_{s_i}p_x \mu_{x+s_i}$, and read as "multiplied over all deaths".

Of course the $n_x - d_x$ survivors contribute $(p_x)^{n_x - d_x} = (1-q_x)^{n_x - d_x}$ to L, so we have the total likelihood

$$L = (1-q_x)^{n_x - d_x} \cdot \prod_{\mathfrak{D}} {}_{s_i}p_x \mu_{x+s_i} \qquad (7.11)$$

for our Special Case A full data situation.

To solve (7.11) for $\hat{q}_x$ it is necessary to make a distribution assumption which will express $_{s_i}p_x\mu_{x+s_i}$ in terms of q_x. We will consider two such assumptions.

Under the linear, or uniform, assumption, we find from (3.58) that for all s_i, $0 < s_i \leq 1$, $_{s_i}p_x\mu_{x+s_i} = q_x$. Then the contribution to L would be q_x for all d_x deaths, so the term $\prod_{\mathcal{D}} {}_{s_i}p_x\mu_{x+s_i}$ in (7.11) becomes $(q_x)^{d_x}$, and (7.11) becomes $q^d \cdot (1-q)^{n-d}$, which is (7.4). Thus (7.11) also leads to estimator (7.7). That is, full data Special Case A, evaluated under the uniform distribution assumption, produces the same estimator as does the partial data Special Case A, which requires no assumption for its evaluation.

Under the exponential assumption, we recall that μ_{x+s_i} is a constant, namely $\mu = -\ln p_x$, and, from (3.64), $_{s_i}p_x = (p_x)^{s_i} = e^{-\mu s_i}$, so that (7.11) becomes

$$L = (p_x)^{n_x - d_x} \cdot \prod_{\mathcal{D}} (p_x)^{s_i} \cdot \mu$$

$$= \mu^d \cdot \exp\left[-\mu(n-d) - \mu \cdot \sum_{\mathcal{D}} s_i\right]. \tag{7.12}$$

Then

$$\ell = \ln L = d \cdot \ln \mu - \mu\left[(n-d) + \sum_{\mathcal{D}} s_i\right], \tag{7.13}$$

and

$$\frac{d\ell}{d\mu} = \frac{d}{\mu} - \left[(n-d) + \sum_{\mathcal{D}} s_i\right] = 0, \tag{7.14}$$

which is easily solved for

$$\hat{\mu} = \frac{d}{(n-d) + \sum_{\mathcal{D}} s_i}. \tag{7.15}$$

The denominator of (7.15) is the exact exposure mentioned earlier in the text. Thus (7.15) estimates m_x, which is the same as μ under the exponential (constant force) assumption. In turn,

$$\hat{q}_x = 1 - e^{-\hat{\mu}} \tag{7.16}$$

is the MLE of q_x. Since q_x and μ have a one-to-one correspondence, we can write (7.11) in terms of μ, solve for the MLE $\hat{\mu}$, and then obtain the MLE $\hat{q}_x$ by (7.16). Alternatively, and more mathematically complex, we could write (7.11) in terms of q_x and proceed to the same $\hat{q}_x$. The demonstration of this is left as Exercise 7.4.

7.2.3 *Summary of Special Case A*

We have derived two Special Case A MLE's in this section: (7.15) for the full data, exponential distribution, and (7.7) for both the full data, uniform distribution and the partial data situations. We have shown the mathematics of these derivations in considerable detail to make the reader feel comfortable with the MLE approach. In future derivations we will not need to show each step in such detail.

We now want to show an alternate way to write the likelihood function for the full data model. Let us define t_i to be the time at which the ith person in n_x ceases observation, either by reaching age x+1 (so that $t_i=1$ and person i is a survivor), or by death (so that $t_i \leq 1$ and person i is a death). Define δ_i to be an indicator variable where

$$\delta_i = \begin{cases} 1 & \text{if person i dies in } (x, x+1] \\ 0 & \text{otherwise} \end{cases} . \tag{7.17}$$

Then the contribution to L by the ith person in n_x is

$$L_i = {}_{t_i}p_x \left(\mu_{x+t_i}\right)^{\delta_i} . \tag{7.18}$$

The structure of (7.18) shows that $L_i = {}_{t_i}p_x \mu_{x+t_i}$ if the ith person is a death (since $\delta_i=1$), and $L_i = {}_{t_i}p_x$ if the ith person is a survivor (since $\delta_i=0$). Of course $t_i=1$ for all i for which $\delta_i=0$ in Special Case A, so it might not seem as if this approach to writing L_i has any advantage in this case. But we are introducing it at this time, since we will use it extensively to write L_i for more complex cases where its advantage will be more easily seen.

 EXAMPLE 7.3 :   Of 100 lives exactly age x, 2 are observed to die in (x, x+1] and 98 survive to age x+1. The deaths occur at precise ages x+.2 and x+.6.   Estimate q_x assuming the force of mortality is constant over (x, x+1].

 SOLUTION : From (7.15), $\hat{\mu} = \dfrac{2}{98+.2+.6} = \dfrac{5}{247}$ is the MLE of μ when μ is constant. Then $\hat{q}_x = 1 - e^{-5/247} = .020039$.

7.3 *SINGLE-DECREMENT ENVIRONMENT, GENERAL CASE*

We will now use the ideas developed in Section 7.2.3 to develop a general form for the likelihood function in a single-decrement environment, and then show how Special Cases B and C, defined in Section 6.2.2, are contained in the general form. Of course Special Case A is contained in the general form as well.

7.3.1 *General Form for Full Data*

We recall that n_x is the total number of persons in the sample who contribute to the estimation interval $(x, x+1]$, and $x+r_i$ is the age at which the ith person enters $(x, x+1]$, $0 \leq r_i < 1$. Let $x+t_i$ be the age at which the ith person leaves $(x, x+1]$, $0 < t_i \leq 1$, whether as a scheduled, and observed, ender, as an interval survivor, or as a death. Let δ_i be the indicator variable for person i defined by (7.17). Then if $t_i = 1$ and $\delta_i = 0$, person i is a survivor; if $t_i < 1$ and $\delta_i = 0$, person i is an observed ender; if $t_i \leq 1$ and $\delta_i = 1$, person i is a death.

As of age $x+r_i$, person i is *scheduled* to leave observation at some age not later than $x+1$, but the possibility of prior death implies that the age at which observation actually does cease is a random result. Thus t_i is the realization of a random variable T_i. On the other hand, r_i, the time of entry, is not a random variable.

We can now see that if $r_i = 0$ for all i, we have either Special Case A or Special Case C. Similarly, if $t_i = 1$ for all i for which $\delta_i = 0$ (i.e., for all i who do not die), we have either Special Case A or Special Case B. This is summarized in Table 7.1.

TABLE 7.1

	$t_i = 1$ for *all* i for which $\delta_i = 0$	$t_i < 1$ for *some* i for which $\delta_i = 0$
$r_i = 0$ for *all* i	Special Case A	Special Case C
$r_i > 0$ for *some* i	Special Case B	General Case

The general form of the contribution to L by person i is

$$L_i = {}_{t_i-r_i}p_{x+r_i}(\mu_{x+t_i})^{\delta_i}, \tag{7.19}$$

since, if $\delta_i=0$, the likelihood is merely the probability of survival from $x+r_i$ to $x+t_i$, and if $\delta_i=1$, it is the density function for death at $x+t_i$ given alive at $x+r_i$. The overall likelihood is

$$L = \prod_{i=1}^{n} {}_{t_i-r_i}p_{x+r_i} (\mu_{x+t_i})^{\delta_i}. \tag{7.20}$$

To evaluate (7.20) we must make a distribution assumption. We will again consider two cases.

7.3.2 *Full Data, Exponential Distribution*

Under the exponential (constant force) assumption, we find

$$L = (\mu)^d \cdot \prod_{i=1}^{n} e^{-(t_i-r_i)\mu}, \tag{7.21}$$

so

$$\ell = \ln L = d \cdot \ln \mu - \mu \cdot \sum_{i=1}^{n} (t_i-r_i), \tag{7.22}$$

and it is easy to see that $\frac{d\ell}{d\mu} = 0$ produces

$$\hat{\mu} = \frac{d_x}{\sum\limits_{i=1}^{n} (t_i-r_i)}. \tag{7.23}$$

Estimator (7.23) is of the same form as estimator (7.15), namely the ratio of d_x to the exact exposure of the sample, which is the sample central rate. (This will be the result for all cases of full data evaluated under the exponential assumption.) Thus (7.23) is the general full data MLE, and Special Cases A, B, and C are all contained within it.

7.3.3 *Full Data, Uniform Distribution*

To evaluate (7.20) under the uniform distribution assumption, we first note that

$$_{t_i-r_i}p_{x+r_i} \;=\; 1 - {}_{t_i-r_i}q_{x+r_i} \;=\; 1 - \frac{(t_i-r_i)q_x}{1-r_i\cdot q_x} \;=\; \frac{1-t_i\cdot q_x}{1-r_i\cdot q_x}, \qquad (7.24)$$

and

$$\mu_{x+t_i} \;=\; \frac{q_x}{1-t_i\cdot q_x}. \qquad (7.25)$$

When (7.24) and (7.25) are substituted into (7.20), we find that (7.20) will contain q_x for each death, $(1-t_i\cdot q_x)$ for each interval survivor ($t_i=1$) and observed ender ($t_i<1$), and $(1-r_i\cdot q_x)^{-1}$ for everyone. Thus (7.20) becomes

$$L \;=\; (q_x)^d \cdot \prod_{i=1}^{n} (1-r_i\cdot q_x)^{-1} \cdot \prod_{\mathscr{S}\&\mathscr{E}} (1-t_i\cdot q_x). \qquad (7.26)$$

Then $\dfrac{d}{dq}\ln L = 0$ produces

$$\frac{d_x}{q_x} + \sum_{i=1}^{n} \frac{r_i}{1-r_i\cdot q_x} - \sum_{\mathscr{S}\&\mathscr{E}} \frac{t_i}{1-t_i\cdot q_x} \;=\; 0. \qquad (7.27)$$

In general, equation (7.27) must be solved for $\hat{q}_x$ by iteration. We note that if r_i were different for all n_x persons, and if t_i were different for all $n_x - d_x$ non-deaths, then there would be $1+n+(n-d) = 2n-d+1$ distinct denominators in (7.27), producing an equation in q_x of degree $2n-d$. Of course we expect many $r_i=0$ and many $t_i=1$, so the degree of the polynomial will not be that big.

Since (7.27) is a polynomial in q_x, we can see that a convenient solution is possible if that polynomial is of degree one or two. How can this be accomplished?

If $r_i=0$ for all n_x persons in the sample, and if $t_i=1$ for all $n_x - d_x$ non-deaths, then we have Special Case A, and (7.27) becomes (7.6), which has two terms, so it solves linearly for estimator (7.7).

If $t_i=1$ for all $n_x - d_x$ non-deaths, $r_i=0$ for b_x of the n_x persons in the sample, and $r_i>0$ for the remaining $k_x = n_x - b_x$, then we have Special Case B. If $r_i=r$, a constant, for all k_x persons, then we have the grouped Special Case B defined in Section 6.2.4. Then (7.27) becomes

$$\frac{d}{q} + k\left(\frac{r}{1-r\cdot q}\right) - (n-d)\left(\frac{1}{1-q}\right) \;=\; 0, \qquad (7.28)$$

from which we obtain the quadratic equation

$$r(n-k)q^2 - (n-rk+rd)q + d = 0, \qquad (7.29)$$

which leads to the result

$$\hat{q}_x = \frac{b - \sqrt{b^2 - 4r(n_x - k_x)d_x}}{2r(n_x - k_x)}, \qquad (7.30)$$

where $b = n - rk_x + rd_x$. The negative radical is used in (7.30) because the positive radical would result in $\hat{q}_x > 1$. This is also true for formulas (7.32) and (7.70).

Similarly, for grouped Special Case C with common ending age x+s for all scheduled enders, (7.27) will again become quadratic. This time $r_i = 0$ for all n_x persons in the sample, $t_i = s$ for all e_x observed enders, and $t_i = 1$ for the $n_x - e_x - d_x$ interval survivors. Then (7.27) becomes

$$\frac{d}{q} - e\left(\frac{s}{1 - s \cdot q}\right) - (n - e - d)\left(\frac{1}{1 - q}\right) = 0, \qquad (7.31)$$

which leads to the result

$$\hat{q}_x = \frac{b - \sqrt{b^2 - 4sn_x d_x}}{2sn_x}, \qquad (7.32)$$

where $b = n_x - (1-s)e_x + sd_x$. Note that (7.32) is similar to (7.30), with r replaced by s, k replaced by $-e$, and $n-k$ replaced by n.

To complete our analysis of (7.27), we note that in the general case, even if all k_x entrants with $r_i > 0$ are at a common entry age x+r and all e_x observed enders are at a common exit age x+s, the presence of an $n_x - k_x$ group at $r_i = 0$ and an $n_x - e_x - d_x$ group at $t_i = 1$ as well, means that there are four distinct denominators in (7.27), which produces a cubic equation in q_x.

EXAMPLE 7.4 : (a) For the estimation interval (x, x+1], suppose $b_x = 5$ persons enter at age x, $k_x = 3$ persons enter at age x+.25, $e_x = 2$ persons are observed enders at age x+.50, one death occurs at age x+.25, and a second death occurs at age x+.75. Calculate $\hat{q}_x$ under the exponential assumption. (b) Let the $k_x = 3$ entrants occur at age x rather than age x+.25, and calculate $\hat{q}_x$ under the uniform assumption.

SOLUTION : (a) Since the ordered pair (r_i, t_i) is not given for each person, we find the exact exposure of the sample by crediting each person with exposure to age x+1, and then deducting the portion of credited exposure not realized. In this manner the exact exposure of the sample is found to be $5 + .75(3) - .50(2) - .75 - .25 = 5.25$. Under full data, exponential,

$$\hat{\mu} = \frac{\text{Deaths}}{\text{Exact Exposure}} = \frac{2}{5.25} = \frac{8}{21}. \text{ Then } \hat{q}_x = 1 - e^{-8/21} = .31678.$$

(b) We now have Special Case C, with n=8, d=2, and e=2 with all enders at age x+$\frac{1}{2}$. Then (7.32) gives $\hat{q}_x = \dfrac{8 - \sqrt{64 - 32}}{8} = .29289.$

7.3.4 Partial Data, Special Case C

Suppose all n_x persons who enter (x, x+1] do so at exact age x (i.e., $r_i = 0$), and suppose that c_x of them have a common, or average, scheduled ending age of x+s, $0 < s < 1$. The remaining $n_x - c_x$ are scheduled to remain in the sample to age x+1. This situation is illustrated in Figure 6.3.

We note that c_x and $n_x - c_x$ form separate binomial samples. A member of c_x can die before age x+s, or can survive to that age and exit observation; a member of $n_x - c_x$ can die before age x+1, or survive to that age and exit observation there. Let d'_x be the observed number of deaths out of the c_x sample, and let d''_x be the observed number of deaths out of the $n_x - c_x$ sample, so that the total number of observed deaths is $d_x = d'_x + d''_x$. Note also that $e_x = c_x - d'_x$ is the observed number of enders at age x+s.

The contribution to the likelihood of the c_x sample is

$$L_c = ({}_sq_x)^{d'} \cdot (1 - {}_sq_x)^{c-d'} \tag{7.33}$$

and the contribution of the $n_x - c_x$ sample is

$$L_{n-c} = (q_x)^{d''} \cdot (1 - q_x)^{n-c-d''}. \tag{7.34}$$

Since the two groups are independent binomial samples, the overall likelihood is the product of L_c and L_{n-c}. Thus

$$L = ({}_sq_x)^{d'} \cdot (1 - {}_sq_x)^{c-d'} \cdot (q_x)^{d''} \cdot (1 - q_x)^{n-c-d''}. \tag{7.35}$$

If this likelihood is evaluated under the uniform assumption, so that ${}_sq_x = s \cdot q_x$, we find

$$L = (s)^{d'} \cdot (q_x)^{d'} \cdot (1 - s \cdot q_x)^{c-d'} \cdot (q_x)^{d''} \cdot (1 - q_x)^{n-c-d''}. \tag{7.36}$$

Dropping the multiplicative constant $s^{d'}$, and combining the two terms $q^{d''}$ and $q^{d'}$, we have

$$L = q^d \cdot (1 - s \cdot q)^{c-d'} \cdot (1 - q)^{n-c-d''}, \tag{7.37}$$

from which we obtain

$$\frac{d \ln L}{dq} = \frac{d}{q} - (c-d')\left(\frac{s}{1-s \cdot q}\right) - (n-c-d'')\left(\frac{1}{1-q}\right) = 0. \qquad (7.38)$$

But $c - d' = e$, and $n - c - d'' = n - c - (d-d') = n - d - e$, so we see that (7.38) is the same as (7.31), so estimator (7.32) will again result. Thus we have found that the grouped Special Case C MLE under the uniform assumption is the same whether full data or partial data is available with respect to the deaths.

If the likelihood given by (7.35) is evaluated under the exponential assumption, with $_sp_x = (p_x)^s$, we find

$$L = (1 - p_x{}^s)^{d'} \cdot (p_x{}^s)^{c-d'} \cdot (q_x)^{d''} \cdot (1 - q_x)^{n-c-d''}. \qquad (7.39)$$

Using $e = c - d'$, we see that the second factor in (7.39) can be written as $(p_x)^{se}$, and then combined with the last factor to produce

$$L = p^{se+n-c-d''} \cdot (1-p)^{d''} \cdot (1-p^s)^{d'}, \qquad (7.40)$$

from which we obtain

$$\frac{d \ln L}{dp} = \frac{se+n-c-d''}{p} - \frac{d''}{1-p} - \frac{d' \cdot sp^{s-1}}{1-p^s} = 0. \qquad (7.41)$$

The likelihood equation (7.41) will, in general, have to be solved by numerical methods for the MLE $\hat{p}_x$ (and hence $\hat{q}_x = 1 - \hat{p}_x$). A special case exists if $s = \frac{1}{2}$; equation (7.41) will then be quadratic in $x = p^{1/2}$ and can be solved for $\hat{p}_x$. The details are left as an exercise.

If the available information does not include the observed deaths d'_x and d''_x separately, nor show the subdivision of n_x into c_x and $n_x - c_x$, then a more intricate partial data likelihood is created. We assume that the data consists only of the facts that, out of n_x persons at age x, there were e_x observed enders at x+s, d_x observed deaths, and $n_x - e_x - d_x$ survivors at age x+1.

The expression

$$L = (q_x)^d \cdot (1 - q_x)^{n-e-d} \cdot (1 - {}_sq_x)^e \qquad (7.42)$$

is not entirely correct for the likelihood, since we know that not all of the d_x deaths had the entire interval (x, x+1] in which to die (although we don't know exactly how many did, and how many had only (x, x+s] in which to die and be observed).

The unknown proportion of n_x which are scheduled to exit at x+s can be incorporated into the random structure of the model. Let ϕ represent this unknown proportion; that is, $c_x = \phi \cdot n_x$. Then the probability of an observed death is $\phi \cdot {}_s q_x + (1-\phi) \cdot q_x$, and the first term of the likelihood would be $[\phi \cdot {}_s q_x + (1-\phi) \cdot q_x]^d$, rather than merely $(q_x)^d$.

We would then proceed to find the MLE of ϕ, as well as the MLE of q_x. Note that ϕ appears only in the first term of L. Since ln L is a decreasing function of ϕ, under both the uniform and the exponential distributions, it follows that ln L, and hence L, is maximized by $\phi=0$. Thus the same $\hat{q}_x$ which maximizes the correct likelihood will also maximize (7.42), so we may work from (7.42) anyway!

When evaluated under the uniform assumption, (7.42) is easily seen to be the same as (7.37), so estimator (7.32) again results.

When evaluated under the exponential assumption, a nice simplification occurs. We can write (7.42) as

$$L = (1-p_x)^d \cdot (p_x)^{\,n-e-d} \cdot (p_x)^{se} , \qquad (7.43)$$

and then combine the two terms in p_x to obtain

$$L = p^{n-d-(1-s)e} \cdot (1-p)^d . \qquad (7.44)$$

Then

$$\frac{d \ln L}{dp} = \frac{n-d-(1-s)e}{p} - \frac{d}{1-p} = 0 , \qquad (7.45)$$

which solves linearly for

$$\hat{q}_x = \frac{d_x}{n_x - (1-s)e_x} . \qquad (7.46)$$

We recognize (7.46) as the actuarial estimator for Special Case C, as described in Section 6.4.

EXAMPLE 7.5 : Out of $n_x = 14{,}200$ persons in a sample at age x, $c_x = 4400$ are scheduled to end at age $x+\frac{1}{4}$. We observe $d'_x = 360$ deaths, prior to age $x+\frac{1}{4}$ from the c_x sample, and $d''_x = 3439$ deaths, prior to age $x+1$ from the remaining $n_x - c_x$. Assuming that the force of mortality is constant over $(x, x+1)$, find the MLE of q_x.

SOLUTION : We have $c = 4400$, $n-c = 9800$, $d' = 360$, $d'' = 3439$, $s=\frac{1}{4}$. From (7.35), the likelihood is $L = (1-p)^{3439} \cdot (p)^{6361} \cdot (1-p^{\frac{1}{4}})^{360} \cdot (p^{\frac{1}{4}})^{4040}$, or $L = (p)^{7371} \cdot (1-p)^{3439} \cdot (1-p^{\frac{1}{4}})^{360}$, combining second and fourth terms.

The log-likelihood is $\ln L = 7371 \cdot \ln p + 3439 \cdot \ln(1-p) + 360 \cdot \ln(1-p^{\frac{1}{4}})$,

and the derivative equation is $\dfrac{d\ln L}{dp} = \dfrac{7371}{p} - \dfrac{3439}{1-p} - \dfrac{90p^{-\frac{3}{4}}}{1-p^{\frac{1}{4}}} = 0$. This leads

to $7371(1-p)(1-p^{\frac{1}{4}}) - 3439p(1-p^{\frac{1}{4}}) - 90p^{\frac{1}{4}}(1-p) = 0$, which can be written as $10{,}900x^5 - 10{,}810x^4 - 7461x + 7371 = 0$, where $x = p^{\frac{1}{4}}$. An iterative solution yields $\hat{x} = \hat{p}_x^{1/4} = .9$, so we have $\hat{q}_x = 1 - (\hat{p}_x^{1/4})^4 = .3439$.

7.3.5 *Special Case C with Random Censoring*

As an alternative to recording, and using, exact or average values of s_i, for the c_x persons with $0 < s_i < 1$, it is sometimes assumed that the values of s_i are randomly distributed over $(x, x+1]$. Then scheduled ending time is a random variable, S, and we let $g(s)$ denote its PDF. In survival data analysis, where termination of observation due to the ending of the observation period is called *censoring*, this structure is referred to as a *random censoring mechanism*.

To construct the likelihood for Special Case C with partial data, we need the probability that a person in c_x will die before the scheduled ending age. If a precise scheduled ending age is not used, and a random distribution of scheduled ending ages is assumed instead, then we must first calculate the marginal probability of death before scheduled ending age. If we let $\overline{q}_x$ denote this marginal probability, then

$$\overline{q}_x = 1 - \overline{p}_x = 1 - \int_0^1 g(s) \cdot {}_sp_x \, ds. \tag{7.47}$$

The integral in (7.47) shows that the marginal probability $\overline{p}_x$ is a weighted average value of ${}_sp_x$, where the sum of the weights is $\int_0^1 g(s)\,ds = 1$.

To evaluate (7.47), we must make a distribution assumption with respect to mortality, and specify the distribution of S as well. If we make the linear assumption for mortality, and the uniform distribution for S (so that $g(s) = 1$), then (7.47) evaluates to

$$\overline{q}_x = \tfrac{1}{2} \cdot q_x. \tag{7.48}$$

The Special Case C likelihood is

$$L = (q_x)^{d''} \cdot (1 - q_x)^{n-c-d''} \cdot (\overline{q}_x)^{d'} \cdot (1 - \overline{q}_x)^{c-d'} \tag{7.49}$$

under random censoring, as opposed to (7.35) for the likelihood when an average (fixed) value of s is assumed. Of course if (7.48) is used for $\bar{q}_x$, then (7.49) becomes the same as (7.35) evaluated under the uniform assumption with $s = \frac{1}{2}$, and the resulting MLE is given by estimator (7.32) with $s = \frac{1}{2}$.

The evaluation of (7.47) assuming other mortality distributions, and the resulting MLE's, is pursued in the exercises.

7.3.6 Summary of Single-Decrement MLE's

We have derived a general, full data, exponential distribution MLE, given by estimator (7.23), which, of course, is applicable to Special Cases A, B, and C as well.

Similarly, estimator (7.27) is the general, full data, uniform distribution MLE, with Special Cases A, B, and C versions given by (7.7), (7.30) and (7.32), respectively.

For partial data, we have developed results for Special Cases A and C only, under each of the exponential and uniform distributions. The partial data MLE's for Special Case B are derived analogously to those for Special Case C, and are left to the exercises. The general case, partial data, MLE's are considerably more complex, and are not pursued in this text.

7.4. DOUBLE-DECREMENT ENVIRONMENT

If both death and withdrawal are random events operating in the estimation interval $(x, x+1]$, then we seek to estimate $q_x = q_x'^{(d)}$ within a double-decrement environment. The basic mathematics and notation for double-decrement theory was presented in Section 5.3, and employed in Section 6.3 in connection with moment estimation. Now we will explore maximum likelihood estimation in a double-decrement environment.

7.4.1 General Form for Full Data

As before, let $x+r_i$ be the age at which person i enters $(x, x+1]$, $0 \le r_i < 1$, and let n_x be the total number of persons in the sample. Let $x+t_i$ be the age at which person i leaves $(x, x+1]$, $0 < t_i \le 1$, whether as an interval survivor $(t_i = 1)$, as an observed ender $(t_i < 1)$, or as a result of one of the random events death or withdrawal.

Thus each person is under observation from age $x+r_i$ to age $x+t_i$, and the probability of this is $_{t_i - r_i}p_{x+r_i}^{(\tau)}$. For interval survivors and enders, this "total survival" (i.e., neither dying nor withdrawing) is the contribution to the likelihood. For each death and withdrawal, the respective density functions, given by (5.15) and (5.16), are needed, so $_{t_i-r_i}\text{p}^{(\tau)}_{x+r_i}$ must be multiplied by the appropriate force. Thus the overall likelihood is

$$L = \prod_{i=1}^{n} {}_{t_i-r_i}\text{p}^{(\tau)}_{x+r_i} \cdot \prod_{\mathcal{D}} \mu^{(d)}_{x+t_i} \cdot \prod_{\mathcal{W}} \mu^{(w)}_{x+t_i} \qquad (7.50\text{a})$$

$$= \prod_{i=1}^{n} {}_{t_i-r_i}\text{p}^{(d)}_{x+r_i} \cdot \prod_{i=1}^{n} {}_{t_i-r_i}\text{p}^{(w)}_{x+r_i} \cdot \prod_{\mathcal{D}} \mu^{(d)}_{x+t_i} \cdot \prod_{\mathcal{W}} \mu^{(w)}_{x+t_i}. \qquad (7.50\text{b})$$

Recall the indicator variable δ_i defined by (7.17). We now introduce a second indicator variable γ_i, where

$$\gamma_i = \begin{cases} 1 & \text{if person i withdraws in (x, x+1]} \\ 0 & \text{otherwise} \end{cases}. \qquad (7.51)$$

Using these two indicator variables, the likelihood can be written as

$$L = \prod_{i=1}^{n} {}_{t_i-r_i}\text{p}'^{(d)}_{x+r_i} \cdot {}_{t_i-r_i}\text{p}'^{(w)}_{x+r_i} \cdot \left(\mu^{(d)}_{x+t_i}\right)^{\delta i} \cdot \left(\mu^{(w)}_{x+t_i}\right)^{\gamma_i}, \qquad (7.50\text{c})$$

since $\mu^{(d)}_{x+t_i}$ is needed in the likelihood function only if person i is a death ($\delta_i=1$), and $\mu^{(w)}_{x+t_i}$ is needed only if person i is a withdrawal ($\gamma_i=1$).

Suppose our objective is to estimate $q'^{(d)}_x$. Since we have assumed that death and withdrawal are independent, then the terms superscripted with (w) are constant with respect to $q'^{(d)}_x$, and can be dropped from the likelihood. Thus we have

$$L = \prod_{i=1}^{n} {}_{t_i-r_i}\text{p}'^{(d)}_{x+r_i} \cdot \left(\mu^{(d)}_{x+t_i}\right)^{\delta i}. \qquad (7.52)$$

Since the unadorned $_{t_i-r_i}\text{p}_{x+r_i}$ and μ_{x+t_i} in (7.20) are the same mortality functions as are $_{t_i-r_i}\text{p}'^{(d)}_{x+r_i}$ and $\mu^{(d)}_{x+t_i}$ in (7.52), it follows that (7.52) is exactly the same as (7.20).

7.4.2 *Full Data, Exponential Distribution for Mortality*

Since (7.52) is the same as (7.20), it follows that the maximization of (7.52) under the exponential distribution will produce the MLE for $\mu^{(d)}$, the constant force over $(x, x+1)$, given by (7.23).

7.4.3 *Full Data, Uniform Distribution for Mortality*

Under the uniform distribution, (7.52), being the same as (7.20), is maximized by the value of q_x which satisfies

$$\frac{d_x}{q_x} + \sum_{i=1}^{n} \frac{r_i}{1 - r_i \cdot q_x} - \sum_{\mathfrak{D}} \frac{t_i}{1 - t_i \cdot q_x} = 0, \tag{7.53}$$

where the last summation is taken over all persons who do not die. Equation (7.53), like its single-decrement counterpart (7.27), must, in general, be solved by iteration.

A quadratic solution is found for (7.53) under Special Case A, with $r_i = 0$ for all i, $t_i = 1$ for all enders, and $t_i = t$, a constant, for all withdrawals. (The derivation of this result is left as an exercise.) For all other situations, we must solve a higher order polynomial equation to obtain $\hat{q}_x = \hat{q}_x'^{(d)}$, with the attendant possibility of multiple roots. Under the exponential assumption, on the other hand, all cases have a unique solution for $\hat{\mu}$ given by (7.23), and thus a unique solution for $\hat{q}_x$.

7.4.4 *Partial Data, Special Case A*

Estimation of $q_x'^{(d)}$ from partial data in the presence of random withdrawals is more complex than with full data. We consider only Special Case A, where $r_i = 0$ for all i and $s_i = 1$ for all i who do not die or withdraw. Suppose our only information is that from a sample of n_x persons at exact age x, d_x died and w_x withdrew in $(x, x+1]$, so that $n_x - d_x - w_x$ survived to age $x+1$. Ages at death and withdrawal are not available.

The likelihood of this sample result is

$$L = \left[q_x^{(d)}\right]^{d_x} \cdot \left[q_x^{(w)}\right]^{w_x} \cdot \left[1 - q_x^{(d)} - q_x^{(w)}\right]^{n_x - d_x - w_x}, \tag{7.54}$$

where $q_x^{(d)}$ and $q_x^{(w)}$ are defined by (5.17) and (5.18), respectively. Recall that our purpose is to estimate $q_x'^{(d)}$. To achieve it we must make distribution assumptions for both of the random events, death and withdrawal.

7.4.5 *Partial Data (Special Case A), Exponential Distributions*

We know that this assumption implies $\mu_{x+t}^{(d)} = \mu^{(d)}$ and $_tp_x'^{(d)} = e^{-t \cdot \mu^{(d)}}$, where $\mu^{(d)}$ is a constant. Similarly $\mu_{x+t}^{(w)} = \mu^{(w)}$ and $_tp_x'^{(w)} = e^{-t \cdot \mu^{(w)}}$, where $\mu^{(w)}$ is likewise a constant.

From (5.17) we find

$$
\begin{aligned}
q_x^{(d)} &= \int_0^1 \mu^{(d)} \cdot e^{-t\left(\mu^{(d)} + \mu^{(w)}\right)} \, dt \\
&= \frac{\mu^{(d)}}{\mu^{(d)} + \mu^{(w)}} \left[1 - e^{-\left(\mu^{(d)} + \mu^{(w)}\right)} \right]
\end{aligned}
\tag{7.55}
$$

Similarly, from (5.18) we find

$$
\begin{aligned}
q_x^{(w)} &= \int_0^1 \mu^{(w)} \cdot e^{-t\left(\mu^{(d)} + \mu^{(w)}\right)} \, dt \\
&= \frac{\mu^{(w)}}{\mu^{(d)} + \mu^{(w)}} \left[1 - e^{-\left(\mu^{(d)} + \mu^{(w)}\right)} \right]
\end{aligned}
\tag{7.56}
$$

To simplify notation, let $\mu^{(d)} = \alpha$ and $\mu^{(w)} = \beta$. Substituting (7.55) and (7.56) into the likelihood function (7.54), we obtain (suppressing the subscripts on d_x, w_x and n_x)

$$
L = \frac{\alpha^d \cdot \beta^w}{(\alpha + \beta)^{d+w}} \cdot \left[1 - e^{-(\alpha+\beta)} \right]^{d+w} \cdot \left[e^{-(\alpha+\beta)} \right]^{n-d-w},
\tag{7.57}
$$

from which we obtain the log-likelihood

$$
\begin{aligned}
\ln L = {}& d \cdot \ln \alpha + w \cdot \ln \beta - (d+w) \cdot \ln(\alpha+\beta) \\
& + (d+w) \cdot \ln\left[1 - e^{-(\alpha+\beta)} \right] + (n-d-w) \left[-(\alpha+\beta) \right].
\end{aligned}
\tag{7.58}
$$

Next,

$$\frac{\partial \ln L}{\partial \alpha} = \frac{d}{\alpha} - \frac{d+w}{\alpha+\beta} + \frac{(d+w) \cdot e^{-(\alpha+\beta)}}{1 - e^{-(\alpha+\beta)}} - (n-d-w) \tag{7.59}$$

and

$$\frac{\partial \ln L}{\partial \beta} = \frac{w}{\beta} - \frac{d+w}{\alpha+\beta} + \frac{(d+w) \cdot e^{-(\alpha+\beta)}}{1 - e^{-(\alpha+\beta)}} - (n-d-w). \tag{7.60}$$

The MLE's of α and β (i.e., of $\mu^{(d)}$ and $\mu^{(w)}$) are found by setting (7.59) and (7.60) equal to zero and solving the resulting equations simultaneously. Since all terms after the first in (7.59) and (7.60) are the same, it follows that $\frac{d}{\alpha} = \frac{w}{\beta}$, or that

$$\hat{\beta} = \frac{w}{d} \cdot \hat{\alpha} . \tag{7.61}$$

Recall that $\hat{\alpha}$ and $\hat{\beta}$ are the values of α and β that make (7.59) equal to zero. Thus by substituting (7.61) into (7.59), we have

$$\frac{d}{\hat{\alpha}} - \frac{d+w}{\hat{\alpha}+\frac{w}{d}\cdot\hat{\alpha}} + \frac{(d+w) \cdot e^{-(\hat{\alpha} + \frac{w}{d}\cdot\hat{\alpha})}}{1 - e^{-(\hat{\alpha} + \frac{w}{d}\cdot\hat{\alpha})}} - (n-d-w) = 0. \tag{7.62}$$

We note that $\hat{\alpha} + \frac{w}{d}\cdot\hat{\alpha} = \frac{1}{d}(d+w)\cdot\hat{\alpha}$, so the second term of (7.62) reduces to $\frac{d}{\hat{\alpha}}$, thereby cancelling the first term. This allows us to write (7.62) as $\dfrac{(d+w) \cdot e^{-\hat{\alpha}(1 + w/d)}}{1 - e^{-\hat{\alpha}(1 + w/d)}} = (n-d-w)$, which eventually leads to

$$\hat{\alpha} = \hat{\mu}^{(d)} = -\frac{1}{1+\frac{w}{d}} \cdot \ln\left[\frac{n-d-w}{n}\right] = -\ln\left(\frac{n-d-w}{n}\right)^{d/(d+w)}. \tag{7.63}$$

Finally,

$$\hat{q}_x = \hat{q}_x'^{(d)} = 1 - e^{-\hat{\mu}^{(d)}} = 1 - \left(\frac{n-d-w}{n}\right)^{d/(d+w)}. \tag{7.64}$$

Note that the MLE (7.64) is the same as the moment estimator (6.46).

7.4.6   *Partial Data (Special Case A), Uniform Distributions*

Under this assumption we know that $_tq_x'^{(d)} = t \cdot q_x'^{(d)}$ and $\mu_{x+t}^{(d)} = \dfrac{q_x'^{(d)}}{1 - t \cdot q_x'^{(d)}}$.

Similarly $_tq_x'^{(w)} = t \cdot q_x'^{(w)}$ and $\mu_{x+t}^{(w)} = \dfrac{q_x'^{(w)}}{1 - t \cdot q_x'^{(w)}}$. Then from (5.17) we find

$$q_x^{(d)} = \int_0^1 q_x'^{(d)}\left[1 - t \cdot q_x'^{(w)}\right]dt = q_x'^{(d)}\left[1 - \tfrac{1}{2} \cdot q_x'^{(w)}\right], \tag{7.65}$$

and from (5.18) we similarly find

$$q_x^{(w)} = \int_0^1 q_x'^{(w)}\left[1 - t \cdot q_x'^{(d)}\right]dt = q_x'^{(w)}\left[1 - \tfrac{1}{2} \cdot q_x'^{(d)}\right]. \tag{7.66}$$

To simplify notation, let $q_x'^{(d)} = \theta$ and $q_x'^{(w)} = \phi$. Substituting (7.65) and (7.66) into the likelihood function (7.54), we obtain (suppressing the subscripts on d_x, w_x, and n_x)

$$L = \left[\theta(1 - \tfrac{1}{2}\phi)\right]^d \cdot \left[\phi(1 - \tfrac{1}{2}\theta)\right]^w \cdot \left[(1-\theta)(1-\phi)\right]^{n-d-w}, \tag{7.67}$$

and

$$\ln L = d \cdot \ln\theta + d \cdot \ln(1 - \tfrac{1}{2}\phi) + w \cdot \ln\phi + w \cdot \ln(1 - \tfrac{1}{2}\theta)$$
$$+ (n-d-w) \cdot \ln(1-\theta) + (n-d-w) \cdot \ln(1-\phi). \tag{7.68}$$

Then

$$\frac{\partial \ln L}{\partial \theta} = \frac{d}{\theta} - \frac{\tfrac{1}{2}w}{1 - \tfrac{1}{2}\theta} - \frac{n-d-w}{1-\theta} = 0 \tag{7.69}$$

is solved for $\hat{\theta} = \hat{q}_x'^{(d)}$. It is easy to see that (7.69) is the same as (7.31), with $s = \tfrac{1}{2}$ and e replaced by w. Thus our MLE of $q_x = q_x'^{(d)}$, from (7.69), is

$$\hat{q}_x = \frac{b - \sqrt{b^2 - 2n_x d_x}}{n_x}, \tag{7.70}$$

where $b = n_x - \frac{1}{2}w_x + \frac{1}{2}d_x$. The similarity of (7.70) and (7.32) is apparent, and we also note that (7.70) is the same as the moment estimator (6.38).

7.4.7 *Summary of Double-Decrement MLE's*

It should be recognized that it was the independence assumption for the random events death and withdrawal which allowed us to reach the general solutions for $\hat{\mu} = \hat{\mu}^{(d)}$ under the exponential distribution, given by (7.23), and $\hat{q}_x = \hat{q}_x'^{(d)}$ under the uniform distribution, given by (7.53), for the full data case. If the independence assumption is not valid, and a dependent model is assumed, then the estimation of q_x is more complex. For a discussion of this, the interested reader is referred to Robinson [52].

　　We chose to develop the partial data situation only for Special Case A, since it is the only one of the special cases which has a convenient solution for $\hat{q}_x$. The more general partial data situation for the random withdrawal model, which embraces all of our special cases, is given by Broffitt [12].

| EXAMPLE 7.6 |: 100 persons enter the estimation interval $(20, 21]$ at exact age 20. There are two withdrawals; one at exact age 20.2 and the other at exact age 20.7, and there is one death at 20.3. The remaining 97 persons reach age 21. Estimate $q_{20}^{(d)}$ under (a) full data, exponential distribution; (b) full data, uniform distribution; (c) partial data, exponential distribution; (d) partial data, uniform distribution.

| SOLUTION |: (a) From (7.23), $\hat{\mu} = \dfrac{1}{.2+.7+.3+97} = \dfrac{1}{98.2}$, so we have $\hat{q}_{20}'^{(d)} = 1 - e^{-1/98.2} = .0101316$. (b) Looking at (7.53), we find $r_i = 0$ for all persons, $t_i = 1$ for 97 persons, $t_i = .2$ for one person, and $t_i = .7$ for one person. Thus the likelihood equation is $\dfrac{1}{q} - \dfrac{.2}{1-.2q} - \dfrac{.7}{1-.7q} - \dfrac{97}{1-q} = 0$, which leads to a cubic equation in q. If both withdrawals are placed at their average age of 20.45, then (7.53) becomes $\dfrac{1}{q} - \dfrac{2(.45)}{1-.45q} - \dfrac{97}{1-q} = 0$, which solves for $\hat{q}_{20}'^{(d)}$ given by (7.32), with e_x replaced by $w_x = 2$, and with $s = .45$. This gives $\hat{q}_{20}'^{(d)} = \dfrac{99.35 - \sqrt{(99.35)^2 - 180}}{90} = .0101106$. (c) This is the same as the corresponding moment estimator, which was found to be $\hat{q}_{20}'^{(d)} = .0101017$ in Example 6.7. (d) This is also the same as the corresponding moment estimator, found in Example 6.6 to be $\hat{q}_{20}'^{(d)} = .0101015$.

7.5 *PROPERTIES OF MAXIMUM LIKELIHOOD ESTIMATORS*

General properties of estimators are defined and summarized in Appendix A. In this section we briefly observe the application of these properties to maximum likelihood estimators, with further details on the properties of MLE's given in Appendix B.

7.5.1 *Bias*

The general conditions for asymptotic unbiasedness of an MLE are given in Appendix B. In this section we will review the concept of bias by using the familiar example of the MLE of the parameter σ^2 in a normal distribution. It is well known that the MLE is $\hat{\sigma}^2_{MLE} = \frac{1}{n} \cdot \sum_{i=1}^{n} (X_i - \bar{X})^2$, and that this is a biased estimator for σ^2. The unbiased estimator is $\hat{\sigma}^2_U = \frac{1}{n-1} \cdot \sum_{i=1}^{n} (X_i - \bar{X})^2$. Then clearly $\hat{\sigma}^2_{MLE} = \frac{n-1}{n} \cdot \hat{\sigma}^2_U$, so the MLE can be made unbiased by multiplying it by the constant $\frac{n}{n-1}$. Furthermore,

$$E\left[\hat{\sigma}^2_{MLE}\right] = \frac{n-1}{n} \cdot E\left[\hat{\sigma}^2_U\right] = \frac{n-1}{n} \cdot \sigma^2. \tag{7.71}$$

Since $\lim_{n \to \infty} \frac{n-1}{n} = 1$, this MLE is unbiased for infinitely large n, which means it is asymptotically unbiased.

7.5.2 *Variance*

The asymptotic variance of an MLE of q, $\hat{q}$, is given by

$$\text{Var}(\hat{q}) = \left\{ E\left[-\frac{\partial^2 \ln L}{\partial q^2} \right] \right\}^{-1}, \tag{7.72}$$

if certain conditions pertaining to the likelihood function are satisfied. Formula (7.72) is derived in Appendix B.

To apply (7.72), the key step is taking the expectation of $-\frac{\partial^2 \ln L}{\partial q^2}$. One must identify the random variable(s) in $-\frac{\partial^2 \ln L}{\partial q^2}$, and know the expected value(s) of such variable(s). Sometimes the expected value(s) will have to be approximated, so (7.72) gives an approximate variance for this reason as well as for its being used in conjunction with a finite n.

EXAMPLE 7.7: Find the variance of the Special Case A estimator given by (7.7).

SOLUTION: Note first the estimator (7.7) is a binomial proportion, so we know its variance is $\frac{q \cdot (1-q)}{n}$. Now from (7.6) we have $\frac{d \ln L}{dq} = \frac{d}{q} - \frac{n-d}{1-q}$, so $\frac{d^2 \ln' L}{dq^2} = -\frac{d}{q^2} - \frac{n-d}{(1-q)^2}$, and we need $E\left[-\frac{d^2 \ln L}{dq^2}\right]$. Now d is actually the realization of the binomial random variable D, and we should use D instead of d when discussing expectations. We know that $E[D] = nq$ and $E[n-D] = n(1-q)$. Substituting these expectations for D and $n-D$, we have $E\left[-\frac{d^2 \ln L}{dq^2}\right] = \frac{nq}{q^2} + \frac{n(1-q)}{(1-q)^2} = \frac{n}{q} + \frac{n}{(1-q)} = \frac{n(1-q)+nq}{q(1-q)} = \frac{n}{q(1-q)}$.

Finally, Var($\hat{q}$) is the reciprocal of this last expression, as already known. Note that for this Special Case A MLE, (7.72) gives the correct variance for finite n (i.e., not asymptotic only.)

EXAMPLE 7.8: Use (7.72) to approximate the variance of the Special Case B MLE given by (7.30).

SOLUTION The left side of (7.28) gives us $\frac{d \ln L}{dq}$ for this case, so we begin there. $\frac{d^2 \ln L}{dq^2} = -\frac{d}{q^2} + \frac{kr^2}{(1-rq)^2} - \frac{n-d}{(1-q)^2}$, and we seek the expected value of this expression. Note that only d (actually D) is a random variable.

However, since D is not binomial, then E[D] is not obvious. We see that $E[D] = b_x \cdot q_x + k_x \cdot {}_{1-r}q_{x+r}$, so we need to make a distribution assumption to approximate E[D]. Let us say $E[D] \approx \left[b_x + (1-r)k_x\right] \cdot q_x$, from the hyperbolic assumption. Then

$$E\left[-\frac{d^2 \ln L}{dq^2}\right] = \frac{\left[b+(1-r)k\right]q}{q^2} - \frac{kr^2}{(1-rq)^2} + \frac{n - \left[b+(1-r)k\right]q}{(1-q)^2}$$

$$= \frac{n-rk}{q} - \frac{kr^2}{(1-rq)^2} + \frac{n}{1-q} + \frac{rkq}{(1-q)^2},$$

since $n = b+k$, and Var($\hat{q}$) is approximated by the inverse of this expression. To *numerically* approximate the variance, one would probably substitute the estimate $\hat{q}$ obtained from (7.30) for q in the variance expression.

7.5.3 *Consistency and Efficiency*

MLE's are consistent estimators. Furthermore, within the class of asymptotically unbiased estimators, the variance of an MLE is as small or smaller than the variance of any other estimator in the class, so the MLE is said to be an efficient estimator.

7.6 *THE PRODUCT LIMIT ESTIMATOR*

This estimator has been suggested by several writers, but is mainly attributed to Kaplan and Meier [34], and is frequently referred to as the Kaplan-Meier estimator. We have included it in our chapter on maximum likelihood estimators since we will see that it makes use of a sequence of MLE's to produce its estimate of q_x, although the product limit estimator itself is *not* an MLE.

A basic characteristic of the product limit estimator is that it does not require a distribution assumption, such as the uniform or exponential.

7.6.1 *Estimation of q_x*

The product limit estimator can be used in any estimation situation, provided full data are available. It treats enders and random withdrawals alike, and we will use simply "terminations" to include both types. The presence of entrants at any age is also handled by this estimation approach.

The product limit estimator is most easily explained by an example. Suppose a sample of $n_x = 20$ lives at age x is augmented by 2 additional entrants and decremented by 3 terminations and 5 deaths prior to age x+1. Figure 7.1 illustrates this data, using arrows to locate the entrants and terminations, and X's to locate the deaths.

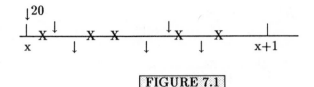

FIGURE 7.1

We have not bothered to indicate the ages within (x, x+1] at which the events of death, entry and termination occur, since this information is not used in computing $\hat{q}_x$. It is only necessary to indicate the events in order of occurrence, but not the precise ages at which they occur.

We now break our basic estimation interval into six subintervals by partitioning $(x, x+1]$ at each point where an entry or termination occurs, as shown in Figure 7.2.

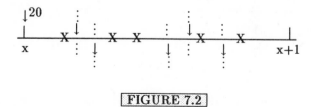

$$\boxed{\text{FIGURE 7.2}}$$

We recognize that each of the six subintervals represents a Special Case A situation, since there are no events *within* the subinterval except (possibly) deaths. If q_i is the conditional probability of death in the ith subinterval, given alive at the beginning of that subinterval, then the MLE of q_i is the simple binomial proportion

$$\hat{q}_i = \frac{d_i}{n_i}, \tag{7.73}$$

where d_i is the number of observed deaths in Subinterval i, and n_i is the binomial sample size for that subinterval. Clearly if $d_i = 0$, as is true for i=2 and i=4, then $\hat{q}_i = 0$ as well.

The product limit estimator of q_x is defined as

$$\hat{q}_x = 1 - \prod_{i=1}^{m} (1-\hat{q}_i) = 1 - \prod_{i=1}^{m} \left(\frac{n_i - d_i}{n_i}\right), \tag{7.74}$$

where m is the number of subintervals in $(x, x+1]$. (m=6 in our example.)

To complete the example, we first note that the subinterval sample sizes are $n_1=20$, $n_2=20$, $n_3=19$, $n_4=16$, $n_5=17$, $n_6=15$. Thus we have

$$\hat{q}_x = 1 - \left(\frac{19}{20}\right)\left(\frac{20}{20}\right)\left(\frac{17}{19}\right)\left(\frac{16}{16}\right)\left(\frac{16}{17}\right)\left(\frac{14}{15}\right) = 1 - \frac{(16)(14)}{(20)(15)} = .25333.$$

The occurrence of a death at the same age as an entrant or termination raises the question of the subinterval to which such death belongs. The usual rule is to consider a death which coincides with an entrant or termination as belonging to the subinterval *preceding* such event. That is, a death at a subinterval boundary is deemed to belong to the subinterval closing at the boundary, rather than the one beginning there. This is consistent with our general notation $(x, x+1]$.

As an alternative to partitioning $(x, x+1]$ at each entry and termination point, we could partition at each death point instead. In that case our example would result in the six subintervals illustrated in Figure 7.3.

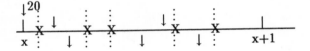

FIGURE 7.3

We call r_j the *risk set* for the jth subinterval, and define it to be the number of persons in the sample immediately preceding the death which marks the end of the jth subinterval. The estimate of the probability of death in the jth subinterval is then

$$\hat{q}_j = \frac{1}{r_j}, \tag{7.75}$$

except for the last subinterval in $(x, x+1]$. Since there is no death in that subinterval (Subinterval 6 in our example), then the $\hat{q}_j$ for that subinterval is zero. Finally,

$$\hat{q}_x = 1 - \prod_{j=1}^{m} (1-\hat{q}_j) = 1 - \prod_{j=1}^{m} \left(\frac{r_j - 1}{r_j} \right) \tag{7.76}$$

gives the estimate of q_x.

EXAMPLE 7.9: Show that the same estimate of q_x results for partitioning at death points as for partitioning at entry and withdrawal points.

SOLUTION: From Figure 7.3, we find the risk sets to be $r_1=20$, $r_2=19$, $r_3=18$, $r_4=17$, $r_5=15$. Then from (7.76), we find the product-limit estimate

$$\hat{q}_x = 1 - \left(\frac{19}{20}\right)\left(\frac{18}{19}\right)\left(\frac{17}{18}\right)\left(\frac{16}{17}\right)\left(\frac{14}{15}\right) = 1 - \frac{(16)(14)}{(20)(15)} = .25333.$$

In the partitioning-at-death approach, if a death and entrant, or death and termination, occur at the same age, we need rules to determine the risk set associated with that death. In order to interpret the risk set as existing "immediately preceding" the death, we treat the death as preceding the entrant or termination. Thus a simultaneous entrant *is not* included in the risk set, whereas a simultaneous termination *is* included (i.e., termination has not yet taken place).

If there is more than one death at the same age, then (7.75) is modified to

$$\hat{q}_j = \frac{d_j}{r_j}, \tag{7.77}$$

where d_j is the number of simultaneous deaths marking the end of the jth subinterval.

Note that if there exists any subinterval for which a study sample does not exist, then the $\hat{q}_j$ for the subinterval does not exist, and so $\hat{q}_x$ does not exist as well. This occurs if all members in the sample terminate before age x+1.

7.6.2 Properties of the Estimator

The product limit estimator is unbiased and consistent.

For the variance of the estimator, let us consider

$$\hat{p}_x = \prod_{i=1}^{m} \hat{p}_i, \tag{7.78}$$

which comes directly from (7.74). Recall that each $\hat{p}_i$ is a binomial proportion, conditional on its sample size n_i. Then all $\hat{p}_i$'s are conditionally mutually independent, and, being binomial proportions, they are unbiased. Therefore, the conditions of Section 6.5 hold here, so by steps analogous to those leading to formula (6.58), we find

$$\text{Var}(\hat{p}_x|\{n_i\}) = (p_x)^2 \cdot \left[\prod_{i=1}^{m} \left(\frac{q_i}{p_i n_i} + 1 \right) - 1 \right]. \tag{7.79}$$

Since $\hat{q}_x = 1 - \hat{p}_x$, it follows that (7.79) is $\text{Var}(\hat{q}_x|\{n_i\})$ as well.

By the same steps as those leading from (6.58) to (6.59), we can obtain the Greenwood approximation

$$\text{Var}(\hat{q}_x|\{n_i\}) = \text{Var}(\hat{p}_x|\{n_i\}) \approx (p_x)^2 \cdot \sum_{i=1}^{m} \left(\frac{q_i}{p_i n_i} \right). \tag{7.80}$$

In either case, a numerical estimate of the variance is obtained by substituting the estimates $\hat{p}_i$, $\hat{q}_i$ and $\hat{p}_x$ just obtained from the sample, along with the n_i's from the sample.

For a very large sample with many entrants and terminations, such as found in insurance company studies, the product limit estimator is not generally used, due to the large number of subintervals that would result. For clinical studies, however, it is commonly used, especially for those situations in which there are no entrants after time t=0. We will now explore this use of the estimator.

7.6.3 Estimation of S(t)

Let us assume a sample of n persons all observed from time t=0 on the follow-up scale. If the study is halted before all have died, then we will have terminations from the sample at various values of t.

In clinical studies it is customary to use the approach of partitioning at each death point. Then if r_j is the risk set immediately preceding the jth death point (which, in general, has d_j deaths, with d_j most frequently being one), we have, as before,

$$\hat{q}_j = \frac{d_j}{r_j}. \tag{7.77}$$

Note that $\hat{q}_j$ estimates the probability of death over the interval which ends at the jth death point, given alive at the beginning of that interval; it is *not* the probability of death over an interval which begins at $t=j$. Then

$$\hat{S}(t_m) = \prod_{j=1}^{m} (1-q_j) = \prod_{j=1}^{m} \left(\frac{r_j - d_j}{r_j} \right) \tag{7.81}$$

estimates the probability of survival from $t=0$ to $t=t_m$, the time of the mth death point. For all t such that $t_m \leq t < t_{m+1}$, the estimate of $S(t)$ is the same as $\hat{S}(t_m)$, since there are no deaths in the sample between t_m and t. Thus

$$\hat{S}(t) = \prod_{j=1}^{m} \left(\frac{r_j - d_j}{r_j} \right) \quad \text{for } t_m \leq t < t_{m+1}, \quad m = 1, 2, \cdots. \tag{7.82}$$

As a special case, $\hat{S}(t) = 1$ for $t < t_1$.

Analogous to (7.80), the variance of $\hat{S}(t)$ is approximated by

$$\text{Var}\left[\hat{S}(t) | \{r_j\} \right] \approx \left[S(t) \right]^2 \cdot \sum_{j=1}^{m} \left(\frac{q_j}{p_j r_j} \right), \tag{7.83}$$

for $t_m \leq t < t_{m+1}$. If (7.83) is then numerically estimated by substituting $\hat{q}_j$ for q_j, $\hat{p}_j$ for p_j, and $\hat{S}(t)$ for $S(t)$, we obtain

$$\text{est. Var}\left[\hat{S}(t) | \{r_j\} \right] \approx \left[\hat{S}(t) \right]^2 \cdot \sum_{j=1}^{m} \left(\frac{d_j}{r_j(r_j - d_j)} \right), \tag{7.84}$$

since $\hat{q}_j = \frac{d_j}{r_j}$.

Finally, if there are no terminations (i.e., complete data), then, for all j, $r_{j+1} = r_j - d_j$. It is then easy to see that (7.81) becomes

$$\hat{S}(t_m) = \prod_{j=1}^{m} \left(\frac{r_{j+1}}{r_j} \right) = \frac{r_{m+1}}{r_1}, \tag{7.85}$$

where $r_1 = n$, the original sample, and r_{m+1} is the number of survivors just preceding the $(m+1)^{st}$ death point, or just after the mth death point. Thus $S(t_m)$ is estimated by the proportion surviving to that time, and we have returned to the approach of Section 4.3.

7.6.4 *The Nelson-Aalen Estimator*

Recall formula (2.13) which states that $S(t) = e^{-\Lambda(t)}$, where $\Lambda(t)$ is called the cumulative hazard function. It would be reasonable to estimate $S(t)$ by first estimating $\Lambda(t)$ and then defining

$$\hat{S}(t) = e^{-\hat{\Lambda}(t)}. \tag{7.86}$$

From (7.86) we have the relationship

$$\hat{\Lambda}(t) = -\ln \hat{S}(t). \tag{7.87}$$

Consider again formula (7.81), the product limit estimator of $S(t)$, for $t_m \leq t < t_{m+1}$. Substituting (7.81) into (7.87) we have

$$\hat{\Lambda}(t) = -\ln \left[\prod_{j=1}^{m} \left(\frac{r_j - d_j}{r_j} \right) \right]$$

$$= -\sum_{j=1}^{m} \ln \left(1 - \frac{d_j}{r_j} \right), \quad t_m \leq t < t_{m+1}. \tag{7.88}$$

Recall that $-\ln \left(1 - \frac{d_j}{r_j} \right) = \frac{d_j}{r_j} + \frac{1}{2} \left(\frac{d_j}{r_j} \right)^2 + \cdots$. By ignoring quadratic and higher power terms, we obtain the approximation

$$-\ln \left(1 - \frac{d_j}{r_j} \right) \approx \frac{d_j}{r_j}, \tag{7.89}$$

thereby approximating the cumulative hazard by

$$\hat{\Lambda}(t) = \sum_{j=1}^{m} \frac{d_j}{r_j}, \quad t_m \leq t < t_{m+1}, \tag{7.90}$$

and, in turn, approximating the survival function by

$$\hat{S}(t) = \exp\left(-\sum_{j=1}^{m} \frac{d_j}{r_j}\right), \quad t_m \leq t < t_{m+1}, \tag{7.91}$$

which is called the Nelson-Aalen estimator (see Nelson [47]).

If there is only one death at any death point (i.e., $d_j = 1$ for all j), and if there are no terminations, then the Nelson-Aalen estimator is particularly easy to calculate. In that case, $r_j = n - j + 1$, so

$$\hat{\Lambda}(t) = \sum_{j=1}^{m} \frac{1}{r_j} = \frac{1}{n} + \frac{1}{n-1} + \cdots + \frac{1}{n-m+1}, \quad t_m \leq t < t_{m+1}. \tag{7.92}$$

EXAMPLE 7.10: In a complete data study, the Nelson-Aalen estimate of $\Lambda(t)$ immediately following the second death is 11/30. Find the estimate of $\Lambda(t)$ immediately following the fourth death.

SOLUTION: After the second death $\hat{\Lambda}(t) = \frac{1}{n} + \frac{1}{n-1}$, where n is the original size of the sample. We are given that $\hat{\Lambda}(t_2) = 11/30$, which implies $\frac{1}{n} + \frac{1}{n-1} = \frac{2n-1}{n(n-1)} = \frac{11}{30}$, or $11n^2 - 71n + 30 = 0$, which solves for $n = 6$. (The other root, $n = 5/11$, is extraneous since n must be an integer.) Thus $\hat{\Lambda}(t_4) = \frac{1}{6} + \frac{1}{5} + \frac{1}{4} + \frac{1}{3} = .95$.

The relationship between the product limit and the Nelson-Aalen estimators is illustrated by the following example.

EXAMPLE 7.11: In a certain complete data study with original sample of size 10, the product limit estimate of S(12) is found to be $\hat{S}(12) = .7$. Find the Nelson-Aalen estimate of S(12).

SOLUTION: Since we have complete data, there must be 7 survivors at $t = 12$ (since the product limit estimator is a simple binomial proportion in this case). Thus there have been 3 deaths by $t = 12$, so the Nelson-Aalen estimate is $\hat{\Lambda}(12) = \frac{1}{10} + \frac{1}{9} + \frac{1}{8} = \frac{242}{720}$, and so $\hat{S}(12) = e^{-242/720} = .71454$. (Note that the Nelson-Aalen estimate exceeds the product limit estimate; see Exercise 7-32.)

7.7 *SUMMARY*

In this chapter we have developed MLE's for q_x (or for the constant μ under the exponential assumption), for various combinations of decrement environment (single or double), type of data (full or partial), and distribution assumption (exponential or uniform). Table 7.2 summarizes the reference numbers of most of the estimators developed in this chapter.

TABLE 7.2

	Full Data Exponential	Full Data Uniform	Partial Data Exponential	Partial Data Uniform
Single-Decrement				
General Case	(7.23)	(7.27)	-----	-----
Special Case A	(7.15)	(7.7)	(7.7)[1]	(7.7)[1]
Special Case B	(7.23)	(7.30)	-----	-----
Special Case C	(7.23)	(7.32)	(7.41) or (7.46)[2]	(7.32)
Double-Decrement				
General Case	(7.23)	(7.53)	-----	-----
Special Case A	(7.23)	**	(7.64)	(7.70)
Special Case B	(7.23)	(7.53)	-----	-----
Special Case C	(7.23)	(7.53)	-----	-----

Notes: [1] No distribution assumption is actually made.
[2] (7.46) is the same as the actuarial estimator.
** See Exercise 7-18.

In addition to these MLE's, we developed product limit estimators for q_x given, equivalently, by (7.74) and (7.76), and for $S(t)$ given by (7.82). The Nelson-Aalen estimator for $S(t)$, given by (7.91), is an alternative to (7.82).

EXERCISES

7.1 *Introduction;*   7.2 *Single-Decrement Environment, Special Case A*

7-1. Find an equation which is satisfied by the MLE of q_x for Special Case A, full data, under the hyperbolic assumption.

7-2.   Solve the equation of Exercise 7-1 for $\hat{q}_x$ if all deaths occur *just before* age x+1 (i.e., if $s_i = 1$ for all deaths).

7-3.   Intuitively, if there are no deaths in our sample we might expect to find $\hat{q}_x = 0$. Similarly, if the entire sample of n_x persons dies, we might expect to find $\hat{q}_x = 1$. It is obvious that these results are obtained for the partial data and the full data, linear distribution, situations.   Are they obtained for the full data, exponential distribution, situation?

7-4.   (a)   Express the likelihood given by (7.11) in terms of q_x under the exponential assumption.
       (b)   Express the log-likelihood for the likelihood in part (a).
       (c)   Solve this log-likelihood for the MLE of q_x.

7-5.   Over the interval (x, x+1] it is assumed that $_sp_x = 1 - \frac{3s^2}{2}(q_x)^2$ for $0 \le s \le \frac{2}{3}$, and that $_sp_x = 1 - s(q_x)^2$ for $\frac{2}{3} \le s < 1$. If $n_x = 300$ and there are two observed deaths, one at x+.40 and one at x+.75, find the MLE of q_x.

7.3   Single-Decrement Environment, General Case

7-6.   Show that the Special Case C, partial data, uniform distribution likelihood, given by (7.36), leads to estimator (7.32).

7-7.   Table 7.3 gives the data for a sample of five lives over the estimation interval (x, x+1].

TABLE 7.3

i	r_i	t_i	δ_i
1	0.0	1.0	0
2	0.0	.6	1
3	0.0	.7	1
4	.5	.9	1
5	.5	1.0	0

Find the MLE of q_x under each of (a) the exponential distribution, and (b) the uniform distribution.

7-8. A sample of 105 individuals were alive at age x. Five died before age x+1, and 10 others were enders at age x+$\frac{1}{2}$. If the force of mortality is constant over (x, x+1), find (a) the actuarial estimator, and (b) the maximum likelihood estimator of q_x.

7-9. Refer to the Schwartz-Lazar moment estimator of Section 6.2.6.
   (a) Of the c_x group, what is the probability of being
      (i)   an observed death?
      (ii)   an observed ender?
      (iii) a survivor to age x+1?
   (b) Write the likelihood, L_c, for the c_x group.
   (c) Of the $(n_x - c_x)$ group, what is the probability of being
      (i)   an observed death?
      (ii)   an observed ender?
      (iii) a survivor to age x+1?
   (d) Write the likelihood, L_{n-c}, for the $(n_x - c_x)$ group.
   (e) Write the overall likelihood, and show that the MLE of q_x is the same as the Schwartz-Lazar estimator given by (6.28). (Note the similarity of (6.28) and (7.32).)

7-10. Solve Equation (7.41) for $\hat{p}_x$ using $s = \frac{1}{2}$.

7-11. Derive the partial data, Special Case B MLE for q_x, assuming (a) the uniform distribution, and   (b) the exponential distribution with $r_i = \frac{1}{2}$ for all i.

7-12. Evaluate (7.47) for $\bar{q}_x$ by assuming a hyperbolic ℓ_{x+s} for mortality, and the uniform distribution for S.

7-13. Evaluate (7.47) for $\bar{q}_x$ by assuming an exponential ℓ_{x+s} for mortality, and the uniform distribution for S.

7-14. The expression for $\bar{p}_x$ found in Exercise 7-13 is commonly approximated by $\bar{p}_x \approx p_x^{1/2}$. Derive this approximation.

7-15. The Special Case C likelihood under random censoring is given by (7.49).   If we assume that scheduled ending ages are uniformly distributed, but mortality follows the exponential distribution, then $\bar{q}_x \approx 1 - (1 - q_x)^{1/2}$ (see Exercise 7-14). Derive the MLE of q_x under these assumptions. (*This is called Drolette's Estimator B* [20].)

7.4   Double-Decrement Environment

7-16. If $_tq_x^{(T)} = 1 - _tp_x^{(T)}$, show that $_tq_x^{(T)} = _tq_x'^{(d)} + _tq_x'^{(w)} - _tq_x'^{(d)} \cdot _tq_x'^{(w)}$, justify this relationship by general reasoning.

7-17. Suppose there are n_x persons in a study sample. Let γ_i be defined by (7.51), and let δ_i be defined by (7.17). Show that the general form for the full data likelihood, given by (7.50b), can also be written as

$$L = \prod_{i=1}^{n} \left[_{t_i}p_x'^{(d)} \right]^{1-\delta_i} \cdot \left[-\frac{d}{dt} _tp_x'^{(d)} \big|_{t=t_i} \right]^{\delta_i} \cdot \left[_{t_i}p_x'^{(w)} \right]^{1-\gamma_i} \cdot \left[-\frac{d}{dt} _tp_x'^{(w)} \big|_{t=t_i} \right]^{\gamma_i}.$$

7-18. Solve equation (7.53) under Special Case A with all withdrawals occurring at $t_i = t$, a constant.

7-19. Find the MLE of $q_x'^{(w)}$ in the Special Case A, partial data, exponential distribution, situation.

7-20. Find the MLE of $q_x'^{(w)}$ in the Special Case A, partial data, uniform distribution, situation.

7.5   Properties of Maximum Likelihood Estimators

7-21. Approximate $\text{Var}(\hat{q}_x)$ for the Special Case B estimator given by (7.30) by using the linear assumption to approximate $E[D]$, rather than the hyperbolic assumption as was done in Example 7.8.

7-22. Find the asymptotic variance of $\hat{\mu}$ given by (7.15).

7-23. Find the asymptotic variance of the estimator derived in Exercise 7-15. [Note that, under the assumptions of the model, $E[D'] = c(1 - p^{1/2})$ and $E[D''] = (n-c)(1-p)$.]

7-24. Find the asymptotic variance of the Schwartz-Lazar estimator derived as an MLE in Exercise 7-9.

7-25. Consider the Special Case A, partial data, situation of Section 7.4.4. Note that both D and W are random variables.
   (a) What is $E[D]$?
   (b) What is $E[W]$?

(c) Under the exponential distribution assumption, $\frac{\partial \ln L}{\partial \alpha}$ and $\frac{\partial \ln L}{\partial \beta}$ are given by (7.59) and (7.60), respectively, where $\alpha = \mu^{(d)}$ and $\beta = \mu^{(w)}$. Find $\frac{\partial^2 \ln L}{\partial \alpha^2}$, $\frac{\partial^2 \ln L}{\partial \beta^2}$, and $\frac{\partial^2 \ln L}{\partial \alpha \partial \beta}$.

(d) (i) Find $E\left[-\frac{\partial^2 \ln L}{\partial \alpha^2}\right]$, and let it be the element f_{11} of matrix f.

   (ii) Find $E\left[-\frac{\partial^2 \ln L}{\partial \beta^2}\right]$, and let it be the element f_{22} of matrix f.

   (iii) Find $E\left[-\frac{\partial^2 \ln L}{\partial \alpha \partial \beta}\right]$, and let it be the elements f_{12} and f_{21} of matrix f.

(e) The inverse of matrix f, $g = f^{-1}$, gives $Var(\hat{\alpha})$ as element g_{11}, $Var(\hat{\beta})$ as element g_{22}, and $Cov(\hat{\alpha}, \hat{\beta})$ as elements g_{12} and g_{21}. Find $Var(\hat{\alpha})$, $Var(\hat{\beta})$ and $Cov(\hat{\alpha}, \hat{\beta})$.

7.6 The Product Limit Estimator

7-26. Show that in a Special Case A, full data, situation, the product limit estimator will be $\hat{q}_x = \frac{d_x}{n_x}$, the same as (7.7) and (6.7).

7-27. One hundred annuitants are observed from attainment of exact age 75 for part or all of the following year of age. There are four deaths, one at the end of each quarter year of age. At the end of the observation period, there were ten annuitants aged $75\frac{2}{3}$, and the other survivors had all attained age 76 or greater.
   (a) Find the product limit estimate of q_{75}.
   (b) Estimate the variance of $\hat{q}_{75}$ by using $\hat{q}_i$ in place of each q_i.

7-28. In a clinical study with n lives at $t = 0$, there are no intermediate entrants. There was one death at time t_7, two deaths at time t_8, and one death at time t_9. The product limit estimate of $S(t)$ is found to be $\hat{S}(t_7) = .75$, $\hat{S}(t_8) = .60$, and $\hat{S}(t_9) = .50$. Determine the number of terminations from the study between times t_8 and t_9.

7-29. Ten nuclear power plant workers were accidentally exposed to a significant dosage of radiation. A death is observed at each of times 2 and 4, and x withdrawals are observed at time 3. Using the product limit estimator of $S(t)$, it is found that $\hat{S}(5) = .75$. Determine x.

7-30. Consider a newborn litter of five mice. As a result of the poor health
       of the mother, they die at times 2, 3, 6, 9, 12. Estimate both S(10)
       and $\Lambda(10)$ by (a) the product limit method, and (b) the Nelson-Aalen
       method.

7-31. In a complete data study, with only one death at each death point,
       $\Lambda(t)$ is estimated by the Nelson-Aalen method. If $\hat{\Lambda}(t_k) = .3101$ and
       $\hat{\Lambda}(t_{k+1}) = .3726$, find $\hat{\Lambda}(t_{k+2})$.

7-32. If $^{PL}\hat{S}(t)$ and $^{NA}\hat{S}(t)$ represent the product limit and Nelson-Aalen
       estimators of S(t), respectively, show that $^{PL}\hat{S}(t) < {}^{NA}\hat{S}(t)$, for
       all $t \geq t_1$.

CHAPTER 8

ESTIMATION OF PARAMETRIC SURVIVAL MODELS

8.1 INTRODUCTION

We now turn our attention to the estimation of survival models in parametric form.   Fewer quantities are to be estimated here than was the case for our tabular models, as described in Chapters 6 and 7.

We will consider two families of parametric models in this chapter. Most of the chapter will deal with estimating the parameters of our familiar univariate model $S(x)$ or $S(t)$.   In turn, we will explore this estimation problem under both complete data and incomplete data samples.   The second kind of parametric model to be considered is the one which involves concomitant variables.   This will include the select model $S(t;x)$, which arises in an actuarial setting, and the more general model $S(t;z)$, which arises in a clinical setting.

Various approaches to parameter estimation will be considered, with emphasis given to least-squares and maximum likelihood methods. Properties of the estimators will be examined, along with some hypothesis testing of the chosen model and its parameters.

8.2 UNIVARIATE MODELS, COMPLETE DATA

As we saw in Chapters 4 through 7, estimation is generally more straightforward with complete data samples. As in Chapter 4, we will distinguish between samples in which exact times of death are known, and those in which times of death have been grouped. We will use $S(t)$ for the underlying survival model to be estimated, rather than $S(x)$, to suggest that complete data samples generally exist in a clinical setting.

8.2.1 Exact Times of Death

Suppose a sample of n lives, all existing at $t=0$, produces observed times of death t_1, t_2, $\cdots$, t_n, assumed to be independent. We wish to use this data to estimate $S(t)$ as a parametric survival model.   In other words, we adopt a particular mathematical function of the variable t, depending on one or more parameters as well, and then use the sample data to estimate these unknown parameters, using a particular estimation procedure.

The simplest parametric models to use are those which depend on only one parameter, such as the exponential distribution with $S(t) = e^{-\lambda t}$. How can we estimate λ from our sample data?

Let us calculate

$$\bar{t} = \frac{1}{n} \cdot \sum_{i=1}^{n} t_i, \tag{8.1}$$

which is the mean time of death of the sample. We know from (2.29) that the mean of T is $E[T] = \frac{1}{\lambda}$ if T has an exponential distribution, so we can estimate λ by equating these two means. Thus

$$\hat{\lambda} = \frac{1}{\bar{t}} = \frac{n}{\sum\limits_{i=1}^{n} t_i}. \tag{8.2}$$

This estimation procedure is called the method of moments, so estimator (8.2) is the *moment estimator* of λ.

EXAMPLE 8.1 : Show that estimator (8.2) is the maximum likelihood estimator of λ as well.

SOLUTION : The likelihood for the ith death is the PDF for death at time t_i, $f(t_i) = \lambda e^{-\lambda t_i}$. The overall likelihood is given by $L = \prod\limits_{i=1}^{n} \lambda e^{-\lambda t_i}$, and the log-likelihood is $\ln L = n \cdot \ln \lambda - \lambda \cdot \sum\limits_{i=1}^{n} t_i$. Then $\frac{d \ln L}{d\lambda} = \frac{n}{\lambda} - \sum\limits_{i=1}^{n} t_i = 0$, which leads to the same result as (8.2).

Since estimator (8.2) is the MLE of λ, we know it is asymptotically unbiased, with asymptotic variance given by

$$\text{Var}(\hat{\lambda}) = \left(E\left[-\frac{d^2 \ln L}{d\lambda^2} \right] \right)^{-1}, \tag{8.3}$$

as stated in Section 7.5.2. The reader is asked to find the variance of estimator (8.2) in Exercise 8-1.

As an alternative to the method of moments, which equated the mean of the distribution ($\frac{1}{\lambda}$) to the mean of the sample ($\bar{t}$), we might instead equate the distribution and sample *medians*. Let $\tilde{t}$ represent the sample median, and let $t_1 < t_2 < \cdots$ be the observed values of t in increasing numerical order. If n is odd, for example n=25, then $\tilde{t}=t_{13}$ is the sample median; if n is even, for example n=24, then $\tilde{t} = \frac{1}{2}(t_{12}+t_{13})$ is usually taken as the median. On the other hand, the median of the distribution is that value of t, $t_{1/2}$ say, for which $S(t_{1/2})=\frac{1}{2}$, or $e^{-\lambda t_{1/2}}=\frac{1}{2}$ under the exponential distribution. Solving for $t_{1/2}$ we find that $t_{1/2} = -\dfrac{\ln\frac{1}{2}}{\lambda}$, and our estimate of λ results from equating $t_{1/2}$ and $\tilde{t}$. Thus

$$t_{1/2} = -\frac{\ln\frac{1}{2}}{\lambda} = \tilde{t}, \tag{8.4}$$

producing

$$\hat{\lambda} = -\frac{\ln\frac{1}{2}}{\tilde{t}}. \tag{8.5}$$

EXAMPLE 8.2: A sample of 10 laboratory mice produces the times of death (in days) 3, 4, 5, 7, 7, 8, 10, 10, 10, 12. Assuming the operative survival model to be exponential, estimate λ by both the method of moments and the method of medians.

SOLUTION: The sample mean is $\bar{t}=7.6$ and the sample median is $\tilde{t}=7.5$. Then $\hat{\lambda} = \frac{1}{\bar{t}} = .13157$ by the method of moments, and $\hat{\lambda} = \dfrac{-\ln\frac{1}{2}}{\tilde{t}} = .09242$ by the method of medians.

For a parametric model with two parameters, the method of moments equates the sample and distribution means, and the sample and distribution second (central) moments. For our sample of times of death t_i, $i = 1, 2, \cdots, n$, the sample second (central) moment, s^2 say, is given by

$$s^2 = \frac{1}{n-1} \cdot \sum_{i=1}^{n} (t_i - \bar{t})^2, \tag{8.6}$$

where $\bar{t}$ is the sample mean. Then if μ and σ^2 are the distribution mean and variance, respectively, in terms of the two unknown parameters of the distribution, we would find estimates of those parameters by solving simultaneously the equations $\mu = \bar{t}$ and $\sigma^2 = s^2$.

This method of parameter estimation is facilitated if we have simple expressions for μ and σ^2 in terms of the distribution parameters. If these do not exist, then the moment equations may require a numerical solution, as would be the case for the popular actuarial parametric models of Gompertz and Makeham. On the other hand, in some cases the moment equations might not have a solution at all, so this method of parameter estimation cannot be used.

EXAMPLE 8.3 : The two-parameter gamma distribution is defined by its PDF as $f(t) = \frac{1}{\beta^\alpha \Gamma(\alpha)} t^{\alpha-1} e^{-t/\beta}$, $t>0$, $\alpha>0$, $\beta>0$, and its mean and variance are $\mu = \beta\alpha$ and $\sigma^2 = \beta^2\alpha$. Using the sample data of Example 8.2, estimate α and β by the method of moments.

SOLUTION : We have $\bar{t} = 7.6$ from Example 8.2, and we find the sample second moment to be $s^2 = \frac{1}{9} \cdot \sum_{i=1}^{10} (t_i - 7.6)^2 = 8.7\dot{1}$. Then our moment equations are $\beta\alpha = 7.6$ and $\beta^2\alpha = 8.7\dot{1}$. Then $8.7\dot{1} = \beta(\beta\alpha) = \beta(7.6)$, so $\hat{\beta} = \frac{8.7\dot{1}}{7.6} = 1.14620$, and $\hat{\alpha} = \frac{7.6}{\hat{\beta}} = 6.63061$.

For two parameters we might also use the method of percentiles, which is an extension of the method of medians (the median is the 50th percentile). If t_p is a value of t such that $S(t_p) = 1 - p$, then t_p is the $100p^{th}$ percentile of the distribution. If $p = \frac{1}{2}$, then t_p is the median, $t_{1/2}$. Note well that if $S(t_p) = .95$, for example, t_p is the 5th percentile, not the 95th. We then observe (or approximate) the corresponding percentiles in the sample, equate them to the distribution percentiles (which are in terms of the unknown parameters), and solve for the parameters. An example will make the procedure clear.

EXAMPLE 8.4 : Estimate the Gompertz parameters B and c (see formula (2.32)) from the sample data of Example 8.2 by the method of percentiles, using the (approximate) 25th and 65th percentiles.

SOLUTION : From the data, let us approximate the desired sample percentiles as 4.5 and 9. (The reader should verify the reasonableness of these values.) For the distribution, $S(t_{.25}) = \exp\left[\frac{B}{\ln c}(1 - c^{t.25})\right] = .75$, so

$$t_{.25} = \frac{\ln\left[1 - \frac{\ln(.75)\cdot \ln c}{B}\right]}{\ln c}. \quad \text{Similarly,} \quad t_{.65} = \frac{\ln\left[1 - \frac{\ln(.35)\cdot \ln c}{B}\right]}{\ln c}. \quad \text{When}$$

we equate $t_{.25} = 4.5$ and $t_{.65} = 9$, the resulting equations produce $\hat{B} = .03777$ and $\hat{c} = 1.24173$. The details of this solution are left as an exercise.

The method of maximum likelihood may also be used for models with two parameters. Here we would take the partial derivative of ln L with respect to each parameter, set each derivative to zero, and solve the resulting pair of equations simultaneously. Frequently these equations are not convenient ones in the unknown parameters, and a numerical solution must be obtained.

EXAMPLE 8.5 : Estimate the Weibull parameters k and n from the sample data of Example 8.2 by the method of maximum likelihood.

SOLUTION : Recall that $L = \prod_{i=1}^{10} f(t_i)$, so that $\ln L = \sum_{i=1}^{10} \ln f(t_i)$. Now $f(t) = S(t) \cdot \lambda(t)$, so, from (2.35) and (2.36) we find the PDF of the Weibull distribution to be $f(t) = k \cdot t^n \cdot \exp\left[-\dfrac{k \cdot t^{n+1}}{n+1}\right]$. Then the log-likelihood is

$$\ln L = 10 \cdot \ln k + n \cdot \sum_{i=1}^{10} \ln t_i - \frac{k}{n+1} \cdot \sum_{i=1}^{10} t_i^{n+1}.$$ Differentiating, we obtain

$$\frac{\partial \ln L}{\partial n} = \sum_{i=1}^{10} \ln t_i - \frac{k}{(n+1)^2}\left[(n+1) \cdot \sum_{i=1}^{10} (\ln t_i) \cdot t_i^{n+1} - \sum_{i=1}^{10} t_i^{n+1}\right] = 0,$$ as well

as $\dfrac{\partial \ln L}{\partial k} = \dfrac{10}{k} - \dfrac{1}{n+1} \cdot \sum_{i=1}^{10} t_i^{n+1} = 0$. From this second equation we then find

$$k = \frac{10 \cdot (n+1)}{\sum_{i=1}^{10} t_i^{n+1}}.$$ This is substituted into the first equation which is then

solved numerically for $\hat{n}$. Finally, this $\hat{n}$ is used to find $\hat{k}$.

We next consider a technique of parameter estimation that does not directly use the observed times of death. Suppose we have produced, from the exact times of death t_i, $i = 1, 2, \cdots, n$, the estimated survival distribution $S^o(t)$ given by equation (4.1), and illustrated in Figure 4.2 for a sample with n=5. Note that this $S^o(t)$ is "parametric" in sense that it is defined for all $t \geq 0$, but not in the sense that we are using the term in this chapter. Since $S^o(t)$ is a representation of the survival pattern observed for the sample to which it relates, it is frequently called the *observed* survival function, which explains the superscript "o". We will now use $\hat{S}(t)$ for our parametric model with estimated parameters; the distinction between $\hat{S}(t)$ and $S^o(t)$ should be clearly understood.

We assume a parametric model for S(t), with unknown parameters, of course. We could then consider the sum of squares

$$SS = \sum_{i=1}^{n} \left[S(t_i) - S^o(t_i) \right]^2. \qquad (8.7a)$$

The only unknowns in (8.7a) are the parameters in $S(t_i)$, so we could differentiate SS with respect to each parameter, set each derivative to zero, and solve for the *least-squares* estimates of the parameters.

   To illustrate, let us fit a uniform distribution (with unknown ω) to the data of Example 8.2. $S^o(t)$ for this data is shown in Figure 8.1, with the adopted uniform $S(t)$ superimposed. For this data, although there are 10 deaths, there are only 7 distinct *times* of death, due to the multiple deaths at $t=7$ and $t=10$.

   Note that formula (8.7a) defines the deviations, whose squares are to be minimized, to be those between $S(t)$ and $S^o(t)$ at the *bottom left corners* of $S^o(t)$. (E.g., $t_1=3$ in Figure 8.1, and $S^o(3) = .90$; similarly, $t_7=12$ and $S^o(12) = 0$.) This procedure exerts a downward bias on $\hat{\omega}$. Conversely,

$$SS = \sum_{i=1}^{n} \left[S(t_i) - S^o(t_{i-1}) \right]^2 \qquad (8.7b)$$

fits $S(t)$ to $S^o(t)$ at the *top right corners* of $S^o(t)$, thereby exerting an upward bias on $\hat{\omega}$. The best procedure is to fit $S(t)$ to $S^o(t)$ at the *midpoints* of the vertical line segments in Figure 8.1. Thus

$$SS = \sum_{i=1}^{n} \left\{ S(t_i) - \tfrac{1}{2}\left[S^o(t_i) + S^o(t_{i-1}) \right] \right\}^2 \qquad (8.7)$$

will be minimized to find the least-squares estimates.

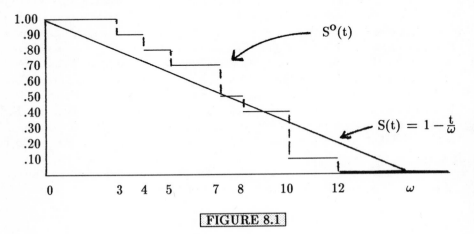

FIGURE 8.1

Applying (8.7) to find $\hat{\omega}$ from the data shown in Figure 8.1, we have

$$\text{SS} = \sum_{i=1}^{7} \left\{ 1 - \frac{t_i}{\omega} - \tfrac{1}{2}\left[S^o(t_i) + S^o(t_{i-1}) \right] \right\}^2 . \tag{8.8}$$

Differentiating, we find

$$\frac{d\,\text{SS}}{d\omega} = 2 \cdot \sum_{i=1}^{7} \left\{ 1 - \frac{t_i}{\omega} - \tfrac{1}{2}\left[S^o(t_i) + S^o(t_{i-1}) \right] \right\} \cdot \frac{t_i}{\omega^2} = 0,$$

or

$$\sum_{i=1}^{7} t_i - \frac{1}{\omega} \cdot \sum_{i=1}^{7} t_i^2 - \sum_{i=1}^{7} t_i \cdot \tfrac{1}{2}\left[S^o(t_i) + S^o(t_{i-1}) \right] = 0,$$

or

$$\hat{\omega} = \frac{\displaystyle\sum_{i=1}^{7} t_i^2}{\displaystyle\sum_{i=1}^{7} t_i - \sum_{i=1}^{7} t_i \cdot \tfrac{1}{2}\left[S^o(t_i) + S^o(t_{i-1}) \right]} . \tag{8.9}$$

Table 8.1 gives the values needed to evaluate (8.9) for $\hat{\omega}$.

TABLE 8.1

i	t_i	$S^o(t_i)$	t_i^2	$t_i \cdot \tfrac{1}{2}\left[S^o(t_i) + S^o(t_{i-1}) \right]$
1	3	.9	9	2.85
2	4	.8	16	3.40
3	5	.7	25	3.75
4	7	.5	49	4.20
5	8	.4	64	3.60
6	10	.1	100	2.50
7	12	0.0	144	.60
	49		407	20.90

Then $\hat{\omega} = \dfrac{407}{49 - 20.9} = 14.48399$.

Least-squares estimation of parameters is facilitated if the parameters are linear within SS, so that the derivative equations are linear. Since this is frequently not the case, a transformation, usually logarithmic, might be used.

EXAMPLE 8.6: Fit the data of Example 8.2 to an exponential distribution, estimating λ by the method of least squares.
SOLUTION: We have

$$SS = \sum_{i=1}^{7} \left\{ e^{-\lambda t_i} - \tfrac{1}{2}\left[S^o(t_i) + S^o(t_{i-1}) \right] \right\}^2, \tag{8.10}$$

so $\dfrac{d\,SS}{d\lambda} = 0$ will be an exponential equation in λ. To avoid this we will fit $\ln S(t_i) = -\lambda t_i$ to $\ln\left\{\tfrac{1}{2}\left[S^o(t_i) + S^o(t_{i-1})\right]\right\}$. We now have

$$SS = \sum_{i=1}^{7} \left(-\lambda t_i - \ln\left\{\tfrac{1}{2}\left[S^o(t_i) + S^o(t_{i-1})\right]\right\} \right)^2, \tag{8.10a}$$

which leads to

$$\frac{d\,SS}{d\lambda} = 2 \cdot \sum_{i=1}^{7} \left(-\lambda t_i - \ln\left\{\tfrac{1}{2}\left[S^o(t_i) + S^o(t_{i-1})\right]\right\} \right)(-t_i) = 0, \tag{8.11}$$

or

$$\lambda \cdot \sum_{i=1}^{7} t_i^2 + \sum_{i=1}^{7} t_i \cdot \ln\left\{\tfrac{1}{2}\left[S^o(t_i) + S^o(t_{i-1})\right]\right\} = 0, \tag{8.11a}$$

which produces the estimator

$$\hat{\lambda} = \frac{ -\sum_{i=1}^{7} t_i \cdot \ln\left\{\tfrac{1}{2}\left[S^o(t_i) + S^o(t_{i-1})\right]\right\} }{ \sum_{i=1}^{7} t_i^2 }. \tag{8.12}$$

Table 8.2 gives the values needed to evaluate (8.12) for $\hat{\lambda}$.

TABLE 8.2

i	t_i	$S^o(t_i)$	t_i^2	$t_i \cdot \ln\left\{\frac{1}{2}\left[S^o(t_i) + S^o(t_{i-1})\right]\right\}$
1	3	.9	9	$-$ .15387
2	4	.8	16	$-$ .65007
3	5	.7	25	$-$ 1.43841
4	7	.5	49	$-$ 3.57578
5	8	.4	64	$-$ 6.38806
6	10	.1	100	$-$13.86294
7	12	0.0	144	$-$35.94879
	49		407	$-$62.01792

Then $\hat{\lambda} = \dfrac{62.01792}{407} = .15238$.

For some survival models, such as Gompertz and Makeham, a transformation to make S(t) linear in its parameters does not exist. The method of least squares could still be used, of course, with the derivative equations being solved numerically, but some of the advantages of this method of estimation would thereby be lost.

Note that unweighted least squares were used in our discussion. If values of $S^o(t_i)$ are felt to be more reliable for some t_i than for others, we could use greater weights on the squared deviations $\left\{S(t_i) - \frac{1}{2}\left[S^o(t_i) + S^o(t_{i-1})\right]\right\}^2$ for such values.

In summary, we have described three methods (moments, percentiles, and maximum likelihood), for estimating survival model parameters directly from exact times of death, and have illustrated these methods for one-parameter models (such as uniform and exponential), and for two-parameter models (gamma, Gompertz, and Weibull). We also explored estimation of one-parameter models from values of $S^o(t_i)$ using least squares.

8.2.2 Grouped Times of Death

This study design was described in Section 4.4, along with techniques for estimating a tabular survival model from such data. We are now interested in the estimation of parametric models, and we will consider the methods of maximum likelihood and least squares for this purpose.

Suppose n persons are alive at t=0, and we observe their deaths in k non-overlapping intervals of equal length. Let d_i be the number of deaths observed in (i, i+1]. The probability of death in (i, i+1] for a person alive at t=0 is $_i|q_0 = S(i) - S(i+1)$, so the contribution of the $(i+1)^{st}$ interval to the likelihood is

$$L_i = \left[S(i) - S(i+1) \right]^{d_i}. \tag{8.13}$$

The overall likelihood is

$$L = \prod_{i=0}^{k-1} \left[S(i) - S(i+1) \right]^{d_i}. \tag{8.14}$$

Then $S(i) - S(i+1)$ is written in terms of the unknown parameters of the chosen parametric model, and the parameters are found by maximizing L.

If the chosen $S(t)$ is sufficiently simple, such as a one-parameter uniform or exponential model, then convenient expressions for the MLE's of the parameters can be found. Otherwise, as frequently occurs, the likelihood equations must be solved numerically, or the likelihood is maximized numerically without taking derivatives.

EXAMPLE 8.7 :   Fit an exponential model to the grouped data of Example 4.4, estimating λ by maximum likelihood.

SOLUTION :   In general, $S(i) - S(i+1) = e^{-\lambda i} - e^{-\lambda(i+1)} = e^{-\lambda i}(1 - e^{-\lambda})$.

Then $L = \prod_{i=0}^{4} \left[e^{-\lambda i}(1 - e^{-\lambda}) \right]^{d_i}$, so $\ln L = -\lambda \cdot \sum_{i=0}^{4} i \cdot d_i + \ln(1 - e^{-\lambda}) \cdot \sum_{i=0}^{4} d_i$.

Next $\dfrac{d \ln L}{d\lambda} = -\sum_{i=0}^{4} i \cdot d_i + \dfrac{e^{-\lambda} \cdot \sum_{i=0}^{4} d_i}{1 - e^{-\lambda}} = 0$, from which we then find

$e^{-\hat{\lambda}} = \dfrac{\sum_{i=0}^{4} i \cdot d_i}{\sum_{i=0}^{4} d_i + \sum_{i=0}^{4} i \cdot d_i}$.   Since $d_0 = 2$, $d_1 = 3$, $d_2 = 8$, $d_3 = 6$, $d_4 = 1$, we find

that $\sum_{i=0}^{4} d_i = 20$ and $\sum_{i=0}^{4} i \cdot d_i = 41$, which produces $\hat{\lambda} = .39730$.

For a two-parameter Weibull distribution, the probability of death in

$(i, i+1]$ is $S(i) - S(i+1) = \exp\left[-\dfrac{k}{n+1} \cdot i^{n+1} \right] - \exp\left[-\dfrac{k}{n+1} \cdot (i+1)^{n+1} \right]$,

so from (8.14),

$$L = \prod_{i=0}^{k-1} \left\{ \exp\left[-\frac{k}{n+1} \cdot i^{n+1} \right] - \exp\left[-\frac{k}{n+1} \cdot (i+1)^{n+1} \right] \right\}^{d_i}. \tag{8.15}$$

We can see that $\frac{\partial \ln L}{\partial k} = 0$ and $\frac{\partial \ln L}{\partial n} = 0$ will not produce equations that are easily solved for $\hat{n}$ and $\hat{k}$. Since numerical computer routines are in existence to directly find the $\hat{n}$ and $\hat{k}$ which maximize L, there is no need to take the partial derivatives of ln L.

We recognize that $S(i) - S(i+1) = S(i) \cdot q_i$ is the multinomial probability that a person in the original sample of n at t=0 will die in (i, i+1]. Then

$$E[D_i] = n[S(i) - S(i+1)] \qquad (8.16)$$

is the expected number of deaths in (i, i+1]. Since d_i is the actual number of such deaths, then least-squares estimates of the parameters of S(t) can be found by minimizing

$$SS = \sum_{i=0}^{k-1} \left\{ n\left[S(i) - S(i+1)\right] - d_i \right\}^2. \qquad (8.17)$$

EXAMPLE 8.8 : From the grouped data of Example 4.4, estimate the uniform distribution parameter ω by unweighted least squares.

SOLUTION : $n=20$ and $S(i) - S(i+1) = \frac{1}{\omega}$, so $SS = \sum_{i=0}^{4} \left[\frac{20}{\omega} - d_i\right]^2$, leading to $\frac{dSS}{d\omega} = 2 \cdot \sum_{i=0}^{4} \left[\frac{20}{\omega} - d_i\right] \cdot \left(-\frac{20}{\omega^2}\right) = 0$, which yields $\hat{\omega} = 5$. (The results of Example 4.4 for $_2|\hat{q}_0 \cdot \hat{S}(3)$ and $\hat{q}_3$ could be compared with those produced by the parametric models estimated in Examples 8.7 and 8.8.)

As an alternative to minimizing the total squared deviations of actual from expected grouped deaths, we could approximate the hazard rate at the midpoint of each interval (see page 193), and define SS to be the sum of squared deviations of (approximate) observed hazard from the parametric model hazard, in terms of the unknown parameters, of course, That is

$$SS = \sum_{i=0}^{k-1} \left[\lambda^o\left(i+\tfrac{1}{2}\right) - \lambda\left(i+\tfrac{1}{2}\right)\right]^2, \qquad (8.18)$$

from which the least-squares estimates of the $\lambda(t)$ parameters can be found. This is frequently easier to do than the grouped deaths approach considered above, since $\lambda(i)$ is frequently a simpler function of the parameters than is $S(i) - S(i+1)$.

The hazard rate approach will be considered further in Section 8.3.2.

8.3 UNIVARIATE MODELS, INCOMPLETE DATA

We now explore the estimation of parametric survival models in the presence of incomplete data. We will consider two estimation approaches, namely, the methods of maximum likelihood and least squares. The former will be used in cases where we estimate our parameters directly from the data. The latter will be used where we first process the basic data to obtain estimates $\hat{q}_x$ (or more likely a constant $\hat{\mu}$) for the interval $(x, x+1]$, as described in Chapters 6 and 7, and then estimate our model parameters by fitting our model to this sequence of initial estimates.

8.3.1 *Maximum Likelihood Approaches*

As a first example, consider a sample of n laboratory mice all alive at $t=0$. We observe the exact time of each death up to time $t=r$, and cease observation at that time with some of the mice still alive. Since not all have died we have an incomplete data situation. Note that the study design is longitudinal (not cross-sectional), and those that are not observed to die are enders, not random withdrawals. In a clinical setting this type of study is said to be *truncated*.

The contribution of each death to the likelihood is the PDF for death at the time that death actually occurs. The contribution for each survivor at $t=r$ is simply the probability of living to $t=r$, namely $S(r)$. If there are d deaths in total, out of the original sample of size n, then we have

$$L = \left[S(r)\right]^{n-d} \cdot \prod_{i=1}^{d} f(t_i), \tag{8.19}$$

where t_i is the time of the ith death.

EXAMPLE 8.9: Suppose the study described in Example 8.2 had been truncated at $t=9$. Estimate the exponential parameter λ in this case.
SOLUTION: At $t=9$, 6 deaths have occurred and 4 are still alive, so we have $L = \left[S(9)\right]^4 \cdot \prod_{i=1}^{6} f(t_i)$. In this case, $S(9) = e^{-9\lambda}$ and $f(t_i) = \lambda e^{-\lambda t_i}$, $t_i = 3,4,5,7,7,8$, giving us $L = \lambda^6 \cdot e^{-34\lambda} \cdot e^{-36\lambda} = \lambda^6 \cdot e^{-70\lambda}$. This produces $\ln L = 6 \cdot \ln \lambda - 70\lambda$, so $\dfrac{d \ln L}{d\lambda} = \dfrac{6}{\lambda} - 70 = 0$, and $\hat{\lambda} = \dfrac{6}{70} = .08571$.

More generally, suppose the ith individual in our study comes under observation at time r_i and leaves observation at time t_i. An individual can leave observation by death or by the ending of the observation period (i.e., as a scheduled ender), but we assume, for now, that there are no random withdrawals. In other words, death is the only random event that can occur, so we are operating in a single-decrement environment.

The probability of living from r_i to t_i is $_{t_i - r_i}p_{r_i} = \dfrac{S(t_i)}{S(r_i)}$, and this is the total contribution to the likelihood for those alive at r_i who cease observation at t_i without dying. For the deaths, we need the PDF at time t_i, so $_{t_i - r_i}p_{r_i}$ must be multiplied by $\lambda(t_i)$. Thus we have

$$L = \prod_{\mathfrak{D}} \frac{S(t_i) \cdot \lambda(t_i)}{S(r_i)} \cdot \prod_{\overline{\mathfrak{D}}} \frac{S(t_i)}{S(r_i)}, \qquad (8.20)$$

where the first product includes all deaths and the second includes all who exit alive.

Recall the indicator variable δ_i defined by (7.17). Since (8.20) contains $\dfrac{S(t_i)}{S(r_i)}$ for all n persons in our study, and contains $\lambda(t_i)$ only for the deaths, we can write the likelihood as

$$L = \prod_{i=1}^{n} \frac{S(t_i) \cdot \left[\lambda(t_i)\right]^{\delta i}}{S(r_i)} . \qquad (8.21)$$

Furthermore, since $\lambda(t_i) = f(t_i)/S(t_i)$, we could write

$$L = \prod_{i=1}^{n} \frac{\left[S(t_i)\right]^{1-\delta_i} \cdot \left[f(t_i)\right]^{\delta_i}}{S(r_i)} . \qquad (8.22)$$

The reader should be able to see that (8.20), (8.21) and (8.22) are equivalent expressions.

EXAMPLE 8.10 : Consider the following sample of six patients who received artificial hearts on the dates shown. Four died by December 31, 1986.

Patient	Date of Transplant	Date of Death
1	Jan. 1, 1985	Apr. 1, 1986
2	Apr. 1, 1985	Apr. 1, 1986
3	July 1, 1985	***
4	Oct. 1, 1985	July 1, 1986
5	Jan. 1, 1986	***
6	Apr. 1, 1986	Oct. 1, 1986

Estimate the exponential parameter λ from the data of this sample, using calendar year 1986 as the observation period.

$\boxed{\text{SOLUTION}}$:   At time of entry into the study, the six patients have the following values of r_i: $r_1 = 1$, $r_2 = .75$, $r_3 = .50$, $r_4 = .25$, $r_5 = 0$, $r_6 = 0$.   At time of exit from the study, the values of t_i are as follows: $t_1 = 1.25$, $t_2 = 1$, $t_3 = 1.50$, $t_4 = .75$, $t_5 = 1$, $t_6 = .50$.   (Note that t_3 and t_5 are *ending* times, and the other t are death times.)   From (8.21) we find the log-likelihood

$$\ln L = \sum_{i=1}^{6} \left[-\lambda \cdot t_i + \lambda \cdot r_i + \ln \lambda \cdot \delta_i \right].$$ When $\dfrac{d \ln L}{d\lambda}$ is set to zero, we obtain

$$\hat{\lambda} = \frac{\displaystyle\sum_{i=1}^{6} \delta_i}{\displaystyle\sum_{i=1}^{6} (t_i - r_i)} = \frac{4}{3.5} = 1.1486.$$ The formula for $\hat{\lambda}$ is similar to those

obtained in Chapter 7 for MLE's under the exponential assumption because, in both cases, λ is assumed to be constant throughout the study interval.

Now suppose withdrawal is a random event along with death, so that we are in a double-decrement environment.   The probability of living from r_i to t_i is now called

$$t_i - r_i \mathrm{p}_{r_i}^{(\tau)} = {}_{t_i - r_i}\mathrm{p}_{r_i}^{(d)} \cdot {}_{t_i - r_i}\mathrm{p}_{r_i}^{(w)}, \tag{8.23}$$

as introduced in Section 5.3, if death and withdrawal are independent.   In terms of survival distribution notation, let $S_d(t)$ denote "survival against death" and let $S_w(t)$ denote "survival against withdrawal".   Then

$$t_i - r_i \mathrm{p}_{r_i}^{(\tau)} = \frac{S_d(t_i) \cdot S_w(t_i)}{S_d(r_i) \cdot S_w(r_i)}. \tag{8.24}$$

Further, let $\lambda_d(t) = \mu_t^{(d)}$ and $\lambda_w(t) = \mu_t^{(w)}$ denote the hazard rates (forces) of death and withdrawal, respectively.

In this situation t_i is the time of death, random withdrawal, or scheduled ending from the sample, recalling that scheduled ending is not a random event.

Clearly all three categories of exit will each contribute $_{t_i - r_i}\mathrm{p}_{r_i}^{(\tau)}$ to the likelihood.   As well, each death will contribute $\lambda_d(t_i)$ and each withdrawal will contribute $\lambda_w(t_i)$.   Thus we have

$$L = \prod_{\mathcal{D}} {}_{t_i - r_i}\mathrm{p}_{r_i}^{(\tau)} \cdot \mu_{t_i}^{(d)} \cdot \prod_{\mathcal{W}} {}_{t_i - r_i}\mathrm{p}_{r_i}^{(\tau)} \cdot \mu_{t_i}^{(w)} \cdot \prod_{\mathcal{E}} {}_{t_i - r_i}\mathrm{p}_{r_i}^{(\tau)}, \tag{8.25}$$

$$= \prod_{i=1}^{n} {}_{t_i - r_i}\mathrm{p}_{r_i}^{(\tau)} \cdot \prod_{\mathcal{D}} \mu_{t_i}^{(d)} \cdot \prod_{\mathcal{W}} \mu_{t_i}^{(w)}. \tag{8.26}$$

Let us introduce a second indicator variable, γ_i, where

$$\gamma_i = \begin{cases} 1 & \text{if person i is a random withdrawal} \\ 0 & \text{otherwise} \end{cases}. \qquad (8.27)$$

Then in terms of survival distribution notation, our likelihood can be written as

$$L = \prod_{i=1}^{n} \frac{S_d(t_i) \cdot S_w(t_i) \cdot \left[\lambda_d(t_i)\right]^{\delta_i} \cdot \left[\lambda_w(t_i)\right]^{\gamma_i}}{S_d(r_i) \cdot S_w(r_i)}. \qquad (8.28)$$

Now the survival model for death depends on certain parameters, say θ_1 and θ_2. Similarly the model for random withdrawal depends on certain parameters, say ϕ_1 and ϕ_2. If the θ-parameters and the ϕ-parameters are mathematically independent of each other, then the terms $S_w(t)$ and $\lambda_w(t)$ are multiplicative constants when we estimate the θ-parameters, and so can be ignored. Similarly $S_d(t)$ and $\lambda_d(t)$ can be ignored when we estimate the ϕ-parameters. In other words, when we estimate the θ-parameters, (8.28) produces the same results as does (8.21) under the independence assumption.

If the independence assumption is not valid, then the estimation of parameters is much more complex. We will not consider such situations in this text.

EXAMPLE 8.11 : Suppose Patient 4 in Example 8.10 withdrew on July 1, 1986, instead of dying. Suppose mortality follows an exponential model and withdrawal follows a uniform model. Estimate λ and ω, assuming independence.

SOLUTION : We first note that $S_d(t) = e^{-\lambda t}$, $\lambda_d(t) = \lambda$, $S_w(t) = \frac{\omega - t}{\omega}$, and $\lambda_w(t) = \frac{1}{\omega - t}$. From (8.28), we find the log-likelihood to be

$$\ln L = \sum_{i=1}^{6} [\ln S_d(t_i) + \ln S_w(t_i) - \ln S_d(r_i) - \ln S_w(r_i) \\ + \delta_i \cdot \ln \lambda_d(t_i) + \gamma_i \cdot \ln \lambda_w(t_i)],$$

so that $\frac{\partial \ln L}{\partial \lambda} = \sum_{i=1}^{6} \left[\frac{d}{d\lambda} \ln S_d(t_i) - \frac{d}{d\lambda} \ln S_d(r_i) + \delta_i \cdot \frac{d}{d\lambda} \ln \lambda_d(t_i) \right]$, since $\frac{\partial}{\partial \lambda} S_w(t) = \frac{\partial}{\partial \lambda} \lambda_w(t) = 0$. This yields the same likelihood equation as in Example 8.10, except that here we have $\sum_{i=1}^{6} \delta_i = 3$ rather than 4. Thus we have $\hat{\lambda} = \frac{3}{3.5} = .85714$. Similarly, $\frac{\partial}{\partial \omega} S_d(t)$ and $\frac{\partial}{\partial \omega} \lambda_d(t)$ are zero, so the derivative equation $\frac{\partial \ln L}{\partial \omega} = 0$ leads, after some simplification, to

$$\sum_{i=1}^{6} \frac{1}{\omega - t_i} - \sum_{i=1}^{6} \frac{1}{\omega - r_i} - \frac{1}{\omega - .75} = 0,$$ where the last term results from $\gamma_4 = 1$ and $t_4 = .75$. This equation must be solved for $\hat{\omega}$ by numerical methods.

8.3.2 Least-Squares Approaches

Let us suppose that one of the estimation procedures of Chapters 6 and 7, actuarial, moment or maximum likelihood, has been used to produce a sequence of $\hat{q}_x$ for each estimation interval $(x, x+1]$. From $\hat{q}_x$ we obtain an estimate of the force of mortality at $x+\frac{1}{2}$, the midpoint of $(x, x+1]$, from

$$\hat{\mu}_{x+1/2} = -\ln(1 - \hat{q}_x), \tag{8.29}$$

by making the exponential assumption for ℓ_{x+s}, $0 < s < 1$, or from

$$\hat{\mu}_{x+1/2} = \frac{\hat{q}_x}{1 - \frac{1}{2} \cdot \hat{q}_x}, \tag{8.30}$$

by making either the uniform or hyperbolic assumption. Of course, if we use estimator (7.23), a full data estimator under the exponential assumption, then we obtain $\hat{\mu}_{x+1/2}$ directly.

We now wish to fit this sequence of $\hat{\mu}_{x+1/2}$, from Chapter 6 or 7, to a chosen functional form, such as Gompertz, Weibull or Makeham. Once the chosen model's parameters have been estimated, then we can calculate our estimate of $\mu_{x+1/2}$ from this parametric survival model. Since we will want to reserve the notation $\hat{\mu}_{x+1/2}$ for such an estimate, the $\hat{\mu}_{x+1/2}$ result from the Chapter 6 or 7 approach must be renamed to avoid confusion. Let us denote such preliminary estimate by $\mu^o_{x+1/2}$, where the superscript means "observed." Thus "o" denotes an estimate calculated directly from the sample data, and the familiar "⌃" denotes an estimate obtained from the parametric model fitted to the $\mu^o_{x+1/2}$ sequence.

To fit a Gompertz model to the $\mu^o_{x+1/2}$ sequence, we recall, from (2.31), that $\mu_x = \lambda(x) = Bc^x$, which is not linear in the unknowns B and c. However, the transformation

$$\ln \mu_x = \ln B + x \cdot \ln c = \alpha + \beta x \tag{8.31}$$

is linear in α and β. If the domain of $\mu^o_{x+1/2}$ is from x=a to x=b, then we have

$$SS = \sum_{x=a}^{b} w_x \left[\alpha + \beta(x+\tfrac{1}{2}) - \ln \mu^o_{x+1/2} \right]^2 \tag{8.32}$$

as the general weighted sum of squares to be minimized by the least-squares estimates $\hat{\alpha}$ and $\hat{\beta}$.

It should be mentioned that the estimates of B and c found from

$$\hat{B} = e^{\hat{\alpha}} \quad \text{and} \quad \hat{c} = e^{\hat{\beta}} \tag{8.33}$$

will be somewhat different from those found by minimizing the sum of squared differences between $Bc^{x+1/2}$ and $\mu^o_{x+1/2}$, without making the log transformation.

If $w_x = 1$ for all x we have unweighted least-squares estimation. Some evidence exists that the unweighted approach gives better estimates of the true parameters (see, for example, Gehan and Siddiqui [25]), and it is certainly easier to apply.

[EXAMPLE 8.12]: Estimate the Gompertz parameters B and c by an unweighted least-squares fit to the following central rates observed from sample data.

x	m^o_x
31	.02639
32	.02914
33	.03557
34	.04121
35	.04966

[SOLUTION]: An observed central rate over (x, x+1] is the same as the (constant) force over (x, x+1) under the exponential assumption. Thus we take $\mu^o_{x+1/2} = m^o_x$. The least-squares equations, which result from differentiating (8.32) with respect to α and β, respectively, are

$$5.0 \cdot \alpha + 167.50 \cdot \beta = -16.69830$$

and

$$167.5 \cdot \alpha + 5621.25 \cdot \beta = -557.78192 ,$$

which solve for $\hat{\alpha} = -8.73694$ and $\hat{\beta} = .16111$. This in turn produces $\hat{B} = .00016054$ and $\hat{c} = 1.17482$.

To fit a Weibull model, we again find that $\mu_x = \lambda(x) = k \cdot x^n$, from

(2.35), is not linear in k and n. Again the log transformation

$$\ln \mu_x \;=\; \ln k + n \cdot \ln x \;=\; \alpha + \beta \cdot \ln x \qquad (8.34)$$

is linear in α and β, so we have

$$SS \;=\; \sum_{x=a}^{b} w_x \Big[\alpha + \beta \cdot \ln (x + \tfrac{1}{2}) - \ln \mu_{x+1/2}^{o} \Big]^2 \qquad (8.35)$$

as the general weighted sum of squares to be minimized by the least-squares estimates $\hat{\alpha}$ and $\hat{\beta}$. Then estimates of k and n are obtained from

$$\hat{k} \;=\; e^{\hat{\alpha}} \quad \text{and} \quad \hat{n} \;=\; \hat{\beta}. \qquad (8.36)$$

Fitting a Makeham model, with $\mu_x = \lambda(x) = A + Bc^x$, from (2.33), is a greater challenge, since the log transformation $\ln \mu_x$ does not produce a linear function in the parameters to be estimated. The following approach, which was suggested by Nesselle [48], might be used.

We begin by approximating $\mu_x = A + Bc^x$ by a Taylor series. Let

$$\mu_x \;=\; \mu_x^0 + (A - A_0) \cdot \frac{\partial \mu_x}{\partial A} \Big|_0 + (B - B_0) \cdot \frac{\partial \mu_x}{\partial B} \Big|_0 + (c - c_0) \cdot \frac{\partial \mu_x}{\partial c} \Big|_0 + \cdots .(8.37)$$

The method requires initial estimates of A, B, c, which we call A_0, B_0, c_0. In (8.37) the notation $|_0$ means that the indicated partial derivative of μ_x is evaluated at A_0, B_0, c_0. Since $\mu_x = A + Bc^x$, the indicated partials are

$$\frac{\partial \mu_x}{\partial A} \;=\; 1, \quad \frac{\partial \mu_x}{\partial B} \;=\; c^x, \quad \frac{\partial \mu_x}{\partial c} \;=\; Bxc^{x-1}. \qquad (8.38)$$

Letting $A - A_0 = d_A$, $B - B_0 = d_B$, $c - c_0 = d_c$, we have

$$SS \;=\; \sum_{x=a}^{b} w_x \Big[\mu_{x+1/2}^0 + d_A + d_B \cdot c_0^{x+1/2} + d_c \cdot B_0(x + \tfrac{1}{2}) c_0^{x-1/2} - \mu_{x+1/2}^o \Big]^2$$

$$(8.39)$$

as the general weighted sum of squares to be minimized by the least-squares estimates $\hat{d}_A$, $\hat{d}_B$, $\hat{d}_c$. Note that $\mu_{x+1/2}^0 = A_0 + B_0 c_0^{x+1/2}$, whereas $\mu_{x+1/2}^o$ is the value observed from sample data. The derivatives of SS with respect to d_A, d_B and d_c are equated to zero to produce $\hat{d}_A$, $\hat{d}_B$, $\hat{d}_c$, which are added to A_0, B_0, c_0, respectively, to produce A_1, B_1, c_1, say. Now these last values could be taken as our estimates of A, B, c, but they are not the true least-squares estimates since (8.37) is only an approximation. We consider A_1, B_1, c_1 to be *improved* estimates from A_0, B_0, c_0, and use them in place of A_0,

B_0, c_0 in (8.39) to solve again for $\hat{d}_A$, $\hat{d}_B$, $\hat{d}_c$ and hence other estimates called A_2, B_2, c_2. Continued use of this iterative approach will show a convergence of the successive estimates to the least-squares estimates $\hat{A}$, $\hat{B}$, $\hat{c}$.

8.4 HYPOTHESIS TESTING OF PARAMETRIC MODELS

We now wish to explore briefly the area of formal statistical tests that can be performed to determine the acceptability of a fitted parametric model as an adequate representation of the true underlying model. We wish to do this first for the case of grouped times of death and then for the case of exact times of death. In both cases we are assuming the complete data situation of Chapter 4.

8.4.1 Grouped Times of Death

Suppose, in the grouped times of death situation of Section 8.2.2, the parameters of the chosen parametric model have been estimated by some procedure such as maximum likelihood. We are then hypothesizing that the fitted model, $\hat{S}(t)$, is a good representation of the real $S(t)$, and we wish to test this hypothesis. Let

$$\hat{E}_i = n\left[\hat{S}(i) - \hat{S}(i+1)\right] \tag{8.40}$$

represent the expected number of deaths in $(i, i+1]$ according to the hypothesized model. Recall that d_i is the number observed in $(i, i+1]$ from our sample. The quantity

$$\chi^2 = \sum_{i=0}^{k-1} \frac{(\hat{E}_i - d_i)^2}{\hat{E}_i} , \tag{8.41}$$

has approximately a χ^2 distribution with $k-1-r$ degrees of freedom, where r is the number of parameters in $S(t)$ which were estimated from the data. If the hypothesized model is fully specified including its parameters (i.e., if the parameters are *not* estimated from the data), then the approximate χ^2 statistic defined by (8.41) has $k-1$ degrees of freedom.

EXAMPLE 8.13 : Test the hypothesis that the $\hat{S}(t)$ determined in Example 8.7 is a good representation of $S(t)$.

SOLUTION : Since $\hat{\lambda} = .3973$, then $\hat{E}_i = 20\left[e^{-.3973i}(1-e^{-.3973})\right]$, for $i = 0, \cdots, 4$, producing $\hat{E}_0 = 6.5574$, $\hat{E}_1 = 4.4074$, $\hat{E}_2 = 2.9624$, $\hat{E}_3 = 1.9911$, $\hat{E}_4 = 1.3383$. In addition, $\hat{E}_{5+}$, the expected number of deaths in $(5, \infty)$, is

$20 \cdot e^{-5\lambda} = 2.7435$, and the number observed is $d_{5+} = 0$. Using (8.41) with $k=6$, we find $\chi^2 = 23.0839$. Since only one parameter was estimated, then χ^2 has $6-1-1 = 4$ degrees of freedom. A table of χ^2 values shows that the probability of obtaining a departure measure of 23.0839 or more is less than .001, so we find very significant evidence against our $\hat{S}(t)$ as a representation of $S(t)$.

Since a small χ^2 value indicates a good fit of $\hat{S}(t)$ to the data, one might determine the parameters of $\hat{S}(t)$ so as to minimize (8.41). Parameters determined in this way are called the *minimum χ^2 estimators* of the parameters.

Since the unknown parameters would appear in both the numerator and denominator of (8.41), the minimization mathematics could be quite complex. As an alternative, we might find the parameters by minimizing

$$\chi'^2 = \sum_{i=0}^{k-1} \frac{(\hat{E}_i - d_i)^2}{d_i} \, , \tag{8.42}$$

instead of (8.41). Parameters determined in this way are called the *minimum modified χ^2 estimators* of the parameters. Note that (8.42) is a weighted version of (8.17), with weights of $w_i = \frac{1}{d_i}$. As the sample size approaches infinity, minimization of (8.41) and (8.42) will produce the same parameters estimates.

EXAMPLE 8.14 : Repeat Example 8.8 using $w_i = \frac{1}{d_i}$ to find the minimum modified χ^2 estimator of ω.

SOLUTION : We have SS $= \sum_{i=0}^{4} \frac{1}{d_i} \left[\frac{20}{\omega} - d_i \right]^2$, so the derivative equation $\frac{d\,SS}{d\omega} = 0$ leads to $\hat{\omega} = 4 \cdot \sum_{i=0}^{4} \frac{1}{d_i} = 8.5$.

8.4.2 *Exact Times of Death*

In this case we wish to compare our $\hat{S}(t)$, which is hypothesized as a representation of $S(t)$, with the observed $S^o(t)$. To do so we need a measure of the departure of $\hat{S}(t)$ from $S^o(t)$.

A fairly simple departure measure is the Kolmogorov-Smirnov (K–S) statistic, defined as

$$D_n = \max_t |\hat{S}(t) - S^o(t)| \, , \tag{8.43}$$

the largest absolute deviation between $\hat{S}(t)$ and $S^o(t)$ to be found over the domain of t. The subscript of D_n reminds us that this measure depends on the sample size n. We then calculate

$$Y = \sqrt{n} \cdot D_n \tag{8.44}$$

as the actual departure measure to be tested.

For small n, tables of critical values of y for various significance levels can be found in some books of tables or textbooks (see, for example, Hollander and Wolfe [31]). As $n \to \infty$, the probabilities can be calculated from

$$\Pr(Y > y) = 2 \sum_{j=1}^{\infty} (-1)^{j+1} e^{-2j^2 y^2}, \tag{8.45}$$

so, in effect, (8.45) gives approximate probabilities for large values of n.

EXAMPLE 8.15: Let us hypothesize that $S(t)$ has the uniform distribution $\hat{S}(t) = 1 - \frac{t}{15}$ for the sample of Example 8.2. Test this hypothesis using the K–S statistic.

SOLUTION: Figure 8.2 shows $S^o(t)$ for that data, along with the hypothesized $\hat{S}(t)$.

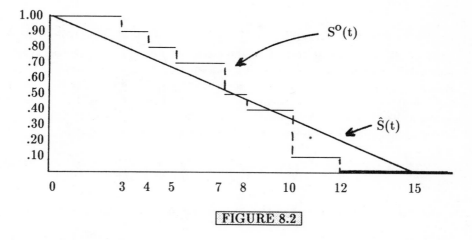

FIGURE 8.2

Table 8.3 on page 198 compares values of $\hat{S}(t)$ with values of $S^o(t)$, where $S^o(t^-)$ denotes the value of $S^o(t)$ *just before* t, and $S^o(t^+)$ denotes the value *just after* t.

TABLE 8.3

t	$\hat{S}(t)$	$S^o(t^-)$	$S^o(t^+)$	max $\lvert \hat{S}(t) - S^o(t) \rvert$
3	.80000	1.00	.90	.20000
4	.73333	.90	.80	.16667
5	.66667	.80	.70	.13333
7	.53333	.70	.50	.16667
8	.46667	.50	.40	.06667
10	.33333	.40	.10	.23333
12	.20000	.10	0.00	.20000
15	0.0000	0.00	---	0.00000

From the table we see that the maximum deviation is .23333. Then $y = (.23333) \cdot \sqrt{10} = .73786$, and we seek $\Pr(Y > .73786)$. From (8.45) we obtain $2\left[e^{-2(.73786)^2} - e^{-8(.73786)^2} + e^{-18(.73786)^2} - \cdots \right] = .64762$. (The first omitted term in the summation is $-e^{-32(.73786)^2}$, which is -2.71×10^{-8}.) Thus we find no significant evidence against our hypothesis of $\hat{S}(t) = 1 - \frac{t}{15}$, although our result here is suspect since we have only $n = 10$. Use of (8.45) for $\Pr(Y > y)$ should probably be restricted to cases where $n \geq 50$, say.

In Example 8.15, $\hat{S}(t) = 1 - \frac{t}{15}$ was fully specified, including the value of $\omega = 15$, without regard to the data. If we only assume the type of parametric model, and estimate its parameters from the data, then the departure measure $Y = \sqrt{n} \cdot D_n$ has different probability values than in the case above. Furthermore, Stephens [59] has suggested that the departure measure itself should be modified in such cases. For example, if an exponential model is suggested, with λ estimated from the data, then

$$Y = \left(D_n - \frac{0.2}{n} \right)\left(\sqrt{n} + 0.26 + \frac{0.5}{\sqrt{n}} \right) \qquad (8.46)$$

is a better measure to use than the unmodified $Y = \sqrt{n} \cdot D_n$.

EXAMPLE 8.16: Evaluate (8.46) for the exponential $\hat{S}(t)$, found by the method of moments in Example 8.2, compared to the data of the sample.
SOLUTION: Our hypothesized model is $\hat{S}(t) = e^{-.13157t}$. Values of $\hat{S}(t)$ are compared with values of $S^o(t)$ in Table 8.4, where $S^o(t^-)$ and $S^o(t^+)$ were defined in Example 8.15.

TABLE 8.4

t	$\hat{S}(t)$	$S^o(t^-)$	$S^o(t^+)$	$\max\limits \|\hat{S}(t) - S^o(t)\|$
3	.67387	1.00	.90	.32613
4	.59079	.90	.80	.30921
5	.51796	.80	.70	.28204
7	.39812	.70	.50	.30188
8	.34904	.50	.40	.15096
10	.26828	.40	.10	.16828
12	.20621	.10	0.00	.20621
>12	< .20621	0.00	0.00	<.20621

The maximum deviation occurs at $t=3^-$, so we have $D_{10} = .32613$. Then $y = (.32613 - \frac{.2}{10})\left(\sqrt{10} + 0.26 + \frac{0.5}{\sqrt{10}}\right) = 1.09607$. Stephens also found that the critical value $y = 1.094$ corresponds to the .05 significance level. Since our $y = 1.09607$ is very close to 1.094, we could reject the hypothesized $\hat{S}(t)$ with approximately 95% confidence.

Recall that the K–S test is based simply on the largest deviation between $\hat{S}(t)$ and $S^o(t)$. A better measure of the departure between $\hat{S}(t)$ and $S^o(t)$ is given by the A^2 statistic, proposed by Anderson and Darling [2], which is the weighted expected squared deviation of $\hat{S}(t)$ from $S^o(t)$, where the deviations are weighted by the inverse variance of $S^o(t)$. That is

$$A^2 = \int_0^\infty \frac{n}{S(t) \cdot F(t)} \cdot \left[S^o(t) - \hat{S}(t)\right]^2 \cdot f(t)\,dt, \qquad (8.47)$$

since, from (4.4b), $\text{Var}\left[S^o(t)\right] = \frac{S(t) \cdot F(t)}{n}$, and $f(t)$ is the PDF for death at time t. Of course $f(t)$, $S(t)$ and $F(t)$ are not known; since $\hat{S}(t)$ is being hypothesized as representing $S(t)$, then (8.47) is evaluated by using $\hat{S}(t)$, $\hat{F}(t)$ and $\hat{f}(t)$ in place of $S(t)$, $F(t)$ and $f(t)$. Furthermore, since $f(t) = 0$ for $t<0$, then we can use $\int_{-\infty}^{\infty}$ in place of $\int_0^{\infty}$. Thus we have

$$A^2 = n\int_{-\infty}^\infty \left[\hat{S}(t) \cdot \hat{F}(t)\right]^{-1} \cdot \left[S^o(t) - \hat{S}(t)\right]^2 \cdot \hat{f}(t)\,dt. \qquad (8.48)$$

Finally, it can be shown (see Appendix C) that (8.48) is equivalent to

$$A^2 = -n - \frac{1}{n} \cdot \sum_{i=1}^{n} (2i-1) \left\{ \ln\left[\hat{F}(t_i) \cdot \hat{S}(t_{n-i+1}) \right] \right\}, \qquad (8.49)$$

which is a more convenient formula for calculating A^2 than is (8.48).

EXAMPLE 8.17 : Let us hypothesize $\hat{S}(t) = e^{-.05t}$ for the sample of Example 8.2. Calculate the A^2 statistic.

SOLUTION : Table 8.5 shows the evaluation of the summation in (8.49).

TABLE 8.5

i	t_i	$\hat{F}(t_i)$	$\hat{S}(t_{11-i})$	$(2i-1)\left\{ \ln\left[\hat{F}(t_i) \cdot \hat{S}(t_{11-i}) \right] \right\}$
1	3	.13929	.54881	− 2.57120
2	4	.18126	.60653	− 6.62347
3	5	.22120	.60653	− 10.04345
4	7	.29531	.60653	− 12.03812
5	7	.29531	.67032	− 14.57757
6	8	.32967	.70469	− 16.05626
7	10	.39346	.70469	− 16.67605
8	10	.39346	.77880	− 17.74165
9	10	.39346	.81873	− 19.25721
10	12	.45118	.86070	− 17.97207
				−133.55705

Then $A^2 = -10 - \frac{1}{10}(-133.55705) = 3.35571$. Stephens [59] found that $y = 3.070$ corresponds to the .025 significance level, and $y = 3.857$ corresponds to the .01 level for this A^2 statistic, so our $y = 3.356$ corresponds roughly to the .019 level.

If the hypothesized $\hat{S}(t)$ has parameters estimated from the data, then the A^2 statistic should be modified. For example, an exponential model with λ estimated from the data should use the modified measure

$$Y = A^2(1 + \frac{0.6}{n}), \qquad (8.50)$$

according to Stephens [60].

8.5 *CONCOMITANT VARIABLES IN PARAMETRIC MODELS*

Throughout most of this text we have only considered survival models that were a function of chronological age, S(x), or those that were a function of time since some initial event, S(t). In both cases the model was univariate.

Many cases arise in which survival probabilities are a function of two or more variables, such as those used for insurance premium calculations which depend on age at issue as well as time since issue. This leads us to the select survival model S(t;x) defined in Section 1.2.1. The tabular form of S(t;x) was described in Section 3.6, and illustrated in Table 3.5. There we saw that the concomitant variable age at issue, denoted [x], was taken into account by having a *separate* S(t;x) for that value of x. In other words, each row in a select table constitutes a separate univariate model (varying with t only); age at selection is reflected by choice of the appropriate row. For this reason we say that the concomitant variable has been taken into account through *separation*.

Similarly, suppose we consider the survival of cancer patients as a function of time since diagnosis. We might believe that type of cancer, sex of the patient, and type of treatment all affect survival, so we would estimate a separate S(t) for each type/sex/treatment combination. Again S(t) is univariate, with concomitant variables taken into account by separation.

We now wish to consider parametric models, in which survival probabilities are determined as a function of both time and the accepted concomitant variables. In this type of model the concomitant variables have been taken into account by *inclusion*, rather that by separation.

The functional form for the multivariate parametric model should allow the variables to interact in a logical manner, *a priori* to testing a proposed model vis-a-vis sample data. That is, the model should be plausible in light of our knowledge of physiology, gerontology, and so forth. In this text we will not be concerned with the question of model appropriateness, but rather with the mathematical question of estimating the parameters of such models from sample data.

8.5.1 *Bivariate (Select) Models*

First let us explore the idea of estimating the parameters of a bivariate parametric model S(t;x), where x is the age at selection and t is duration (time) since selection. (Note that if *different* S(t;x) are estimated for males and females, then sex is accounted for by separation. Allowing for sex by inclusion will be considered in the following section.)

As mentioned above, a logical form for S(t;x) will depend on the nature of the aging process, the nature of the selection process, and the interaction between the two. This has been studied by Tenenbein and

Vanderhoof [61], who then proposed the forms for S(t;x) which we will consider in this section.

As mentioned earlier in this chapter, it is frequently easier to work with the hazard rate function than with the survival function for purposes of parameter estimation. Thus we will consider

$$\lambda(t;x) \;=\; -\frac{d}{dt}\ln S(t;x), \tag{8.51}$$

which, in actuarial notation, is denoted by $\mu_{[x]+t}$.

Consider the model

$$\mu_{[x]+t} \;=\; Br^t c^{x+t}, \tag{8.52}$$

where x+t is the attained age. To estimate B, r and c, we assume that we have values of $\mu^O_{[x]+t+1/2}$ from sample data, and we will fit (8.52) to these values by least squares.

As in Section 8.3.2, we will use a log transformation and actually fit

$$\ln \mu_{[x]+t} \;=\; \ln B + t\cdot\ln r + (x+t)\cdot\ln c \;=\; \alpha + \beta t + \gamma(x+t) \tag{8.53}$$

to the values of $\ln \mu^O_{[x]+t+1/2}$. Thus

$$SS \;=\; \sum_{x=a}^{b}\sum_{t=0}^{k-1} w_{x,t}\Big[\alpha + \beta(t+\tfrac{1}{2}) + \gamma(x+t+\tfrac{1}{2}) - \ln \mu^O_{[x]+t+1/2}\Big]^2 \tag{8.54}$$

is the general weighted sum of squares to be minimized by the least-squares estimates $\hat{\alpha}$, $\hat{\beta}$ and $\hat{\gamma}$, where the select period is k years.

The three equations which solve for $\hat{\alpha}$, $\hat{\beta}$ and $\hat{\gamma}$ are found by setting $\frac{\partial SS}{\partial \alpha}$, $\frac{\partial SS}{\partial \beta}$ and $\frac{\partial SS}{\partial \gamma}$ to zero. To simplify notation, let $u_{x,t} = \ln \mu^O_{[x]+t+1/2}$. Then our least-squares equations are

$$\alpha\cdot\Sigma\Sigma w_{x,t} \qquad\quad + \beta\cdot\Sigma\Sigma(t+\tfrac{1}{2})w_{x,t} \qquad\quad + \gamma\cdot\Sigma\Sigma(x+t+\tfrac{1}{2})w_{x,t}$$
$$=\Sigma\Sigma w_{x,t}u_{x,t}$$

$$\alpha\cdot\Sigma\Sigma(t+\tfrac{1}{2})w_{x,t} \quad + \beta\cdot\Sigma\Sigma(t+\tfrac{1}{2})^2 w_{x,t} \quad + \gamma\cdot\Sigma\Sigma(t+\tfrac{1}{2})(x+t+\tfrac{1}{2})w_{x,t}$$
$$=\Sigma\Sigma(t+\tfrac{1}{2})w_{x,t}u_{x,t},$$

$$\alpha\cdot\Sigma\Sigma(x+t+\tfrac{1}{2})w_{x,t} + \beta\cdot\Sigma\Sigma(t+\tfrac{1}{2})(x+t+\tfrac{1}{2})w_{x,t} + \gamma\cdot\Sigma\Sigma(x+t+\tfrac{1}{2})^2 w_{x,t}$$
$$=\Sigma\Sigma(x+t+\tfrac{1}{2})w_{x,t}u_{x,t}$$
$$\tag{8.55}$$

where $\Sigma\Sigma$ denotes $\displaystyle\sum_{x=a}^{b}\sum_{t=0}^{k-1}$.

EXAMPLE 8.18 : Let a=40, b=42, and k=2. Find the coefficients of α, β, γ in the equation which results from $\frac{\partial SS}{\partial \beta} = 0$, in an unweighted least squares approach.

SOLUTION : For α, we have $\sum\limits_{40}^{42} \sum\limits_{0}^{1} \left(t+\tfrac{1}{2}\right) = \sum\limits_{40}^{42} (2) = 6$. For β, we have $\sum\limits_{40}^{42} \sum\limits_{0}^{1} \left(t+\tfrac{1}{2}\right)^2 = \sum\limits_{40}^{42} \left(\tfrac{1}{4}+\tfrac{9}{4}\right) = 7\tfrac{1}{2}$. Finally, for γ we have $\sum\limits_{40}^{42} \sum\limits_{0}^{1} \left(t+\tfrac{1}{2}\right)\left(x+t+\tfrac{1}{2}\right) = \sum\limits_{40}^{42} \left[\tfrac{1}{2}\left(x+\tfrac{1}{2}\right)+1\tfrac{1}{2}\left(x+1\tfrac{1}{2}\right)\right] = 253\tfrac{1}{2}$.

As a second example of a bivariate model, consider the model

$$\mu_{[x]+t} = Bc^{x+t}\left(Hd^{x+t}\right)^{1/(t+1)}. \tag{8.56}$$

The log transformation gives

$$\ln \mu_{[x]+t} = \ln B + (x+t)\cdot \ln c + \left(\tfrac{1}{t+1}\right)\cdot \ln H + \left(\tfrac{x+t}{t+1}\right)\cdot \ln d$$

$$= \alpha + \beta(x+t) + \gamma\left(\tfrac{1}{t+1}\right) + \delta\left(\tfrac{x+t}{t+1}\right), \tag{8.57}$$

and $\hat{\alpha}$, $\hat{\beta}$, $\hat{\gamma}$, $\hat{\delta}$ are found so as to minimize

$$SS = \sum_{x=a}^{b} \sum_{t=0}^{k-1} w_{x,t}\left[\alpha + \beta\left(x+t+\tfrac{1}{2}\right) + \gamma\left(\tfrac{1}{t+1\frac{1}{2}}\right) + \delta\left(\tfrac{x+t+\frac{1}{2}}{t+1\frac{1}{2}}\right) - u_{x,t}\right]^2, \tag{8.58}$$

where $u_{x,t} = \ln \mu^{o}_{[x]+t+1/2}$.

8.5.2 *General Multivariate Models*

Now let us consider the general case where there are s concomitant variables, z_1, z_2, $\cdots$, z_s. We will use z to denote the column vector of concomitant variables, and will denote the survival function by $S(t;z)$ and the hazard function by $\lambda(t;z)$. As usual,

$$\lambda(t;z) = -\frac{d}{dt}\ln S(t;z), \tag{8.59}$$

so

$$S(t;z) = \exp\left(-\int_0^t \lambda(u;z)\,du\right), \qquad (8.60)$$

and

$$f(t;z) = S(t;z) \cdot \lambda(t;z). \qquad (8.61)$$

Each person in the group to which $S(t;z)$ applies will have his or her own hazard rate, wherein the values of z apply specifically to that person. For example, suppose z_1 is age at selection, and z_2 and z_3 are indicator variables defined by

$$z_2 = \begin{cases} 0 & \text{if male} \\ 1 & \text{if female} \end{cases} \qquad (8.62)$$

and

$$z_3 = \begin{cases} 0 & \text{if smoker} \\ 1 & \text{if nonsmoker} \end{cases}. \qquad (8.63)$$

If person i is a 40-year-old, nonsmoking female, then her hazard rate function is $\lambda(t;z_i)$, where $z_i' = [40, 1, 1]$.

In many cases, of which the above example is one, the concomitant variables are factors which exist at time $t=0$, and do not change as t increases. This concept of z being constant with respect to t is easier to deal with, and is the only case we will consider in this text.

In addition to the variables t and z, a parametric $S(t;z)$ will also depend on a set of parameters. Just as we did for univariate models earlier in this chapter, we will choose a parametric form for $S(t;z)$, and then estimate its parameters from sample data, using the method of maximum likelihood.

To construct the likelihood function, let us assume that person i comes under observation at time r_i and leaves observation at time t_i, either alive or by death. We will assume that either withdrawals do not occur at random, or, if they do, they are independent of mortality. In either case they can be ignored in the likelihood function as we saw in Section 7.4.1. The contribution to the likelihood by the ith life is

$$L_i = \frac{f(t_i;z_i)}{S(r_i;z_i)} \qquad (8.64)$$

if that life is observed to die, or

$$L_i = \frac{S(t_i; z_i)}{S(r_i; z_i)} \tag{8.65}$$

if the life terminates observation alive at t_i. Both cases can be incorporated by writing

$$L_i = \frac{S(t_i; z_i) \cdot \left[\lambda(t_i; z_i)\right]^{\delta_i}}{S(r_i; z_i)}, \tag{8.66}$$

where δ_i is the familiar indicator variable defined by (7.17). The overall likelihood is given by

$$L = \prod_{i=1}^{n} \left[\lambda(t_i; z_i)\right]^{\delta_i} \cdot \frac{S(t_i; z_i)}{S(r_i; z_i)}. \tag{8.67}$$

In theory, we can always estimate the parameters in (8.67) so as to maximize L, where the difficulty of the maximization will depend on the complexity of $\lambda(t; z)$, and thus of $S(t; z)$. We now consider two models for $\lambda(t; z)$, and explore the maximization of (8.67) under each of them.

8.5.3 *The Additive Model*

In this model the total hazard $\lambda(t; z)$ is made up of an underlying hazard which is a function of time, $\lambda(t)$, and additional hazards arising from the concomitant variables, all added together. If, in general,

$$\lambda(t; z_j) = h_j(t) \cdot g_j(z_j) \tag{8.68}$$

represents the extra hazard at time t due to the jth concomitant variable, then the total hazard is

$$\lambda(t; z) = \lambda(t) + \sum_{j=1}^{s} h_j(t) \cdot g_j(z_j). \tag{8.69}$$

Now (8.68) is written to suggest the most general form for $\lambda(t; z_j)$, expressed as the product of a function of time and a function of z_j. (By subscripting the functions h and g with j, we allow them to vary with j.) As a special case, we might have $g_j(z_j) = z_j$ for all j. Similarly we might let $h_j(t) = a_j$, say. If these two simplifications are combined, we then have

$$\lambda(t; z_j) = a_j z_j, \tag{8.70}$$

so that the additive model becomes

$$\lambda(t;z) = \lambda(t) + \sum_{j=1}^{s} a_j z_j. \qquad (8.71)$$

As a final simplification of the additive model, we consider the underlying hazard $\lambda(t)$ to be a constant, say a_0, which implies that the underlying survival function is exponential. Then by defining the dummy variable $z_0 = 1$, (8.71) can be written as

$$\lambda(t;z) = \sum_{j=0}^{s} a_j z_j = a'z, \qquad (8.72)$$

where $a' = [a_0, a_1, \cdots, a_s]$ and $z' = [z_0, z_1, \cdots, z_s]$. Since the hazard is constant, the overall survival function is exponential. Furthermore, since (8.72) is linear in z, this $\lambda(t;z)$ is sometimes called the *linear-exponential* model.

To estimate the parameters a of (8.72), we construct the likelihood given by (8.67). Note that, for this case,

$$\frac{S(t_i;z_i)}{S(r_i;z_i)} = \exp\left(-\int_{r_i}^{t_i} \lambda(u;z_i)\,du\right) = \exp\left[-a'z_i(t_i-r_i)\right], \qquad (8.73)$$

since $\lambda(u;z_i) = a'z_i$ is a constant. Then we have

$$L = \prod_{i=1}^{n} \left((a'z_i)^{\delta_i} \cdot \exp\left[-a'z_i(t_i-r_i)\right]\right), \qquad (8.74)$$

which leads to

$$\ln L = \sum_{i=1}^{n} \delta_i \cdot \ln(a'z_i) - \sum_{i=1}^{n} (t_i-r_i)(a'z_i). \qquad (8.75)$$

Finally, $\frac{\partial \ln L}{\partial a_j} = 0$ leads to the equation

$$\sum_{i=1}^{n} \frac{\delta_i \cdot z_{ji}}{a'z_i} - \sum_{i=1}^{n} (t_i-r_i)z_{ji} = 0, \qquad (8.76)$$

where z_{ji} is the jth concomitant variable for person i. The $(s+1)$ equations of this form, $j = 0,1,\cdots,s$, are then solved simultaneously for $\hat{a}_0, \hat{a}_1, \cdots, \hat{a}_s$, which must usually be done by numerical methods.

EXAMPLE 8.19 : The survival of patients with a certain lung disorder is believed to depend on age at onset and smoking habits, as well as time since onset. Assume that a linear-exponential survival model is appropriate. Let z_1 be the age at onset, and $z_2 = 1$ if a smoker, 0 if a nonsmoker. A sample of six patients was observed from t=0. Table 8.6 gives the values of z_1, z_2, the times of death for those who died, and the survival times for those alive when the study was terminated. Determine the equations to be solved for $\hat{a}_0$, $\hat{a}_1$, and $\hat{a}_2$.

TABLE 8.6

Patient	z_1	z_2	Time of Death	Time at Study Termination
1	50	1	6.0	★
2	52	0	★	4.8
3	53	0	★	2.2
4	55	1	9.2	★
5	58	1	★	8.0
6	60	0	5.5	★

SOLUTION : Note that $r_i = 0$ for all i, $\delta_i = 1$ for $i = 1, 4, 6$, and the $\mathbf{a}'\mathbf{z}_i$ vector is $\mathbf{a}'\mathbf{z}_i = a_0 + a_1 z_{1i} + a_2 z_{2i}$. (Recall that $z_{0i} = 1$ for all i.) We first calculate $\mathbf{a}'\mathbf{z}_1$ for $i = 1, 2, \cdots, 6$. The results of this are $\mathbf{a}'\mathbf{z}_1 = a_0 + 50a_1 + a_2$; $\mathbf{a}'\mathbf{z}_2 = a_0 + 52a_1$ $(z_2=0)$; $\mathbf{a}'\mathbf{z}_3 = a_0 + 53a_1$ $(z_2=0)$; $\mathbf{a}'\mathbf{z}_4 = a_0 + 55a_1 + a_2$; $\mathbf{a}'\mathbf{z}_5 = a_0 + 58a_1 + a_2$; $\mathbf{a}'\mathbf{z}_6 = a_0 + 60a_1$ $(z_2=0)$. Now for j=0, (8.76) becomes

$$\frac{1}{a_0 + 50a_1 + a_2} + \frac{1}{a_0 + 55a_1 + a_2} + \frac{1}{a_0 + 60a_1} = 35.7,$$ since $\delta_i = 0$

for $i = 2, 3, 5$, and $z_{0i} = 1$ for all i. Next, for j=1, (8.76) becomes

$$\frac{50}{a_0 + 50a_1 + a_2} + \frac{55}{a_0 + 55a_1 + a_2} + \frac{60}{a_0 + 60a_1} = 1966.2.$$ For j=2,

we have $z_{ji} = 0$ for $i = 2, 3, 6$, and $\delta_i = 0$ for $i = 2, 3, 5$. Thus the first summation in (8.76) has nonzero terms only for i=1 and i=4, yielding

$$\frac{1}{a_0 + 50a_1 + a_2} + \frac{1}{a_0 + 55a_1 + a_2} = 23.2,$$ where only $i = 1, 4, 5$ contribute to

the second summation.

8.5.4 *The Multiplicative Model*

In this model the underlying hazard and the additional hazards from the concomitant variables are multiplied together, rather than added.

The most popular model in this family is the Cox model (see Cox [18]), where

$$\lambda(t;z_j) = \exp(a_j z_j), \qquad (8.77)$$

so the entire hazard is

$$\lambda(t;z) = \lambda(t) \cdot \prod_{j=1}^{s} \lambda(t;z_j) = \lambda(t) \cdot \exp\left(\sum_{j=1}^{s} a_j z_j\right). \qquad (8.78)$$

Furthermore, if the underlying hazard is constant over time, then we can let $\lambda(t) = \lambda = e^{a_0}$, so that

$$\lambda(t;z) = \exp\left(\sum_{j=0}^{s} a_j z_j\right) = e^{a'z}, \qquad (8.79)$$

where $a' = [a_0, a_1, \cdots, a_s]$, $z' = [z_0, z_1, \cdots, z_s]$, and $z_0 = 1$, necessarily.

The hazard rate is again constant, so the survival model is exponential. Furthermore, $\ln \lambda(t;z)$ is linear in z, so (8.79) is sometimes called a *log-linear exponential* model.

To estimate the parameters a of (8.79), we construct the likelihood given by (8.67). Since $\lambda(t;z_i) = e^{a'z_i}$ is constant, then

$$\frac{S(t_i;z_i)}{S(r_i;z_i)} = \exp\left[-(t_i - r_i) \cdot e^{a'z_i}\right], \qquad (8.80)$$

so that

$$L = \prod_{i=1}^{n} \left[e^{a'z_i}\right]^{\delta_i} \cdot \exp\left[-(t_i - r_i) \cdot e^{a'z_i}\right], \qquad (8.81)$$

leading to

$$\ln L = \sum_{i=1}^{n} \delta_i \cdot a'z_i - \sum_{i=1}^{n} (t_i - r_i) \cdot e^{a'z_i}. \qquad (8.82)$$

Finally, $\frac{\partial \ln L}{\partial a_j} = 0$ leads to the equation

$$\sum_{i=1}^{n} \delta_i \cdot z_{ji} - \sum_{i=1}^{n} z_{ji}(t_i - r_i) \cdot e^{a'z_i} = 0. \tag{8.83}$$

Again we recognize that there are $(s+1)$ equations of this form, for $j = 0, 1, \cdots, s$, which must be solved, usually numerically, for $\hat{a}_0, \hat{a}_1, \cdots, \hat{a}_s$.

EXAMPLE 8.20 : Repeat Example 8.19 by assuming a log-linear exponential model.

SOLUTION : Recall that $r_i = 0$ for all i, and $\delta_i = 1$ for $i = 1, 4, 6$. For $j = 0$, $z_{ji} = z_{0i} = 1$ for all i, producing, for the derivative equation (8.83),
$3 - 6 \cdot \exp(a_0 + 50a_1 + a_2) - 4.8 \cdot \exp(a_0 + 52a_1) - \cdots - 5.5 \cdot \exp(a_0 + 60a_1) = 0$,
where the six values of $a'z_i$ were recorded in Example 8.19. For $j = 1$ we have
$(50 + 55 + 60) - (6)(50) \cdot \exp(a_0 + 50a_1 + a_2) - \cdots - (5.5)(60) \cdot \exp(a_0 + 60a_1) = 0$.
For $j = 2$, $z_{ji} = z_{2i} = 1$ for $i = 1, 4, 5$, so derivative equation (8.83) becomes
$2 - 6 \cdot \exp(a_0 + 50a_1 + a_2) - 9.2 \cdot \exp(a_0 + 55a_1 + a_2) - 8 \cdot \exp(a_0 + 58a_1 + a_2) = 0$.

8.6 *SUMMARY*

In this chapter we presented several approaches to the estimation of the parameters in a chosen survival model from sample data, considering various ways in which the data might be available (e.g., exact times of death, grouped deaths, initial estimates of values of $S(t)$ or $\lambda(t)$, etc.). We also explored our estimation problem under both complete and incomplete data.

Two major techniques were emphasized in this chapter, namely maximum likelihood and least squares. Both are popular methods with available computational packages to handle the otherwise formidable (or even prohibitive) number of calculations required to obtain numerical results in many cases.

The reader should bear in mind that maximum likelihood estimates are not guaranteed to result from the standard calculus approach to maximizing the likelihood function. The function may be unbounded (i.e., a maximum does not exist), or it could have several local maxima.

We have given only a brief treatment of hypothesis testing and models with concomitant variables. Many other texts are available which give a complete treatment of these topics.

The general concomitant variable model would appear to have a natural life insurance application. In addition to the obvious concomitant variable of age at issue, already incorporated into the select $S(t;x)$ model, other concomitant variables (or covariates) such as sex, smoker/nonsmoker, blood pressure, weight, and other underwriting factors could be incorporated into a parametric hazard function applicable to the particular insurance applicant. From this personal hazard function, the insurance premium and other policy values could be calculated specifically for this applicant. This interesting possibility has been explored by Brown and Brown [14].

EXERCISES

8.1 Introduction;   8.2 Univariate Models, Complete Data

8-1.   Find the asymptotic variance of estimator (8.2).

8-2.   Since $\frac{1}{\lambda}$ is the mean of T, the time of death, then $\lambda^{-1} = \zeta$, say, is the average time at death of the exponential survival model. Consider the sample of independent exact times of death t_i, i = 1,2,$\cdots$,n.
   (a)   Estimate ζ from this sample data by the method of moments.
   (b)   Show that $\hat{\zeta}$ is an unbiased estimate of ζ.
   (c)   Find the variance of $\hat{\zeta}$. (*Note that this is* $Var(\hat{\zeta})$ *for finite n as well as the asymptotic variance.*)

8-3.   In an experiment involving 6 newborn mice, the following exact times of death were observed: 0.6, 2.2, 2.3, 3.1, 4.6, 7.2. An exponential survival model is to be fitted to the data. Determine the MLE of λ.

8-4.   For a group of five impaired individuals followed from birth, the force of mortality is assumed to be a linear function of age such that $\mu_x = bx$. If the deaths occurred at exact ages 1, 2, 3, 4 and 5, find the MLE of b.

8-5.   Using the sample data of Example 8.2, estimate the parameter ω of the uniform distribution (a) by the method of moments, and (b) by the method of medians.

8-6.   The survival times of 10 persons, each age 75 at diagnosis of a disease, were 0.5, 1.3, 1.4, 1.6, 1.7, 2.2, 2.9, 3.8, 3.9 and 4.2 years. Using the method of moments, a gamma distribution (see Example 8.3) with $\alpha=2$ is fit to the data. Find the moment estimator of β.

8-7.   Verify the numerical results of Example 8.4.

8-8.   Verify the numerical results of Example 8.6.

8-9 In a study of 12 individuals from birth, the following times of death (in years) are observed: 0.38, 0.82, 1.23, 1.61, 1.86, 2.20, 2.70, 2.95, 3.47, 4.25, 5.16, 5.99. The Nelson-Aalen method is to be used to obtain approximate values of $\Lambda(t)$. We then wish to fit the data to an extreme value distribution for which $\Lambda(t) = \exp[\ln(R/a) + at]$, by matching the fitted values of $\Lambda(t)$ to the Nelson-Aalen approximate values at the times of the third and ninth deaths. What is the resulting estimate of a?

8-10. Two different studies each have a sample of 3 persons at $t=0$. For Study 1, two persons die in $(0,1]$ and one person dies in $(1,2]$. For Study 2, one person dies in $(0,1]$ and two persons die in $(1,2]$. For Study 1 we assume an exponential model with parameter λ_1, and for Study 2 we assume an exponential model with parameter λ_2. The MLE's for λ_1 and λ_2 are $\hat{\lambda}_1$ and $\hat{\lambda}_2$, respectively. Find the value of $\exp(\hat{\lambda}_1 - \hat{\lambda}_2)$.

8-11. Of ten lightbulbs tested, two fail before time $t=3$. The distribution of failure time is assumed to be exponential. Determine the MLE of λ.

8.3 Univariate Models, Incomplete Data

8-12. Show that (8.25), (8.26) and (8.28) are equivalent.

8-13. Show that the likelihood given by (8.28) can also be written as

$$L = \prod_{i=1}^{n} \frac{[f_d(t_i)]^{\delta_i} \cdot [S_d(t_i)]^{1-\delta_i} \cdot [f_w(t_i)]^{\gamma_i} \cdot [S_w(t_i)]^{1-\gamma_i}}{S_d(r_i) \cdot S_w(r_i)}.$$

8-14. An exponential distribution with mean 50 years in truncated from above at an unknown age z. A sample of five lifetimes from the truncated distribution is 40.2, 55.7, 55.7, 60.5 and 72.1. From this data, find the MLE of z.

8-15. A population is believed to be subject to a uniform survival distribution with parameter ω. A sample of five lives was observed from time 5 to time 10. One death occurred at time 8, another death occurred at time 9, and the other three lives survived to time 10. Find the MLE of ω.

8-16. From equation (8.32), derive the equations which produce $\hat{\alpha}$ and $\hat{\beta}$.

8-17.   Derive the equations for $\hat{\alpha}$ and $\hat{\beta}$ which minimize (8.35).

8-18.   Using the data of Example 8.12, estimate the Weibull parameters k and n by unweighted least squares.

8-19.   Derive the three equations in d_A, d_B and d_c by differentiating (8.39).

8-20.   A Gompertz distribution is to be fit to a set of observed μ_x^o. The parameter $B = .0001$ has been specified, and the parameter $\beta = \ln c$ is to be estimated by least squares. Give a formula for $\hat{\beta}$.

8.4   Hypothesis Testing of Parametric Models

8.21.   From the $\hat{S}(t)$ determined in Example 8.8, calculate the value of the χ^2 statistic. At what significance level could we reject the hypothesis that S(t) is uniform?

8.22.   Repeat Exercise 8-21 for the $\hat{S}(t)$ determined in Example 8.14.

8.23.   A sample of n persons is observed from exact age x until all die, and deaths are grouped into quinquennial age groupings. $_5d_{x+t}$ denotes the observed deaths in (x+t, x+t+5]. The last person died at age x+44. An exponential distribution is to be fit to the data, with the parameter determined as the minimum modified χ^2 estimator. Given an expression for the function to be minimized by this estimator.

8-24.   In the following table, the values of $_t|_5q_x$ are calculated from a fully specified survival model, and the values of $_5d_{x+t}$ are the observed deaths from a complete mortality experience of 100 asthma sufferers, age x at entry to the study.

t	$_t|_5q_x$	$_5d_{x+t}$
0	.05	4
5	.08	6
10	.10	11
15	.15	18
20	.16	24
25	.16	20
30	.15	12
35	.10	4
40	.05	1

We hypothesize that the mortality of asthma sufferers is governed by the specified model. By reference to a table of χ^2 probabilities, with what level of confidence could we reject this hypothesis?

8-25. Suppose the values of $_t|_5q_x$ in Exercise 8-24 are given by a Weibull distribution with parameters estimated from the data. With what level of confidence could we now reject the hypothesis?

8-26. From a group of five cancer patients diagnosed at $t=0$, three died in $(0,1]$ and two died in $(1,2]$. We wish to fit the survival distribution $S(t) = k^t$, $t \geq 0$, $0 < k < 1$, to this data. Assuming there exists a minimum modified χ^2 estimator of k between 0 and 1, it satisfies the equation $30k^3 + ak^2 + bk + c = 0$. Find a, b and c.

8-27. A sample of two lives at $t=0$ experience times of death $t_1 = 5$ and $t_2 = 9$. Let $\hat{S}(t) = 1 - \frac{t}{10}$ be the hypothesized uniform distribution. Calculate A^2 by (8.48), and verify the result by using (8.49).

8-28. Calculate the modified A^2 statistic, from (8.50), for the hypothesized exponential $\hat{S}(t)$ with λ estimated from the data of Example 8.2 by the method of medians.

8-29. The following table gives approximate values of $\Pr(Y > y)$ for certain critical values of y, the Kolmogorov-Smirnov statistic.

y	$\Pr(Y > y)$
1.2238	.100
1.3581	.050
1.4802	.025
1.6276	.010
1.7308	.005
1.9495	.001

For a sample of n lives, a certain survival model has been hypothesized. A complete set of times at death were observed from the sample, and the K-S statistic was calculated. It was found that the hypothesis was rejected at the 5% significance level, but not at the 2.5% level. If the departure measure D_n were increased by .005, then the hypothesis would be rejected at the 1% level, but not at the .5% level. Find the largest possible integral value of n implied by these facts.

8.5　Concomitant Variables in Parametric Models

8-30. Derive equations (8.55).

8-31. Solve the three equations in Example 8.19 for $\hat{a}_0$, $\hat{a}_1$ and $\hat{a}_2$.

8-32. For a linear-exponential survival model, the hazard rate function for person i is of the form $\lambda(t;z_i) = a_1 z_{1i} + a_2 z_{2i}$, where a_1 and a_2 are parameters. All persons enter a study at time t=0. We are given the following table of data concerning the four persons of a study sample.

Person i	Time of Departure	Method of Departure	Concomitant Variables	
			z_{1i}	z_{2i}
1	1	Death	2	1
2	2	Death	1	1
3	3	Termination	4	4
4	5	Termination	8	8

Find the MLE's of a_1 and a_2.

8-33. A *proportional hazard rate model* is one in which $\lambda(t;z_i)$ and $\lambda(t;z_j)$, the hazard rates for persons i and j, have a constant ratio regardless of the value of t. If the underlying hazard $\lambda(t)$ is *not* a constant function of t, show that the Cox model (8.78) is a proportional hazard model, whereas model (8.71) is not.

8-34. The Gompertz model $\lambda(t) = Bc^t$ can be modified to include s concomitant variables by replacing B with $B \cdot \exp\left(\sum_{j=1}^{s} a_j z_j\right)$.

　(a)　If the model is expressed as $\lambda(t;z) = e^{kt + a'z}$, what are k, a_0 and z_0, in terms of B and c?

　(b)　Show whether or not this new Gompertz model is a proportional hazard model.

CHAPTER 9

SURVIVAL MODELS ESTIMATED FROM
GENERAL POPULATION DATA

9.1 *INTRODUCTION*

Having considered various statistical approaches to the estimation of survival models from clinical data and from actuarial data, we turn now to the question of estimating such models from the general population data of a nation, state or province, or city.

This topic is part of the general field of demography, and in this text we present only a brief treatment of it. The topic is covered in greater detail in standard demography texts (e.g., Spiegelman [58], Pollard, et al. [50]).

General population data is characterized by the presence of large samples. In light of this, it is usually not practical (or even possible) to have detailed information on each life in the sample, so the estimation techniques described in Chapters 4 through 8 are usually not applicable. Instead we will use an estimation approach that makes use of a *census*, or count of the population, at one or more points of time, along with a tabulation of the deaths which occur during the observation period. This approach will tend to produce an estimate of the central rate of mortality, m_x, rather than an estimate of the probability, q_x, so a way of estimating q_x from an estimate of m_x will then be needed.

Furthermore, in demographic approaches to model estimation, it is common to tabulate the deaths and the census enumeration in age intervals of greater than one year, with five-year intervals frequently being used. This will lead to estimates of $_5m_x$, from which estimates of $_5q_x$ must be obtained. The relationships developed in Section 3.3.6 will be useful here.

A consequence of this use of quinquennial estimation intervals is that values of the life table function ℓ_x are then produced at every fifth age only. To obtain values at every integral age, it is common to interpolate among the ℓ_x values obtained from the estimates of $_5q_x$. For this purpose, smooth-junction interpolation is particularly useful. (For a review of such interpolation formulas, the reader is referred to Chapter 15 of Kellison [35] or to Chapter 7 of London [41].)

In this chapter we will illustrate the construction of life tables from general population data by the case study approach. In Sections 9.3 and 9.4 we describe the construction of the 1979-81 U.S. Life Tables and the 1980-82 Canadian Life Tables, respectively, Before those case studies are presented, however, some basic demographic notation and concepts are explained in the next section.

9.2 *DEMOGRAPHIC NOTATION AND CONCEPTS*

In this section we present some basic theory regarding the estimation of q_x or m_x from population data.   In Sections 9.3 and 9.4 we will see how that theory was applied, with modifications, in the construction of the most recent U.S. and Canadian Life Tables.

9.2.1 *Census Population Available on Each January* 1

Suppose the following information is available for a certain population:

P_x^z — number living on January 1 of calendar year z who are age x last birthday on that date (i.e., are between exact ages x and x+1).

E_x^z — number attaining exact age x during calendar year z.

D_x^z — number dying in calendar year z who are age x last birthday at death (i.e., die between exact ages x and x+1).

(We use the standard demographic symbols P, E and D for these values, notwithstanding our preference to reserve capital letters for random variables.) These quantities are illustrated in Figure 9.1.

CALENDAR YEAR

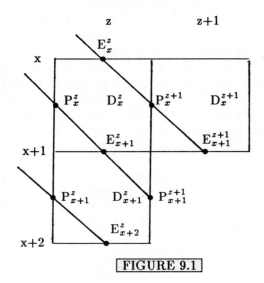

FIGURE 9.1

In Figure 9.1 we have assumed that

(1) the average age of the population represented by P_x^z on January 1, z is age $x+\frac{1}{2}$, and
(2) the average birthday of the group represented by E_x^z occurs on July 1, z.

Note that the population represented by P_x^z all turned age x in calendar year $z-1$, so they were all born in calendar year $z-x-1$. Similarly, the population represented by E_x^z was born in calendar year $z-x$, and the one represented by P_{x+1}^z was born in calendar year $z-x-2$. Thus each diagonal line in Figure 9.1 carries the "flow" of the population from a different calendar year of birth (CYB), and it will be useful to label each diagonal with respect to that CYB. This is illustrated in Figure 9.2.

Next we note that D_x^z, for example, represents the "deaths in the square," which are those occurring in calendar year z at ages in (x, x+1]. (D_x^{z+1} and D_{x+1}^z are similarly defined.) Thus it follows that some of the D_x^z deaths arose out of the E_x^z group (CYB $= z-x$), and some arose from the P_x^z group (CYB $= z-x-1$). For the purpose of estimating q_x, we would like to know the subdivision of D_x^z between these two different CYB's.

First let us define symbols to represent this subdivision. We define $_\alpha D_x^z$ to be the deaths out of E_x^z, but before the end of calendar year z, and $_\delta D_x^z$ to be the deaths out of P_x^z, but before attaining age x+1. Then all deaths represented by $_\alpha D_x^z$ have CYB $= z-x$, and all deaths represented by $_\delta D_x^z$ have CYB $= z-x-1$. It is clear that

$$_\alpha D_x^z + {}_\delta D_x^z = D_x^z. \tag{9.1}$$

These new symbols are illustrated in Figure 9.2 on the following page.

If it is assumed that there is no *migration* (i.e., no new persons are admitted to our populations, and no one leaves other than by death), then it is clear that

$$E_x^z - {}_\alpha D_x^z = P_x^{z+1} , \tag{9.2}$$

$$P_x^z - {}_\delta D_x^z = E_{x+1}^z , \tag{9.3}$$

and

$$P_x^{z+1} - {}_\delta D_x^{z+1} = E_{x+1}^{z+1} . \tag{9.4}$$

CALENDAR YEAR

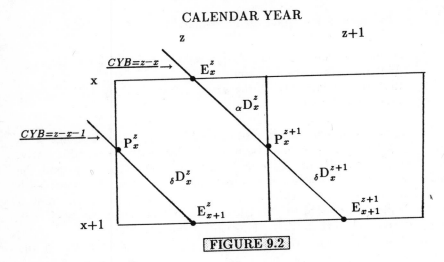

FIGURE 9.2

If the values shown in Figure 9.2 are available, it is then quite easy to produce an estimate of q_x. However, studies using general population data will not normally produce actual values of E_x^z for the population, but rather will produce only P_x^z and D_x^z. If the deaths are reported by CYB, as well as by calendar year of death and age last birthday at death, then separate values of $_\alpha D_x^z$ and $_\delta D_x^z$ are directly available, and values of E_x^z, etc., can be obtained from equations (9.2), etc., by assuming no migration.

EXAMPLE 9.1: Table 9.1 represents a classification of the deaths occurring in a certain community each year, classified by year of birth and age last birthday at death.

TABLE 9.1

CYB	Deaths Occurring in 1985 at Age Last Birthday			Deaths Occurring in 1986 at Age Last Birthday		
	20	21	22	20	21	22
1963	a	b	c	j	k	l
1964	d	e	f	m	n	o
1965	g	h	i	p	q	r

(i)   Which letters in Table 9.1 can represent nonzero entries?
(ii) What letter represents $_\alpha D_{20}^{1985}$?
(iii) What letter represents $_\delta D_{21}^{1986}$?
(iv) What letters together represent D_{21}^{1985}?

: Figure 9.3 presents the data of Table 9.1 graphically.

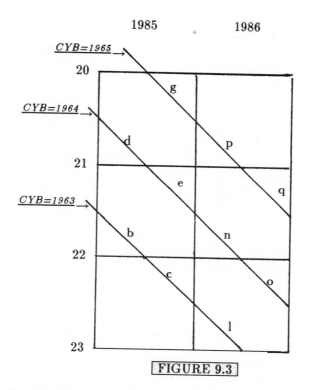

FIGURE 9.3

(i) Only the letters shown in Figure 9.3 can represent nonzero entries. The other letters in Table 9.1 represent impossible classification combinations.

(ii) From Figure 9.1, we obtain $_\alpha D_{20}^{1985} = g$.

(iii) Similarly, we directly find $_\delta D_{21}^{1986} = n$.

(iv) $D_{21}^{1985} = {_\alpha D_{21}^{1985}} + {_\delta D_{21}^{1985}} = e + b$.

If the CYB is *not* reported for the deaths in D_x^z, then an approximate separation of D_x^z into $_\alpha D_x^z$ and $_\delta D_x^z$ must be obtained. This is usually accomplished by using *separation factors*, which are presumably derived from other data. We define f_x^z to be the proportion of deaths in calendar year z at age x last birthday who had their x^{th} birthday in calendar year z−1. Thus we have

$$_\delta D_x^z = f_x^z \cdot D_x^z \tag{9.5}$$

and
$$_{\alpha}D_x^z \;=\; (1 - f_x^z) \cdot D_x^z. \tag{9.6}$$

If no reliable separation factors are available from other data, $f_x^z = \frac{1}{2}$ is frequently used.

With values of E_x^z, $_{\alpha}D_x^z$ and $_{\delta}D_x^{z+1}$ available, either exactly or approximately, it is then natural to estimate q_x by

$$\hat{q}_x \;=\; \frac{_{\alpha}D_x^z + {_{\delta}}D_x^{z+1}}{E_x^z}\;. \tag{9.7}$$

The reader will recognize that estimator (9.7) is a simple binomial proportion. This estimation situation is the one which we called Special Case A in Chapter 5, where the observation period runs from the birthday in calendar year z to the birthday in calendar year z+1.

It will be useful to write estimator (9.7) in a different way. Let us define $_{\alpha}P_x^z$ to be the probability of surviving from age x, attained in year z, to the beginning of year z+1, and $_{\delta}P_x^z$ to be the probability of surviving from the beginning of year z to the attainment of age x+1 later in that year. Then it is clear that

$$q_x \;=\; 1 - {_{\alpha}}P_x^z \cdot {_{\delta}}P_x^{z+1}. \tag{9.8}$$

(Note that the values of $_{\alpha}P_x^x$ and $_{\delta}P_x^z$ depend on the date of the birthday in year z. In most applications it is understood that an average (or common) birth date applies to all persons in a sample. This average birth date is frequently, but not necessarily, taken to be July 1.) Again it is natural to estimate both $_{\alpha}P_x^z$ and $_{\delta}P_x^{z+1}$ as binomial proportions, so that

$$_{\alpha}\hat{P}_x^z \;=\; \frac{P_x^{z+1}}{E_x^z} \tag{9.9}$$

and

$$_{\delta}\hat{P}_x^{z+1} \;=\; \frac{E_{x+1}^{z+1}}{P_x^{z+1}}\;. \tag{9.10}$$

Then if q_x is estimated by

$$\hat{q}_x \;=\; 1 - {_{\alpha}}\hat{P}_x^z \cdot {_{\delta}}\hat{P}_x^{z+1}, \tag{9.8a}$$

it is easy to see that when we substitute (9.9) and (9.10) into (9.8a), we will again obtain (9.7).

EXAMPLE 9.2: Given that $P_x^{z+1} = 1000$, $_\alpha D_x^z = 42$, $_\delta D_x^{z+1} = 48$, and that there is no migration, estimate $_\alpha p_x^z$, $_\delta p_x^{z+1}$ and q_x.

SOLUTION: First note that $E_x^z = P_x^{z+1} + _\alpha D_x^z = 1042$, and also that $E_{x+1}^{z+1} = P_x^{z+1} - _\delta D_x^{z+1} = 952$. From these values $_\alpha \hat{p}_x^z = \dfrac{P_x^{z+1}}{E_x^z} = .9597$, $_\delta \hat{p}_x^{z+1} = \dfrac{E_{x+1}^{z+1}}{P_x^{z+1}} = .9520$, and $\hat{q}_x = 1 - _\alpha \hat{p}_x^z \cdot _\delta \hat{p}_x^{z+1} = .0864$.

If the observation period is only calendar year z, rather than birthdays in year z to birthday in year z+1, so that P_x^z and $_\delta D_x^z$ are given rather than $_\delta D_x^{z+1}$, then estimator (9.7) does not apply. Instead we would estimate $_\delta p_x^z$ by

$$_\delta \hat{p}_x^z = \frac{E_{x+1}^z}{P_x^z}, \qquad (9.11)$$

and then estimate q_x by

$$\hat{q}_x = 1 - _\alpha \hat{p}_x^z \cdot _\delta \hat{p}_x^z. \qquad (9.12)$$

Note the similarity of (9.12) to (9.8a). In (9.12), two different birth groups contribute to our estimate of q_x, whereas in (9.8a) the estimate is based on the experience of the CYB $= z - x$ group only.

Substituting (9.9) and (9.11) into (9.12) produces

$$\hat{q}_x = 1 - \frac{P_x^{z+1}}{E_x^z} \cdot \frac{E_{x+1}^z}{P_x^z}. \qquad (9.13)$$

It should be noted that $_\delta P_x^z = _\delta P_x^{z+1}$, without approximation, in a stationary population (see Section 9.2.4). Thus if the population under study is approximately stationary, estimators (9.13) and (9.8a) will produce nearly identical results.

A different estimate of q_x is obtained by the following set of assumptions. By assuming a stationary population, we have $_\delta D_x^z = _\delta D_x^{z+1}$; by assuming a uniform distribution of deaths over the year of age, with no migration and birthdays on July 1 on the average, we have $_\alpha D_x^z = _\delta D_x^{z+1}$. Putting these two together, we have

$$_\alpha D_x^z = _\delta D_x^z = \tfrac{1}{2} \cdot D_x^z. \qquad (9.14)$$

Under the assumptions, we also have

$$E_x^z = P_x^{z+1} + _\alpha D_x^z = P_x^{z+1} + \tfrac{1}{2} \cdot D_x^z \qquad (9.15)$$

and

$$E^z_{x+1} \;=\; P^z_x \,-\, {}_\delta D^z_x \;=\; P^z_x - \tfrac{1}{2} \cdot D^z_x \,. \qquad (9.16)$$

Then if (9.13) is used to estimate q_x, we have

$$\hat{q}_x \;=\; 1 - \frac{P^{z+1}_x}{P^{z+1}_x + \tfrac{1}{2} \cdot D^z_x} \cdot \frac{P^z_x - \tfrac{1}{2} \cdot D^z_x}{P^z_x} \,, \qquad (9.17)$$

by substituting (9.15) and (9.16) into (9.13). Recalling that, under the assumption of a stationary population, $P^z_x = P^{z+1}_x$, formula (9.17) is easily simplified to

$$\hat{q}_x \;=\; \frac{D^z_x}{\tfrac{1}{2}(P^z_x + P^{z+1}_x) + \tfrac{1}{2} \cdot D^z_x} \,, \qquad (9.18)$$

a popular formula for estimating q_x from P^z_x, P^{z+1}_x and D^z_x.

$\boxed{\text{EXAMPLE 9.3}}$: Assume that a population is approximately stationary and that there is no migration. Given that $E^z_x = 685$, $P^z_x = 712$, ${}_\alpha D^z_x = 3$, ${}_\delta D^z_x = 1$, estimate q_x (a) by formula (9.13), and (b) by formula (9.18).

$\boxed{\text{SOLUTION}}$: First note that $P^{z+1}_x = E^z_x - {}_\alpha D^z_x = 682$, and also that $E^z_{x+1} = P^z_x - {}_\delta D^z_x = 711$. Then (a) $\hat{q}_x = 1 - \dfrac{682}{685} \cdot \dfrac{711}{712} = .00578$, and (b) $\hat{q}_x = \dfrac{4}{\tfrac{1}{2}(712 + 682) + 2} = .00572$.

9.2.2 *Census Population Available on One Date Only*

The estimators for q_x described in Section 9.2.1 are not generally applicable in practice, because census populations are not available on each January 1. These estimators were presented here mainly to lay a theoretical foundation. (In Chapter 11 we will present a situation using insurance company data in which populations *are* available at the end, and thus beginning, of each calendar year.)

The more common situation is one in which the census population is available on only one date, normally near or at the middle of the observation period. We can illustrate this situation with a one-year observation period with census population taken on July 1, as shown in Figure 9.4.

CALENDAR YEAR

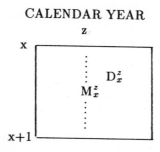

FIGURE 9.4

If M_x^z is the midyear population that is age x last birthday, and D_x^z is, as before, deaths in year z at age x last birthday, then a natural estimator for the central rate m_x is

$$\hat{m}_x = \frac{D_x^z}{M_x^z}. \qquad (9.19)$$

Estimator (9.19) is easily justified. The central rate m_x, in a survival model, is the ratio of the deaths in (x, x+1] to the life-years of exposure out of which those deaths arose (see Section 3.3.5). Thus m_x is naturally estimated by the ratio of deaths in (x, x+1] during year z to the exact exposure from which those deaths arose. In turn, the exposure is found by integrating the function which measures the number alive at time t within year z over the domain of t. That is, if $\lambda_{x,t}^z$ is a function which gives the population at time t within year z that is age x last birthday, then

$$\Lambda_x^z = \int_0^1 \lambda_{x,t}^z \, dt \qquad (9.20)$$

is the exposure for this population. But $\lambda_{x,t}^z$ is not known, so Λ_x^z cannot be found by (9.20). Instead we recognize that the integral in (9.20) also represents the average value of $\lambda_{x,t}^z$ within year z, and we approximate this average value by the midyear value $M_x^z = \lambda_{x,1/2}^z$.

EXAMPLE 9.4 : If M_x^z in used to approximate Λ_x^z, how good is the approximation if (a) $\lambda_{x,t}^z = 100{,}000(1.01)^t$; (b) $\lambda_{x,t}^z = 100{,}000(1+.01t)$?

SOLUTION : (a) $\Lambda_x^z = \int_0^1 \lambda_{x,t}^z \, dt = \left. \frac{100{,}000(1.01)^t}{\ln(1.01)} \right|_0^1 = 100{,}499.17$, and

$M_x^z = \lambda_{x,1/2}^z = 100{,}000(1.01)^{1/2} = 100{,}498.76$, so the error of approximation is $-.41$. (b) $\Lambda_x^z = \int_0^1 \lambda_{x,t}^z \, dt = 100{,}000t + 500t^2 \Big|_0^1 = 100{,}500.00$, and $M_x^z = \lambda_{x,1/2}^z = 100{,}000(1.005) = 100{,}500.00$ as well. The midyear population exactly equals the exposure when the population function is linear.

If the population were stationary, then $\lambda_{x,t}^z$ is the same for all t, $0 \leq t \leq 1$, so that $M_x^z = \Lambda_x^z = \lambda_{x,t}^z$.

This principle is easily extended to the case where quinquennial age intervals are used. If $_5D_x^z$ represents the deaths in year z in $(x, x+5]$, and if $_5M_x^z$ represents the midyear population between ages x and x+5, then, by interpreting $_5M_x^z$ as an approximation to $_5\Lambda_x^z$, the exposure of this sample, it follows that

$$_5\hat{m}_x = \frac{_5D_x^z}{_5M_x^z} \tag{9.21}$$

is a natural estimator of $_5m_x$.

If the observation period is more than one year, as is the case for both the U.S. and the Canadian Life Tables where a three-year period is used, then the natural estimator for $_5m_x$ is

$$_5\hat{m}_x = \frac{_5D_x^{z-1, z, z+1}}{3 \cdot {}_5M_x^z}, \tag{9.22}$$

where $_5D_x^{z-1, z, z+1}$ represents the observed deaths in $(x, x+5]$ during calendar years $z-1$, z and z+1 combined, and $_5M_x^z$ is the *mid-period* population (at or near July 1, z) that is between ages x and x+5. The multiple of 3 in the denominator of (9.22) is necessary because $_5m_x$ is an average *annual* rate. Since $_5D_x^{z-1, z, z+1}$ represents "three years' worth" of deaths, division by 3 is necessary to obtain an annual central rate. This situation is illustrated by Figure 9.5 on page 225.

Interestingly, neither the U.S. Census nor the Canadian Census is taken on July 1 of the middle year, since it is believed that many people are not at their regular residence on that date, mainly due to summer vacations. The U.S. Census is taken on April 1, and the Canadian Census on June 1.

EXAMPLE 9.5 : A certain country takes a census on January 1, 1986, by quinquennial age, and records deaths by quinquennial ages as well. If $_5D_{35}^{1981-1990} = 2174$ denotes observed deaths between ages 35 and 40 in calendar years 1981 through 1990, and the census population on January 1, 1986 of those alive between ages 35 and 40 is 195,855, estimate $_5m_{35}$.

SOLUTION : By formula (9.22), adapted to a ten-year observation period,

$$_5\hat{m}_{35} = \frac{2174}{(10)(195{,}855)} = .00111.$$

CALENDAR YEARS

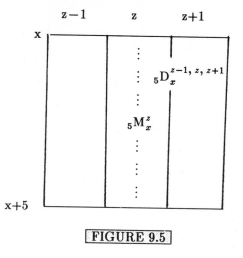

FIGURE 9.5

9.2.3 *Estimating Infant Mortality Rates*

For the first year of life, Figure 9.2 applies with $x=0$. Then P_0^z represents the survivors on January 1, z of the births in year $z-1$, and E_0^z represents the births in year z. It is common to use the symbol B^z in place of E_0^z.

The estimators developed in Sections 9.2.1 and 9.2.2 are equally applicable for the $x=0$ case. However, it is common, in developing life tables from population data, to show values of ℓ_x at various ages less than one year. Thus a table constructed from such data might show values of ℓ_0 (the table radix), $\ell_{1/365}$ (survivors after one day), $\ell_{7/365}$ (survivors after one week), $\ell_{30/365}$ (survivors after one month), and ℓ_1 (survivors after one year).

To estimate the probabilities needed to produce such values of ℓ_x, deaths in the first year of life must be reported in such age intervals. The required probabilities are then estimated from such reported deaths and births from several years. This is illustrated in Section 9.3 by the 1979-81 U.S. Life Tables.

9.2.4 *Stationary Population*

The theory of stationary populations is described in many textbooks, including Jordan [32], Bowers, et al. [10], Pollard, et al. [50], and Keyfitz and Beekman [36].

The assumptions of a stationary population are threefold:

(1)   That there is a constant number of births each year,
       uniformly   distributed over the year of birth;

(2)   That the force of mortality at a given age is constant
       over time;

(3)   That there is no migration.

The consequence of these three assumptions is that all characteristics of a population at any given age (or in any given age interval) stay the same *over time*.   Thus   we   would   have $P_x^z = P_x^{z+1}$, $E_x^z = E_x^{z+1}$, $D_x^z = D_x^{z+1}$, $_\alpha D_x^z = {_\alpha}D_x^{z+1}$, and $_\delta D_x^z = {_\delta}D_x^{z+1}$. Several of these equalities were assumed in developing the estimators in the preceding sections of this chapter.

The use of estimator (9.19) to estimate m_x is also related to an assumption of stationarity.   This can be seen by reference to Figure 9.6, in which standard life table symbols are used.

1 year

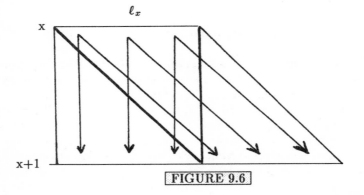

FIGURE 9.6

If ℓ_x is the number of persons turning age x in a year, then d_x of them die, and exactly L_x life years are lived prior to age x+1. These values of d_x and L_x are associated with the parallelogram denoted by the diagonal arrows, and the central rate $m_x = \dfrac{d_x}{L_x}$, defined in Chapter 3, also has its meaning "down the diagonal."

Now if a population is stationary, then there are also d_x deaths in the square denoted by the vertical arrows. Furthermore, at *any* point of time within the year which defines the square there are exactly L_x persons alive. Therefore, to the extent that a population is stationary, the ratio of "deaths in the square" to "midyear population" is a good approximation to the lifetable concept of central rate.

9.3 *THE* 1979-81 *UNITED STATES LIFE TABLES*

These tables are based on the 1980 U.S. Census and the deaths which occurred in 1979 through 1981. In all, twelve national life tables were developed: tables for males, females, and both sexes combined for each of the four racial groups of whites, blacks, all other-than-white, and all races combined. In addition to the national tables, state tables were developed by sex and by race for those states with significant other-than-white populations.

The methodology used in developing these tables is reported by Armstrong and Curtin [3], upon which most of this section is based.

9.3.1 *Available Data*

For the different sex/race categories, the available data consisted of

(1) deaths in 1979 through 1981,
(2) population as of April 1, 1980, and
(3) births in years 1977 through 1981.

The reported deaths were tabulated by age last birthday in one-year intervals for $x = 1, 2, 3, 4$, and in five-year intervals for $x = 5, 10, \cdots, 95$, with a final group for all deaths at age 100 and over. For the first year of life, the $D_0^{1979-81}$ deaths were subdivided into those occurring under 1 day, 1-6 days, 7-27 days, and 28-364 days. (Those completing 365 days prior to death would be contained in $D_1^{1979-81}$.)

The census populations were available in one-year intervals for ages $x = 0, 1, \cdots, 5$ (denoted by M_x^{1980}), and in five-year intervals for ages $x = 5, 10, \cdots, 95$ (denoted by $_5M_x^{1980}$), with $_\infty M_{100}^{1980}$ denoting the population aged 100 and over. Note the overlap situation in which M_5^{1980} is also contained in $_5M_5^{1980}$.

9.3.2 *Estimation of Life Table Values Under Age 2*

For ages up to age 2, the census population figures were not used, and estimates of q_x or m_x were not directly obtained. Instead estimates of $_{x|t}q_0$ were obtained from the tabulated deaths and reported births in years 1977 through 1981. This is illustrated in Figure 9.7 on page 228, where, of necessity, the horizontal lines for ages 1/365, 7/365 and 28/365 are not located to scale.

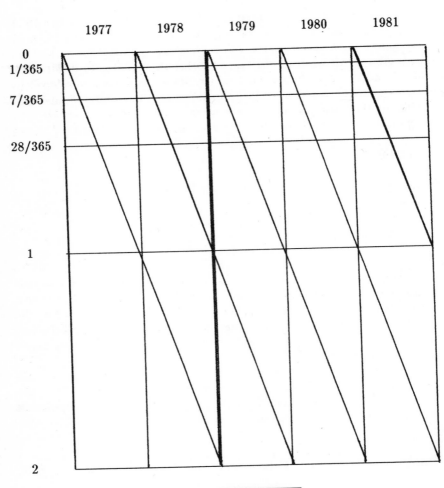

FIGURE 9.7

Recall that the deaths are in years 1979-81 only. By assuming that births in each year are evenly distributed over that year, it is easy to approximate the number of births from which each group of deaths arose. For example, *all* births in 1979 and 1980 were exposed to the risk of death in the first day of life during the observation period. Births from the last day of 1978 were exposed to this risk for half a day on the average, so half of 1/365 of the 1978 births (i.e., $\frac{1}{730}B^{1978}$) is the approximate exposure for first-day deaths from this birth group. Similarly, *all but* 1/730 of the 1981 births is part of this exposure. Putting these pieces together, we have

$$_{1/365}E_0 = \frac{1}{730}(B^{1978} + 730B^{1979} + 730B^{1980} + 729B^{1981}) \qquad (9.23)$$

as the exposure for the deaths in the 0-1 day interval.

A similar argument leads to the other values for $_tE_x$, the approximate exposure for the deaths in age interval x to x+t. For deaths in the 1-7 day interval,

$$_{6/365}E_{1/365} = \frac{1}{730}(8B^{1978} + 730B^{1979} + 730B^{1980} + 722B^{1981}). \qquad (9.24)$$

For deaths in the 7-28 day interval,

$$_{21/365}E_{7/365} = \frac{1}{730}(35B^{1978} + 730B^{1979} + 730B^{1980} + 695B^{1981}). \qquad (9.25)$$

For deaths in the 28-365 day interval,

$$_{337/365}E_{28/365} = \frac{1}{730}(393B^{1978} + 730B^{1979} + 730B^{1980} + 337B^{1981}). \qquad (9.26)$$

Finally, for deaths in the 1-2 year interval, all of the 1978 and 1979 births, and approximately half of the 1977 and 1980 births, represent the births from which the $D_1^{1979-81}$ deaths arose, so we have

$$_1E_1 = \tfrac{1}{2}(B^{1977} + 2B^{1978} + 2B^{1979} + B^{1980}). \qquad (9.27)$$

With these approximate values for $_tE_x$, and the tabulated deaths $_tD_x^{1979-81}$, the natural estimator for $_x|_tq_0$ is

$$_x|_t\hat{q}_0 = \frac{_tD_x^{1979-81}}{_tE_x}, \qquad (9.28)$$

which is obtained for x=0, t=1/365; x=1/365, t=6/365; x=7/365, t=21/365; x=28/365, t=337/365; and x=1, t=1. From these estimates of $_x|_tq_0$, life table values of $_td_x$ were found from

$$_td_x = \ell_0 \cdot {_x|_t\hat{q}_0}, \qquad (9.29)$$

using $\ell_0 = 100{,}000$ as the table radix, and values of ℓ_x at x = 1/365, 7/365, 28/365, 1 and 2 follow immediately from the values of $_td_x$.

9.3.3 Ages 2 to 4 (Age Last Birthday)

For these ages deaths were available in one-year age intervals, represented by $D_x^{1979\text{-}81}$, for $x = 2, 3, 4$, as were the census populations, represented by M_x^{1980}. As described in Section 9.2.2, a natural estimator for m_x in this situation would be

$$\hat{m}_x = \frac{D_x^{1979\text{-}81}}{3 \cdot M_x^{1980}} . \tag{9.30}$$

For somewhat obscure reasons, it was felt that better estimates of m_x could be obtained from

$$\hat{m}_x = \frac{D_x^{1979\text{-}81}}{M_{x-1}^{1980} + M_x^{1980} + M_{x+1}^{1980}} . \tag{9.31}$$

Then, by assuming a uniform distribution of death over each year of age, estimates of q_x were obtained from these estimates of m_x by

$$\hat{q}_x = \frac{\hat{m}_x}{1 + \frac{1}{2} \cdot \hat{m}_x} . \tag{9.32}$$

By substituting (9.31) into (9.32) we obtain the formula actually used to estimate q_x, namely

$$\hat{q}_x = \frac{D_x^{1979\text{-}81}}{M_{x-1}^{1980} + M_x^{1980} + M_{x+1}^{1980} + \frac{1}{2} \cdot D_x^{1979\text{-}81}} , \tag{9.33}$$

for $x = 2, 3, 4$. It was for this estimate of q_4 that M_5^{1980} was needed.

9.3.4 Ages 5 to 94 (Age Last Birthday)

Recall that the basic data consisted of quinquennial sums of deaths and populations, $_5D_x^{1979\text{-}81}$ and $_5M_x^{1980}$, for ages $x = 5, 10, \cdots, 90, 95$, as well as $_\infty D_{100}^{1979\text{-}81}$ and $_\infty M_{100}^{1980}$. From these grouped values, one-year interval values were approximated, for deaths and populations separately, using Beers' smooth-junction interpolation formula (see Beers [8]), with some minor modifications. Since the last group was at $x=100$, the last single-age value that could be obtained from Beers' central formula was at $x=94$; interpolation for single-age values at $x=95$ would either have required grouped values at $x=105$, or the use of a non-central interpolation formula. Letting D_x' and M_x' denote these single age interpolated values, the natural estimator for m_x is then

$$\hat{m}_x = \frac{D'_x}{3 \cdot M'_x}. \tag{9.30a}$$

Substituting (9.30a) into (9.32) produces

$$\hat{q}_x = \frac{D'_x}{3 \cdot M'_x + \frac{1}{2} \cdot D'_x}, \tag{9.34}$$

which was then used for x=5 through 94.

9.3.5 *Ages 95 and Over*

As described in Section 9.3.4, the census population data was used to estimate values of q_x only as far as x=94. At ages 95 and over, values of q_x were estimated from data amassed under the Medicare program, which is considered to be more accurate than census data. Because we wish to concentrate on population-based estimation in this chapter, we will give only a brief description of the procedure used at ages 95 and over for the 1979-81 U.S. Life Tables.

Initial estimates of q_x for $x = 66, \cdots, 105$ were obtained from the Medicare data by methods discussed in Chapter 6, and were then graduated by Whittaker's method (see formula (4.1) of London [41]), with z=3, h=140,000, and weights as approximate inverse variances. Some adjustments were then made to assure a smooth increase of q_x values at higher ages. This was accomplished by replacing some of the graduated values with new ones generated by the formula

$$q_x = q_{x-1}\left\{0.9\left[\frac{q_{x-1}}{q_{x-2}} - 1\right] + 1\right\}. \tag{9.35}$$

Formula (9.35) was also used to calculate extrapolated values of q_x as far as x=111. Finally, the Medicare-based values, which were on an age nearest birthday basis, were adjusted to an age last birthday basis (to be consistent with the census-based values), with the last value produced as q_{109}.

The Medicare-based values for ages 66 through 84 were then discarded. For ages 85 through 94, the Medicare-based values, q_x^M, and the census-based values, q_x^C, were blended by the formula

$$q_x = \frac{1}{11}\left[(95-x)q_x^C + (x-84)\,q_x^M\right], \tag{9.36}$$

for $x = 85, \cdots, 94$. Thus the final life table shows q_x values estimated from the census data for $x = 0, \cdots, 84$, values estimated from the Medicare data for $x = 95, \cdots, 109$, and blended values from each source for $x = 85, \cdots, 94$.

9.3.6 *Calculation of Other Values*

With the life table values of q_x now available for $x = 0, \cdots, 109$, values of ℓ_x were calculated, using $\ell_0 = 100,000$, for $x = 1, \cdots, 110$, as well as for $x = 1/365,\ 7/365$ and $28/365$. The values of q_x were extrapolated to $x = 132$ by use of formula (9.35), and adjusted to an age last birthday basis (ending with q_{130}), from which ℓ_x was determined as far as ℓ_{130}.

Next L_x was determined for $x = 110, \cdots, 130$ by assuming a constant force of mortality over $(x, x+1)$. Under that assumption the formula is

$$L_x = \frac{d_x}{-\ln p_x}, \qquad (9.37)$$

as developed in Chapter 3.

For ages 109 back to age 1, L_x was determined under the uniform distribution of deaths assumption. Under that assumption the formula is

$$L_x = \tfrac{1}{2}(\ell_x + \ell_{x+1}), \qquad (9.38)$$

which was also developed in Chapter 3.

Values of T_x were then developed. Beginning with $T_{131} = 0$, other values of T_x were calculated from age 130 back to age 1 by the formula

$$T_x = T_{x+1} + L_x, \qquad (9.39)$$

for $x = 130, \cdots, 1$. For $x = 0$, T_0 was calculated by a formula using previously calculated information during the first year of life.

With values of T_x and ℓ_x available, the complete expectation of life was calculated by the formula

$$\overset{o}{e}_x = \frac{T_x}{\ell_x}. \qquad (9.40)$$

Finally, an approximate variance of each value of q_x and $\overset{o}{e}_x$ was determined.

9.4 *THE* 1980-82 *CANADIAN LIFE TABLES*

These tables are based on the deaths observed in calendar years 1980 through 1982, and the census population of June 1, 1981. The Adult Tables begin at age 0, but do not show values for subdivisions of the first year of life as do the U.S. tables. Instead, special Infant Tables are prepared for the first year of life, showing values by day up to 7 days, then by week up to 28 days, then by month up to 1 year.

Provincial, as well as national, tables are produced. Because of its small population, abridged tables only are produced for Prince Edward Island.

9.4.1 *Infant Tables*

As was true for the U.S. tables in the first year of life, the Canadian Infant Tables are derived from birth and death records, and do not make use of actual census populations.

Figure 9.8 shows the representative age interval from x to x+t for which we wish to estimate $_tq_x$. Note that the births, from which the deaths $_tD_x^{1980-82}$ arise, take place throughout all of 1980 and 1981, the latter part of 1979, and the first part of 1982.

CALENDAR YEARS

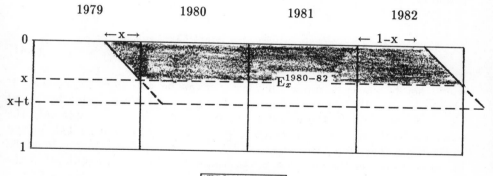

FIGURE 9.8

In Figure 9.8, $E_x^{1980-82}$ represents the number reaching exact age x during the three-year period. Since this number is not enumerated exactly in the census, it must be approximated. Viewing x as a fraction of a year, it is clear that the births which would reach age x in 1980-82 occurred in the last x (a fraction) of 1979, all of 1980 and 1981, and the first $1-x$ (a fraction) of 1982. The births for 1979 and 1982 were tabulated by month of birth. By assuming an even distribution of births over the month of birth, it is possible to ascertain the number of births for which $E_x^{1980-82}$ is the number still surviving at age x. To find $E_x^{1980-82}$ from these births, the deaths prior to age x from these births would be needed. These deaths (those in the shaded parallelogram of Figure 9.8) are not precisely known, but are assumed to be the same as those in the rectangle (between ages 0 and x, and years 1980-82), such deaths being part of our basic data.

To recapitulate, two basic assumptions are needed in order to calculate $E_x^{1980-82}$ from the given birth and death data:

(1)   That births in each month of 1979 and 1982 are evenly distributed over the month;

(2)   That deaths between 0 and x "down the parallelogram" are equal to deaths "in the rectangle" (note that the areas of the two figures are equal).

For x less than one month, only births in December of 1979, denoted by B_{12}^{1979}, would affect $E_x^{1980-82}$. Thus $E_x^{1980-82}$ is $B^{1980-82}$, plus a fraction of B_{12}^{1979}, minus the same fraction of B_{12}^{1982}, minus observed deaths at ages between 0 and x. For x greater than one month, births from the last several months of 1979 are added to $B^{1980-82}$, with births from the corresponding period in 1982 deleted.

To estimate $_tq_x$ by

$$_t\hat{q}_x = \frac{_tD_x^{1980-82}}{E_x^{1980-82}} \tag{9.41}$$

would not be precisely correct, however, as can be seen from Figure 9.8. If $_tD_x^{1980-82}$ were the observed deaths in the *parallelogram* bounded by x and x+t, then formula (9.41) would be correct. But $_tD_x^{1980-82}$ represents the observed deaths in the *rectangle* bounded by x and x+t (and by 1/1/80 and 12/31/82). Therefore, the value of $E_x^{1980-82}$ in the denominator must be increased to reflect the fact that births from a fraction t of 1979 do affect the exposure, and correspondingly decreased to reflect the fact that births from a fraction t of 1982 do not affect the exposure for the entire (x, x+t] interval (shown by the triangle extending to the right of 1/1/83 in Figure 9.8).

Thus we have seen that $B^{1980-82}$ is adjusted for some 1979 births (+) and for some 1982 births (−) to reach $E_x^{1980-82}$. In turn, $E_x^{1980-82}$ must be adjusted in the same manner to reach the proper denominator in the estimator for $_tq_x$. Usually these two sets of adjustments are combined, so that we reach

$$_t\hat{q}_x = \frac{_tD_x^{1980-82}}{B^{1980-82} + s(B_{12}^{1979} - B_{12}^{1982}) - _xD_0^{1980-82}}, \tag{9.42}$$

where s depends on x and t, and $_xD_0^{1980-82}$ are the observed deaths prior to age x. Note that (9.42) only holds when x+t is less than one month. When x+t exceeds one month, several months' births from 1979 and 1982 are involved. For example, to estimate $_tq_x$ for the interval from one month to two months, we would have

$$(9.43)$$

$$_{1/12}\hat{q}_{1/12} = \frac{_{1/12}D_{1/12}^{1980-82}}{B^{1980-82} + \frac{1}{2}\cdot B_{11}^{1979} + B_{12}^{1979} - \frac{1}{2}\cdot B_{11}^{1982} - B_{12}^{1982} - _{1/12}D_0^{1980-82}}$$

where B_{11}^{1979} and B_{12}^{1979} are births in November and December of 1979, respectively.

9.4.2 *Adult Tables, Ages* 0 *to* 4

The basic approach to estimating q_x, for $x = 0, \cdots, 4$, is the method presented in Section 9.2.1, with the estimator given by formula (9.13).

The reader will recall that this approach requires the census population to be available on each January 1 in the observation period. Thus preliminary steps were taken to estimate P_x^z for $x = 0, \cdots, 4$, and for $z = 1980, \cdots, 1983$, given the census population on June 1, 1981, and the birth and death records.

Since deaths up to age 4 last birthday were available by year of birth, the subdivision of D_x^z into $_\alpha D_x^z$ and $_\delta D_x^z$ was easily obtained. This, in turn, facilitated the approximate determination of the required values of P_x^z and E_x^z.

Figure 9.9 illustrates the estimation situation for the representative age interval $(x, x+1]$.

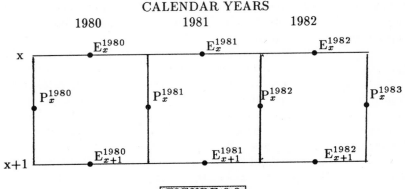

CALENDAR YEARS

FIGURE 9.9

First we define

$$P'_x = \sum_{z=1981}^{1983} P^z_x, \tag{9.44}$$

$$P''_x = \sum_{z=1980}^{1982} P^z_x, \tag{9.45}$$

and

$$E_y = \sum_{z=1980}^{1982} E^z_y, \tag{9.46}$$

for $y = x$ and $y = x+1$. Then we estimate

$$_\alpha\hat{P}_x = \frac{P'_x}{E_x} \tag{9.47}$$

and

$$_\delta\hat{P}_x = \frac{E_{x+1}}{P''_x}. \tag{9.48}$$

Finally, we estimate q_x as

$$\hat{q}_x = 1 - {}_\alpha\hat{P}_x \cdot {}_\delta\hat{P}_x, \tag{9.49}$$

for $x = 0,1,2,3,4$.

9.4.3 *Adult Tables, Ages 5 and Over*

Following a common demographic practice, the census populations and deaths were grouped in quinquennial age intervals even though they were available by single years of age. The basic reason for this is to help smooth out heapings which occur at certain ages due to age misreporting. The quinquennial intervals used were 5-9, 10-14, $\cdots$, 95-99, along with a final group for ages 100 and higher.

The overall approach was to use smooth-junction interpolation to obtain the values of q_x for the resulting life table (see London [41]).

First a sequence of single-age values, called *pivotal values*, are obtained from the grouped data, separately for deaths and populations. Note that a pivotal value is associated with the age in the middle of the quinquennial interval. Thus the pivotal value associated with the quinquennial group of deaths ${}_5D_5$ will be called D^P_7; the pivotal value associated with the quinquennial population group ${}_5M_{10}$ will be called M^P_{12}, etc. The available ${}_5D_x$ and ${}_5M_x$ values are subscripted at $x = 5, 10, \cdots, 95, 100$.

The basic pivotal value formula employed was

$$D_{x+2}^P = \frac{1}{4500}\Big[900 \cdot {}_5D_x - 36 \cdot \delta^2 {}_5D_x - 19 \cdot \delta^4 {}_5D_x\Big], \qquad (9.50)$$

where δ denotes the central difference taken over a quinquennial interval. Since $\delta^4 {}_5D_x$ involves ${}_5D_{x-10}$, ${}_5D_{x-5}$, ${}_5D_x$, ${}_5D_{x+5}$ and ${}_5D_{x+10}$, it follows that the lowest subscripted pivotal value that could be obtained from the available ${}_5D_x$ values by formula (9.50) was D_{17}^P, and the highest subscripted one was D_{92}^P.

Special formulas were used to obtain the pivotal values at ages 12 and 7, namely

$$D_{12}^P = -\frac{1}{125}\Big[{}_5D_5 - 27 \cdot {}_5D_{10} + {}_5D_{15}\Big], \qquad (9.51)$$

and

$$D_7^P = \frac{1}{125}\Big[23 \cdot {}_5D_5 + 5 \cdot {}_5D_{10} - 4 \cdot {}_5D_{15} + {}_5D_{20}\Big]. \quad (9.52)$$

The same formulas were used to produce the pivotal values, M_{x+2}^P, from the grouped population values ${}_5M_5$, ${}_5M_{10}$, $\cdots$, ${}_5M_{95}$, ${}_\infty M_{100}$.

Then pivotal mortality probabilities were obtained by the formula

$$q_{x+2}^P = \frac{D_{x+2}^P}{3 \cdot M_{x+2}^P + \frac{1}{2} \cdot D_{x+2}^P}, \qquad (9.53)$$

which was derived in the same manner as formula (9.34). The general subscript x+2 can be written as x, and we will now make that notational change. Thus we now have pivotal probabilities q_x^P, for $x = 7, 12, 17, \cdots, 92$. Note that q_{92}^P is the highest subscripted q_x^P that was derived directly from the data.

Before proceeding to the interpolation, four additional values of q_x^P were obtained by extrapolation, using the formula

$$q_x^P = 4 \cdot q_{x-5}^P - 6 \cdot q_{x-10}^P + 4 \cdot q_{x-15}^P - q_{x-20}^P, \qquad (9.54)$$

for $x = 97, 102, 107, 112$.

The basic interpolation formula used was the Karup-King four-point tangential reproducing formula (see Section 7.3 of London [41] for the derivation of this formula). Being a four-point formula, Karup-King will yield interpolated values, $\hat{q}_x$, at $x=12$ through 107 from the pivotal values. Since the formula is reproducing $\hat{q}_x \equiv q_x^P$ for $x = 12, 17, \cdots, 102, 107$.

To obtain $\hat{q}_x$ for $x = 7, 8, 9, 10, 11$, the Jenkins six-point osculatory smoothing formula (see Section 7.4 of London [41]) was used. This formula requires values of $\delta^4 q_7^P$ and $\delta^4 q_{12}^P$ in order to interpolate at $x = 7, 8, 9, 10, 11$. In this application, $\delta^4 q_7^P$ was arbitrarily set equal to zero, and $\delta^4 q_{12}^P$ was calculated by using the estimate $\hat{q}_2$, determined as described in Section 9.4.2, along with q_7^P, q_{12}^P, q_{17}^P and q_{22}^P.

Finally, the estimates $\hat{q}_3$ and $\hat{q}_4$, determined as described in Section 9.4.2, and the interpolated values $\hat{q}_7$ and $\hat{q}_8$ were used to determine a third degree polynomial, from which $\hat{q}_5$ and $\hat{q}_6$ were obtained.

9.4.4 The Final Table

Estimates $\hat{q}_x$, for $x = 5, 6, \cdots 107$, were obtained by the various interpolation approaches described in Section 9.4.3. Along with the values of $\hat{q}_x$, for $x = 0, 1, 2, 3, 4$, obtained as described in Section 9.4.2, a complete set of single-age estimates of q_x were then available.

Using a radix of $\ell_0 = 100,000$, The Canadian Life Tables for 1980-82 were then developed. The tables were arbitrarily truncated by setting $\hat{q}_{102} = 1$.

The methodology used to develop these tables is reported by Nagnur [46], upon which most of this section is based.

9.5 SUMMARY

In this chapter we have examined an approach to survival model estimation that is considerably different from the estimation procedures discussed in earlier chapters. The fundamental characteristic of this approach, which gives it its different nature, is the use of census populations, as opposed to the use of detailed information on individual lives. We will return to this approach in Chapter 11, using data available from the records of an insurance company or a pension fund.

In dealing with the two case studies of the Canadian and United States Life Tables, we went beyond merely describing the procedures used to obtain estimates of q_x directly from the sample data, and dealt as well with certain modifications of these initial estimates to obtain the final tables. Such modifications included graduation, extrapolation, blending of rates to create a smooth transition from one section of the table to another, and adjustments from age nearest birthday to age last birthday basis.

The reader should understand that these particular steps to a final table represent only one example of how such table construction might be accomplished, and are not to be considered as the only approach.

EXERCISES

9.1 Introduction; 9.2 Demographic Notation and Concepts

9-1. Show that the substitution of (9.9) and (9.10) into (9.8a) produces estimator (9.7).

9-2. (a) Derive estimator (9.17) by substituting (9.15) and (9.16) into (9.13).
 (b) Simplify (9.17) into (9.18).

9-3. Given the following information, calculate D_x^z.
 (i) The number of deaths at age x last birthday out of the $CYB = z - x$ group is 10.
 (ii) The number of deaths in calendar year z out of the $CYB = z - x$ group is 11.
 (iii) $_\delta D_x^{z+1} = 2(_\alpha D_{x+1}^z)$ (iv) $_\delta D_{x-1}^z = 5$ (v) $_\delta D_x^z + _\alpha D_{x+1}^z = 7$.

9-4. In a certain country, there were 34,950 deaths in 1982 in age interval (40,45], and the estimated population on July 1, 1982 in that age range was 5,205,000. If other studies suggest that $_5f_{40} = .535$, estimate $_5q_{40}$.

The following information is used for questions 5, 6 and 7:

	Calendar Year		
	1985	1986	1987
Births	5275	5237	7210
Deaths at Age 0 Last Birthday	200	210	300
Deaths at Age 1 Last Birthday	100	120	210
f_0^z	.3	.3	.3
f_1^z	.4	.4	.4

9-5. Calculate E_1^{1987}.

9-6. Calculate $_\alpha D_1^{1986}$.

9-7. Estimate q_1^{1987}.

9.3   The 1979-81 United States Life Tables

9-8.   Consider the following data:

Number of Deaths in Age Interval

Year	Births	0-1 day	1-7 days	7-28 days	28-365 days
1977	350	--	--	--	--
1978	375	--	--	--	--
1979	400	7	10	6	15
1980	425	6	12	6	13
1981	450	9	16	5	17

Using a radix of $\ell_0 = 100{,}000$ and the methodology employed in the development of the 1979-81 United States Life Tables, calculate ℓ_x for $x = 1/365, 7/365, 28/365$, and 1.

9-9.   Consider the following data:

x	M_x^{1980}	$D_x^{1979-81}$
2	1000	2
3	980	2
4	960	3

Estimate q_3 by the method used for the 1979-81 U.S. Life Tables.

9-10.   The following table shows hypothetical estimates of q_x based on census data and on Medicare data:

x	$\hat{q}_x^C$	$\hat{q}_x^M$
80	.070	.072
90	.190	.185
100	.336	.320

By the method used for the 1979-81 U.S. Life Tables, what values of q_x would be used in the final table for $x = 80, 90$ and 100?

9-11. Consider the following data:
$$\overset{\circ}{e}_{110} = 2.20 \qquad \ell_{107} = 1300 \qquad \ell_{108} = 1000 \qquad \ell_{109} = 700 \qquad \ell_{110} = 500$$
Using the method of the 1979-81 U.S. Life Tables, determine $\overset{\circ}{e}_{107}$.

9.4 The 1980-82 Canadian Life Tables

9-12. For the Infant Canadian Life Tables, $_tq_x$ is estimated as $\dfrac{_tD_x^{1980-82}}{_t(\text{Exposure})_x}$, where t and x are fractions of a *year*. Values of $_tD_x^{1980-82}$ are given, but values of $_t(\text{Exposure})_x$ must be estimated from birth and death data. Estimate each of the following values of $_t(\text{Exposure})_x$:

(a) $_{1/365}(\text{Exposure})_{4/365}$, the exposure used to estimate $_{1/365}q_{4/365}$, the conditional probability of death between ages 4 and 5 days.

(b) $_{1/52}(\text{Exposure})_{2/52}$, the exposure used to estimate $_{1/52}q_{2/52}$, the conditional probability of death between ages 2 and 3 weeks.

[*Hint: For parts (a) and (b), note that only December's births are involved in the adjustment terms. Use the facts of 7 days in a week, and 31 days in December, rather than considering a week to be $\frac{1}{4}$ of a month.*]

(c) $_{1/12}(\text{Exposure})_{7/12}$, the exposure used to estimate $_{1/12}q_{7/12}$, the conditional probability of death between ages 7 and 8 months.

9-13. Using the method of the Infant Canadian Life Tables, estimate $_{1/52}q_{1/52}$, the probability of dying during the second week of life, from the following data:

Year z	Births in Year z	Births in December of Year z	Deaths in First Week of Life	Deaths in Second Week of Life
1979	378,000	33,000	1,735	160
1980	377,000	32,000	1,730	164
1981	376,000	31,000	1,725	159
1982	375,000	30,000	1,720	157

9-14. Estimate q_2 by the approach used in the Adult Canadian Life Tables, using the following data and assuming no migration:

Year z	P_2^z	$_\alpha D_2^z$	$_\delta D_2^z$
1980	350,000	321	330
1981	352,000	319	332
1982	354,000	326	340
1983	356,000		

9-15. The following hypothetical values of populations and deaths are to be used to estimate q_{50} by the method used in the Adult Canadian Life Tables:

x	$_5D_x$	$_5M_x$
30	946	529,500
35	1,178	477,700
40	2,026	507,100
45	3,495	520,500
50	5,348	506,100
55	7,564	439,300
60	10,113	378,800
65	11,668	297,100
70	12,483	211,700
75	12,861	145,300

(a) Calculate D_x^P and M_x^P, for $x = 42, 47, 52, 57$.
(b) Calculate q_x^P, for $x = 42, 47, 52, 57$
(c) Calculate $\hat{q}_{50}$.
   [*Note: The Karup-King formula, adapted to unit intervals, is*
   $$\hat{q}_{x+s} = s \cdot q_{x+1}^P + \tfrac{1}{2}(s^3 - s^2) \cdot \delta^2 q_{x+1}^P$$
   $$+ t \cdot q_x^P + \tfrac{1}{2}(t^3 - t^2) \cdot \delta^2 q_x^P, \quad 0 \le s \le 1, \text{ where } t = 1 - s.]$$

PART III

PRACTICAL ASPECTS OF SURVIVAL MODEL ESTIMATION

In this final part of the text we wish to address aspects of survival model estimation that are not directly related to the statistical theory of the topic, which has been our concern for most of the text.

The very practical issue concerning procedures for processing large amounts of data naturally arises. In other words, with the derivation and analysis of estimators having been completed, how does one then obtain numerical results from sample data, especially in the case of large samples. This practical question is addressed in Chapter 10, with primary focus on life insurance company and pension fund data.

Finally, in Chapter 11, a popular actuarial variation on the Chapter 10 approach is presented. Similarity between this procedure and the demographic procedures of Chapter 9 is apparent. Some final observations of a practical nature are also presented in Chapter 11.

CHAPTER 10

EVALUATION OF ESTIMATORS FROM SAMPLE DATA

10.1 INTRODUCTION

In Chapter 5 we briefly described how basic data about persons in a study sample could be processed to obtain the ordered pair (y_i, z_i), the ages (or times) at which person i entered and was scheduled to exit observation.

Chapters 6 and 7 were then devoted to the problem of estimating q_x, the conditional probability of death over $(x, x+1]$, given alive at age x, and in Chapter 8 we considered the estimation of the parameters in a functional form of $S(x)$ or $\lambda(x)$. In both cases we saw how the ordered pairs (y_i, z_i) were used to obtain the desired estimates.

Before the advent of the computer age, the use of exact ages into and out of a study for all persons in a large-sample study involved a prohibitive amount of hand-calculation. As a result, grouping methods were developed which reduced the level of computation without sacrificing much accuracy.

In this text, however, we make the reasonable assumption that all large-scale studies are completely computerized, which allows us to take the exact age approach to estimation. Furthermore, the exercises in this chapter anticipate that the reader has access to computing facilities .

We will first describe the data processing steps involved in a large-sample study in which each person's actual date of birth is utilized. With insurance company or pension fund data, however, a person's actual date of birth is not used, for reasons that will be explained later. In these cases, the use of a hypothetical date of birth will simplify the data processing. We will present two different insurance cases here:

(1) The case of individual policies, in which an *insuring* date of birth is substituted for the actual date of birth.
(2) The case of group policies or pension plans, in which a *fiscal* date of birth is substituted for actual date of birth.

10.2 ACTUAL AGES

In Examples 5.1 and 5.2 we saw how the exact age y_i at which person i came under observation could be obtained from the date of birth and the latter of the date on which the observation period opened and the date person i joined the study sample. Now let us see how to streamline such calculations.

10.2.1 *Decimal Years*

A convenient way to obtain exact ages is to first express dates of events in terms of decimal years. These, in turn, are easily obtained from a day-of-the-year table, illustrated by Table 10.1, which has been stored in the computer.

TABLE 10.1

Day of the Year Represented by a Calendar Date

Date	Jan	Feb	Mar	Apr	May	Jun	Jul	Aug	Sep	Oct	Nov	Dec
1	1	32	60	91	121	152	182	213	244	274	305	335
2	2	33	61	92	122	153	183	214	245	275	306	336
3	3	34	62	93	123	154	184	215	246	276	307	337
4	4	35	63	94	124	155	185	216	247	277	308	338
5	5	36	64	95	125	156	186	217	248	278	309	339
6	6	37	65	96	126	157	187	218	249	279	310	340
7	7	38	66	97	127	158	188	219	250	280	311	341
8	8	39	67	98	128	159	189	220	251	281	312	342
9	9	40	68	99	129	160	190	221	252	282	313	343
10	10	41	69	100	130	161	191	222	253	283	314	344
11	11	42	70	101	131	162	192	223	254	284	315	345
12	12	43	71	102	132	163	193	224	255	285	316	346
13	13	44	72	103	133	164	194	225	256	286	317	347
14	14	45	73	104	134	165	195	226	257	287	318	348
15	15	46	74	105	135	166	196	227	258	288	319	349
16	16	47	75	106	136	167	197	228	259	289	320	350
17	17	48	76	107	137	168	198	229	260	290	321	351
18	18	49	77	108	138	169	199	230	261	291	322	352
19	19	50	78	109	139	170	200	231	262	292	323	353
20	20	51	79	110	140	171	201	232	263	293	324	354
21	21	52	80	111	141	172	202	233	264	294	325	355
22	22	53	81	112	142	173	203	234	265	295	326	356
23	23	54	82	113	143	174	204	235	266	296	327	357
24	24	55	83	114	144	175	205	236	267	297	328	358
25	25	56	84	115	145	176	206	237	268	298	329	359
26	26	57	85	116	146	177	207	238	269	299	330	360
27	27	58	86	117	147	178	208	239	270	300	331	361
28	28	59	87	118	148	179	209	240	271	301	332	362
29	29		88	119	149	180	210	241	272	302	333	363
30	30		89	120	150	181	211	242	273	303	334	364
31	31		90		151		212	243		304		365

Sufficient accuracy can be obtained by ignoring leap years. Any events which do occur on February 29 will be presumed to have occurred on February 28.

The decimal part of a decimal year is then obtained by dividing the day of the year by 365.

EXAMPLE 10.1: Find the decimal year for October 11, 1943.

SOLUTION: October 11 is day 284 of the year, so the decimal year is $1943 + 284/365 = 1943.78$. (In the examples and exercises of this text, decimal years will be rounded to two places.)

10.2.2 *Exact Ages*

It is easily seen that the exact age at which an event takes place is found by subtracting the decimal year of birth from the decimal year of the event.

EXAMPLE 10.2: If person i was born on October 11, 1943, and comes under observation on August 1, 1982, find y_i, the exact age that observation begins.

SOLUTION: August 1, 1982 is decimal year $1982 + 213/365 = 1982.58$. Then $y_i = 1982.58 - 1943.78 = 38.80$.

Example 10.2 illustrates the general approach to finding the exact age at which an event occurs. For each person in the sample, three ages are important: y_i, the age into a study; z_i, the *scheduled* age out of the study; and the *actual* age out of the study, due to death or withdrawal before age z_i, if this does, in fact, occur. We denote the exact age at death by θ_i and the exact age at withdrawal by ϕ_i, and adopt the convention that $\theta_i = 0$ if person i is not a study death, and $\phi_i = 0$ if person i is not a study withdrawal.

Therefore each person in a study is assigned an *age vector* $v'_i = [y_i, z_i, \theta_i, \phi_i]$ which contains all the information needed to process person i's contribution to the estimators presented in previous chapters.

EXAMPLE 10.3: An observation period runs from August 1, 1982 to December 31, 1987. Person i was born on October 11, 1943, and dies on April 12, 1986. Find the age vector v_i for this person.

SOLUTION: The age into the study is $y_i = 38.80$, from Example 10.2. December 31, 1987 is decimal year $1987 + 365/365 = 1988.00$, so the scheduled age out of the study is $z_i = 1988 - 1943.78 = 44.22$. April 12, 1986 is decimal year $1986 + 102/365 = 1986.28$, so the age at death is found to be $\theta_i = 1986.28 - 1943.78 = 42.50$. The age at withdrawal is $\phi_i = 0$. Thus $v'_i = [38.80, 44.22, 42.50, 0]$.

To estimate q_x over the interval $(x, x+1]$, it is necessary to first determine person i's contribution, if any, to $(x, x+1]$. We note first that if $y_i \geq x+1$, then person i enters the study beyond age $x+1$ and does not contribute to $(x, x+1]$. Similarly, if $z_i \leq x$, then person i leaves the study before age x and does not contribute to $(x, x+1]$. Even if $y_i < x+1$ and $z_i > x$, which implies that person i is *scheduled* to contribute to $(x, x+1]$, the occurrence of death or withdrawal before age x would prevent this scheduled contribution from being realized. This would be evidenced either by $0 < \theta_i < x$ or by $0 < \phi_i < x$.

Once the age vectors for persons who do not contribute to $(x, x+1]$ have been eliminated from consideration, the next step is to convert each age vector v_i into a *duration vector* for the interval $(x, x+1]$, showing the fractional duration within $(x, x+1]$ at which observation begins, is scheduled to end, or actually ends due to death or withdrawal prior to scheduled ending. We denote the duration vector by $u'_{i,x} = [r_i, s_i, \iota_i, \kappa_i]$, where, necessarily, at least one of ι_i and κ_i must be zero. The double subscript on u' identifies both the person and the estimation interval to which it relates.

The reader should verify the following conversion relationships for person i known to contribute to $(x, x+1]$.

$$r_i = \begin{cases} 0 & \text{if } y_i \leq x \\ y_i - x & \text{if } x < y_i < x+1 \end{cases} \tag{10.1a}$$

$$s_i = \begin{cases} z_i - x & \text{if } x < z_i < x+1 \\ 1 & \text{if } z_i \geq x+1 \end{cases} \tag{10.1b}$$

$$\iota_i = \begin{cases} 0 & \text{if } \theta_i = 0 \\ \theta_i - x & \text{if } x < \theta_i \leq x+1 \\ 0 & \text{if } \theta_i > x+1 \end{cases} \tag{10.1c}$$

$$\kappa_i = \begin{cases} 0 & \text{if } \phi_i = 0 \\ \phi_i - x & \text{if } x < \phi_i \leq x+1 \,. \\ 0 & \text{if } \phi_i > x+1 \end{cases} \tag{10.1d}$$

EXAMPLE 10.4: Convert the age vector of Example 10.3 into duration vectors for the estimation intervals $(38, 39]$, $(39, 40]$, and $(42, 43]$.

SOLUTION: For $(38, 39]$, we have $r_i = y_i - 38 = .80$, $s_i = 1$ (since $z_1 > 39$), $\iota_i = 0$ (since $\theta_i > 39$), and $\kappa_i = 0$ (since $\phi_i = 0$); thus $u'_{i,38} = [.80, 1, 0, 0]$. For $(39, 40]$, $r_i = 0$ (since $y_i < 39$), $s_i = 1$ (since $z_i > 40$), $\iota_i = 0$ (since $\theta_i > 40$), and $\kappa_i = 0$ (since $\phi_i = 0$); thus $u'_{i,39} = [0, 1, 0, 0]$. For the interval $(42, 43]$, $r_i = 0$ (since $y_i < 42$), $s_i = 1$ (since $z_i > 43$), $\iota_i = \theta_i - 42 = .50$, and $\kappa_i = 0$ (since $\phi_i = 0$); thus $u'_{i,42} = [0, 1, .50, 0]$. $u'_{i,39} = u'_{i,40} = u'_{i,41}$ and $u'_{i,x}$ is not defined for $x < 38$ or for $x > 42$, since person i does not contribute to any such intervals.

10.2.3 *Calculation of Exposure*

Many of the estimators developed in Chapters 6 and 7 are of the general form $\hat{q}_x = \dfrac{\text{Deaths}}{\text{Exposure}}$. This includes the moment estimators (which use scheduled exposure), the actuarial estimators (which use actuarial exposure), and the full data, exponential assumption MLE's (which use exact exposure).

Estimators of this form are particularly easy to apply when the basic data is represented by $u_{i,x}$ for person i within interval $(x, x+1]$. We first note that the number of observed deaths in $(x, x+1]$ is simply the number of $u_{i,x}$ vectors for which $\iota_i \neq 0$. Similarly the number of observed withdrawals in $(x, x+1]$ is the number of $u_{i,x}$ vectors for which $\kappa_i \neq 0$.

The exact exposure over $(x, x+1]$ contributed by person i is simply

$$(\text{Exact Exposure})_{i,x} = \begin{bmatrix} s_i \\ \iota_i \\ \kappa_i \end{bmatrix} - r_i, \tag{10.2}$$

where $\begin{bmatrix} s_i \\ \iota_i \\ \kappa_i \end{bmatrix}$ represents the minimum of s_i, ι_i, κ_i that exceed zero. In other words, if $\iota_i = \kappa_i = 0$, so that person i neither dies nor withdraws in $(x, x+1]$, then we have $(\text{Exact Exposure})_{i,x} = s_i - r_i$. But if person i dies in $(x, x+1]$, so that $\iota_i < s_i$ and $\kappa_i = 0$, then $(\text{Exact Exposure})_{i,x} = \iota_i - r_i$. Finally, if person i withdraws in $(x, x+1]$, so that $\kappa_i < s_i$ and $\iota_i = 0$, then $(\text{Exact Exposure})_{i,x} = \kappa_i - r_i$.

To find the scheduled exposure for estimating the mortality probability $q_x^{(d)}$ under Hoem's moment approach, exact exposure is still used for those who withdraw and for those who neither die nor withdraw in $(x, x+1]$, but those who die are exposed to age $x+s_i$. Thus we have

$$(\text{Scheduled Exposure})_{i,x} = \begin{bmatrix} s_i \\ \kappa_i \end{bmatrix} - r_i, \tag{10.3}$$

where κ_i is used if person i withdraws in $(x, x+1]$, and s_i is used otherwise.

The actuarial exposure differs from the other two types by the convention of exposing deaths in $(x, x+1]$ to age $x+1$. Thus we have

$$\text{(Actuarial Exposure)}_{i,x} = \begin{bmatrix} s_i \\ \kappa_i \\ 1 \end{bmatrix} - r_i, \tag{10.4}$$

where κ_i is used if person i withdraws in $(x, x+1]$, s_i is used if person i does not die or withdraw in $(x, x+1]$, and 1 is used if person i dies in $(x, x+1]$.

EXAMPLE 10.5 :   Consider the age vector $v'_i = [39.85, 40.75, 40.25, 0]$. Find each of (a) (Exact Exposure)$_{i,40}$, (b) (Scheduled Exposure)$_{i,40}$, and (c) (Actuarial Exposure)$_{i,40}$.
SOLUTION :   First we convert v'_i to $u'_{i,40} = [0, .75, .25, 0]$. Then we find (a) (Exact Exposure)$_{i,40} = .25$, $(\iota_i < s_i)$; (b) (Scheduled Exposure)$_{i,40} = .75$, where we use $s_i - r_i$, rather than $\iota_i - r_i$; (c) (Actuarial Exposure)$_{i,40} = 1$, where we use $1 - r_i$ rather than $\iota_i - r_i$.

The total exposure over $(x, x+1]$ is then found by summing over all persons who contribute to $(x, x+1]$. Thus

$$\text{(Exposure)}_x = \sum_i \text{(Exposure)}_{i,x}, \tag{10.5}$$

where (10.5) holds for all three types of exposure. The reader should recognize that the three types of exposure differ from each other only with respect to the treatment accorded to deaths within $(x, x+1]$.

10.2.4 *Grouping*

In many cases an average age at event might be substituted for the exact age at event for all persons whose exact age at event falls within a certain age range. For example, consider all persons whose exact y_i's fall between the integers x and x+1. We might substitute a common age y' for all such y_i, frequently using $y' = x + \frac{1}{2}$ as the assumed average value of the y_i's. When we do this the entrants to the study have been grouped by *age last birthday*, since it is those with a common age last birthday (x) that are being considered together.

A second type of grouping is one that is done by *calendar age*. Calendar age at event is defined to be the integral age y obtained on the birthday in the same calendar year in which the event takes place. For example, if a person's date of birth is September 14, 1950, and date of withdrawal is June 26, 1984, then the calendar age at withdrawal is 34, since this person would be integral age 34 on the birthday in the calendar year of withdrawal. Calendar ages at event are easily found by

$$CA = CYE - CYB, \tag{10.6}$$

where CYE is the calendar year of the event and CYB is the calendar year of birth.

It is easy to see that a person with calendar age w at event has an exact age at event that falls within $(w-1, w+1)$. If the wth birthday is January 1, and the event is December 31 of the same year, then the calendar age at event is w but the exact age is practically $w+1$. Conversely, if the wth birthday is December 31, and the event is January 1 of the same year, then the calendar age at event is still w, but the exact age is virtually $w-1$.

The advantage of a calendar age grouping is that an *integral* age w can then be reasonably substituted for the various exact fractional ages. When withdrawals are grouped by calendar age, and assumed to occur at the integral age w, then all withdrawals are occurring at the boundaries of the various estimation intervals. The occurrence of withdrawals *only* at estimation interval boundaries greatly simplifies the estimation work.

EXAMPLE 10.6 : An observation period begins on January 1, 1980. Consider a person born on April 12, 1960 who joins the group under observation on February 2, 1981. What is this person's exact age at entry to the study? What age would be substituted for the exact age if calendar age grouping is used? If age last birthday grouping is used?

SOLUTION : From Table 10.1, April 12, 1960 is 1960.28 and February 2, 1981 is 1981.09. Then the exact age is $y_i = 1981.09 - 1960.28 = 20.81$. The calendar age is $CA = 1981 - 1960 = 21$. The age last birthday is 20, so the substituted age would be $20\frac{1}{2}$.

10.2.5 *Actual Age Summary*

Here we recapitulate the steps involved in processing basic data for the purpose of estimating q_x (or a constant force of mortality) over the estimation interval $(x, x+1]$. We assume that the basic data for each person consists of the date of birth, date of joining the group under study (e.g., date of insurance policy issue), and date of death or withdrawal, if applicable. In addition, the opening and closing dates of the observation period (O.P.) must be specified. Actual ages are used.

(1) Any person whose death or withdrawal occurs before the O.P. opens, or whose date of joining the group occurs after the O.P. closes, is not part of the study sample.

(2) Dates of birth, joining the group, and death or withdrawal are converted to decimal years.

(3) Age at entry to study, y_i, is found as age when O.P. opens, or age when person i joins group, whichever is later.

(4)   Scheduled age at exit from study, z_i, is found as age on closing date of O.P.

(5)   Age at death or withdrawal, θ_i or ϕ_i, is found from date of event and date of birth; steps (3), (4) and (5) produce the age vector $v_i' = [y_i,\ z_i,\ \theta_i,\ \phi_i]$.

(6)   The duration vector $u_{i,x}' = [r_i,\ s_i,\ \iota_i\ \kappa_i]$ is obtained from v_i' with respect to the estimation interval $(x,\ x+1]$.

(7)   The estimators presented in Chapters 6, 7 and 8 can then be evaluated from the $u_{i,x}$ vectors for all persons in the study.

In Section 10.2.3 we discussed the evaluation of all estimators of the form $\dfrac{\text{Deaths}}{\text{Exposure}}$. Estimators for Special Case C, such as (6.19), which make use of c_x, the number scheduled to end observation in $(x,\ x+1]$, can also be easily evaluated from the $u_{i,x}$ vectors. Recall that Special Case C has $r_i = 0$ for all i. Then all vectors which show $s_i < 1$ belong to c_x for the estimation interval $(x,\ x+1]$.

The v_i vectors also contain all the information needed to evaluate the various Chapter 8 estimators for the parameters of a hypothesized parametric survival model. In this case it is not necessary to convert v_i into $u_{i,x}$. As seen in Chapter 8, it will frequently be necessary to evaluate these estimators by numerical methods.

The exercises presented at the end of this chapter give the reader ample opportunity to become comfortable with the required data processing steps. As already mentioned, it is assumed that the reader has access to adequate computing facilities.

10.3 *INSURING AGES*

Since most people do not purchase individual insurance policies on their actual birthdays, it follows that they are various fractional attained ages when their policies are issued. The insurance company, on the other hand, will not calculate a premium for the policy that depends on the insured's actual fractional age at issue. Instead an integral *insuring age* is substituted for the insured's actual age as of the policy issue date. Most commonly this insuring age will be the insured's actual age on the birthday nearest the policy issue date. In other words,

$$\text{IA} = \text{Actual Age Nearest Birthday}, \qquad (10.7)$$

where IA stands for Insuring Age.

Less commonly, the insuring age could be taken as the actual age on the birthday preceding the policy issue date, in which case we say that IA = Actual Age Last Birthday. Note that the examples and exercises in this chapter all use the Age Nearest Birthday basis.

10.3.1 *Valuation Year of Birth*

Assigning an integral insuring age to the insured as of the policy issue date implies that a hypothetical date of birth, called the *insuring date of birth*, has been substituted for the actual date of birth. Clearly the month and day of this insuring date of birth are the same as the policy issue date. The hypothetical year of birth, called the *valuation year of birth* (VYB), is then found as

$$VYB \ = \ CYI - IA, \tag{10.8}$$

where CYI is the calendar year of policy issue. It should be recognized that VYB will frequently be the same as CYB, but it can also be one year earlier or one year later than CYB.

[EXAMPLE 10.7]: An insurance policy is issued on August 22, 1988. Find the IA and the VYB if the actual date of birth is (a) January 12, 1968; (b) July 4, 1967.
[SOLUTION]: (a) As of August 22, 1988 the nearest birthday is the one coming up on January 12, 1989, when this person will be IA = 21. Then VYB = 1988 − 21 = 1967, which is one year less than the actual CYB. (b) As of August 22, 1988 the nearest birthday is the one just passed on July 4, 1988, when this person was IA = 21. Then VYB = 1988 − 21 = 1967, the same as the actual CYB.

10.3.2 *Anniversary-to-Anniversary Studies*

When insuring ages are used, a natural choice for the observation period is one that opens on the policy anniversary in a designated year for each insured person involved in the study. Similarly, the observation period would close on the policy anniversary in a later year. For example, an observation period might be defined as running from policy anniversaries in 1984 to those in 1988. Note that each person involved in the study has his or her own observation period.

Observation periods that run from a fixed date to a later fixed date can be used with insuring ages, but there are definite advantages to the anniversary-to-anniversary study when insuring ages are used. In this text we emphasize anniversary-to-anniversary studies with insuring ages.

The major convenient consequence of anniversary-to-anniversary studies with insuring ages is that all persons enter the study at an integral age y_i. This is true whether the person enters the study by joining the group via policy issue during the O.P. (at an integral insuring age), or by already being in the group when the O.P. opens. In the latter case, entry is at a policy anniversary which is always the attainment of an integral (insuring) age. Since y_i is an integer, it follows that $r_i = 0$ for any estimation interval $(x, x+1]$, since x is integral.

Similarly, with the O.P. ending on a policy anniversary, all scheduled ending ages z_i are integers, from which it follows that $s_i = 1$ for all estimation intervals $(x, x+1]$. Hence all vectors $u_{i,x}$ are of the form $[0, 1, \iota_i, \kappa_i]$, and all anniversary-to-anniversary insuring age studies belong to our Special Case A.

If there are no withdrawals, then the estimate $\hat{q}_x$ is found from (6.7) simply by counting the number of vectors $u_{i,x}$ with $r_i = 0$, which gives n_x, and the number with $\iota_i \neq 0$, which gives d_x, for $(x, x+1]$. If there are withdrawals, the number of them in $(x, x+1]$, w_x, is the number of vectors $u_{i,x}$ with $\kappa_i \neq 0$. With n_x, d_x and w_x available, $q_x'^{(d)}$ and $q_x'^{(w)}$ can be estimated by (6.38) or (6.46). Of course any of the exposure-based estimators could be used as well. Note that since all $s_i = 1$, the moment estimator and the actuarial estimator are the same.

Another approach that is frequently followed when withdrawals are present in an anniversary-to-anniversary insuring age study is to group the withdrawals by calendar insuring age. This is similar to actual calendar age, as defined by (10.6), except that VYB is used instead of CYB. Thus

$$CIA = CYW - VYB, \tag{10.9}$$

where CIA stands for Calendar Insuring Age, and CYW is the calendar year of withdrawal. Then all withdrawals with $CIA = w$, an integer, are assigned $\phi_i = w$ in place of their actual ϕ_i ages. Since *all* withdrawals are then viewed as occurring at an integral insuring age, which is an estimation interval boundary, so that none occur *within* $(x, x+1]$, then the simplified Special Case A again results, and q_x can be easily estimated by (6.7).

It should be noted that grouping by CIA is the same as assuming that all withdrawals occur on policy anniversaries. Since withdrawal from an insured group generally means policy surrender, which frequently occurs on a policy anniversary anyway, the assumption of *all* withdrawals on policy anniversaries is not unreasonable.

EXAMPLE 10.8 : For the sample of ten policyholders shown below, estimate q_{30} under the following conditions:

(1) The observation period runs from anniversaries in 1983 to those in 1988.
(2) Insuring ages are used throughout.
(3) Withdrawals are grouped by CIA.

Person	Date of Birth	Date of Policy Issue	Date of Death	Date of Withdrawal
1	Mar 17, 1954	Jun 20, 1982	---	---
2	May 6, 1954	Aug 6, 1982	Jun 12, 1983	---
3	Aug 12, 1954	Dec 18, 1982	---	Jun 18, 1985
4	Oct 27, 1954	Jan 4, 1983	---	---
5	Jan 4, 1955	Apr 28, 1983	Aug 29, 1986	---
6	Apr 18, 1955	Jun 16, 1983	---	Dec 12, 1985
7	May 20, 1955	Oct 29, 1983	Apr 21, 1986	---
8	Jul 4, 1955	Feb 16, 1984	---	---
9	Sep 16, 1955	Aug 22, 1984	---	Feb 22, 1987
10	Dec 11, 1955	Mar 6, 1985	Feb 17, 1987	---

SOLUTION : Each person is first assigned an IA by (10.7) and a VYB by (10.8). Then the VYB, Date of Policy Issue, and dates of the O.P. imply an integral y_i and z_i for all persons involved in the study. The grouping assumption for withdrawals implies that an integral ϕ_i replaces the exact, fractional ϕ_i. Exact ages at death, θ_i, are fractional. The vector v_i then implies the vector $u_{i,30}$. The data are summarized in the following table.

Person	IA	VYB	y_i	z_i	Age Vector v_i θ_i	ϕ_i	Duration Vector $u_{i,30}$ r_i	s_i	ι_i	κ_i
1	28	1954	29	34	0	0	0	1	0	0
2	28	1954	---	---	---	---	---	---	---	---
3	28	1954	29	34	0	31	0	1	0	1
4	28	1955	28	33	0	0	0	1	0	0
5	28	1955	28	33	31.34	0	0	1	0	0
6	28	1955	28	33	0	30	---	---	---	---
7	28	1955	28	33	30.48	0	0	1	.48	0
8	29	1955	29	33	0	0	0	1	0	0
9	29	1955	29	33	0	32	0	1	0	0
10	29	1956	29	32	30.95	0	0	1	.95	0

Note that Persons 2 and 6 do not contribute to (30,31]. Person 2 is not even in the study, since death precedes the O.P., and Person 6 withdraws at $CIA = 30$, so does not enter (30,31]. The remaining $n_{30} = 8$ persons all enter (30, 31] at age 30 (i.e., $r_i = 0$), and stay until age 31 (i.e., $s_i = 1$ and $\kappa_i \not< s_i$), except for the $d_{30} = 2$ deaths (Persons 7 and 10). As expected, this study design produces a Special Case A estimation situation. Using estimator (6.7), we find $\hat{q}_{30} = \frac{2}{8} = .25$.

EXAMPLE 10.9: Repeat Example 10.8, calculating the full data MLE of q_{30}, assuming a constant force of mortality over (30,31).
SOLUTION: This time we calculate exact exposure as 1 year for all 6 persons who do not die in (30, 31], .48 for Person 7, and .95 for Person 10. Then $\hat{\mu} = \frac{2}{7.43}$, and $\hat{q}_{30} = 1 - e^{-2/7.43} = .23599$.

10.3.3 *Select Studies*

For the purpose of estimating $S(t;x)$, as defined in Section 1.2, we consider only those policies issued at $IA = x$. Again assuming an anniversary-to-anniversary observation period, the data processing is quite similar to that described for insuring age studies, with the following parallel features:

(1) The vector $\mathbf{v}_i$ now represents the policy *duration* at entry, scheduled exit, death or withdrawal, rather than the insuring age of the insured at such events. Note that for policies issued during the O.P., the duration at entry to the study is 0.

(2) The vector $\mathbf{u}_{i,t}$ represents the location of these events within estimation interval $(t, t+1]$.

(3) Withdrawals are grouped by *calendar duration*, instead of calendar insuring age. Note that calendar duration is defined by

$$CD = CYW - CYI. \qquad (10.10)$$

An example will show the similarity of select studies to insuring age studies.

EXAMPLE 10.10: Consider the policies of Example 10.8 with $IA = 28$. Estimate $q_{[28]+2}$ using an observation period that runs from anniversaries in 1984 to those in 1989, grouping withdrawals by calendar duration.
SOLUTION: Again we expect Special Case A as a result of the study design. In Example 10.8, Policies 1 through 7 have $IA = 28$, and Policy 2 is not involved in the study due to death before the O.P. opens. The other policies have duration vectors for the study, $\mathbf{v}_i$, as follows:

| | | Duration Vector $\mathbf{v}_i$ | | |
Policy	y_i	z_i	θ_i	ϕ_i
1	2	7	0	0
3	2	7	0	3
4	1	6	0	0
5	1	6	3.34	0
6	1	6	0	2
7	1	6	2.48	0

For estimation interval (2,3], all policies enter at $t=2$ (i.e., $r_i = 0$), except for Policy 6 which does not contribute to (2,3] do to the calendar duration grouping of withdrawals. All policies which enter are *scheduled* to complete (2,3], and all do except Policy 7. Using any of the moment estimator, the partial data MLE, or the full data MLE with uniform distribution assumption, we have $\hat{q}_{[28]+2} = \frac{1}{5} = .20000$. Using the full data MLE with exponential distribution assumption, we have $\hat{q}_{[28]+2} = 1 - e^{-1/4.48} = .20005$.

10.3.4 *Insuring Age Summary*

In this section we have shown how the combination of insuring ages with an anniversary-to-anniversary observation period, the insuring age analogy to an actual age birthday-to-birthday study, considerably simplifies the estimation of q_x over the interval (x, x+1]. Note that basic data was available on each insured life in the sample.

If a date-to-date observation period is used, then ages at entry to and exit from the study, y_i and z_i, will no longer be integral. This situation is the same as that presented in Section 10.2 using actual ages.

Instead of grouping withdrawals by calendar insuring age, we might group them by age last birthday. That is, all withdrawals occurring in (x, x+1], i.e., at age x last birthday, are assumed to occur at some average age, commonly $x+\frac{1}{2}$.

In this text we take the point of view that an anniversary-to-anniversary observation period, with withdrawals grouped by calendar insuring age, are the features of a standard insuring age study using data from a sample of individual life insurance policyholders. Date-to-date studies and/or withdrawals grouped by age last birthday constitute variations of the standard study design. The date-to-date variation will be considered briefly in Section 11.2.2.

10.4   *FISCAL AGES*

In the case of group insurance or group pension plans, a large number of individual persons are covered under a single policy or plan. There will exist a key date for such a plan, called the plan anniversary or plan valuation date.   On such a date it will be necessary to calculate premium rates, actuarial present values of accrued benefits, or other financial values.   For this purpose it will be convenient for all members of the plan to be an integral age on this key date. This integral age is called the *fiscal age*.

Note that this situation is similar to that under insuring ages, where each individual insured was an integral insuring age on that person's policy anniversary.   Here the same idea holds, with the further condition that the policy anniversary is the same date for all persons. It is traditional to refer to this date as the *T-date*.

Historically the terms T-date and fiscal ages were adopted to indicate that the T-date was the terminal date of the fiscal year of an enterprise.   In this text we feel that the major application of the fiscal age concept is to studies of mortality under group insurance or pension plans.   Thus the T-date is the plan anniversary.   The term fiscal age is not particularly descriptive, but we will retain it for the sake of tradition.

10.4.1   *Fiscal Year of Birth*

Analogous to the definitions of insuring age and valuation year of birth (VYB) in Section 10.3, we assign each person in a group plan a fiscal age (FA) as of some particular T-date, say the T-date in calendar year z. This fiscal age would likely be the actual age nearest birthday on that date, or it could be the actual age last birthday, or the actual calendar age. Regardless of how it is assigned, we then define the *fiscal year of birth* (FYB) as

$$FYB = z - FA. \tag{10.11}$$

Just as was true for VYB under insuring ages, FYB could be the same as the person's actual CYB, or it could be one year less or one year greater. Once the FYB has been assigned, the T-date in the FYB is then the hypothetical date of birth for each person in the group plan.

EXAMPLE 10.11: A pension plan has its anniversary on March 31. A new employee becomes a member of the plan on March 31, 1988. This employee's actual date of birth is November 17, 1956. If the fiscal age is assigned as actual age last birthday, find this employee's FYB.

SOLUTION : The actual age last birthday as of March 31, 1988, is 31, which was attained on November 17, 1987. Then FYB $= 1988 - 31 = 1957$. Note that FYB $=$ CYB $+ 1$.

10.4.2 *Observation Periods for Fiscal Age Studies*

The natural choice of an observation period is one that runs from the T-date in a certain year to the T-date in a later year. Note that the T-date is the anniversary for all members of the group plan, so a T-to-T study is both a date-to-date study and an anniversary-to-anniversary study.

The principal benefit of using a T-to-T observation period is that all members in the plan when the O.P. opens enter the study at an integral age y_i. Similarly, all members in the study sample will have an integral scheduled exit age z_i. In turn, we know that integral y_i and z_i imply $r_i = 0$ and $s_i = 1$ for any estimation interval $(x, x+1]$.

Another reason to use a T-to-T O.P. is that certain summary information, prepared for valuation or pricing purposes on a T-date, can be used in the estimation of q_x. This will be pursued further in Chapter 11.

Although dates other than T-dates can be used in date-to-date fiscal age studies, there is no particular advantage to this, and only T-to-T studies will be considered in this chapter. One variation from T-to-T will be presented in the next chapter.

10.4.3 *New Members and Withdrawals*

If new employees can only join the group plan under study on a T-date, then such new employees would enter the study at integral fiscal ages, just as was true under insuring ages. However such a restriction does not usually hold, so persons joining the group during the observation period could do so at any fractional age. Similarly, persons might withdraw from the group plan by terminating employment at any date, and hence at any fractional fiscal age.

Recall that y_i is the age at which person i enters the study, whether as a member when the O.P. opens (in which case y_i is an integer), or as a new member during the O.P. (in which case y_i can be fractional).

The procedures using exact actual ages described in Section 10.2 can be used with exact fiscal ages as well. On the other hand, grouping procedures could be used for the new members and withdrawals. If calendar fiscal age grouping is used, then an integral fiscal age is substituted for the exact fractional fiscal ages. If age last fiscal birthday grouping is used, then usually $y + \frac{1}{2}$ is substituted for all exact fractional ages in $(y, y+1]$. Whether calendar age or age last birthday is used, it is customary to use the same grouping for both new members and withdrawals. The major reason for this will be illustrated in the next chapter.

EXAMPLE 10.12: A group life insurance plan has a June 30 anniversary date. From the following sample data, estimate q_{40} using an O.P. that runs from June 30, 1980 to June 30, 1985. Group new members and withdrawals by fiscal age last birthday, assume an average age of $y+\frac{1}{2}$, and use the actuarial estimator.

Member	FYB	Date of Plan Membership	Date of Death	Date of Withdrawal
1	1942	May 12, 1979	---	Sep 30, 1983
2	1942	Aug 24, 1979	---	---
3	1941	Oct 3, 1979	Mar 17, 1984	---
4	1941	Jan 30, 1980	---	Apr 30, 1980
5	1941	May 18, 1980	---	---
6	1940	Jan 3, 1981	---	---
7	1941	Jul 15, 1980	---	Feb 15, 1982
8	1941	Apr 7, 1982	Jun 22, 1982	---
9	1943	Sep 15, 1984	---	---
10	1943	Jul 1, 1985	---	---

SOLUTION: Note that Member 4 withdrew from the plan before the O.P. opened, and Member 10 did not join the plan until after the O.P. closed, so neither member is involved in this study. Members 6 through 9 are new members during the O.P., whereas the others all come under observation on June 30, 1980. The following table gives y_i, the fiscal age into the study (exact age for starters, grouped age for new members); z_i, the scheduled fiscal age at exit from the study; θ_i, the fiscal age last birthday at death; ϕ_i, the grouped fiscal age at withdrawal.

Member	y_i	z_i	θ_i	ϕ_i
1	38	43	0	41.5
2	38	43	0	0
3	39	44	42	0
5	39	44	0	0
6	40.5	45	0	0
7	39.5	44	0	40.5
8	40.5	44	40	0
9	41.5	42	0	0

Member 9 does not contribute to $(40, 41]$, since $y_i > 41$. Members 6 and 8 enter $(40, 41]$ at 40.5, and the 5 others enter at 40. Member 7 leaves at 40.5, and all others leave at 41, except Member 8 who dies in $(40, 41]$. But under the actuarial estimator, Member 8 is exposed to age 41 nonetheless. Thus we have $\hat{q}_{40} = \dfrac{1}{5 + 2(\frac{1}{2}) - \frac{1}{2}} = \dfrac{1}{5.5} = .18182$.

10.4.4 *Fiscal Age Summary*

The use of fiscal ages gains an advantage over the use of insuring ages in that all persons in the study sample attain integral ages on the same date. Thus date-to-date and anniversary-to-anniversary studies become identical whenever T-to-T is used for the O.P.

On the other hand, under insuring ages persons who join the group under study during the O.P. do so at an integral age, so only withdrawals can occur at fractional ages. Under fiscal ages, both new members during the O.P. and withdrawals can occur at fractional ages. When grouping is used, it is customary to consider both categories together. This practice is widely used in the actuarial approach to estimation described in the next chapter.

10.5 *SUMMARY*

With considerable attention having been paid to the *theory* of estimation in prior chapters, our purpose in this chapter has been to describe the *practice* of estimating q_x over $(x, x+1]$, with emphasis given to insurance company and pension plan situations. In particular the use of hypothetical insuring ages (for individual policy studies) and fiscal ages (for group studies) was introduced, and certain practical advantages were seen to follow from this practice.

Considerable emphasis was given to the use of exact ages, with age grouping considered as well. In the exercises which follow, both approaches will be used. We repeat that most of the exercises assume that the reader has access to adequate computing facilities.

EXERCISES

The exercises for this chapter are quite different from those presented at the end of previous chapters. It is our expectation that the twelve examples in this chapter have provided the reader with an adequate reinforcement of the relevant theory and procedures. Accordingly, the following exercises provide the reader with an opportunity to deal with our topic in a macro, rather than micro, sense.

On pages 262 and 263 the basic data are given for a sample of 70 persons, showing Date of Birth, Date of Entry, Date of Withdrawal, and Date of Death. The sample data will be used in three different contexts in the exercises, where each context requires a slightly different meaning for the concept of Entry. This will be made clear in each of the three sets of exercises that follow.

BASIC DATA

Person Number	Date of Birth	Date of Entry	Date of Withdrawal	Date of Death
1	Apr 12, 1950	Jan 16, 1978	---	---
2	Jul 2, 1946	Mar 29, 1978	---	Jan 4, 1980
3	Jun 11, 1948	Aug 1, 1978	Dec 1, 1980	---
4	Feb 28, 1944	Aug 20, 1978	Aug 27, 1979	---
5	Nov 28, 1951	Jan 11, 1979	---	Dec 25, 1981
6	Jun 6, 1941	Jan 6, 1979	May 3, 1979	---
7	Mar 15, 1947	Dec 9, 1978	---	---
8	Aug 24, 1948	May 3, 1979	Mar 4, 1980	---
9	Jun 25, 1950	Jan 31, 1980	Dec 31, 1980	---
10	Feb 23, 1949	Sep 22, 1979	---	May 10, 1988
11	Dec 15, 1947	Oct 8, 1979	May 16, 1981	---
12	Jul 6, 1948	Feb 18, 1980	Aug 10, 1989	---
13	Jun 10, 1950	Apr 5, 1980	---	---
14	Feb 19, 1949	Jun 2, 1980	---	Apr 14, 1986
15	Oct 15, 1950	Nov 24, 1980	May 10, 1988	---
16	Apr 14, 1951	Feb 10, 1981	---	---
17	Aug 10, 1948	Dec 20, 1980	---	Oct 10, 1987
18	Oct 8, 1951	Jul 7, 1981	Apr 6, 1986	---
19	Oct 26, 1949	May 26, 1981	---	---
20	Feb 5, 1950	Dec 16, 1981	Aug 25, 1984	---
21	Dec 14, 1951	Dec 12, 1981	---	Mar 6, 1987
22	Dec 10, 1950	May 2, 1982	---	---
23	Jul 31, 1952	Apr 22, 1982	---	---
24	Jan 24, 1951	Sep 9, 1982	Sep 9, 1983	---
25	Jul 18, 1953	Jan 28, 1983	Nov 16, 1989	---
26	Oct 2, 1952	Oct 14, 1982	---	Nov 14, 1984
27	Sep 5, 1950	Aug 24, 1982	Jun 4, 1987	---
28	Mar 21, 1951	Nov 12, 1982	---	Dec 2, 1987
29	Apr 10, 1953	Mar 4, 1983	---	---
30	May 25, 1952	Dec 30, 1982	Jun 21, 1985	---
31	Aug 6, 1952	May 26, 1983	---	---
32	Nov 20, 1953	Jun 13, 1983	---	---
33	Dec 10, 1951	Apr 6, 1983	---	Feb 15, 1988
34	Aug 4, 1953	Sep 2, 1983	Aug 19, 1984	---
35	Sep 10, 1953	Feb 28, 1984	---	---

BASIC DATA (Continued)

Person Number	Date of Birth	Date of Entry	Date of Withdrawal	Date of Death
36	Jun 30, 1952	Nov 1, 1983	Mar 10, 1988	---
37	Feb 28, 1953	Jul 15, 1984	---	Jul 16, 1987
38	Jan 31, 1954	Aug 8, 1984	---	---
39	Sep 5, 1952	Nov 2, 1984	Aug 6, 1986	---
40	Nov 2, 1953	Jan 21, 1985	---	---
41	Jul 15, 1955	Mar 16, 1985	---	---
42	Apr 20, 1954	May 4, 1985	---	Jan 20, 1986
43	Jul 27, 1955	Sep 17, 1985	Jul 6, 1988	---
44	Dec 3, 1955	Apr 10, 1986	---	---
45	Jan 4, 1954	Dec 23, 1985	---	---
46	Nov 6, 1954	Mar 10, 1986	Jun 21, 1986	---
47	May 19, 1956	Jul 12, 1986	Jul 12, 1987	---
48	Aug 16, 1956	Jul 6, 1986	Jul 6, 1989	---
49	Jan 4, 1955	Aug 19, 1986	---	---
50	Mar 10, 1956	Jun 25, 1986	---	Sep 24, 1988
51	Sep 24, 1956	Feb 7, 1987	Dec 21, 1988	---
52	Nov 15, 1956	Apr 14, 1987	---	---
53	Sep 6, 1954	Dec 8, 1986	---	Jun 4, 1988
54	Sep 14, 1957	May 21, 1987	Sep 21, 1987	---
55	Nov 21, 1955	Aug 27, 1987	---	---
56	Aug 19, 1957	Sep 16, 1987	---	---
57	Jan 6, 1957	Aug 9, 1987	---	---
58	Apr 6, 1957	Nov 30, 1987	---	Aug 19, 1988
59	Aug 4, 1955	Oct 23, 1987	Nov 23, 1987	---
60	Feb 3, 1956	Dec 4, 1987	---	---
61	Apr 27, 1958	Jan 4, 1988	Jun 4, 1988	---
62	Feb 26, 1957	May 10, 1988	---	---
63	Aug 13, 1958	Jul 25, 1988	---	Sep 5, 1989
64	Jul 6, 1956	Sep 16, 1988	Nov 19, 1989	---
65	May 21, 1959	Feb 3, 1989	---	---
66	Sep 15, 1956	Dec 12, 1988	Dec 12, 1989	---
67	Nov 8, 1957	Apr 27, 1989	---	---
68	Jul 21, 1959	Aug 5, 1989	Jan 10, 1990	---
69	Feb 16, 1958	Oct 18, 1989	---	---
70	Nov 13, 1956	Jan 14, 1990	---	---

10.1 *Introduction*;   10.2 *Actual Ages*

For questions 1 through 4, the data refer to members of a fraternal organization. In particular, the Date of Entry is the date of membership in the organization. Values of q_x are to be estimated from this sample data using an observation period of January 1, 1980 to December 31, 1989.

10-1. Determine the exact actual age vector v_i for each member of the sample, indicating any members who are not involved in the study. Round decimal years to two decimal places.

10-2. Find the values of d_x, the number of observed deaths in (x, x+1], for all values of x for which $d_x \neq 0$.

10-3. For all values of x for which exposure exists, use the results of Exercise 10-1 to find each of the following:
   (a) (Exact Exposure)$_x$,
   (b) (Scheduled Exposure)$_x$,
   (c) (Actuarial Exposure)$_x$.

10-4. For all values of x for which $d_x \neq 0$, estimate q_x by each of the following:
   (a) Full data MLE, exponential distribution assumption.
   (b) Grouped actuarial estimator, using age last birthday grouping for study starters and enders, and calendar age grouping for new members and withdrawals during the O.P.

10.3 *Insuring Ages*

For questions 5 through 7, the data refer to a sample of individual life insurance policyholders, and the Date of Entry is the date of policy issue. Insuring age is defined as actual age nearest birthday at issue. The observation period will be policy anniversaries in 1980 to those in 1989. Group withdrawals by calendar insuring age.

10-5. Find the insuring age vector v_i for each policyholder, indicating those not involved in the study. Use the calendar insuring age, rather than exact insuring age, for ϕ_i.

10-6. Recall that this study design produces a Special Case A study where $\hat{q}_x = \frac{d_x}{n_x}$. Calculate d_x and n_x for all x for which $n_x \neq 0$.

10-7. For each of issue ages 30, 31 and 32 separately, a select study is to be performed. Use the observation period of A, 1980 to A, 1989 and group withdrawals by calendar duration, so that Special Case A again results. Calculate $d_{[x]+t}$ and $n_{[x]+t}$, for $x = 30,31,32$, for all t for which $n_{[x]+t} \neq 0$.

10.4 *Fiscal Ages*

For questions 8 through 10, the data refer to the members of a group insurance plan with policy anniversary on June 30. The Date of Entry is the date of employment, at which time insurance coverage begins. A fiscal age is assigned as the actual age nearest birthday as of the June 30 *following* Date of Entry. (E.g., for Date of Entry November 18, 1985, the following June 30 is June 30, 1986. If the member's actual birthday is April 4, 1954, then the fiscal age is the actual age nearest birthday on June 30, 1986, which is 32. Then FYB $= 1986 - 32 = 1954$.) Values of q_x are to be estimated over an observation period of June 30, 1982 to June 30, 1990.

10-8. Find the set of exact fiscal age vectors v_i for all persons who are involved in this study.

10-9. Using the exact fiscal age vectors, estimate q_x by the full data, exponential assumption, MLE, for all x for which $d_x \neq 0$.

10-10. Calculate the actuarial exposure for all intervals $(x, x+1]$ for which the exposure is nonzero, separately for each of the following grouping assumptions for new members and withdrawals during the O.P.:
(a) Fiscal age last birthday.
(b) Calendar fiscal age.

CHAPTER 11

OTHER ISSUES REGARDING ACTUARIAL ESTIMATION

11.1 *INTRODUCTION*

In this final chapter we will address several miscellaneous topics related to our main theme of estimating survival models from sample data. Our focus remains on the general actuarial area of insurance companies and pension funds. No new estimation theory is presented here, but rather a discussion of various practical issues and variations from the standard theory and mathematics presented in earlier chapters.

11.2 *VALUATION SCHEDULE EXPOSURE FORMULAS*

The approach to determination of exposure, and to mortality estimation in general that was presented in earlier chapters, was characterized by the availability of basic information on each individual in the study sample. Such approach is referred to in the actuarial literature as the *individual record* approach.

Not uncommonly, however, insurance companies and pension plans will use a different approach to the calculation of exposure from which to estimate q_x by the actuarial estimator. This approach makes use of tabulations of the number of persons in the study group at various ages last birthday on various dates. These tabulations are prepared primarily for the actuarial functions of pricing or valuation, but they can be used to produce an estimate of the mortality experienced by the group as well. In light of this basic purpose for producing the tabulations, this approach to estimating q_x is called the *valuation schedule* approach.

It must be remembered that valuation schedule formulas are methods of calculating actuarial exposure, and hence the actuarial estimator, but not the other types of exposure defined in Chapter 6. Because this exercise is strictly actuarial, we have chosen to present it in this chapter, rather than in Chapter 10.

When calculating actuarial exposure by valuation schedule formulas, it is common to use certain grouping assumptions, as described in Chapters 6 and 10 in connection with the individual record approach. Since the goal is to calculate actuarial exposure over $(x, x+1]$, it follows that if the *same* grouping and average age assumptions are used with an individual record approach as with a valuation schedule approach for a certain study sample, the same value of actuarial exposure will result. This equivalent pair of exposure formulas, individual record and valuation schedule, are referred to as *counterpart formulas*.

Calculation of actuarial exposure by the valuation schedule approach will first be illustrated using fiscal ages and then using insuring ages. The reader will note some similarity to the general population approaches of Chapter 9, especially in the case of insuring ages.

11.2.1 *Valuation Schedule Approach Using Fiscal Ages*

Recall the properties of fiscal ages as defined in Section 10.4. In particular, the T-date for a pension plan or group insurance policy is the fiscal birthday for all persons in the group, so all persons are integral ages on that date.

Suppose an observation period is defined to run from the T-date in calendar year z to the T-date in calendar year z+1. Then all persons in the study sample are integral fiscal ages when the observation period opens.

Let F_x^z represent the number of persons who are exact fiscal age x on the T-date in calendar year z. It is clear that these persons all have $FYB = z - x$. Similarly, F_x^{z+1} represents those who are exact age x on the T-date in calendar year z+1.

We will use the same type of two-dimensional diagrams that were introduced in Chapter 9, where calendar time increases from left to right, and age increases from top to bottom. Figure 11.1 represents the flow of persons from fiscal age x to fiscal age x+1.

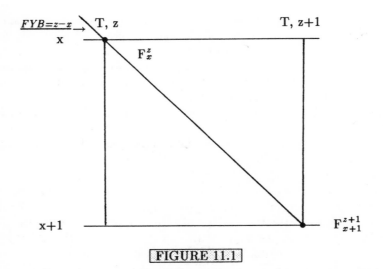

FIGURE 11.1

Note that the persons who move down the illustrated diagonal line all have $FYB = z - x$. Between the T-date in calendar year z and the T-date in calendar year z+1 the composition of the group changes due to three factors:

(1) New persons with FYB $= z - x$ might join the group.
(2) Persons might withdraw from the group.
(3) Persons might leave the group by death.

In the valuation schedule approach it is standard practice to consider the first two factors together. The net effect on the FYB $= z - x$ group, between T, z and T, z+1, resulting from these two factors is called the *net migration* for the group, and is denoted by m_x^z. Note that m_x^z can be positive, negative, or zero.

The number of deaths from the FYB $= z - x$ group between these two T-dates (i.e., between fiscal ages x and x+1) is denoted by d_x^z. It then follows that

$$F_x^z + m_x^z - d_x^z = F_{x+1}^{z+1}. \tag{11.1}$$

Note that the m_x^z migrants enter or exit the FYB $= z - x$ group at ages between x and x+1 (i.e., at fiscal age x last birthday). Instead of keeping track of the exact fiscal age for each migrant, we group them all together at an assumed average age of $x + \frac{1}{2}$. Recall from Chapter 6 that deaths are exposed to age x+1 in the calculation of actuarial exposure over (x, x+1]. Then it follows that

$$(\text{Actuarial Exposure})_x = F_x^z + \frac{1}{2} \cdot m_x^z, \tag{11.2}$$

by the principles described in Chapter 6.

If equation (11.1) is solved for m_x^z, we obtain

$$m_x^z = F_{x+1}^{z+1} - F_x^z + d_x^z, \tag{11.3}$$

which is then substituted into formula (11.2) to obtain

$$(\text{Actuarial Exposure})_x = \frac{1}{2}\left(F_x^z + F_{x+1}^{z+1} + d_x^z\right), \tag{11.4}$$

which is frequently written as

$$(\text{Actuarial Exposure})_x = \bar{F}_x^z + \frac{1}{2} \cdot d_x^z. \tag{11.5}$$

The symbol $\bar{F}_x^z = \frac{1}{2}(F_x^z + F_{x+1}^{z+1})$ denotes a mean, or average, number of persons in the group during the observation period. Formula (11.5) is of the general form "mean population plus half the deaths," a description that is characteristic of valuation schedule formulas.

⎡EXAMPLE 11.1⎤: In a certain pension plan, the number of persons with FYB = 1955 on the T-date in 1985 is 1000. Prior to the T-date in 1986, 22 new persons join this FYB group, 6 withdraw, and 2 die. The observation period is T, 1985 to T, 1986. Calculate (Actuarial Exposure)$_{30}$.

⎡SOLUTION⎤: First we see that $m_{30}^{1985} = 22 - 6 = 16$, and $d_{30}^{1985} = 2$, so that $F_{31}^{1986} = 1000 + 16 - 2 = 1014$. Then, by formula (11.4), we find that (Actuarial Exposure)$_{30} = \frac{1}{2}(1000 + 1014 + 2) = 1008$.

An alternative formula for actuarial exposure over (x, x+1] is derived from the assumptions stated in the following paragraph. Again the observation period runs from T, z to T, z+1.

Let G represent the mid-date between T, z and T, z+1, and let $g_x^{z,z+1}$ represent the number of persons in the FYB = z−x group on that date. The half-year from T, z to G is denoted the a-period, and the half-year from G to T, z+1 is denoted the b-period. Let $_am_x^z$ and $_ad_x^z$ denote the net migration and deaths, respectively, for the FYB = z−x group during the a-period, and let $_bm_x^z$ and $_bd_x^z$ be similarly defined for the b-period. Then it follows that

$$F_x^z + {_am_x^z} - {_ad_x^z} = g_x^{z,z+1}, \tag{11.6}$$

and that

$$g_x^{z,z+1} + {_bm_x^z} - {_bd_x^z} = F_{x+1}^{z+1}. \tag{11.7}$$

These new symbols are illustrated in Figure 11.2.

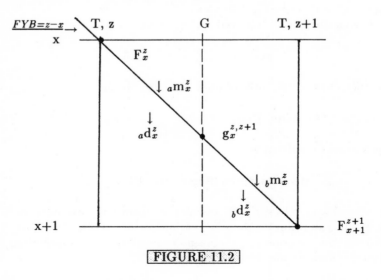

⎡FIGURE 11.2⎤

We note that the $_am_x^z$ migrants do so at ages between x and $x+\frac{1}{2}$, and the $_bm_x^z$ migrants do so at ages between $x+\frac{1}{2}$ and x+1. Our grouping assumptions in this case are that all $_am_x^z$ are grouped at age x and all $_bm_x^z$ are grouped at age x+1. Clearly these are not the average ages at which the migration occurs, but the understatement of average age for the $_am_x^z$ group is assumed to be approximately offset by the overstatement of average age for the $_bm_x^z$ group.

Under these grouping assumptions, the actuarial exposure is

$$(\text{Actuarial Exposure})_x = F_x^z + {_am_x^z}, \qquad (11.8)$$

by the principles of Chapter 6. When equation (11.6) is solved for $_am_x^z$ and substituted into formula (11.8), we obtain

$$(\text{Actuarial Exposure})_x = g_x^{z,z+1} + {_ad_x^z}, \qquad (11.9)$$

which is known as King's formula [37]. Again the general form "mean population plus half the deaths" is apparent.

EXAMPLE 11.2 : Suppose that, for the data of Example 11.1, the new entrants, withdrawals and deaths in the a-period were 10, 4 and 1, respectively. Calculate (Actuarial Exposure)$_{30}$ by formula (11.9).
SOLUTION : We have $_am_{30}^{1985} = 10 - 4 = 6$, and $_ad_{30}^{1985} = 1$, which produces $g_{30}^{1985,1986} = 1000 + 6 - 1 = 1005$. Then by formula (11.9), we have (Actuarial Exposure)$_{30} = 1005 + 1 = 1006$. Since formulas (11.4) and (11.9) embody different grouping assumptions, we are not surprised to see that they produce different answers.

If an observation period covers several fiscal years, the actuarial exposure over (x, x+1] is found by summing the one-year exposure formula over the several years of the observation period. For example, if the period is from T, z to T, z+4, we have the following representation for (x, x+1].

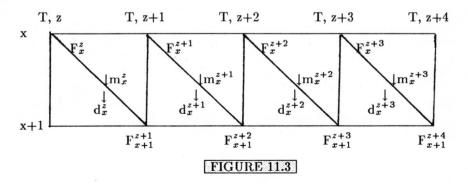

FIGURE 11.3

Using formula (11.5), the total actuarial exposure over $(x, x+1]$ is given by

$$(\text{Actuarial Exposure})_x = \sum_{u=z}^{z+3} \left(\bar{F}_x^u + \tfrac{1}{2} \cdot d_x^u \right), \tag{11.10}$$

and the actuarial estimate of q_x is given by

$$\hat{q}_x = \frac{\sum\limits_{u=z}^{z+3} d_x^u}{\sum\limits_{u=z}^{z+3} \left(\bar{F}_x^u + \tfrac{1}{2} \cdot d_x^u \right)}. \tag{11.11}$$

Note that persons with different FYB contribute to this estimate.

EXAMPLE 11.3: From the following data, estimate q_{50}, q_{51} and q_{52}, using the exposure given by (a) formula (11.4), and (b) formula (11.9). In both cases the observation period is the T-date in 1985 to the T-date in 1988.

Migration and Deaths During the Observation Period

FYB	Members on T, 1985	T, '85 to T, '86 $_am$	$_ad$	$_bm$	$_bd$	T, '86 to T, '87 $_am$	$_ad$	$_bm$	$_bd$	T, '87 to T, '88 $_am$	$_ad$	$_bm$	$_bd$
1935	120	4	2	4	1	2	0	4	1	8	1	4	1
1934	110	8	0	-4	2	8	1	4	0	8	0	4	0
1933	115	4	1	4	0	4	0	8	2	4	0	4	1

SOLUTION: The data are summarized on the diagram shown on page 273. The values shown in parentheses are derived from the T, 1985 membership and the values of $_am$, $_ad$, $_bm$ and $_bd$ by relationships (11.6) and (11.7). Note that only one group (FYB=1935) contributes to (Actuarial Exposure)$_{50}$, two groups (FYB = 1934 and FYB = 1935) contribute to (Actuarial Exposure)$_{51}$, and all three FYB groups contribute to (Actuarial Exposure)$_{52}$. (a) Using formula (11.4), we have (Actuarial Exposure)$_{50} = \tfrac{1}{2}(120+125+3) = 124$; similarly, (Actuarial Exposure)$_{51} = \tfrac{1}{2}(110+112+2) + \tfrac{1}{2}(125+130+1) = 240$; (Actuarial Exposure)$_{52} = \tfrac{1}{2}(115+122+1) + \tfrac{1}{2}(112+123+1) + \tfrac{1}{2}(130+140+2) = 373$. Then $\hat{q}_{50} = 3/124$; $\hat{q}_{51} = 3/240$; $\hat{q}_{52} = 4/373$. (b) Using formula (11.9), we have (Actuarial Exposure)$_{50} = 122 + 2 = 124$; similarly we have (Actuarial Exposure)$_{51} = (118+0) + (127+0) = 245$; using all three FYB groups, (Actuarial Exposure)$_{52} = (118+1) + (119+1) + (137+1) = 377$. Then $\hat{q}_{50} = 3/124$; $\hat{q}_{51} = 3/245$; $\hat{q}_{52} = 4/377$.

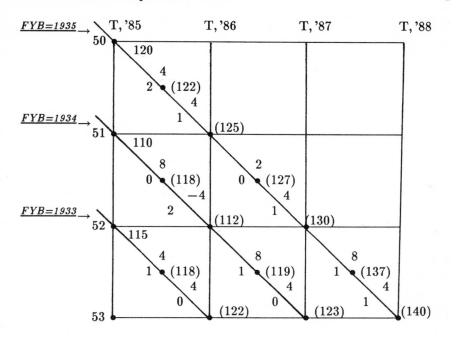

11.2.2 *Valuation Schedule Approach Using Insuring Ages*

Insuring ages are used when the study sample is a collection of individual insured lives, rather than the members of a pension plan or group insurance policy. In this case the valuation schedules are prepared as of December 31 for the purpose of valuing the actuarial liabilities which exist under these individual policies.

Since December 31 is *not* the insuring birthday for all persons, it follows that persons will be various attained insuring ages on that date. We let I_x^z represent the number of persons with policies in force on $12/31/z$ who are insuring age x last birthday on that date. Since these persons all turned insuring age x in calendar year z, it follows that they all have $VYB = z - x$. The flow of persons using insuring ages is represented on Figure 11.5, shown on page 274.

Whereas diagrams using fiscal ages show the flow of one FYB group down a single diagonal line, diagrams using insuring ages show the flow of one VYB group down a unit parallelogram. This results from the presence of a common birthday using fiscal ages, a feature that does not exist for insuring ages. We will normally assume that the average age of those included in I_x^z is $x+\frac{1}{2}$, and will locate I_x^z at that age in our insuring age diagrams, as shown in Figure 11.5 on the following page.

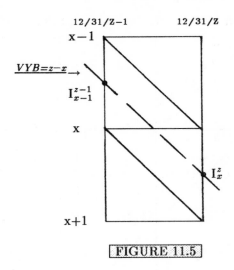

$$\boxed{\text{FIGURE 11.5}}$$

As explained in Chapter 10, insuring age studies normally use observation periods which run from policy anniversaries in calendar year z to those in a later calendar year. We will illustrate the valuation schedule approach to calculating actuarial exposure for a one-year anniversary-to-anniversary insuring age study.

Let the observation period run from policy anniversaries in calendar year z to those in calendar year z+1. This situation is illustrated by Figure 11.6.

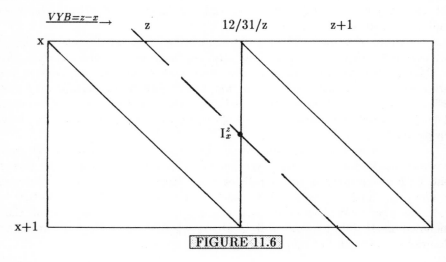

$$\boxed{\text{FIGURE 11.6}}$$

We assume that the I_x^z policyholders in force on $12/31/z$ have an average age of $x+\frac{1}{2}$. (Note that this is equivalent to assuming policy issues, and hence integral insuring ages, occur on July 1, on the average.)

We denote the time interval from the insuring birthday (i.e., policy anniversary) to December 31 as the α-period, and the interval from December 31 to the next insuring birthday as the δ-period. Note the similarity of these concepts to those in Chapter 9 for general population data. Let $_\alpha w_x^z$ and $_\delta w_x^z$ denote the withdrawals in the α-period and δ-period, respectively, of calendar year z, at insuring age x last birthday. Let $_\alpha d_x^z$ and $_\delta d_x^z$ be similarly defined for the deaths. Let i_x^z denote the new policies issued in calendar year z at issue age x. Necessarily the i_x^z persons joining the VYB $= z-x$ group do so at exact age x.

Since migration *into* the VYB $= z-x$ group, in the form of the i_x^z new issues, necessarily occurs at integral ages, we must likewise use integral ages for our grouping assumption for the withdrawals, in order that net migration can be considered together. This is illustrated in Figure 11.7.

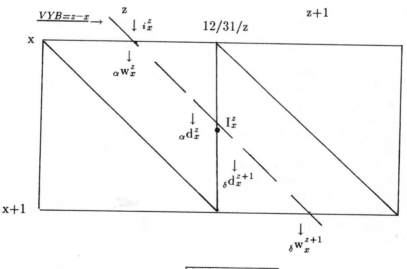

FIGURE 11.7

To derive the valuation schedule formula for actuarial exposure under the described assumptions, we first define A_x^z to be the number of persons, with VYB $= z-x$, who survive to their policy anniversaries in calendar year z. (Note the analogy of A_x^z to E_x^z defined in Section 9.2.1) Then it follows that

$$A_x^z + i_x^z - _\alpha w_x^z - _\alpha d_x^z = I_x^z. \tag{11.12}$$

By the principles defined in Chapter 6 for the calculation of actuarial exposure, we have directly

$$(\text{Actuarial Exposure})_x \ = \ A_x^z + i_x^z - {}_\alpha w_x^z, \qquad (11.13)$$

which becomes

$$(\text{Actuarial Exposure})_x \ = \ I_x^z + {}_\alpha d_x^z, \qquad (11.14)$$

when equation (11.12) is substituted into formula (11.13). Note the similarity of formulas (11.14) and (11.9). Again the obvious understatement of average age at withdrawal for the ${}_\alpha w_x^z$ group is assumed to be offset by the overstatement of average withdrawal age for the ${}_\delta w_x^{z+1}$ group.

$\boxed{\text{EXAMPLE 11.4}}$: An insuring age study from anniversaries in calendar year z to those in calendar year z+1 shows 12 deaths at insuring age x last birthday, equally divided between the α and δ periods. If $A_{x+1}^{z+1} = 967$ and ${}_\delta w_x^{z+1} = 15$, estimate q_x.

$\boxed{\text{SOLUTION}}$: $I_x^z = A_{x+1}^{z+1} + {}_\delta w_x^{z+1} + {}_\delta d_x^{z+1} = 967 + 15 + 6 = 988$. Then we have $(\text{Actuarial Exposure})_x = I_x^z + {}_\alpha d_x^z = 988 + 6 = 994$, and $\hat{q}_x = 12/994$.

The reader should recognize that the grouping assumption for the withdrawals, along with the automatic location of i_x^z at the integral age and the anniversary-to-anniversary observation period, together result in a Special Case A estimation situation. This grouping assumption for withdrawals was called "grouping by calendar insuring age" in connection with the individual record approach in Section 10.3.2. Thus an individual record formula for actuarial exposure, using a calendar insuring age grouping assumption for withdrawals, in an anniversary-to-anniversary insuring age study, is the counterpart formula to valuation schedule formula (11.14).

We also recognize the similarity between formula (11.14), using insuring ages, and formula (11.9), using fiscal ages. This similarity results from the similar grouping assumptions for the migration in both cases.

It is possible to derive an insuring age formula that is analogous to fiscal age formula (11.4) simply by locating *all* migration in Figure 11.7 at the midpoint of the diagonal, which is approximately age $x+\frac{1}{2}$. But this would contradict our understanding that all new issues occur at integral ages, so such a formula is not very logical. In addition, this formula would require values of A_x^z and A_{x+1}^{z+1}, which are not readily available.

Although an anniversary-to-anniversary observation period is more convenient for an insuring age study, a date-to-date observation period can be used. Consider a one-year observation period from $12/31/z-1$ to $12/31/z$. Assuming that policy anniversaries occur on July 1, on the average, we have the situation illustrated in Figure 11.8.

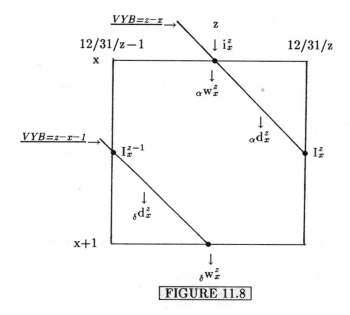

FIGURE 11.8

Note that two different VYB groups contribute to $(x, x+1]$ during this one-year observation period. Note also that A_x^z and i_x^z persons come under observation at exact age x, whereas I_x^{z-1} persons come under observation at age $x+\frac{1}{2}$ and I_x^z persons exit there. Under our standard calendar age grouping assumption for withdrawals, $_\alpha w_x^z$ exit at age x and $_\delta w_x^z$ exit at age $x+1$. When represented on a one-dimensional (age) diagram, Figure 11.8 becomes Figure 11.9.

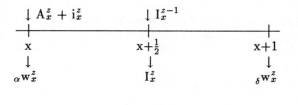

FIGURE 11.9

By the principles defined in Chapter 6, the actuarial exposure over $(x, x+1]$ is given by

$$\text{(Actuarial Exposure)}_x = A_x^z + i_x^z - {}_\alpha w_x^z - \tfrac{1}{2} \cdot I_x^z + \tfrac{1}{2} \cdot I_x^{z-1}. \tag{11.15}$$

But we notice that

$$A_x^z + i_x^z - {}_\alpha w_x^z = I_x^z + {}_\alpha d_x^z; \tag{11.16}$$

when this substitution is made in formula (11.15), and simplified, we obtain

$$\text{(Actuarial Exposure)}_x = \tfrac{1}{2}(I_x^{z-1} + I_x^z) + {}_\alpha d_x^z. \tag{11.17}$$

Again the general from "mean population plus half the deaths" is apparent. If ${}_\alpha d_x^z$ is not precisely known, and is approximated by $\tfrac{1}{2} \cdot d_x^z$, then we have the convenient approximate formula

$$\text{(Actuarial Exposure)}_x \approx \tfrac{1}{2}(I_x^{z-1} + I_x^z) + \tfrac{1}{2} \cdot d_x^z . \tag{11.18}$$

The similarity between formulas (11.18) and (9.18) should be noted.

 EXAMPLE 11.5 : Estimate q_{50} and q_{51}, given the following values: $P_{50}^{1985} = 1000$; $P_{50}^{1986} = 1010$; $d_{50}^{1985} = 2$; $P_{51}^{1985} = 990$; $P_{51}^{1986} = 1030$; $d_{51}^{1985} = 4$.

 SOLUTION : Since values of ${}_\alpha d_x^z$ are not given, we approximate them by $\tfrac{1}{2} \cdot d_x^z$. Using formula (11.18), we have $\hat{q}_{50} = \dfrac{2}{\tfrac{1}{2}(1000 + 1010) + 1} = \dfrac{2}{1006}$, and $\hat{q}_{51} = \dfrac{4}{\tfrac{1}{2}(990 + 1030) + 2} = \dfrac{4}{1012}$.

If an observation period covers more than one year, the total actuarial exposure over $(x, x+1]$ is found by summing the one-year exposure formula (formula (11.14) for anniversary-to-anniversary studies or formula (11.17) for calendar year studies) over all years in the observation period. For example, a study from anniversaries in z to those in z+6, using insuring ages with calendar age grouping for withdrawals, would have total actuarial exposure given by

$$\text{(Actuarial Exposure)}_x = \sum_{u=z}^{z+5} \left(I_x^u + {}_\alpha d_x^u \right). \tag{11.19}$$

The actuarial estimate of q_x would then be given by

$$\hat{q}_x = \frac{\sum\limits_{u=z}^{z+5}\left(\alpha d_x^u + {}_\delta d_x^{u+1}\right)}{\sum\limits_{u=z}^{z+5}\left(I_x^u + {}_\alpha d_x^u\right)}. \qquad (11.20)$$

EXAMPLE 11.6 : The following table gives the number of persons living on December 31 of the several years shown, classified by Valuation Year of Birth:

VYB	1985	1986	1987	1988	1989
1935	4800	4600	4500	4400	4000
1936	5100	4900	4800	4800	4700
1937	5400	5200	5000	4700	4600
1938	6000	5900	5800	5500	5300
1939	6600	5600	5600	5400	5000

The number of deaths in each calendar year, classified by age last birthday at death and by α and δ type, are given in the following table:

Year z	$_\alpha d_{48}$	$_\delta d_{48}$	$_\alpha d_{49}$	$_\delta d_{49}$	$_\alpha d_{50}$	$_\delta d_{50}$
1986	16	14	12	15	14	11
1987	15	12	17	13	13	12
1988	11	10	19	18	16	20
1989	14	13	16	17	19	18

Using a calendar insuring age grouping for withdrawals in all cases, estimate q_{48}, q_{49} and q_{50}, separately under each of the two following observation periods:

(a) Anniversaries in 1986 to anniversaries in 1989.
(b) January 1, 1986 to December 31, 1989.

SOLUTION : The data are summarized in the diagram shown on page 280.
(a)   For the anniversary-to-anniversary study, the observed deaths are $d_{48} = 16 + 12 + 15 + 10 = 53$, where two VYB groups contribute to (48, 49)]; $d_{49} = 12 + 13 + 17 + 18 + 19 + 17 = 96$, where three VYB groups contribute to (49, 50]; $d_{50} = 14 + 12 + 13 + 20 + 16 + 18 = 93$, with three VYB groups contributing to (50, 51].   Using formula (11.14) for actuarial exposure, we have (Actuarial Exposure)$_{48}$ = $(5900 + 16)$ + $(5600 + 15)$ = 11,531; (Actuarial Exposure)$_{49}$ = $(5200+12) + (5800+17) + (5400+19)$ = 16,448; (Actuarial Exposure)$_{50}$ = $(4900+14) + (5000+13) + (5500+16)$ = 15,443. Thus we have $\hat{q}_{48} = 53/11{,}531$; $\hat{q}_{49} = 96/16{,}448$; $\hat{q}_{50} = 93/15{,}443$.

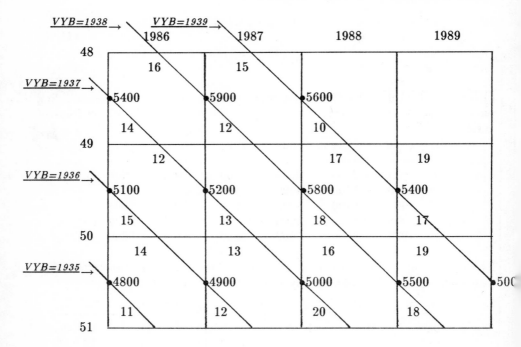

(b)   For the date-to-date study, the observed deaths are easily found to be $d_{48} = 16 + 14 + 15 + 12 = 57$; $d_{49} = 12 + 15 + 17 + 13 + 19 + 18 = 94$; and $d_{50} = 14 + 11 + 13 + 12 + 16 + 20 + 19 + 18 = 123$.   Note the extra year of experience that gets used in the date-to-date study, as compared to the anniversary-to-anniversary study, in the interval (50, 51]. Using formula (11.17) for the actuarial exposure, we have the following values:

(Actuarial Exposure)$_{48} = \frac{1}{2}(5400+5900) + 16 + \frac{1}{2}(5900+5600) + 15 = 11,431$;

(Actuarial Exposure)$_{49} = \frac{1}{2}(5100) + 5200 + 5800 + \frac{1}{2}(5400)$
$$+ 12 + 17 + 19 = 16,298;$$

(Actuarial Exposure)$_{50} = \frac{1}{2}(4800) + 4900 + 5000 + 5500 + \frac{1}{2}(5000)$
$$+ 14 + 13 + 16 + 19 = 20,362.$$

Thus we have $\hat{q}_{48} = 57/11,431$; $\hat{q}_{49} = 94/16,298$; $\hat{q}_{50} = 123/20,362$.

11.2.3 *Summary of Valuation Schedule Approach*

In this section we have only been concerned with the calculation of actuarial exposure, using an approach that is common in actuarial studies to estimate q_x from insurance company or pension fund data. Under insuring ages (individual insurance policies) we considered both anniversary-to-anniversary and date-to-date observation periods. Under fiscal ages (group insurance policies or pension plans) these two types of observation periods are the same.

Under fiscal ages we considered both calendar age and age last birthday grouping assumptions for migration; under insuring ages we considered only calendar age grouping for withdrawals, since new issues were necessarily located at integral ages.

The reference numbers of the four main valuation schedule formulas for actuarial exposure derived in this section are summarized in Table 11.1.

TABLE 11.1

	Fiscal Ages T-to-T O.P.	Insuring Ages A-to-A O.P.	D-to-D O.P.
Age Last Birthday Grouping	(11.4)	---	---
Calendar Age Grouping	(11.9)	(11.14)	(11.17)

Remember that the formulas referenced in Table 11.1 are for unit (i.e., one-year) observation periods. For multiple-year observation periods, the total actuarial exposure is easily found by summation of the unit formula over all years, as illustrated in Examples 11.3 and 11.6.

Finally, the reader should note that three different symbols have been defined for the similar concept of number of persons in a group as of a certain date. These are summarized in Table 11.2.

TABLE 11.2

Symbol	Section	Meaning
P_x^z	9.2.1	Number of persons at *actual age x last birthday* on January 1, z.
I_x^z	11.2.2	Number of persons at *insuring age x last birthday* on December 31, z.
F_x^z	11.2.1	Number of persons at *exact fiscal age x* on T, z.

11.3   *PRACTICAL ISSUES IN ACTUARIAL SURVIVAL MODEL ESTIMATION*

Chapters 5 through 9 were devoted to the statistical estimation theory involved in the estimation of q_x over $(x, x+1]$, or the estimation of $S(x)$ in parametric form, with consideration given to several different estimation environments. Chapter 10 and Section 11.2 dealt with the data processing steps required to execute this estimation theory in large-sample studies, mainly actuarial studies using insurance company or pension fund data.

The earlier discussion assumed that certain decisions regarding the study had already been made, so that we could concentrate on the applicable mathematics. These decisions included length and location of the observation period, which policies to include (or exclude) from the study, which policy years to include, what to use for the exposure unit (lives, policies or amounts of insurance), and so on. In this section we will very briefly address these practical issues.

It should be stated at the beginning that there are no "right" ways to resolve these issues, and considerable difference of opinion has been expressed in the literature. In addition, this text is intended to deal mainly with the mathematics of survival model estimation, and does not purport to be an authoritative work on these practical issues. Therefore we will concentrate more on making the reader aware of the issues to be considered, and less on advocating specific resolutions of those issues.

By way of illustration, however, we can consider how these issues were addressed in various recent studies that have been conducted. In particular, the development of the 1980 CSO Tables might be taken as representative. This methodology is reported by Ormsby, et al. [49].

11.3.1 *Observation Period*

An initial decision of a practical nature regards the selection of the observation period for the study. Since the values of q_x derived from the study will be used as estimates of prevailing survival probabilities, it is important that the chosen period be free of any unusual mortality influences, such as wars or epidemics. The period chosen for the 1980 CSO Tables ran from policy anniversaries in 1970 to those in 1975, in part because it was free of any unusual mortality events. Any deaths in the experience from the war in Vietnam were simply excluded from the study.

If an estimated survival model is viewed as representative of current prevailing mortality, then it should have been derived from *recent* experience, subject to the concern expressed in the previous paragraph.

Regarding the appropriate length of an observation period, it is clear that the period must be long enough to provide a sufficient volume of data. The 1980 CSO Tables are based on five policy years, which is one year longer than the four years used for a previous major study (1958 CSO). This decision was made specifically to include more data, especially for the female table.

11.3.2 *Separation of Policies*

Provided that a sufficient volume of experience exists, the lives involved in a study should be separated into several different categories from which separate survival models are estimated. The basis for separating the data is with respect to the various concomitant variables that may be present, as described in Section 1.2.

An obvious division of data is with respect to sex, so that separate models are estimated for males and females. In earlier studies, including the preparation of the 1958 CSO Table, the volume of female data was not sufficiently large to support the estimation of a separate female table. Instead, a special female table was derived from the male table by an age-setback approach. This is not an ideal method of estimating a female survival model. Fortunately, the increased volume of insurance written on female lives by the 1970's allowed for a female model to be estimated directly from female data.

A second variable which is considered in the subdivision of data is with respect to policies which were, or were not, issued subject to a medical examination. The 1958 CSO Table was estimated from data which included medical issues only, except that a small amount of nonmedical experience was included beyond the fifteenth policy year. The 1980 CSO Tables, however, did not make this separation; that is, both medical and nonmedical data were included at all durations. It was considered appropriate to include nonmedical data in the new tables because of the industry trend, since the development of the 1958 CSO Table, toward the writing of nonmedical business for higher amounts and at higher ages. The nonmedical experience was also needed to provide sufficient data for the female table.

A third issue of some importance is the separation of policies that are fully paid up from those still in a premium-paying status. This is particularly significant if the paid-up policy is a result of the exercise of the nonforfeiture provision of the policy. It has been shown that the survival experience of premium-paying policies is notably different from that of policies in force under nonforfeiture options, especially the extended term option, so these policies are frequently eliminated from the study. Separate male and female tables for extended term insurance, called the KET Tables, accompany the regular 1980 CSO Tables.

Finally, a decision must be made as to the policy years of experience included in the basic data. In the case of a model based on data gathered from several insurance companies, the estimated q_x can be affected by differences in intercompany underwriting rules, nonmedical limits, and suicide and incontestable provisions. Accordingly, the first five policy years of experience were eliminated from the data used to estimate the 1980 CSO Tables.

11.3.3 *Exposure Unit*

The estimation theory presented in this text, and the statistical analysis of the resulting estimators, assumed that the entities exposed to the risk of death over (x, x+1] were individual persons. The significance of this is that an assumption of independence among exposure entities is then very reasonable. In turn, the independence assumption is required in order to reach many of the conclusions that were found in the analysis of the estimators.

In the case of individual insurance policies, however, actuarial studies might not be based on individual lives. This arises because a policyholder might have several individual insurance policies, issued at various times, and the identification of multiple policies on one life might not be easy to achieve. Clearly multiple policies create a situation of nonindependent exposure units if the study is based on policies.

Another case of nonindependent exposure units arises if the study is based on amounts of insurance, as was the case for the 1980 CSO Tables. In order to analyze the effect of mortality on a company's financial results, many actuaries feel that amounts is the most meaningful basis for the study. On the other hand, several deaths involving exceptionally large amounts of coverage can produce a misleading estimate of q_x. In addition, a practical matter arises in the case of non-level amount policies, for which careful documentation would be required to assure that the correct exposure is calculated each estimation year.

The analysis of estimators for q_x, when the study is based on policies or amounts of insurance, is pursued by Klugman [38]. An earlier work addressing this issue is that of Cody [17].

11.4 *OTHER TYPES OF ACTUARIAL STUDIES*

Actuarial studies in an insurance company setting are frequently not directed toward the development of new estimated survival models. In many cases a study of the mortality experience under special classes of policies is undertaken to discover how those mortality levels compare with standard mortality levels. In these cases, a complete life table is not constructed; rather the results are expressed as ratios of the actual number of deaths to the number that would be expected according to an adopted standard table.

The tables frequently used as the standards, against which special mortality experiences are compared, are referred to as Basic Tables. These complete life tables are estimated from large amounts of intercompany data every ten years by the Society of Actuaries. The most recent are the 1975-80 Basic Tables, which used an observation period of policy anniversaries in 1975 to those in 1980. The development of these tables is reported by Ferguson, et al. [23].

There are many examples of special mortality experiences for which studies might be conducted. These include the experience of insurance policies issued under term conversion or guaranteed insurability options, policies issued only to nonsmokers, policies issued on substandard lives, and policies in force under a nonforfeiture option. Various types of annuity contracts constitute an area requiring special mortality studies. Special studies are also conducted to investigate the level of mortality experienced under policies of unusually large amounts, or policies issued to persons with particular impairments. Variations in mortality levels by occupation, or by involvement in aviation or hazardous sports, are also investigated.

In addition to the above examples of special mortality studies, actuaries specializing in health insurance also study the experience under various types of individual or group health coverage. These include medical expense policies, short-term and long-term disability income coverages, and major medical policies.

Results of these special studies, of both mortality and morbidity experiences are reported periodically in the Reports of the Transactions of the Society of Actuaries.

11.5 *SUMMARY*

This final chapter has addressed mortality estimation from a practical, rather than theoretical, point of view. In particular, the approaches of the actuarial practitioner in a life insurance company setting have been summarized. As this text is primarily concerned with the mathematics of survival model estimation, our survey has been appropriately brief. A more thorough treatment of these important topics is left for another text, and another writer, to undertake.

EXERCISES

11.1 Introduction;   11.2 Valuation Schedule Exposure Formulas

11-1   Prepare a schedule showing the number of persons in our group as of
       each June 30, from June 30, 1982 to June 30, 1990, inclusive, at exact
       fiscal age.   (I.e., a schedule of F_x^z, for $z = 1982, \cdots , 1990$.)   Also
       prepare a schedule of values of $_ad_x^z$ and $_bd_x^z$ for all relevant x and z.

11-2   Use the schedules from Exercise 11-1 to calculate the actuarial exposure
       for a fiscal age study from June 30, 1982 to June 30, 1990, separately
       for each of the following grouping assumptions for net migration:
       (a) Fiscal age last birthday.
       (b) Calendar fiscal age.
       Compare the results to those of Exercise 10-10.

11-3. Prepare a schedule showing the number of persons in our group as of
       each December 31, from December 31, 1979 to December 31, 1989,
       inclusive, at insuring age last birthday.   (I.e., a schedule of values of
       I_x^z, for $z = 1979, 1980, \cdots, 1989$.)   Also prepare a schedule of values of
       $_ad_x^z$ and $_\delta d_x^z$ for all relevant x and z.

11-4. Use the schedules from Exercise 11-3 to calculate the actuarial
       exposure for an insuring age study from anniversaries in 1980 to those
       in 1989, using calendar insuring age grouping for withdrawals.
       Compare the results to those of Exercise 10-6.

PROPERTIES OF ESTIMATORS

In this appendix we give formal definitions of the various properties of estimators which we have cited throughout the text. The extent to which specific estimators do or do not satisfy these properties has been noted in the text when such specific estimators were defined, and reference has been made to other sources for further information regarding the properties of specific estimators. In particular, Broffitt [12] gives a good analysis of the properties of the actuarial estimator, the product limit estimator, and the full data MLE under the exponential assumption.

It should always be kept in mind that estimators are random variables. In this appendix we use $\hat{\theta}$ to denote the estimator random variable for the quantity θ which we wish to estimate. Note that θ could be a parameter of a parametric survival model (e.g., λ of an exponential model), or it could represent a q_x value of a tabular survival model.

A.1 BIAS

Since $\hat{\theta}$, the estimator of θ, is a random variable, some useful information is supplied by its expected value $E[\hat{\theta}]$. Of particular interest is the question of how $E[\hat{\theta}]$ compares of θ. If

$$E[\hat{\theta}] \;=\; \theta, \tag{A.1}$$

then $\hat{\theta}$ is said to be an *unbiased* estimator of θ. Alternatively, if

$$E[\hat{\theta}] \;>\; \theta, \tag{A.2}$$

then $\hat{\theta}$ is said to be *positively biased*, and if

$$E[\hat{\theta}] \;<\; \theta, \tag{A.3}$$

then $\hat{\theta}$ is said to be *negatively biased*. In general, the bias of $\hat{\theta}$ is given by

$$\text{Bias}(\hat{\theta}) \;=\; E[\hat{\theta}] - \theta. \tag{A.4}$$

287

In some cases $E[\hat{\theta}]$ is a function of the sample size, n, from which the estimate of θ was produced. In these cases we do not strictly have $E[\hat{\theta}] = \theta$, so $\hat{\theta}$ is not strictly unbiased. However, if it is true that

$$\lim_{n \to \infty} E[\hat{\theta}] = \theta, \tag{A.5}$$

then we say that $\hat{\theta}$ is *asymptotically unbiased.*

A.2   MEAN SQUARE ERROR AND VARIANCE

Another characteristic of an estimator that gives some information about its quality is the extent to which the outcome of an estimator differs from the true value θ which it seeks to estimate. Remember that the estimator, $\hat{\theta}$, is a random variable, whereas the true value of θ is fixed, albeit unknown. We define the expected squared difference between $\hat{\theta}$ and θ to be the *mean square error* of the estimator $\hat{\theta}$. That is,

$$\text{MSE}(\hat{\theta}) = E\left[(\hat{\theta} - \theta)^2\right], \tag{A.6}$$

where the expectation is taken with respect to the random variable $\hat{\theta}$. We see that $\text{MSE}(\hat{\theta})$ gives an average, or expected, squared departure of $\hat{\theta}$ from θ, *a priori* to a consideration of actual data.

Similar *a priori* measure of departure of $\hat{\theta}$ from θ is given by the *variance*, defined as

$$\text{Var}(\hat{\theta}) = E\left[(\hat{\theta} - E[\hat{\theta}])^2\right]. \tag{A.7}$$

There is a convenient relationship between the mean square error and the variance of $\hat{\theta}$. Beginning with (A.6), we subtract and add $E[\hat{\theta}]$ inside the parentheses to obtain

$$\begin{aligned}
\text{MSE}(\hat{\theta}) &= E\left[(\hat{\theta} - E[\hat{\theta}] + E[\hat{\theta}] - \theta)^2\right] \\
&= E\left[(\hat{\theta} - E[\hat{\theta}])^2 + 2(E[\hat{\theta}] - \theta)(\hat{\theta} - E[\hat{\theta}]) + (E[\hat{\theta}] - \theta)^2\right] \\
&= E\left[(\hat{\theta} - E[\hat{\theta}])^2\right] + 2(E[\hat{\theta}] - \theta) \cdot E\left[\hat{\theta} - E[\hat{\theta}]\right] + E\left[(E[\hat{\theta}] - \theta)^2\right],
\end{aligned}$$

since $2(E[\hat{\theta}] - \theta)$ is a constant. In the middle term,

$$E\left[\hat{\theta} - E[\hat{\theta}]\right] = E[\hat{\theta}] - E\left[E[\hat{\theta}]\right] = 0,$$

since $E\big[E[\hat{\theta}]\big] = E[\hat{\theta}]$. Thus we have

$$\begin{aligned}
\text{MSE}(\hat{\theta}) &= E\big[(\hat{\theta} - E[\hat{\theta}])^2\big] + E\big[(E[\hat{\theta}] - \theta)^2\big] \\
&= E\big[(\hat{\theta} - E[\hat{\theta}])^2\big] + \big(E[\hat{\theta}] - \theta\big)^2,
\end{aligned} \qquad (A.8)$$

since $E[\hat{\theta}] - \theta$ is a constant. Finally, by using (A.7) and (A.4), we see that (A.8) becomes

$$\text{MSE}(\hat{\theta}) = \text{Var}(\hat{\theta}) + \big[\text{Bias}(\hat{\theta})\big]^2. \qquad (A.9)$$

A.3 CONSISTENCY

Instead of looking at the expected difference between an estimator and the quantity which it estimates, let us consider the probability that such difference (in absolute value) is less than a given number ϵ. That is, we wish to consider $\Pr\{|\hat{\theta} - \theta| < \epsilon\}$.

Now let $\hat{\theta}_n$ represent the estimator of θ when the sample from which it is derived is of size n. As n increases, it would be desirable for $\hat{\theta}_n$ to become closer to θ. To investigate this, we will consider the probability that $\hat{\theta}_n$ is close to θ, which is the same as the probability that $|\hat{\theta}_n - \theta| < \epsilon$. If this probability approaches one as n approaches infinity, we say that $\hat{\theta}_n$ is a *consistent* estimator of θ. Formally, $\hat{\theta}_n$ is a consistent estimator of θ if

$$\lim_{n \to \infty} \Pr\big\{|\hat{\theta}_n - \theta| < \epsilon\big\} = 1 \qquad (A.10)$$

for any ϵ.

A.4 EFFICIENCY

An *efficient* estimator is one which has a variance as small as, or smaller than, the variance of any other estimator in the class with which it is being compared. The class could be all consistent estimators, all asymptotically unbiased estimators, etc. In other words, an efficient estimator is one that is of minimum variance within the class.

A.5 DISTRIBUTION

In some cases the actual distribution of the estimator random variable $\hat{\theta}$ can be determined. A simple example of this is the binomial proportion estimator.   This discrete random variable takes on the values $\frac{0}{n}$, $\frac{1}{n}$, $\cdots$, $\frac{n}{n}$, with probabilities given by a binomial distribution with parameters n and θ.

Generally the precise distribution of $\hat{\theta}$ for finite n is extremely complex.   In many cases, however, this distribution approaches a normal distribution as $n \to \infty$.   If this is so, we say that $\hat{\theta}$ is asymptotically normally distributed, or that $\hat{\theta}$ possesses the property of *asymptotic normality*.   Broffitt [12] shows that the actuarial estimator, the product limit estimator, and the full data, exponential distribution MLE are all asymptotically normal.

In discussing asymptotic distributions, it is customary to consider the random variable

$$Z_n = \sqrt{n}(\hat{\theta} - \theta). \tag{A.11}$$

If $\hat{\theta}$ is asymptotically unbiased, its asymptotic mean is θ, so the asymptotic mean of Z_n is 0.   Then if Z_n is asymptotically normal, its asymptotic distribution is defined by its asymptotic variance.

Derivation of asymptotic variance can be quite complex, and we will consider it only for maximum likelihood estimators.   This is pursued in Appendix B

ASYMPTOTIC PROPERTIES OF
MAXIMUM LIKELIHOOD ESTIMATORS

In this appendix we discuss the general conditions under which maximum likelihood estimators will possess the asymptotic properties of consistency, unbiasedness and normality. We will state these conditions and results without proof. The interested reader is referred to Rao [51] or to Rohatgi [53] for further details. The development below follows that given on pages 384-385 of Rohatgi.

We assume an exact age at death model so that the likelihood for one observation is the PDF, $f(x;\theta)$. We use this notation to remind us that the PDF is a function of both θ, the parameter whose MLE we seek, and x.

B.1 CONDITIONS

Consider the following five conditions to be satisfied by $f(x;\theta)$:

(i) $\ln f(x;\theta)$ is thrice differentiable with respect to θ. That is, the derivatives $\frac{\partial}{\partial\theta} \ln f(x;\theta)$, $\frac{\partial^2}{\partial\theta^2} \ln f(x;\theta)$ and $\frac{\partial^3}{\partial\theta^3} \ln f(x;\theta)$ all exist.

(ii) $\int_{-\infty}^{\infty} \frac{\partial}{\partial\theta} f(x;\theta) \, dx = 0$. (This is the same as $E[\frac{\partial}{\partial\theta} \ln f(x;\theta)] = 0$.)

(iii) $\int_{-\infty}^{\infty} \frac{\partial^2}{\partial\theta^2} f(x;\theta) \, dx = 0$.

(iv) $-\infty < \int_{-\infty}^{\infty} \frac{\partial^2}{\partial\theta^2} \ln f(x;\theta) \cdot f(x;\theta) \, dx < 0$.

(Note that the integral represents $E\left[\frac{\partial^2}{\partial\theta^2} \ln f(x;\theta)\right]$. The purpose of the condition is to establish that this expectation exists.)

(v)   There exists a function $H(x)$ such that $\left|\frac{\partial^3}{\partial\theta^3} \ln f(x;\theta)\right| < H(x)$, where $E[H(x)] < \infty$.

Let Θ be an open interval, on the real number axis, which contains the true value of θ. Conditions (i), (ii), (iii) and (v) need hold only for all θ in Θ, whereas Condition (iv) is to hold for all θ.

291

B.2 RESULTS

If $f(x;\theta)$ satisfies the five conditions, then we have the following results for a a sample of size n:

(a)   The likelihood equation has (with probability one) at least one solution (i.e., $\hat{\theta}$ exists).

(b)   There exists a sequence of solutions, $\{\hat{\theta}_n\}$, with $\hat{\theta}_n$ denoting the member of the sequence for sample size n, that is a consistent estimator of θ. That is, $\Pr\{|\hat{\theta}_n - \theta| < \epsilon\}$ approaches one as n approaches infinity.

(c)   As $n \to \infty$, the distribution of $\hat{\theta}_n$ approaches a normal distribution (i.e., $\hat{\theta}_n$ is asymptotically normal), with

      (i) $E[\hat{\theta}_n] = \theta$ (i.e., $\hat{\theta}_n$ is asymptotically unbiased), and

      (ii) $Var(\hat{\theta}_n) = \dfrac{1}{n \cdot E\left[\left\{\frac{\partial}{\partial\theta}\ln f(x;\theta)\right\}^2\right]}.$

    Note that an equivalent way to express (c) is to say that $Z_n = \sqrt{n}(\hat{\theta}_n - \theta)$ is asymptotically normal with mean 0 and variance $\left[E[\{\frac{\partial}{\partial\theta}\ln f(x;\theta)\}^2]\right]^{-1}$.

    It should be kept in mind that the $\hat{\theta}_n$ referred to above is a solution of the likelihood equation, but not *necessarily* an MLE of θ, although in most cases it will also be an MLE.

B.3 DERIVATION OF FORMULA (7.72)

We now need to show that the expression for $Var(\hat{\theta}_n)$ given by (c), (ii) is the same as that given by formula (7.72) on page 162. That is, we wish to show that

$$E\left[-\frac{\partial^2}{\partial\theta^2}\ln L(x;\theta)\right] = n \cdot E\left[\left\{\frac{\partial}{\partial\theta}\ln f(x;\theta)\right\}^2\right]. \tag{B.1}$$

    We note first that the likelihood is $L(x;\theta) = \prod\limits_{i=1}^{n} f(x_i;\theta)$, so that $\ln L(x;\theta) = \sum\limits_{i=1}^{n} \ln f(x_i;\theta)$. Since both E and $\frac{\partial}{\partial\theta^2}$ are distributive operators, we have

$$E\left[-\frac{\partial^2}{\partial\theta^2}\ln L(x;\theta)\right] = \sum_{i=1}^{n} E\left[-\frac{\partial^2}{\partial\theta^2}\ln f(x_i;\theta)\right]. \tag{B.2}$$

$f(x_i;\theta)$ is the same PDF for all i, so $E[-\frac{\partial^2}{\partial\theta^2}\ln f(x_i;\theta)]$ is the same for all i. Thus the left side of (B.1) is $n \cdot E[-\frac{\partial^2}{\partial\theta^2}\ln f(x;\theta)]$, so it remains for us to show that

$$E\left[-\frac{\partial^2}{\partial\theta^2}\ln f(x;\theta)\right] = E\left[\left\{\frac{\partial}{\partial\theta}\ln f(x;\theta)\right\}^2\right]. \tag{B.3}$$

Beginning with the left side of (B.3), we see that

$$\frac{\partial^2}{\partial\theta^2}\ln f(x;\theta) = \frac{\partial}{\partial\theta}\left[\frac{\partial}{\partial\theta}\ln f(x;\theta)\right]$$

$$= \frac{\partial}{\partial\theta}\left[\frac{f'(x;\theta)}{f(x;\theta)}\right]$$

$$= \frac{f(x;\theta) \cdot f''(x;\theta) - \left[f'(x;\theta)\right]^2}{\left[f(x;\theta)\right]^2}, \tag{B.4}$$

where $f'(x;\theta) = \frac{\partial}{\partial\theta}f(x;\theta)$ and $f''(x;\theta) = \frac{\partial^2}{\partial\theta^2}f(x;\theta)$. Then

$$E\left[-\frac{\partial^2}{\partial\theta^2}\ln f(x;\theta)\right] = E\left[\frac{[f'(x;\theta)]^2}{[f(x;\theta)]^2} - \frac{f''(x;\theta)}{f(x;\theta)}\right]$$

$$= E\left[\left\{\frac{\partial}{\partial\theta}\ln f(x;\theta)\right\}^2\right] - E\left[\frac{f''(x;\theta)}{f(x;\theta)}\right]. \tag{B.5}$$

Finally we see that the first expectation in (B.5) *is* the right side of (B.3), and the second expectation is equivalent to $\int_{-\infty}^{\infty}\frac{\partial^2}{\partial\theta^2}f(x;\theta)\,dx$, which is zero if Condition (iii) holds.

In this appendix we show how the conceptual definition of the A^2 statistic, given by (8.47) is evolved into (8.49), the formula from which A^2 would be calculated.

We begin by noting the definition of $S^o(t)$, the observed distribution defined by (4.1). Substituting this expression into (8.47), we have

$$A^2 = \sum_{i=0}^{n-1} \int_{t_i}^{t_{i+1}} \frac{n}{S(t) \cdot F(t)} \left[\frac{n-i}{n} - S(t) \right]^2 f(t) \, dt$$

$$+ \int_{t_n}^{\infty} \frac{n}{S(t) \cdot F(t)} \left[0 - S(t) \right]^2 f(t) \, dt \tag{C.1}$$

$$= \sum_{i=0}^{n-1} \int_{t_i}^{t_{i+1}} \frac{n}{S(t) \cdot F(t)} \left[\left(\frac{n-i}{n}\right)^2 - 2\left(\frac{n-i}{n}\right) \cdot S(t) + \left[S(t)\right]^2 \right] f(t) \, dt$$

$$+ \int_{t_n}^{\infty} \frac{n}{S(t) \cdot F(t)} \left[S(t) \right]^2 f(t) \, dt$$

$$= \int_0^{\infty} \frac{n}{S(t) \cdot F(t)} \left[S(t) \right]^2 f(t) \, dt \tag{C.2}$$

$$+ \sum_{i=0}^{n-1} \int_{t_i}^{t_{i+1}} \frac{n}{S(t) \cdot F(t)} \left[\left(\frac{n-i}{n}\right)^2 - 2\left(\frac{n-i}{n}\right) \cdot S(t) \right] f(t) \, dt,$$

by combining the two terms involving $\left[S(t) \right]^2$ into one integral. Then (C.2) simplifies to

$$A^2 = n \cdot \int_0^{\infty} \frac{S(t) \cdot f(t)}{F(t)} \, dt$$

$$- \sum_{i=0}^{n-1} 2(n-i) \cdot \int_{t_i}^{t_{i+1}} \frac{f(t)}{F(t)} \, dt$$

$$+ \sum_{i=0}^{n-1} \frac{(n-i)^2}{n} \cdot \int_{t_i}^{t_{i+1}} \frac{f(t)}{S(t) \cdot F(t)} \, dt. \tag{C.3}$$

Consider the three integrals in (C.3). Let the indefinite integrals be represented by

$$I_1 = \int \frac{S(t) \cdot f(t)}{F(t)} dt$$

$$I_2 = \int \frac{f(t)}{F(t)} dt$$

$$I_3 = \int \frac{f(t)}{S(t) \cdot F(t)} dt.$$

Integration by parts produces $I_1 = \ln F(t) - F(t)$. Straightforward integration produces $I_2 = \ln F(t)$. Integration by partial fractions is used to produce $I_3 = \ln F(t) - \ln S(t)$. Substitution of these results into (C.3) produces

$$A^2 = n\Big[\ln F(t) - F(T)\Big]\Big|_0^\infty$$

$$- \sum_{i=0}^{n-1} 2(n-i)\Big[\ln F(t)\Big]\Big|_{t_i}^{t_{i+1}}$$

$$+ \sum_{i=0}^{n-1} \frac{(n-i)^2}{n}\Big[\ln F(t) - \ln S(t)\Big]\Big|_{t_i}^{t_{i+1}}. \quad (C.4)$$

Next we simplify the three terms in (C.4). For convenience we call them A, B and C, so that $A^2 = A - B + C$.

A: This easily simplifies to $n\Big[\ln F(\infty) - F(\infty) - \ln F(0) + F(0)\Big]$. Recall that $F(\infty) = 1$, $F(0) = 0$, and $\ln(1) = 0$. Thus we have

$$A = -n - n \cdot \ln F(0). \quad (C.5)$$

We notice that $F(0) = 0$ so we have the term $\ln(0)$, which is awkward to define. For now we will retain the notation $\ln F(0)$.

B: This term simplifies to $2 \cdot \sum_{i=0}^{n-1}(n-i) \cdot \Big[\ln F(t_{i+1}) - \ln F(t_i)\Big]$, which

expands to $2\left[n \cdot \ln F(t_1) - n \cdot \ln F(t_0) + (n-1) \cdot \ln F(t_2)\right.$
$$\left[- (n-1) \cdot \ln F(t_1) + \cdots + \ln F(t_n) - \ln F(t_{n-1})\right],$$

which simplifies to $2\left[\ln F(t_1) + \ln F(t_2) + \cdots + \ln F(t_n) - n \cdot \ln F(t_0)\right].$
Thus we have

$$B = 2 \cdot \sum_{i=1}^{n} \ln F(t_i) - 2n \cdot \ln F(0), \qquad (C.6)$$

since $t_0 = 0$.

C: This term can be written as

$$\frac{1}{n} \cdot \sum_{i=0}^{n-1} (n-i)^2 \cdot \left[\ln F(t_{i+1}) - \ln F(t_i) + \ln S(t_i) - \ln S(t_{i+1})\right].$$

Expanding the summation we have

$$\frac{1}{n} \left\{ n^2 \left[\ln F(t_1) - \ln F(0) + \ln S(0) - \ln S(t_1)\right] \right.$$
$$+ (n-1)^2 \left[\ln F(t_2) - \ln F(t_1) + \ln S(t_1) - \ln S(t_2)\right]$$
$$+ \cdots + 1^2 \left[\ln F(t_n) - \ln F(t_{n-1}) + \ln S(t_{n-1}) - \ln S(t_n)\right]$$
$$\left. + 0^2 \left[\ln S(t_n) - \ln F(t_n)\right] \right\}, \qquad (C.7)$$

where the zero-value last line is added for symmetry. Now each of $\ln F(t_i)$ and $\ln S(t_i)$, $t = 1, \cdots, n$, appears twice in (C.7). Grouping these terms we find that (C.7) becomes

$$\frac{1}{n}\left[\ln F(t_1)\{n^2 - (n-1)^2\} + \ln F(t_2)\{(n-1)^2 - (n-2)^2\}\right.$$
$$\left[+ \cdots + \ln F(t_n)\{1^2 - 0^2\}\right]$$

$$- \frac{1}{n}\left[\ln S(t_1)\{n^2 - (n-1)^2\} + \ln S(t_2)\{(n-1)^2 - (n-2)^2\}\right.$$
$$\left[+ \cdots + \ln S(t_n\{1^2 - 0^2\}\right]$$

$$+ n \cdot \ln S(0) - n \cdot \ln F(0).$$

Since $S(0) = 1$ and $\ln(1) = 0$, this expression can be written as

$$\frac{1}{n} \cdot \sum_{i=1}^{n} \left[(n-i+1)^2 - (n-i)^2 \right] \cdot \ln F(t_i)$$

$$- \frac{1}{n} \cdot \sum_{i=1}^{n} \left[i^2 - (i-1)^2 \right] \cdot \ln S(t_{n-i+1}) - n \cdot \ln F(0). \qquad \text{(C.8)}$$

Next we make the simplifications $\left[(n-i+1)^2 - (n-1)^2 \right] = 2(n-i)+1$ and $\left[i^2 - (i-1)^2 \right] = 2i-1$. Finally we can write term C as

$$C = -n \cdot \ln F(0) + \frac{1}{n} \cdot \sum_{i=1}^{n} (2n-2i+1) \cdot \ln F(t_i)$$

$$- \frac{1}{n} \cdot \sum_{i=1}^{n} (2i-1) \cdot \ln S(t_{n-i+1}). \qquad \text{(C.9)}$$

Combining $A^2 = A - B + C$, we have

$$A^2 = -n - n \cdot \ln F(0) - 2 \cdot \sum_{i=1}^{n} \ln F(t_i) + 2n \cdot \ln F(0) - n \cdot \ln F(0)$$

$$+ \frac{1}{n} \cdot \sum_{i=1}^{n} (2n-2i+1) \cdot \ln F(t_i) - \frac{1}{n} \cdot \sum_{i=1}^{n} (2i-1) \cdot \ln S(t_{n-i+1})$$

$$= -n - \frac{1}{n} \cdot \sum_{i=1}^{n} (2i-1) \cdot \ln F(t_i) - \frac{1}{n} \cdot \sum_{i=1}^{n} (2i-1) \cdot \ln S(t_{n-i+1})$$

$$= -n - \frac{1}{n} \cdot \sum_{i=1}^{n} (2i-1) \left\{ \ln \left[F(t_i) \cdot S(t_{n-i+1}) \right] \right\}, \qquad \text{(C.10)}$$

which becomes (8.49) when $F(t_i)$ and $S(t_{n-i+1})$ are evaluated by $\hat{F}(t_i)$ and $\hat{S}(t_{n-i+1})$, respectively.

ANSWERS TO THE EXERCISES

CHAPTER 2

2-1   (a) .00625   (b) .01   (c) .69315   (d) 66.6̇6   (e) 888.8̇8

2-2   (a) $e^{-(at + bt^2/2)}$ (b) $(a + bt)e^{-(at + bt^2/2)}$ (c) $b^{-1/2} - ab^{-1}$

2-3 $45\sqrt{2}$

2-4   Because $\lim\limits_{t \to \infty} S(t) = e^{-1/r} \neq 0$

2-5 $\frac{1}{3}$

2-7 $-\frac{1}{2} \ln .3$

2-8   (a) constant   (b) decreasing   (c) increasing

2-9   (a) (i) r   (ii) 2r   (iii) $\frac{1}{r-2}$, r > 2   (b) $\frac{1}{2}$

2-11 $\frac{1}{4}$

2-12   4.7504

2-13   15.4822

2-14 $\dfrac{\lambda}{1 - e^{-\lambda(z-x)}}$; truncation from above increases the hazard rate, so it must become a function of remaining *possible* lifetime (which is $z-x$). Note that the truncated HRF increases as x increases, i.e., as $z-x$ decreases.

2-15   (b) They are the same

2-16 $S_Y(y) = \exp\left[-\dfrac{k}{n+1} \cdot e^{y(n+1)}\right]$; $\lambda_Y(y) = k \cdot e^{y(n+1)}$. Let $k = B$ and $(n+1) = \ln c$, so that $c = e^{n+1}$. Then we recognize the Type 1 Least Value distribution defined in Exercise 2-15.

2-18   Y is exponential with parameter $\lambda = \frac{1}{a}$

2-19 $f_Y(y) = \dfrac{1}{\pi(1+y)y^{1/2}}$, $0 \le y \le \infty$

2-20   (a) $\frac{1}{2}\sqrt{\pi}$; $1 - \frac{1}{4}\pi$ (b) $\frac{7}{8}$; $\frac{1}{4}$

2-21   2; 1

2-22   (a) $\sigma^2 \cdot e^{2\mu}$ (b) $\dfrac{3\sigma^4}{2}$

2-23   Exact: $E[Y] = .4$; $\mathrm{Var}(Y) = .04$

       Approximate: $E[Y] = .4$; $\mathrm{Var}(Y) = .037̇7$

CHAPTER 3

3-1   (a) S(x): 1, .9, .72, .432, .1296, 0   (b)

x	ℓ_x	d_x
0	10,000	1000
1	9,000	1800
2	7,200	2880
3	4,320	3024
4	1,296	1296
5	0	---

      (c) $\omega=5$, the first age for
           which S(x) = 0.

3-2   (a) 5680   (b) .52   (c) .144   (d) 1.00

3-3   (a) $S(x) - S(x+1) = \dfrac{\ell_x - \ell_{x+1}}{\ell_0} = \dfrac{d_x}{\ell_0}$

3-4   (a) 90   (b) .2   (c) 5/24
3-5   2081.61

3-6   (a) $-{}_sp_x\mu_{x+s}$ (b) ${}_sp_x(\mu_x - \mu_{x+s})$

3-7   .0012749

3-8   (a) $\frac{1}{15}(64 - .8x)^{-2/3}$ (b) 60   (c) 514.286

3-9   (a) $\dfrac{\mu_x T_x}{\ell_x} - 1$ (b) $-\dfrac{\ell_x}{T_x} = -\dfrac{1}{\overset{\circ}{e}_x}$

3-10 7.5; 8.03571

3-12 2/15

3-13 (a) $-{}_nd_x$ (b) ℓ_{x+n}

3-14 (a) T_x (b) $T_x - T_{x+n}$ (c) $\frac{1}{\ell_x}(T_x - T_{x+n})$ (d) ℓ_{x+n} (e) $n\cdot\ell_{x+n}$

      (f) $T_x - T_{x+n} - n\cdot\ell_{x+n}$ (g) $\ell_x - \ell_{x+n}$ (h) $\dfrac{T_x - T_{x+n} - n\cdot\ell_{x+n}}{\ell_x - \ell_{x+n}}$

3-18 (b) and (c)
3-19 .5214

3-20 2

3-22 Exact: .0078431;   Approximate: .0078905, .0079061, .0079217

3-23 13,440

3-24 .46

3-25 2.78084

3-26 .1(1−k)

3-27   All are correct

3-29   (a) 25.1   (b) 25.096819

3-31   150,000

CHAPTER 4

4-1   7

4-2   3.75

4-3 $7\frac{1}{2}$; $4\frac{1}{2}$

4-4 $E[T]$; $\dfrac{Var(T)}{n}$

4-5   11/16

4-6 $-\dfrac{(_t|q_0)(_r|q_0)}{n}$

4-7 $\frac{1}{n} \cdot S(r) \cdot \left[1 - S(t)\right]$

4-8   9/10

4-9   .00009

4-11   .000084

4-12   Reading down $d_t = $ 200, 150, 150, 50, 50, 100, 100, 100, 100
each column: $n_t = $ 1000, 800, 650, 500, 450, 400, 300, 200, 100
$\hat{q}_t = $ .200, .188, .231, .100, .111, .250, .333, .500, 1.000
$\hat{S}(t) = $ 1.000, .800, .650, .500, .450, .400, .300, .200, .100

4-14   (a) $\dfrac{2(1 - p_t)}{1 + p_t}$ (b) $\dfrac{2(n_t - N_{t+1})}{n_t + N_{t+1}}$ (c) $\dfrac{16 \cdot p_t(1 - p_t)}{n_t(1 + p_t)^4}$ (d) Biased

4-16   Exponential: $\hat{m}_i = .040821$;   est.$Var(\hat{m}_i) = .00041667$
Uniform: $\hat{m}_i = .040816$;   est.$Var(\hat{m}_i) = .00041631$

4-17   32.4

4-20 $\dfrac{n_t(n - n_t)}{n^3}$

CHAPTER 5

5-1   Date of joining the pension plan.

5-2   (a) 25.75   (b) 28   (c) Undefined

5-3   (a) 31.75   (b) 31.75

5-4 $x \le y_i < x+1$

5-5 $x < z_i \le x+1$

5-6   (a) $(.75, 1)$ (b) $(0, 1)$ (c) $(0, .75)$

5-7   (a) Special Case B   (b) Special Case A   (c) Special Case C

5-8   .28

5-9 $\dfrac{20 - t}{600}$

5-10   .18

CHAPTER 6

6-1 $\dfrac{(s-r) \cdot q_x}{1 - r \cdot q_x}$

6-2 $\dfrac{(s-r) \cdot q_x}{1 - (1-s) \cdot q_x}$

6-5 $\dfrac{d_x}{n_x - r \cdot k_x}$

6-6   .01487

6-8   (b) Positive

6-9   (a) $\dfrac{q_x(1-q_x)}{n_x}$

(b) $\dfrac{\sum\limits_{i=1}^{n} {}_{1-r_i}q_{x+r_i}(1 - {}_{1-r_i}q_{x+r_i})}{\left[\sum\limits_{i=1}^{n}(1-r_i)\right]^2}$ (c) $\dfrac{\sum\limits_{i=1}^{n} s_i q_x(1 - s_i q_x)}{\left[\sum\limits_{i=1}^{n} s_i\right]^2}$

6-10   (a) s   (b) $\dfrac{1 - (1-q_x)^s}{q_x}$ (c) $\dfrac{s}{1 - (1-s) \cdot q_x}$

6-11   (b) $d_x^{\frac{1}{2}}$ (b) $\dfrac{1}{q_x} + \dfrac{1}{\ln p_x}$

6-12 $\dfrac{}{n_x - c_x}$, where $d_x'' = d_x \overset{=}{} d_x'$

6-13 $\dfrac{d_x}{\sum\limits_{i=1}^{n}(s_i - r_i) - \frac{1}{2} \cdot w_x}$

6-14 $\dfrac{b - \sqrt{b^2 - 2n_x w_x}}{n_x}$, where $b = n_x - \frac{1}{2}d_x + \frac{1}{2}w_x$

6-15   (a) $\dfrac{b - \sqrt{b^2 - 4ad}}{2a}$, where $a = \left[\frac{1}{2}n(1-r^2) - \frac{1}{2}wr(1-r) + \frac{1}{2}dr(1+r)\right]$

              and $b = \left[n(1-r) - \frac{1}{2}w(1-r) + \frac{1}{2}d(1+3r)\right]$

  (b) $\dfrac{b - \sqrt{b^2 - 4aw}}{2a}$, where $a = \left[\frac{1}{2}n(1-r^2) - \frac{1}{2}dr(1-r) + \frac{1}{2}wr(1+r)\right]$

              and $b = \left[n(1-r) - \frac{1}{2}d(1-r) + \frac{1}{2}w(1+3r)\right]$

6-16   (a) $\dfrac{b - \sqrt{b^2 - 2ns^4 d}}{ns^3}$, where $b = ns^2 - \frac{1}{2}s^2 w + \frac{1}{2}s^2 d$

  (b) $\dfrac{b - \sqrt{b^2 - 2ns^4 w}}{ns^3}$, where $b = ns^2 - \frac{1}{2}s^2 d + \frac{1}{2}s^2 w$

6-17 $1 - \left[\dfrac{n_x - d_x - w_x}{n_x}\right]^{w_x/(d_x + w_x)}$

6-18   (a) $1 - \left[\dfrac{n_x - d_x - w_x}{n_x}\right]^{d_x/(1-r)(d_x + w_x)}$

  (b) $1 - \left[\dfrac{n_x - d_x - w_x}{n_x}\right]^{w_x/(1-r)(d_x + w_x)}$

6-19   (a) $1 - \left[\dfrac{n_x - d_x - w_x}{n_x}\right]^{d_x/s(d_x + w_x)}$

  (b) $1 - \left[\dfrac{n_x - d_x - w_x}{n_x}\right]^{w_x/s(d_x + w_x)}$

6-20   Hyperbolic: .01739;   Linear: .01737;   Exponential: .01738

6-21   .3439

6-22 $\hat{m}^w = 1/16$; $\hat{q}^w = 2/33$

6-23 $2/7$

6-24   .25

6-26   (a) $n_x \cdot q_x$ (b) (i) $c_x \cdot {}_s q_x \cdot {}_{1-s}q_{x+s}$ (ii) $e_x \cdot {}_{1-s}q_{x+s}$

6-27   (a) No. D_n and D_c are not independent (since $D_c \le D_n$), so

          $\text{Var}(D_x) = \text{Var}(D_n) + \text{Var}(D_c) - 2 \cdot \text{Cov}(D_n, D_c)$.

    (b) $n_x \cdot q_x (1 - q_x) + c_x \left[{}_s q_x (1 - {}_s q_x) - q_x (1 - q_x)\right]$

CHAPTER 7

7-1 $-\dfrac{n}{1-q} + \dfrac{d}{q} + \sum_{\mathfrak{D}}\left[\dfrac{2(1-s_i)}{1-(1-s_i)q}\right] = 0$

7-2 $\dfrac{d}{n+d}$

7-3 $\hat{q}_x = 0$ if none die. $\hat{q}_x = 1$ only if all die *and* $s_i = 0$ for all i;   thus, in general, $\hat{q}_x < 1$ even if all die.

7-4   (a) $(1-q)^{n-d} \cdot \prod_{\mathfrak{D}}\left[(1-q)^{s_i} \cdot -\ln(1-q)\right]$

      (b) $(n-d)\cdot\ln(1-q) + \sum_{\mathfrak{D}} s_i \cdot \ln(1-q) + \sum_{\mathfrak{D}} \ln\left[\ln(1-q)^{-1}\right]$

      (c) $1 - \exp\left[\dfrac{-d}{(n-d) + \sum_{\mathfrak{D}} s_i}\right]$

7-5 $2/151$

7-7   (a) .60839   (b) .66667

7-8   (a) .05   (b) .05

7-9   (a) (i) $\alpha \cdot q_x$ (ii) $1 - \alpha \cdot q_x$ (iii) 0   (b) $(\alpha \cdot q_x)^{d'_x} \cdot (1-\alpha \cdot q_x)^{c_x - d'_x}$

      (c) (i) q_x (ii) 0   (iii) $1-q_x$ (d) $(q_x)^{d''_x} \cdot (1-q_x)^{n_x - c_x - d''_x}$

7-10 $1 - \dfrac{-\frac{1}{2}d'_x + \sqrt{\frac{1}{4}d'^2_x + 4(n_x - \frac{1}{2}c_x)(n_x - c_x - d''_x + \frac{1}{2}e_x)}}{2(n_x - \frac{1}{2}c_x)}$

7-11   (a) $\dfrac{b - \sqrt{b^2 - 4rd_x(n_x - k_x)}}{2r(n_x - k_x)}$, where $b = (n_x - rk_x + rd_x)$

      (b) $1 - \dfrac{-\frac{1}{2}d^*_x + \sqrt{\frac{1}{4}d^{*2}_x + 4(n_x - \frac{1}{2}k_x)(n_x - d_x - \frac{1}{2}k_x + \frac{1}{2}d^*_x)}}{2(n - \frac{1}{2}k_x)}$,

      where d^*_x is the number of observed deaths out of the k_x entrants at age x+r.

7-12 $1 + \dfrac{p_x \cdot \ln p_x}{q_x}$

7-13 $1 + \dfrac{q_x}{\ln p_x}$

7-15 $\quad 1 - \left[\dfrac{-\frac{1}{2}d' + \sqrt{\frac{1}{4}d' + 4(n-\frac{1}{2}c)(n-\frac{1}{2}c-\frac{1}{2}d'-d'')}}{2(n-\frac{1}{2}c)}\right]^2$

7-18 $\quad \dfrac{b - \sqrt{b^2 - 4tn_x d_x}}{2tn_x}$, where $b = n_x + td_x - (1-t)w_x$

7-19 $\quad 1 - \left[\dfrac{n-d-w}{n}\right]^{w/(w+d)}$

7-20 $\quad \dfrac{(n-\frac{1}{2}d+\frac{1}{2}w) - \sqrt{(n-\frac{1}{2}d+\frac{1}{2}w)^2 - 2nw}}{n}$

7-21 $\quad \left[\dfrac{b}{q(1-q)} + \dfrac{br^2 q}{(1-rq)^2} + \dfrac{k(1-r)}{q(1-q)(1-rq)^2}\right]^{-1}$

7-22 $\quad \dfrac{\mu^2}{n(1-e^{-\mu})}$

7-23 $\quad \left[\dfrac{n-c}{p(1-p)} + \dfrac{\frac{1}{4}c}{p^{3/2}(1-p^{1/2})}\right]^{-1}$

7-24 $\quad \dfrac{q(1-q)(1-\alpha q)}{n(1-\alpha q) - c(1-\alpha)}$

7-25 $\quad$ (a) $\quad n_x \cdot q_x^{(d)}$ $\qquad$ (b) $\quad n_x \cdot q_x^{(w)}$ $\quad \Big[$In parts (c), (d), (e), $k = e^{-(\alpha+\beta)}.\Big]$

$\qquad$ (c) $\quad -\dfrac{d}{\alpha^2} + \dfrac{d+w}{(\alpha+\beta)^2} - \dfrac{(d+w)k}{(1-k)^2};$ $\qquad -\dfrac{w}{\beta^2} + \dfrac{d+w}{(\alpha+\beta)^2} - \dfrac{(d+w)k}{(1-k)^2};$

$\qquad\qquad \dfrac{d+w}{(\alpha+\beta)^2} - \dfrac{(d+w)k}{(1-k)^2}$

$\qquad$ (d) $\quad$ (i) $\quad \dfrac{\frac{n\alpha}{\alpha+\beta}(1-k)}{\alpha^2} - \dfrac{n(1-k)}{(\alpha+\beta)^2} + \dfrac{nk}{1-k}$

$\qquad\qquad$ (ii) $\quad \dfrac{\frac{n\beta}{\alpha+\beta}(1-k)}{\beta^2} - \dfrac{n(1-k)}{(\alpha+\beta)^2} + \dfrac{nk}{1-k}$ $\qquad$ (iii) $\quad -\dfrac{n(1-k)}{(\alpha+\beta)^2} + \dfrac{nk}{1-k}$

(e)   From part (d), $f_{11} = \dfrac{n(1-k)^2(\alpha+\beta) - \alpha n(1-k)^2 + \alpha nk(\alpha+\beta)^2}{\alpha(\alpha+\beta)^2(1-k)}$

$$f_{12} = f_{21} = \frac{-n(1-k)^2 + nk(\alpha+\beta)^2}{(\alpha+\beta)^2(1-k)}$$

$$f_{22} = \frac{n(1-k)^2(\alpha+\beta) - \beta n(1-k)^2 + \beta nk(\alpha+\beta)^2}{\beta(\alpha+\beta)^2(1-k)}$$

Let $\Delta = f_{11} \cdot f_{22} - f_{12} \cdot f_{21}$.

Then $\mathrm{Var}(\hat{\alpha}) = \dfrac{f_{22}}{\Delta};$ $\mathrm{Var}(\hat{\beta}) = \dfrac{f_{11}}{\Delta};$ $\mathrm{Cov}(\hat{\alpha}, \hat{\beta}) = \dfrac{-f_{12}}{\Delta}$

7-27   (a) .04227   (b) .00042963

7-28   2

7-29   3

7-30   (a)   .20000;   1.60944   (b) .27711;   1.28333

7-31   .43926

CHAPTER 8

8-1 $\dfrac{\lambda^2}{n}$

8-2   (a) $\dfrac{1}{n} \cdot \sum\limits_{i=1}^{n} t_i$ (c) $\dfrac{\zeta^2}{n}$

8-3   .3

8-4   2/11

8-5   (a) 15.2   (b) 15.0

8-6   1.175

8-9   .68422

8-10   1.6

8-11   .07438

8-14   72.1

8-15   17.5

8-16 $\quad \alpha \cdot \sum_a^b w_x \qquad\qquad + \beta \cdot \sum_a^b w_x(x+\tfrac{1}{2}) \qquad = \sum_a^b w_x \cdot \ln \mu^o_{x+1/2}$

$\qquad\quad \alpha \cdot \sum_a^b w_x(x+\tfrac{1}{2}) \quad + \beta \cdot \sum_a^b w_x(x+\tfrac{1}{2})^2 \quad = \sum_a^b w_x(x+\tfrac{1}{2}) \cdot \ln \mu^o_{x+1/2}$

8-17 $\quad \alpha \cdot \sum_a^b w_x \qquad\qquad + \beta \cdot \sum_a^b w_x \cdot \ln(x+\tfrac{1}{2}) \qquad = \sum_a^b w_x \cdot \ln \mu^o_{x+1/2}$

$\qquad\quad \alpha \cdot \sum_a^b w_x \cdot \ln(x+\tfrac{1}{2}) + \beta \cdot \sum_a^b w_x[\ln(x+\tfrac{1}{2})]^2 \quad = \sum_a^b w_x \cdot \ln(x+\tfrac{1}{2}) \cdot \ln \mu^o_{x+1/2}$

8-18 $\quad \hat{k} = 2.1583 \times 10^{-10}; \qquad \hat{n} = 5.3884$

8-19 $\quad d_A \cdot \Sigma w_x \qquad\qquad + d_B \cdot \Sigma w_x c_0^{x+\frac{1}{2}} \qquad\qquad + d_c \cdot \Sigma w_x B_0(x+\tfrac{1}{2})c_0^{x-\frac{1}{2}}$

$$= \Sigma w_x(u_{x+\frac{1}{2}})$$

$\quad d_A \cdot \Sigma w_x c_0^{x+\frac{1}{2}} \qquad\qquad + d_B \cdot \Sigma w_x(c_0^{x+\frac{1}{2}})^2 \qquad + d_c \cdot \Sigma w_x B_0(x+\tfrac{1}{2})c_0^{2x}$

$$= \Sigma w_x c_0^{x+\frac{1}{2}}(u_{x+\frac{1}{2}})$$

$\quad d_A \cdot \Sigma w_x B_0(x+\tfrac{1}{2})c_0^{x-\frac{1}{2}} + d_B \cdot \Sigma w_x B_0(x+\tfrac{1}{2})c_0^{2x} + d_c \cdot \Sigma w_x[B_0(x+\tfrac{1}{2})c_0^{x-\frac{1}{2}}]^2$

$$= \Sigma w_x B_0(x+\tfrac{1}{2})c_0^{x-\frac{1}{2}}(u_{x+\frac{1}{2}})$$

where Σ represents $\sum_{x=a}^b$, and $u_{x+\frac{1}{2}} = \mu^o_{x+\frac{1}{2}} - \mu^0_{x+\frac{1}{2}}$.

8-20 $\quad \dfrac{\sum\limits_{x=a}^b x \cdot w_x \cdot \ln(10{,}000\,\mu^o_x)}{\sum\limits_{x=a}^b x^2 \cdot w_x}$

8-21 $\quad$ 8.5; $\quad$ approximately .039

8-22 $\quad$ 20.215; $\quad$ approximately .0002

8-23 $\quad \sum\limits_{t=0}^8 \dfrac{\left[n \cdot e^{-5t\lambda}(1-e^{-5\lambda}) - {}_5d_{x+5t}\right]^2}{{}_5d_{x+5t}}$

8-24 $\quad \chi^2 = 13.8$; reject with approximately 91% confidence

8-25 $\quad$ Reject with approximately 96.5% confidence

8-26 $\quad a = -45; \quad b = 37; \quad c = -10$

8-27 $\quad$ .69563

8-28 $\quad$ 1.58043

8-29   5556

8-31   .015740;   .001071;   .014322

8-32   53/54;   −52/54

8-34   (a) ln c;   ln B;   1   (b) It is

CHAPTER 9

9-3   11

9-4   .03306

9-5   5000

9-6   72

9-7   .04165

9-8   98,274;   95,292;   93,955;   90,310

9-9   2/2941

9-10   .070;   .187;   .320

9-11   2.846

9-12   (a) $B^{1980-82} + \frac{9}{62}(B_{12}^{1979} - B_{12}^{1982}) - {}_{4/365}D_0^{1980-82}$

(b) $B^{1980-82} + \frac{35}{62}(B_{12}^{1979} - B_{12}^{1982}) - {}_{2/52}D_0^{1980-82}$

(c) $B^{1980-82} + (B_{12}^{1979} + B_{11}^{1979} + \cdots + B_6^{1979} + \frac{1}{2}\cdot B_5^{1979})$

$- (B_{12}^{1982} + B_{11}^{1982} + \cdots + B_6^{1982} + \frac{1}{2}\cdot B_5^{1982}) - {}_{7/12}D_0^{1980-82}$

9-13   .000427

9-14   .001857

9-15   (a) D_x^P: 401.25;   695.02;   1066.73;   1515.61

M_x^P: 101,187.42;   104,376.44;   101,287.49;   88,173.56

(b)   .001321;   .002217;   .003504;   .005713

(c)   .002904

CHAPTER 10

10-1	i	y_i	z_i	θ_i	ϕ_i	i	y_i	z_i	θ_i	ϕ_i
	1	29.72	39.72	0	0	36	31.34	37.50	0	35.69
	2	33.50	43.50	33.51	0	37	31.38	36.84	34.38	0
	3	31.56	41.56	0	32.48	38	30.52	35.92	0	0
	4	****	****	****	****	39	32.25	37.41	0	34.01
	5	28.09	38.09	30.07	0	40	31.22	36.16	0	0
	6	****	****	****	****	41	29.67	34.46	0	0
	7	32.80	42.80	0	0	42	31.04	35.70	31.75	0
	8	31.35	41.35	0	31.52	43	30.14	34.43	0	32.94
	9	29.79	39.52	0	30.52	44	30.35	34.08	0	0
	10	30.85	40.85	39.21	0	45	31.97	35.99	0	0
	11	32.0	42.04	0	33.41	46	31.34	35.15	0	31.62
	12	31.62	41.49	0	41.10	47	30.15	33.62	0	31.15
	13	29.82	39.56	0	0	48	29.89	33.38	0	32.89
	14	31.28	40.86	37.14	0	49	31.62	34.99	0	0
	15	30.11	39.21	0	37.57	50	30.29	33.81	32.54	0
	16	29.83	38.72	0	0	51	30.37	33.27	0	32.24
	17	32.36	41.39	39.17	0	52	30.41	33.13	0	0
	18	29.75	38.23	0	34.49	53	32.26	35.32	33.74	0
	19	31.58	40.18	0	0	54	29.69	32.30	0	30.02
	20	31.86	39.90	0	34.55	55	31.76	34.11	0	0
	21	30.00	38.05	35.23	0	56	30.08	32.37	0	0
	22	31.39	39.06	0	0	57	30.59	32.98	0	0
	23	29.73	37.42	0	0	58	30.66	32.74	31.37	0
	24	31.62	38.93	0	32.62	59	32.22	34.41	0	32.31
	25	29.53	36.45	0	36.33	60	31.84	33.91	0	0
	26	30.04	37.25	32.12	0	61	29.69	31.68	0	30.10
	27	31.97	39.32	0	36.74	62	31.20	32.84	0	0
	28	31.65	38.78	36.70	0	63	29.94	31.38	31.06	0
	29	29.90	36.73	0	0	64	32.20	33.49	0	33.37
	30	30.60	37.60	0	33.07	65	30.54	30.61	0	0
	31	30.80	37.40	0	0	66	32.23	33.29	0	33.24
	32	29.56	36.11	0	0	67	31.47	32.15	0	0
	33	31.32	38.06	36.19	0	68	30.04	30.45	0	0
	34	30.08	36.41	0	31.04	69	31.67	31.87	0	0
	35	30.47	36.31	0	0	70	****	****	****	****

**** Member is not involved in the study.

10-2

x	d_x
30	1
31	3
32	2
33	2
34	1
35	1
36	2
37	1
39	2

10-3

Interval	Exact Exposure	Scheduled Exposure	Actuarial Exposure
(28,29]	.91	.91	.91
(29,30]	4.49	4.49	4.49
(30,31]	23.68	24.61	24.61
(31,32]	35.33	36.57	37.19
(32,33]	44.12	45.46	45.46
(33,34]	35.88	36.63	36.63
(34,35]	28.07	28.69	28.69
(35,36]	23.83	24.60	24.60
(36,37]	16.27	17.38	17.38
(37,38]	10.53	11.39	11.39
(38,39]	8.72	8.72	8.72
(39,40]	4.72	6.34	6.34
(40,41]	2.18	2.18	2.18
(41,42]	1.10	1.10	1.10
(42,43]	.80	.80	.80

10-4

x	(a): q_x^M	(b): q_x^A
30	.04135	.03922
31	.08141	.08067
32	.04432	.04444
33	.05422	.05479
34	.03500	.03448
35	.04110	.04167
36	.11567	.11111
37	.09060	.08333
39	.34539	.30770

10-5

i	y_i	z_i	θ_i	ϕ_i
1	30	39	0	0
2	*	*	*	*
3	32	41	0	32
4	*	*	*	*
5	28	37	29.95	0
6	*	*	*	*
7	34	43	0	0
8	*	*	*	*
9	30	39	0	30
10	32	41	39.62	0
11	33	42	0	34
12	32	41	0	41
13	30	39	0	0
14	31	40	36.86	0
15	30	39	0	38
16	30	38	0	0
17	32	41	38.81	0
18	30	38	0	35
19	32	40	0	0
20	32	40	0	35
21	30	38	35.23	0
22	31	38	0	0
23	30	37	0	0
24	32	39	0	33
25	30	36	0	36
26	30	37	32.08	0
27	32	39	0	37
28	32	39	37.05	0
29	30	36	0	0
30	31	38	0	34
31	31	37	0	0
32	30	36	0	0
33	31	37	35.87	0
34	30	36	0	31
35	30	35	0	0

i	y_i	z_i	θ_i	ϕ_i
36	31	37	0	36
37	31	36	34.01	0
38	31	36	0	0
39	32	37	0	34
40	31	35	0	0
41	30	34	0	0
42	31	35	31.71	0
43	30	34	0	33
44	30	33	0	0
45	32	36	0	0
46	31	34	0	31
47	30	33	0	31
48	30	33	0	33
49	32	35	0	0
50	30	33	32.25	0
51	30	32	0	31
52	30	32	0	0
53	32	35	33.48	0
54	30	32	0	30
55	32	34	0	0
56	30	32	0	0
57	31	33	0	0
58	31	33	31.71	0
59	32	34	0	32
60	32	34	0	0
61	30	31	0	30
62	31	32	0	0
63	30	31	0	0
64	32	33	0	33
65	*	*	*	*
66	32	33	0	33
67	*	*	*	*
68	*	*	*	*
69	*	*	*	*
70	*	*	*	*

* Policyholder is not involved in the study

10-6

x	d_x	n_x
28	0	1
29	1	1
30	0	23
31	2	32
32	2	43
33	1	35
34	1	29
35	2	23
36	1	15
37	1	11
38	1	7
39	1	4
40	0	2
41	0	1
42	0	1

10-7

t	x=30 $d_{[x]+t}$	x=30 $n_{[x]+t}$	x=31 $d_{[x]+t}$	x=31 $n_{[x]+t}$	x=32 $d_{[x]+t}$	x=32 $n_{[x]+t}$
0	0	22	2	13	0	15
1	0	18	0	11	1	13
2	2	16	0	10	0	9
3	0	11	1	9	0	7
4	0	10	1	7	0	6
5	1	8	1	4	1	5
6	0	4	0	2	1	4
7	0	3	1	1	0	3
8	0	1	0	1	0	2
9					0	1
10					0	1

10-8

i	y_i	z_i	θ_i	ϕ_i	i	y_i	z_i	θ_i	ϕ_i
1	32	40	0	0	36	31.34	38	0	35.69
2	*	*	*	*	37	31.04	37	34.04	0
3	*	*	*	*	38	30.10	36	0	0
4	*	*	*	*	39	32.34	38	0	34.10
5	*	*	*	*	40	31.56	37	0	0
6	*	*	*	*	41	29.71	35	0	0
7	35	43	0	0	42	30.84	36	31.55	0
8	*	*	*	*	43	30.21	35	0	33.01
9	*	*	*	*	44	30.77	35	0	0
10	33	41	38.86	0	45	31.48	36	0	0
11	*	*	*	*	46	31.69	36	0	31.97
12	34	42	0	41.11	47	30.03	34	0	31.03
13	32	40	0	0	48	30.01	34	0	33.01
14	33	41	36.78	0	49	31.13	35	0	0
15	32	40	0	37.86	50	29.98	34	32.23	0
16	31	39	0	0	51	30.60	34	0	32.47
17	34	42	39.28	0	52	30.78	34	0	0
18	31	39	0	34.76	53	32.44	36	33.92	0
19	33	41	0	0	54	29.89	33	0	30.22
20	32	40	0	34.15	55	32.15	35	0	0
21	31	39	35.68	0	56	30.21	33	0	0
22	32	40	0	0	57	30.11	33	0	0
23	30	38	0	0	58	30.42	33	31.13	0
24	31.19	39	0	32.19	59	32.31	35	0	32.40
25	29.58	37	0	36.38	60	31.43	34	0	0
26	30.29	38	32.37	0	61	29.51	32	0	29.92
27	32.15	40	0	36.92	62	30.86	33	0	0
28	31.37	39	36.42	0	63	30.06	32	31.18	0
29	29.67	37	0	0	64	32.21	34	0	33.38
30	30.50	38	0	32.97	65	30.43	31	0	0
31	30.90	38	0	0	66	32.44	34	0	33.45
32	29.95	37	0	0	67	31.82	33	0	0
33	31.76	39	36.63	0	68	30.09	31	0	30.53
34	30.17	37	0	31.13	69	31.30	32	0	0
35	30.66	37	0	0	70	33.54	34	0	0

* Member is not involved in the study.

10-9	x	q_x
	31	.09553
	32	.04993
	33	.02918
	34	.03384
	35	.04020
	36	.14514
	38	.10673
	39	.14720

10-10	x	Fiscal Age (a) Last Birthday	Calendar (b) Fiscal Age
	29	3	0
	30	16	19
	31	31.5	33
	32	38.5	41
	33	35.5	33
	34	30.5	30
	35	24.5	25
	36	20	20
	37	11.5	12
	38	9	9
	39	7	7
	40	3	3
	41	1.5	1
	42	1	1

CHAPTER 11

11-2   See Exercise 10-10

11-4   See Exercise 10-6

BIBLIOGRAPHY

1. Ackland, T.G., "An Investigation of Some of the Methods for Deducing the Rates of Mortality, and of Withdrawal, in Years of Duration; etc.," *JIA*, XXXIII (1898), 68.

2. Anderson, T.W., and D.A. Darling, "A Test of Goodness of Fit," *JASA*, 49 (1954), 765.

3. Armstrong, R.J., and L.R. Curtin, "Methodology of the National and State Life Tables: 1979-81," *DHHS* Publication No. (PHS)87-1150-3, Department of Health and Human Services, 1987.

4. Balducci, G., "Costruzione e critica della tavola di mortalita," *Gior. degli Economisti e Riv. di Statis.*, 55 (1917), 455.

5. ———, Correspondence, *JIA*, LII (1921), 184.

6. Batten, R.W., *Mortality Table Construction.* Englewood Cliffs: Prentice-Hall, Inc., 1978.

7. Beers, H.S., "Notes on Exposure Formulae," *TASA*, XLIV (1943), 240.

8. ———, "Six-term Formulas for Routine Actuarial Interpolation," *RAIA*, 34 (1945), 60.

9. Benjamin, B., and J.H. Pollard, *The Analysis of Mortality and Other Actuarial Statistics.* London: William Heinemann Ltd., 1980.

10. Bowers, N.R., et al., *Actuarial Mathematics.* Itasca: Society of Actuaries, 1984.

11. Breslow, N., and J. Crowley, "A Large Sample Study of the Life Table and Product Limit Estimates under Random Censorship," *Annals of Statistics*, II (1974), 437.

12. Broffitt, J.D., "Maximum Likelihood Alternatives to Actuarial Estimators of Mortality Rates," *TSA*, XXXVI (1984), 77.

13. Broffitt, J.D., and S.A. Klugman, "Method of Moments Derivation of the Balducci Exposure Formula," *ARCH*, 1983.1, 8.

315

14. Brown, R.L. and K.S. Brown, "Toward Computerized Underwriting - A Biological Age Model," *TSA*, XXXV (1983), 393.

15. Cantelli, F.P., "Genesi e Costruzione della Tavole di Mutualita," *Boll. notiz. sul Credito e sulla Previdenze*, 3-4 (1914).

16. Chiang, C.L., *The Life Table and Its Applications*. Malabar: Robert E. Krieger, Inc,. 1984.

17. Cody, D.D., "Actuarial Note: The Standard Deviation of the Rate of Mortality by Amounts," *TASA*, XLII (1941), 69.

18. Cox, D.R., "Regression Models and Life Tables," *J. Roy. Statist. Soc. Ser. B*, 33 (1972), 187.

19. Dobson, R.H., "Mortality and Morbidity Tables," Society of Actuaries Study Note 7BA-111-83, 1983.

20. Drolette, M.E., "The Effect of Incomplete Follow-up," *Biometrics*, 31 (1975), 135.

21. Elandt-Johnson, R.C., and N.L. Johnson, *Survival Models and Data Analysis*. New York: John Wiley and Sons, 1980.

22. Elveback, L. "Actuarial Estimation of Survivorship in Chronic Disease," *JASA*, 53 (1958), 420.

23. Ferguson, A.N. et al., "1975-80 Basic Tables with Appendix of Age-Last-Birthday Basic Tables," *TSA* Reports, 1982, 55.

24. Gehan, E.A., "Estimating Survival Functions from the Life Table," *J. Chron. Dis.* 21 (1969), 629.

25. Gehan, E.A., and M.M. Siddiqui, "Simple Regression Methods for Survival Time Studies," *JASA*, 68 (1973), 848.

26. Gershenson, H., *Measurement of Mortality*. Chicago: Society of Actuaries, 1961.

27. Gompertz, B., "On the Nature of the Function Expressive of the Law of Human Mortality," *Phil. Trans.*, Royal Society of London, 1825.

28. Greenwood, M. "A Report on the Natural Duration of Cancer," Reports on Public Health and Medical Subjects, H.M. Stationery Office, 33 (1926), 1.

29. Hoem, J.M., "A Flaw in Actuarial Exposed-to-Risk Theory," *Scand Actur. J.*, 1984, 187.

30. Hogg, R.V., and S.A. Klugman, *Loss Distributions*. New York: John Wiley and Sons, 1984.

31. Hollander, M. and D.A. Wolfe, *Nonparametric Statistical Methods*. New York: John Wiley and Sons, 1973.

32. Jordan, C.W., *Life Contingencies*. Chicago: Society of Actuaries, 1967.

33. Kalbfleisch, J.D., and R.L. Prentice, *The Statistical Analysis of Failure Time Data*. New York: John Wiley and Sons, 1980.

34. Kaplan, E.L. and P. Meier, "Nonparametric Estimation from Incomplete Observations," JASA, 53 (1958), 457.

35. Kellison, S.G., *Fundamentals of Numerical Analysis*. Homewood: Richard D. Irwin, Inc., 1975.

36. Keyfitz, N., and J.A. Beekman, *Demography Through Problems*. New York: Springer-Verlag, 1984.

37. King, G., "Actuarial Note: On a New Formula for Deducing the Exposed-to-Risk from the Records of a Life Assurance Company," *JIA*, XXVII (1888), 218.

38. Klugman, S.A., "On the Variance and Mean Squared Error of Decrement Estimators," *TSA*, XXXIII (1981), 301.

39. Lawless, J.F., *Statistical Models and Methods for Lifetime Data*. New York: John Wiley and Sons, 1982.

40. Lee, E.T., *Statistical Methods for Survival Data Analysis*. Belmont: Lifetime Learning Publications, 1980.

41. London, D., *Graduation: The Revision of Estimates*. Winsted: ACTEX Publications, Inc., 1985.

42. Makeham, W.M., "On the Law of Mortality, and the Construction of Annuity Tables," *JIA*, VIII (1860).

43. Marshall, E.W., "Principles Underlying Exposed to Risk Formulae," *TASA*, XLVI (1945), 10.

44. Mereu, J.A., "Some Observations on Actuarial Approximations," *TSA*, XIII (1961), 87.

45. Miller, R.G., *Survival Analysis*. New York: John Wiley and Sons, 1981.

46. Nagnur, D., "Life Table Methodology: Canada and Provinces (1980-1982 Cycle)," Research Paper No. 9, Statistics Canada, 1984.

47. Nelson, W.A., "Theory and Applications of Hazard Plotting for Censored Failure Data," *Technometrics*, 14 (1972), 945.

48. Nesselle, D., "A Least-Squares Method for Determining the Makeham Constants," (unpublished Master's paper). Boston: Northeastern University, 1965.

49. Ormsby, C.A. et al., "Report of the Special Committee to Recommend New Mortality Tables for Valuation," *TSA*, XXXIII (1981), 617.

50. Pollard, A.H. et al., *Demographic Techniques* (Second Edition). Sydney and New York: Pergamon Press, 1981.

51. Rao, C.R., *Linear Statistical Inference*. New York: John Wiley and Sons, 1965.

52. Robinson, J.M., Discussion of "Maximum Likelihood Alternatives to Actuarial Estimators of Mortality Rates," by J.D. Broffitt, *TSA*, XXXVI (1984), 125.

53. Rohatgi, V.K., *An Introduction to Probability Theory and Mathematical Statistics*. New York: John Wiley and Sons, 1976.

54. Schwartz, D. and P. Lazar, "Taux de Mortalite par une Cause Donnee de Deces en Tenant Compte des Autres Causes de Deces ou de Disparition," *Revue Inst. de Stat.*, 29:3 (1961), 15.

55. Seal, H.L., "The Estimation of Mortality and Other Decremental Probabilities," *Skand. Aktuar.*, 1954, 137.

56. _____, "Deaths Among Prospective Existings," *PCAPP*, XI (1962), 308.

57. _____, "An Attempt to Convert American Actuaries," *The Actuary*, March 1981, 4.

58. Spiegelman, M., *Introduction to Demography.* Cambridge: Harvard University Press, 1968.

59. Stephens, M.A., "EDF Statistics for Goodness of Fit and Some Comparisons," *JASA*, 69 (1974), 730.

60. _____, "Goodness of Fit for the Extreme Value Distribution," *Biometrika*, 64 (1977), 583.

61. Tenebein, A. and I. Vanderhoof, "New Mathematical Laws of Select and Ultimate Mortality," *TSA*, XXXII (1980), 119.

62. Wolfenden, H.H., "On the Formulae for Calculating the "Exposed to Risk" in Constructing Mortality and Other Tables from the Individual Records of Insured Lives," *TASA*, XLIII (1942), 234.